WHAT PURE EYES COULD SEE

PRIMITIVISM, RADICALISM, AND THE LAMB'S WAR
The Baptist-Quaker Conflict in Seventeenth-Century England
T. L. Underwood

THE GOSPEL OF JOHN IN THE SIXTEENTH CENTURY
The Johannine Exegesis of Wolfgang Musculus
Craig S. Farmer

CASSIAN THE MONK
Columba Stewart

HUMAN FREEDOM, CHRISTIAN RIGHTEOUSNESS
Philip Melanchthon's Exegetical Dispute
with Erasmus of Rotterdam
Timothy J. Wengert

IMAGES AND RELICS
Theological Perceptions and Visual Images
in Sixteenth-Century Europe
John Dillenberger

THE BODY BROKEN
The Calvinist Doctrine of the Eucharist and the Symbolization
of Power in Sixteenth-Century France
Christopher Elwood

WHAT PURE EYES COULD SEE
Calvin's Doctrine of Faith in Its Exegetical Context
Barbara Pitkin

WHAT PURE EYES COULD SEE

Calvin's Doctrine of Faith
in Its Exegetical Context

Barbara Pitkin

New York   Oxford
OXFORD UNIVERSITY PRESS
1999

Oxford University Press

Oxford   New York
Athens   Auckland   Bangkok   Bogotá   Buenos Aires   Calcutta
Cape Town   Chennai   Dar es Salaam   Delhi   Florence   Hong Kong   Istanbul
Karachi   Kuala Lumpur   Madrid   Melbourne   Mexico City   Mumbai
Nairobi   Paris   São Paulo   Singapore   Taipei   Tokyo   Toronto   Warsaw

and associated companies in
Berlin   Ibadan

Published by Oxford University Press, Inc.
198 Madison Avenue, New York, New York 10016

Oxford is a registered trademark of Oxford University Press

Library of Congress Cataloging-in-Publication Data
Pitkin, Barbara, 1959–
What pure eyes could see : Calvin's doctrine of faith in its
exegetical context / Barbara Pitkin.
p.   cm.—(Oxford studies in historical theology)
Includes bibliographical references and index.
ISBN 0-19-512828-1
1. Calvin, Jean, 1509–1564.   2. Faith—History of doctrines—16th
century.   3. Bible—Criticism, interpretation, etc.—History—16th
century.   I. Title.   II. Series.
BT771.2.P52   1999
234'.23'092—dc21   98-28136

1 3 5 7 9 8 6 4 2

Printed in the United States of America
on acid-free paper

Acknowledgments

In the course of preparing this book for publication, I have benefited from the scholarly, financial, and moral support of numerous institutions, colleagues, and friends, and I wish to acknowledge with gratitude these many contributions. First, I express my appreciation to several people who took time to read earlier versions of the manuscript in parts or in its entirety and to offer suggestions for clarifying and strengthening the argument: Irena Backus, Helmut Feld, Richard Muller, and David Steinmetz. To these last two I am particularly indebted for their thorough and critical readings, which have done much to transform what was originally a doctoral dissertation into a book. I am also grateful to them as a member of the editorial board and editor for Oxford's Studies in Historical Theology series for accepting the book for publication. Along the way I have also benefited greatly from conversations about subjects raised in the various chapters with Max Engammare, Francis Higman, and Gerald Hobbs. Anne Groton cheerfully assisted with several of the translations from the Latin. Finally, the scholarship of my former teachers at the University of Chicago, Susan Schreiner and B. A. Gerrish, has continued to stimulate and inspire my work; I hope to have answered here some of the questions they found lingering in the original version. The argument and presentation are a good deal better as a result of the ideas, suggestions, and criticisms of all these individuals. Any remaining shortcomings are, I must stress, completely my responsibility.

Several institutions provided financial and other assistance that afforded me the time and space to write and revise. The Institute for European History in Mainz, Germany, awarded a three-month postdoctoral fellowship in the early stages of the project. That same summer, the Institute for the History of the Reformation in Geneva, Switzerland, once again welcomed me for a short research visit. St. Olaf College awarded me a summer research grant for the summer of 1996. I am thankful for the College's support of the project, even though I had to decline the grant in order to accept a year-long postdoctoral fellowship at Stanford University. During my tenure as an Andrew W. Mellon Post-Doctoral Fellow in the Humanities at Stanford, I was able to complete the revisions and submit a version that was accepted by Oxford. I am thankful in addition to Cynthia Read and Robert Milks of Oxford University Press and my copy editor, Martha Ramsey, for seeing the manuscript through the review and production process.

A debt of a more personal nature is owed to the many colleagues, friends, and family members who showed interest in the project (without inquiring too often about its progress) and helped me maintain my own enthusiasm, and whose friendship was an important source of support. Here I especially mention Doug and Kathy Schuurman, Stephanie Paulsell, Kevin Madigan, and my husband, Brent Sockness. Finally, I am especially grateful for the longstanding support of my parents, Roy and Marcia Pitkin, to whom this book is dedicated.

Contents

Translations

Translations of Calvin, occasionally modified, are taken from:

Calvin's Commentaries, 45 vols. (Edinburgh: Calvin Translation Society, 1844–1856; reprinted in 22 vols., Grand Rapids: Baker Books, 1981).

Calvin's New Testament Commentaries, ed. D. W. Torrance and T. F. Torrance (Grand Rapids: Eerdmans, 1959–1972).

Calvin: Institutes of the Christian Religion, 2 vols., ed. J. T. McNeill and trans. F. L. Battles, Library of Christian Classics, vols. 20–21 (Philadelphia: Westminster Press, 1960).

Institutes of the Christian Religion: 1536 Edition, trans. and annotated by F. L. Battles (1975; rev. ed., Grand Rapids: Eerdmans, 1986).

WHAT PURE EYES COULD SEE

Faith is the eye that enlightens every conscience and produces understanding.

Cyril of Jerusalem

Introduction

From the earliest days of the Christian church, preachers and theologians capitalized on scriptural images to establish firm bonds between faith and illumination, especially understood as intellectual insight or spiritual understanding. These connections, however, were variously drawn. Cyril of Jerusalem's lenten lectures for the instruction of catechumens (ca. 349) illustrate two common ways of stating the relationship. Commenting on Heb. 11:1, Cyril compares faith to an eye and asserts that the expression "faith" can mean one of two things. First there is a "dogmatic faith" that is knowledge of and assent to a proposition, acquiescence that comes from one's self and is directed toward divine truth. The second kind of faith is a supernaturally bestowed power to behold divine things beyond the natural human capacity: "For when it is enlightened by faith, the soul has visions of God, and contemplates God, as far as it may; it ranges over the bounds of the universe, and before the consummation of this world, beholds the judgment and the payment of promised rewards."[1] For Cyril, this power apparently follows upon the dogmatic assent, and then only when one "cherishes" that first type of faith.

Like Cyril and countless others, John Calvin viewed faith as a special kind of perception that involved new ways of understanding and even seeing. He supported this notion by appealing to scripture and, again quite in keeping with the earlier tradition, sought to make sense of the variety of scriptural expression by distinguishing various aspects of faith. Although he spent much of his career defending his understanding of faith over against traditional and contemporary views that he judged to be false, his attention to the relationship between faith, knowledge, and enlightenment is in many ways conventional. This has not always been recognized in discussions of Calvin's doctrine of faith, where the assumption has often (although not always) been that Calvin's definition of faith as knowledge is really something new.[2] The most important previous treatments of the topic have provided thorough analysis both of the knowledge character of Calvin's idea of faith and of faith's relationship to other aspects of Calvin's soteriology on the basis of the *Institutes*, the biblical commentaries (most limit their view primarily to the commentaries on the New Testament), and the polemical treatises.[3] Their authors have noted various problems and tensions, especially in the concept of faith's certainty and in the relationship between faith and double predestination.[4] Some have been driven by such overt dogmatic interests that the light they shed on Calvin's thought is quite inadequate.[5] And despite acknowledgment of develop-ment in Calvin's thought and attention to discussions of faith outside the *Institutes*, gaps remain in our understanding of how Calvin's views on faith as knowledge developed, the relationship he saw between faith and perception, and what role his exegetical work might have played in this process. This is because earlier studies have, consciously or unconsciously, oriented their presentations exclusively around Calvin's discussion of faith in the 1559 *Institutes*, incorporating citations from the commentaries and sermons into a portrait drawn from the outlines of Calvin's discussion in book 3.[6] Thus while many seek to broaden the picture of Calvin's concept of faith from, in Walter Stuermann's words, "eternal to temporal felicity," they nevertheless restrict faith to soteriology, to God's activity as redeemer, and thereby miss an essential element of Calvin's doctrine of faith.

Recent work has begun to address some of these concerns by locating Calvin's doctrine of faith in its medieval and Renaissance contexts.[7] This investigation complements these efforts by tracing how Calvin's exegetical labors contributed to his understanding of faith. Calvin is part of a long conversation about the knowl-edge of faith and the vision of faith; his peculiar contribution to this tradition can best be seen by considering how he interprets biblical statements about faith and the normative weight he assigns to particular readings. In recent years, many ex-cellent studies of Calvin's exegesis have demonstrated the importance of the com-mentaries and sermons for understanding Calvin's theology and its place in the theological tradition.[8] Thus far, however, none has focused on the central category of faith. Attention to this topic here makes it possible to establish the exegetical underpinnings of Calvin's doctrine and yields additional important insights. Let me suggest several of these.

First, this study underscores the centrality of the twofold knowledge of God for Calvin's theology, if not as a methodological principle at least as an essential theological one.[9] Moreover, this investigation uncovers an important connection between the twofold knowledge of God and faith and highlights a further link to Christology. Calvin's views on faith paralleled his understanding of the knowledge of God in that both evolved in a twofold direction. Each of these strands has a distinct exegetical basis; a correct understanding of Calvin's doctrine of faith must encompass both. For Calvin, it was just as important to know God as creator as it was to know God as redeemer. Faith, likewise, while always grounded in God's specifically redemptive activity, looks also to God's creative and providential ac-tivity. Because the discussion of faith in the 1559 *Institutes* occurs within the context of the discussion of redemption, the discussion of faith there often centers rather narrowly around questions of justification, individual salvation, and eternal life. Yet these issues were not the ultimate focus of Calvin's theology, and at least since Stuermann and Edward Dowey some scholars have stressed that they are not the only focus for faith. Nonetheless, most previous discussions of Calvin's under-standing of faith have neglected the question of faith's relationship to God's activity as creator. A notable exception is the investigation by Josef Bohatec, which points out the relationship between faith and providence for Calvin (providence is known by faith and not by reason) and describes the content of providential faith (*Vorsehungsglaube*). However, since Bohatec approaches faith from the question of providence, he focuses on the relationship between providence and predestination and does not treat at all the relationship between providential faith and saving faith.[10] Closer attention to how Calvin develops faith's relationship to nature and history as realms of the divine activity in his commentary on the Psalms (1557) demonstrates more clearly the existence and nature of providential faith. Moreover, by considering providential faith not simply from the perspective of providence, as Bohatec does, but from the question of faith itself, it will be possible to specify the relationship between providential and saving faith. The discussion will trace the evolution of both strands and determine their influence on the understandings of faith articulated in the *Institutes*, especially in the 1559 edition.

The origins of these connections lie in the development of the idea of the twofold knowledge of God early in Calvin's career as a religious reformer, specifically between the years 1536 and 1539.[11] During this time Calvin's thinking underwent several significant shifts in emphasis, evidenced most strikingly in the differences between the first and second editions of the *Institutes*. In chapter 1 I trace this development in Calvin's thinking about the knowledge of God and its impact on his understanding of faith by comparing his treatment of these topics in the first (1536) and second (1539) editions of the *Institutes* and by considering his expansions of the discussion of faith in the successive Latin editions through 1554. After investigation of his exegesis in chapters 2–4, chapter 5 explores the explicit specification of the twofold knowledge of God in the final edition of the *Institutes* and the corresponding twofold notion of faith and the duplex character of Christ's mediation implied in that edition.

In claiming evolution in Calvin's understanding of faith, I am departing from earlier views that his understanding of faith was essentially in place by 1539 and underwent no significant changes over the next twenty years. Dowey, for example, discusses the "development" of the doctrine of faith "as seen in the development of the *Institutes*, not in the development of the doctrine itself, for it was essentially complete already in 1539, but in the way it took its place along with the other doctrines."[12] Heribert Schützeichel similarly remarks that Calvin's important and foundational formulation of the tractate on faith was already present in the 1539 *Institutes*, before the publication of the first biblical commentary.[13] While I agree that the important features of Calvin's understanding of faith had been laid out in 1539, one should not underestimate the way that these elements were confirmed and cultivated through his exegetical activity. Indeed, his 1539 formulation of faith may have been *published* before the first biblical commentary, but it was certainly being written at the same time that he was preparing his first commentary, on Romans, for publication, not to mention that he had been lecturing on scripture in Geneva and Strasbourg while revising his *Institutes*. Dowey himself argues with Emile Doumergue that a new and, indeed, for Calvin "extremely important" theme (union with Christ) is added to the discussion of faith in 1559. According to Dowey, union with Christ best expresses the character of faith according to Calvin.[14] There are, in my view, other explicit developments evident in 1559 that are implicit in 1539, just as the explicit declaration of the *duplex cognitio dei* is implicit in the second edition of the *Institutes*. This study seeks to determine these themes and to show why they come to expression by indicating their exegetical roots.

To this end, chapters 2, 3, and 4 consider the views on faith in Calvin's exegesis of key texts from the Old and New Testaments. These findings constitute a further contribution, this time to the field of the history of biblical interpretation. In his 1952 book, Walter Stuermann assumed and asserted that Calvin's understanding of faith represented a rediscovery of the Pauline understanding of faith's nature and significance.[15] This was probably an overstatement, since both ancient and medieval tradition held Paul in far greater esteem than is often acknowledged in studies of the Protestant Reformation. Nevertheless, Paul was an important authority—indeed, *the* biblical authority—for Calvin's understanding of faith. This is evident not solely in the copious citations from Paul in Calvin's discussions of faith in the *Institutes* and the correspondence between the view of faith expressed there and that articulated in his commentaries on the Pauline epistles. Rather, the Pauline shape of Calvin's understanding of faith emerges with particular clarity in his use of Paul to interpret other biblical, especially New Testament, passages about faith. Consideration of how Calvin understands Paul and uses him to legitimate his view of faith illuminates the character of his Paulinism and helps situate him in the history of Pauline interpretation.

Though Paul may have been for Calvin the consummate biblical authority, David was the one with whom he most personally identified. In his commentary on the Psalms, Calvin draws on ideas expressed virtually in passing in his commentaries on Paul to develop his view of the relationship between faith, creation, and divine providence. Calvin's exegesis of the Old Testament, but especially the Psalms, enriches and expands his understanding of faith by raising new themes and contexts for viewing faith. In particular, Calvin speaks of faith not primarily in the context of knowledge of God's redemptive activity but in relationship to knowledge of God the creator. He also explores in greater detail the perception of faith in the present world. The literal and "historical" character of Calvin's exegesis of the Old Testament has both offended and intrigued the readers of his commentaries, and his explication of faith without explicit reference to soteriology may well evoke the same response. While none of these things was entirely without precedent in the tradition, Calvin's strategy for recovering the idea of faith in the Psalms for sixteenth-century believers constitutes a significant moment in the history of the interpretation of the Psalms and their authority in the life of the Christian church.

Consideration of the view of faith that emerges in Calvin's biblical commentaries and sermons will contribute to our understanding of his theology in one further way. The exegetical context will underscore the fundamentally noetic and perceptual character of faith according to Calvin. Already in identifying faith as "knowledge" he draws on a biblical theme.[16] Yet this knowledge, as he is at great pains to show, is not bare cognition. It is enlightenment not in the sense that the subject receives and assents to certain data or information but rather in the very literal sense of "illumination."[17] My investigation will confirm the insights of earlier studies, especially those by Simon Pieter Dee, Dowey, and Werner Krusche, which argue that Calvin's understanding of "knowledge of God" is broad and not restricted solely to a function of the intellect. Likewise, the knowledge that is faith, as indicated in Calvin's definition from 1539, is "sealed on our hearts" as well as "revealed to our minds."[18] For Calvin, this illumination is effected by the Holy Spirit, which opens the subject's eyes to perceive the objectively clear revelation of God in the person and work of Christ, in the scriptures, and in creation. In all these ways God has already accommodated God's self to the finite human capacity. And yet fallen humans are still unable on their own power to gain proper knowledge of God through these designated means. In the postlapsarian world, the problem that faith corrects is not so much the ignorance of finite human nature but the blindness of *sinful* human nature.[19] So the question of what needs to and can be known about God is fundamentally the question of how God *appears* to eyes healed by faith. Certain books of the Bible, especially the Psalms, allow Calvin to explore this theme at great length.

The approach taken here should certainly not imply that the *Institutes* are not important for understanding Calvin or even that the exegetical work somehow provides a superior corrective to the discussions there. Rather, as it was Calvin's explicit view that the commentaries and the *Institutes* be read together, his thought cannot be abstracted from one without consideration of the other.[20] What distinguishes this investigation is the attempt to preserve the integrity of each, rather than offering up selected citations from the commentaries to "support" the explication of what Calvin says in the *Institutes*. Only then can one determine not only which biblical texts contributed to Calvin's understanding but also how he read them to arrive at his doctrine. Of course, this alone does not explain Calvin's understanding of faith; polemical, political, social, and traditional theological influences also played important roles in its development. Nevertheless, the significance of Calvin's exegetical labors can scarcely be overstated. Attention to the exegetical underpinnings of his understanding of faith yields a more accurate picture of his discussions in the *Institutes* by illuminating the twofold character of faith, the development of Calvin's doctrine, and its perceptual character.

From Fiducia to Cognitio

This chapter considers the formation of Calvin's views on faith at the beginning of his career and their relationship to developments in his theology as expressed in the Latin editions of the *Institutes* prior to 1559. This overview of Calvin's concept of faith—as expressed in his summary of Christian doctrine 1536–1554—prepares for the investigation of the exegetical underpinnings of that concept in chapters 2, 3, and 4. The discussion will show that Calvin's understanding of faith is an evolving one. The most important stage (1536–1539) reflects a significant development in or solidification of his theology as a whole. In these years he moves beyond the primarily "Lutheran" categories to new theological shores, bringing to expression views that are widely recognized to constitute his own mature position on theology and faith.[1] However, the designation "mature" should not imply that Calvin's views after 1539 remained static. To the contrary, they continued to evolve, though now in a clear direction. By tracing Calvin's treatment of faith in the successive editions of the *Institutes* through the 1554 edition I will show how the expanding polemical context refined and sharpened the distinctions Calvin tried to draw between his definition of faith in 1539 and what he perceived to be false alternatives. Yet this is but one aspect of the continuing evolution of Calvin's concept of faith. In order to gain more comprehensive insight into the blossoming of the view arrived at in 1539, I will need to consider, in subsequent chapters, the exegetical bases of and further influence on Calvin's understanding of faith.

In the Wake of Luther

The 1536 edition of the *Institutes of the Christian Religion* marks Calvin's first major theological publication and clearly takes up the "Lutheran" cause, at least as he perceived it, by fighting on the same front using similar tactics.[2] What is true for Calvin's theology in general in 1536 is true for his understanding of faith in particular. After consideration of the central concern of the 1536 *Institutes* and Calvin's twofold means of presenting it, attention to his first published discussion of faith will show that he employs arguments and tactics similar to those used by Luther, Philip Melanchthon, and Martin Bucer to advance his view. It is, of course, still an open question—and one beyond the scope of this study—how far Calvin's understanding of faith, even in 1536, accurately reflects Luther's views on faith and justification or, indeed, whether Calvin intended to follow Luther's lead. Nonetheless, it will become clear in the analysis of Calvin's treatment of these topics that he was at least, even if implicitly, aiming to further his perception of the Lutheran doctrine of justification by faith.

Calvin's placement within the evangelical mainstream is evident in his understanding of justification by faith in Jesus Christ, his focus on this as the central concern of his work, his method of promoting this cause, and the opponents against whom he directs his arguments. In the Dedicatory Epistle to Francis I, Calvin states his desire to explicate and defend sound doctrine currently under attack in France. Only in the subsequent discussion of the law, with which he begins the work itself, does he cast off his guarded caution and state the particular issue at stake, namely, justification by faith in Christ apart from works of the law. The centrality of this concern becomes fully explicit in the exposition of the Apostles' Creed, where he declares that "the church itself stands and consists in this forgiveness of sins, and is supported by this as by a foundation" and that forgiveness of sin itself is "the hinge of salvation."[3] Indeed, Calvin later designates this doctrine (that Christ was offered on account of sin) as virtually synonymous with the word of God.[4] According to Calvin, this is the "fact" that has been condemned and is being kept from the French people, who he claims are being led astray through meaningless practices, such as the mass and veneration of the saints, that arise out of human traditions. Hence, Calvin's main concern is doctrinal; he criticizes contemporary ecclesiastical practices to the extent that they obscure what he designates as proper teaching. Moreover, the particular doctrines that Calvin finds are being obscured, suppressed, and even persecuted pertain to soteriology and Christology. Thus the 1536 *Institutes* has a soteriological perspective and a christological orientation. By a soteriological perspective, I mean that the question driving the presentation is how human beings are saved, a concern that forms the basis for each of the six chapters of the first edition.[5] By a christological orientation, I refer to what Alexandre Ganoczy has called Calvin's powerful Christocentrism.[6] Ganoczy singles out at least three elements of this christocentric focus. First, Calvin uses the terms "kingdom of God" and "kingdom of Christ" synonymously (one notes that this applies to his use of "God" and "Christ" as well). Second, he underscores the exclusivity of Christ as the only mediator, which is, according to Ganoczy, Calvin's central dogmatic affirmation. Third, he uses the name "Christ" and the phrase "in Christ" constantly and takes eight times as much space to explicate the second article of the Creed as he does for the first or the third.[7] The interrelatedness of these two foci, soteriology and Christocentrism, is especially evident in this discussion of the Creed.[8] In short, the 1536 *Institutes* is a book about the proper teaching about salvation in Jesus Christ. In its emphasis on doctrinal reform and on the particular doctrine of justification by faith and its concern with Christ's exclusive mediation the book echoes the themes of Luther.

The 1536 edition intertwines catechesis and apology to support this endeavor. Calvin models his instruction on Luther's catechisms, discussing in four chapters the Decalogue and the function of the law, the Apostles' Creed, the Lord's Prayer, and the sacraments. His two concluding chapters address the five Roman sacraments that he rejects and the themes of Christian freedom, ecclesiastical power, and political administration. He aims to present an orderly summary of Christian teaching, of all that is needful to know concerning the free forgiveness of sin in Christ and the implications of this fact for Christian existence. Thus even though Calvin's intentions for this edition appear to be initially apologetic, one cannot underestimate the work's instructional value. It is true that Calvin wants to prove the orthodoxy of his doctrine before those in power; namely, the king and intellectuals. Though he gives as his reason for writing the hunger and thirst for Christ among the people of France, he writes in Latin, suggesting that his motivations are at least as apologetic as they are pastoral. Nonetheless, the apology cannot be divorced from Calvin's desire to teach, evident especially in the emphasis on doctrine.[9] This concern also manifests itself in the subtle yet unmistakable stress on knowledge, which appears in every part of the work. We see this emphasis in the Dedicatory Epistle, where Calvin says that of those he sees hungering and thirsting for Christ there were "very few who had been imbued with even a slight knowledge of him."[10] The theme sounds in the famous opening line of the text itself: "Nearly the whole of sacred doctrine consists in these two parts: knowledge of God and of ourselves."[11] Throughout Calvin underscores the cognitive element: what Christians are to learn about God and themselves from the law[12] and from God's revelation in Christ;[13] how this knowledge is summed up and expressed in the Apostles' Creed;[14] how Christians use what they have learned to seek from God in prayer the things that God has promised them;[15] and how the sacraments provide knowledge in a visible way.[16] Even the polemical fifth chapter provides important instruction by exposing, "for simple folk to see," what the remaining sacraments are and how they are falsely considered genuine.[17] Finally, the sixth chapter teaches about Christian freedom, also a subject of utmost importance.[18] Calvin clearly intends the entire book to teach the Christian faith.[19] Nonetheless, he writes not simply to instruct those who share his religious convictions but also to defend their right to hold those convictions and to ease the religious persecution in France by proving the orthodoxy of this faith.

Along with these two ends, however, Calvin also aims to promote the glory of God. This theme, so characteristic of Calvin's later theology, is present in 1536 and underlies the twofold aim just specified.[20] In his appeal to the king he says that this very issue is at stake in his defense of sound doctrine.[21] He accuses the Roman Catholic priests of not being troubled by the "sight of God's glory defiled with manifest blasphemies."[22] He says that God will take "harsh vengeance" on those who "think, say and do things other than those that pertain to his glory."[23] Moreover, the glory of God is, according to Calvin, the chief concern of each petition of the Lord's Prayer.[24] Finally, in discussing the sacraments, Calvin distinguishes between the elements, which serve God's glory by visibly manifesting the divine promise, and the glory of God itself, which alone ought to be worshipped. Related to this important theme is Calvin's concern that people properly acknowledge God's glory by glorifying, that is, worshipping God. He declares that one reason ought to have been sufficient to arouse people to fulfill the law: "that God ought to be glorified in us."[25] He allows singing and speaking in public worship, because the glory of God should be evident in various parts of human bodies. When human tongues are joined together in praising God, God is glorified.[26]

Calvin finds that the failure to proclaim the free forgiveness of sin through faith in Christ both degrades God's glory and imperils human salvation. Yet while the former liability underlies his argument in the 1536 *Institutes*, it is the latter that is most prominent, due in part to the polemical situation in which Calvin found himself. As mentioned, he perceives the doctrine of justification by faith to be under attack by Roman Catholics unsympathetic to the reforming movements and by groups insisting on more radical reforms. In his view, both groups are driven on by Satan.[27] Neither proclaims the truth about human salvation; both, unwittingly perhaps, aim to obscure it. The polemical situation thus helps determine the strong soteriological focus and the christocentric orientation of the first edition of the *Institutes*.

Already I have had occasion to touch on the role of faith in Calvin's theology, insofar as the doctrine that I have claimed is summed up in the 1536 edition of the *Institutes* is the free forgiveness of sin through *faith* in Christ. It is now necessary to consider in more detail how Calvin depicts faith and how it functions in 1536. The actual discussion of the topic appears at the beginning of chapter 2, where it forms one of two short prefatory discussions to the exposition of the Apostles' Creed. But already in the preceding Dedicatory Epistle and discussion of the law there are indications of Calvin's views. In the former, he vehemently rejects the scholastic notion of implicit faith, declaring this to be inconsistent with true godliness.[28] After the exposition of the Decalogue in chapter 1, he reflects in some detail on faith's role in enabling humans to become spiritually free from the curse and condemnation of the law: "When through faith we lay hold on the mercy of God in Christ, we attain this liberation and, so to speak, manumission from subjection to the law, for it is by faith we are made sure and certain of forgiveness of sins, the law having pricked and stung our conscience to the awareness of them."[29] He also sketches the character of faith: "For to have faith is not to waver, to vary, to be borne up and down, to hesitate, to remain in suspense, finally, to despair! Rather, to have faith is to strengthen the mind with constant assurance and perfect confidence, to have a place to rest and plant your foot."[30] These statements prefigure themes that Calvin develops more fully in the discussion of faith in his next chapter, especially faith's reliance on God's mercy rather than on human works, the christocentric element, and the emphasis on faith's certainty.

Having already indicated the crucial role of faith in redemption, Calvin devotes the discussion at the beginning of chapter 2 to a closer examination of the character of faith. This brief but important discussion reveals that Calvin represents a general trend in the sixteenth century that aims to transcend the various medieval distinctions and classifications for faith.[31] Along with Luther, Melanchthon, and Bucer, Calvin posits a simple distinction between a genuine and a false faith in place of the comparatively complex and fluid medieval terminology. Though they hold that their formulations represent the scriptural views of faith, they also implicitly and explicitly refer to medieval understandings of faith, sometimes using the very language and concepts of the scholastic definitions to develop and express what they hold to be the scriptural meaning. As already mentioned, Calvin refers to the scholastic *fides implicita* in the Dedicatory Epistle. Though he does not expressly use scholastic categories and, in fact, wants to reject these distinctions, his discussion reflects several types of faith that one can rather clearly identify by the medieval tags. The commonality with Luther as well as with Melanchthon and Bucer is particularly evident in Calvin's desire to do away with the medieval distinctions and the strategy he employs to do so.

First, one notices that Calvin uses the term *fides* without any further specification to designate both the objective content of faith and the subjective act of believing. Though he is aware that the word embraces at least these two distinct senses, he does not make a precise or at least an explicit distinction between them. However, he uses the term most often in the latter sense, suggesting that he views this as the primary meaning. At the beginning of chapter 2, it appears that Calvin has in mind the equivalent of *fides quae creditur*, for when he tells his readers that they may readily learn what the nature of this faith is from the Apostles' Creed, it seems that he intends to provide an account of the content of Christian faith. However, the rest of the prefatory considerations have to do more with the act of faith, the *fides qua creditur*. By the time that Calvin arrives at a definition of faith as "a firm conviction of mind whereby we determine with ourselves that God's truth is so certain, that it is incapable of not accomplishing what it has pledged to do by his holy Word,"[32] he seems to have forgotten, at least moɪ entarily, about the faith that can be readily learned from the Creed.[33]

Calvin digresses from his opening declaration to look at the Creed in order to elucidate faith as the act of believing in greater detail. He begins by distinguishing between two different forms of faith, faith about God and faith in God. Peter Brunner has shown that this distinction derives from Luther; Ganoczy has pointed to the same distinction in Melanchthon.[34] Calvin's characterization of these two forms also betrays the influence of the Augustinian-scholastic threefold distinction with respect to the act of faith:[35] *credere Deum* (believing that God exists), *credere Deo* (believing what God says), *credere in Deum* (embracing God in knowledge and love.)[36] As I will show, Calvin subtly transforms and critiques this threefold distinction in setting forth his two forms in a way that parallels Bucer's treatment of the same issue.

The first form Calvin identifies is a kind of *fides acquisita* or *historica*: "If someone believes that God is, he thinks that the history related concerning Christ is true." This is a faith acquired by natural means: "Such is the judgment we hold on those things which either are narrated as once having taken place, or we ourselves have seen to be present." Calvin equates this with demons' faith (James 2:19) and says that this kind of faith is not important, not really worthy of the name "faith" at all.[37] The second form of faith is distinct from this in including the subjective attitude of trust and the recognition of God *pro nobis*:

> [W]e not only believe that God and Christ are, but also believe in God and Christ, truly acknowledging him as our God and our Savior. Now this is not only

to adjudge true all that has been written or is said of God and Christ: but to put all hope and trust in one God and Christ, and to be so strengthened by this thought, that we have no doubt about God's good will toward us. Consequently, we have been persuaded that whatever we need, either for the use of the soul or of the body, he will give us; we await with assurance whatever the Scriptures promise concerning him; we do not doubt Jesus is our Christ, that is, Savior.[38]

In this passage, Calvin seems to identify *credere Deum* with his first form of faith (the *fides acquisita* or *historica*) and, by extension, with demons' faith.[39] Simply believing the things written about God or Christ or that God and Christ exist is by itself not really faith at all, nor is it the primary element in the act of faith. Rather, the other two elements of the threefold distinction determine the character of genuine faith. Calvin collapses the concepts *credere Deo* and *credere in Deum*, using the words *credere in Deum et Christum* to reflect both confidence toward God and Christ and believing that God's good will, the promise, is true. The same idea is expressed more explicitly by Bucer in his Romans commentary from 1536.[40]

For Calvin this second kind of faith not only embraces holding God's word to be true and trust in God's goodness but also is inseparable from hope and love. Calvin expresses the inseparability of genuine faith from hope and love after his exposition of the Creed, using terms that recall Luther's favorite term for faith, *fiducia*: "Now indeed wherever this living faith is, which we previously showed to be trust in the one God and Christ, it certainly is a matter of no little significance that faith has at the same time as companions hope and love."[41] Calvin continues this reflection on faith, hope, and love and soon explicitly rejects the use of 1 Cor. 13:2 to prove the medieval notion of unformed faith, which he says is a kind of faith apart from love.[42] This criticism of a so-called faith separate from love also reflects a strategy employed by Luther: Reinhard Schwarz argues that Luther's marginal comments to the *Sentences* in 1509–1510 show him already collapsing the medieval *fides infusa* with the *fides formata* because Luther views the *fides infusa* as inseparably combined with *caritas*.[43]

Calvin's attempt, after his exposition of the Creed, to explain what Paul means by "faith" in 1 Cor. 13:2 ("if anyone has faith so as to remove mountains, but has not love, he is nothing") marks Calvin's only admission in 1536 that scripture uses the word "faith" in different senses. Calvin says that in this passage "faith" means the gift of working miracles.[44] Surely the direct impetus for this singular digression is that this was the text advanced by Roman Catholic polemicists in support of a distinction between a formed and an unformed faith.[45] However, there may be yet another reason why Calvin responded especially to this argument. Calvin is anxious to protect his earlier descriptions of faith in light of this passage in particular because it was written by Paul. His brief comments here point to the fact that Paul was a sixteenth-century battleground. Amid Roman and reformist parties all claiming Pauline authority for their views, Calvin also desires to legitimate his interpretation of Paul. In this section on faith, and in the 1536 *Institutes* as a whole, Paul becomes the lens through which Calvin views the Christian religion. The central concern of the 1536 *Institutes*, the free forgiveness of sins through faith in Christ, derives from Calvin's understanding of this typically Pauline theme. Calvin's preference for Paul is especially evident in the section on faith, where, with the exception of James 2:19, all the scriptural passages that form the basis for Calvin's comments about faith are either from Paul (Romans 8 and 10) or treated by Calvin, at least in 1536, as being of Pauline authorship (Hebrews 11). It is on the basis of these passages in particular that Calvin advances his understanding faith as certain persuasion of God's promise to justify those who believe in Christ (Rom. 10:8–11). As I will show in greater detail in the next chapter, Paul is an important source for Calvin's soteriological perspective and for his Christocentrism, especially as these pertain to faith. Calvin thus takes great pains to interpret this passage in terms of his theological assumptions about faith and in light of what he understands Paul himself to be saying elsewhere about this topic.

Calvin's treatment of Heb. 11:1 merits closer examination, since it not only illustrates some of the forces shaping his views but also is modified in future editions of the *Institutes* in ways that reflect the subsequent development of his early position. In 1536, Calvin understands the term "substance" in Heb. 11:1 to mean that faith is a support that assures believers that they already possess the things God has promised. As the indication or proof of things not appearing, faith is itself the evidence of the divine mystery of salvation, for it is "vision of things which are not seen, the perception of things obscure, the presence of things absent, the proof of things hidden." This, says Calvin, is the only kind of faith that God accepts.[46] This discussion shows similarities with Luther's interpretation in his early lectures on Hebrews (1517–1518). While these lectures, published from student notes for the first time in 1929,[47] could not possibly have had direct influence on Calvin, his repeated use of the term *possessio* suggests an affinity to Luther, who had adopted this term from Jerome.[48] Calvin echoes other voices of the theological tradition: he designates Heb. 11:1 as a "definition," depicts faith as a foundation (*fulcrum*), and offers *probatio* as a translation of *elenchos*.[49] Yet despite this traditional language, Calvin is generally following Luther in understanding the faith in Heb. 11:1 as a possession of the things promised by God; that is, of the future heavenly things that, since they are the objects of hope, are not seen with the eyes but are grasped through faith in the word.[50]

I note here the peculiar perceptual quality that is attributed to faith on the grounds of Hebrews 11 and Rom. 8:24. Faith is a special kind of perception or vision. As Calvin says, "we can only possess those things [pertaining to the last day] if we exceed the total capacity of our own nature, and press our keenness of vision beyond all things which are in the world, in short, surpass ourselves [*nos . . . superemus*]."[51] Faith cannot be acquired by natural means because it involves going out of one's self and exceeding human nature. And yet while faith does grasp certain lofty truths, its reach is limited.

Calvin provides a few more details on what faith can or cannot see when he considers what he calls the fourth part of the Creed, where faith in the church is confessed. First, faith does not make God's incomprehensible wisdom concerning election intelligible; faith does not allow humans to discern who ultimately belongs to the church and who does not, though they may gain a kind of provisional idea by certain marks described in scripture. However, faith does provide ample security for all who through faith possess Christ: "We have a clear enough testimony that we are among God's elect and of the church, if we partake in Christ."[52] Faith also allows believers to ascertain without a doubt the existence of the church, which cannot be surely discerned except by faith, since "by faith are believed things that cannot be seen with the naked eye."[53]

These examples betray an ambiguous attitude toward the physical sense of sight. Actual appearances, for Calvin, cannot fully convey true spiritual reality, and the corruption of human faculties in the Fall has only increased the distortion. For this reason, Calvin often presents the kind of vision involved in faith as opposed to ordinary sense perception and talks about "pressing beyond the keenness of our vision." In keeping with this view, concluding the section on prayer, he assures his readers that faith will make them certain that they have obtained what was expedient, even though their senses fail to perceive it.[54] Finally, Calvin, like Luther, stresses the need to look away from human works, in this instance playing one type of sense perception off against another: "Indeed, the nature of faith is to arouse the ears but close the eyes, to await the promise but turn thoughts away from all human worth or merit."[55]

Discussing the inward character of real knowledge for Calvin, William Bouwsma argues that Calvin suggests, at times, a "bias against visual experience." According to Bouwsma, Calvin preferred the sense of hearing to that of sight for the reason that "we truly *see* after we *hear*."[56] One can see this bias in the examples just cited, which portray faith as the means by which fallen human beings overcome the weakness of their perceptive faculties. However, Calvin does not completely deny the value of physical perception, including the sense of sight. In the case of the elect and the church, there are visible marks and signs that still disclose something of the true character of the spiritual to believers. Faith, in one particular way, appears to rely on visible sense perception: certain sensible or outward signs have been specially joined to the promise, which they visibly manifest. Through earthly things perceptible to the senses, the sacraments lead believers to contemplate spiritual realities and thereby nourish, exercise, and increase faith.[57] Calvin's rejection of the Zwinglian understanding of the sacraments demonstrates his greater appreciation of the things of the flesh and his willingness to admit their utility in spiritual matters.[58]

While faith looks to something that is by nature beyond all sense perception and human capacity (the word of God), this object has been accommodated to human sense capacity. The object of faith comes to humans through the physical senses: hearing the word, reading scripture, seeing and partaking of the sacraments. For this reason Calvin often depicts faith as a kind of perception and can speak appreciatively of the tangible means through which God makes God's self known. Yet the sensible means themselves do not make the promise effective; without the Holy Spirit, the promise remains outside and cannot penetrate to the heart.[59] Moreover, the senses often present an obstacle to faith, for if faith relies improperly on what can be seen with the physical eye, this will detract from the word, the true object of faith. Awareness of this often leads Calvin to speak disparagingly of human faculties of perception. As I will show, this tension in faith's relationship to sensible reality persists throughout the development of Calvin's thinking about faith and, moveover, is greatly expanded and complicated when Calvin begins to extend faith's view beyond the divinely appointed accommodations of the word of grace (the gospel) to God's self-accommodation in creation and history.

This consideration of the perceptual character of faith as well as of what faith can "see" has led this discussion beyond the remarks on faith that preface and conclude the exposition of the Apostles' Creed and, at the same time, from the discussion of the character of faith to a consideration of the content of faith. What Christians believe is the subject of both the comments on the Trinity, which precede the discussion of the Creed, and Calvin's statements about each article of the Creed. It was pointed out earlier that the lengthiest consideration is given to the second article. This is due in part to the fact that this is also the most detailed article. More important, it is perhaps the most significant part of the Creed for Calvin, as one can gather from his statement that "we see the whole sum of our salvation and also all its parts comprehended in Christ."[60] Calvin devotes a great deal of this space to discussing the person of Christ by defending the Chalcedonian formula and the communication of properties. He views this not as an idle, speculative matter but rather as an important soteriological issue. Christians have to know who Christ is so that they can believe what Christ does for them.

In discussing the first article of the Creed, Calvin briefly but emphatically stresses God's ongoing divine providence and says that faith attends to this.[61] Even in times of adversity, faith trusts that God is a propitious and benevolent father who continues to safeguard the salvation of the elect. And yet, as shown with the theme of the glory of God earlier, this aspect of Calvin's teaching on faith is subordinated to his soteriological and christocentric concerns. The question driving the 1536 *Institutes* is not that of God's glory or divine providence but the challenge to salvation in Christ alone. Hence, these other themes are not as prominent as they will become in later works.

In sum, besides the idea of two forms of faith (the first of which is denied the designation of faith proper), the *pro nobis* character of true faith, the characterization of faith as *fiducia*, and the virtual collapsing of genuine faith and love, other typically "Lutheran" or evangelical themes and strategies have left their imprint on Calvin's discussion. In rejecting his first kind of faith, whether this is implicit, acquired, unformed, historical, or demons', Calvin, like Luther, Melanchthon, and Bucer, is interested in restricting the understanding of faith and setting this understanding apart from traditional types of faith that he views as false pretenders. This faith is firm, sure, and certain persuasion that the word of God, God's promise of salvation, is true. Moreover, faith is fundamentally trust.[62] Calvin stresses that the word is the object of faith; by this he means especially God's promises set forth in scripture. The word, according to Calvin, is not only the goal and object but also the basis and foundation of true faith. Hence, faith of this sort cannot be acquired by natural means; it is entirely God's work.[63] Such faith is itself the fulfillment of the law, insofar as singular and certain hope and trust in God alone is what is required by the first commandment.[64] Finally, faith involves a kind of perception but has a primarily negative relationship to the physical sense of sight.

These similarities signal a common theological and exegetical strategy. Theologically, Luther and Calvin share what I have called Calvin's soteriological perspective and christological orientation. Both are concerned with faith as this relates to salvation in Jesus Christ; any form of faith that does not directly pertain to this is dismissed. Whether or not the actual substance of the understanding of faith for Luther and Calvin is the same (a question that can only be approached with care), Calvin's aims and tactics make clear that he at least perceives himself to be within the Lutheran ranks. And while he may not have veered from this self-understanding, his ideas about theology and his language about faith continued to evolve, particularly in the period between the first and second editions of the *Institutes*.

Arriving on the Shores of Knowledge

Through Turbulent Waters

A brief summary of the course of events and Calvin's literary activity surrounding the writing of the first *Institutes* and leading to the revision of the text in 1539 sets the stage for my consideration of these changes.[65] Arriving in Basel in January 1535, Calvin works on his *Institutes*, which he completes in August 1535, and probably has some important contacts with reformists residing in or visiting Basel.[66] Just before the publication of the *Institutes* in March 1536, Calvin and Louis du Tillet set out for Ferrara, Italy, to the court of Duchess Renée of France. However, after just a few weeks, and possibly because of fear of persecution against the evangelicals at the duchess's court, they return to Basel. Calvin goes on to Paris to put his personal affairs in order and, in mid-July, leaves with his brother Antoine and his half-sister Marie. The three intend to seek refuge in Strasbourg, but because of war between the king of France and the emperor, they are forced to detour through Geneva.

Prior to settling in Geneva, Calvin had authored, in addition to his commentary on Seneca, the biblical prefaces for Olivétan's French Bible, and the as yet unpublished *Psychopannychia*, two other epistles, both of which attest to Calvin's increasing hostility toward the papal church and to his growing awareness of his vocation as a reformer. One of these, *On Fleeing the Illicit Rites of the Wicked and Observing Piety in the Christian Religion*, advises an evangelically minded Christian how to act when living "in a place from which the discipline of true religion is banished."[67] Calvin, writing in a prophetic tone, invokes the examples of biblical figures (such as Abraham, Isaac, Daniel, Paul) and early Christian martyrs (such as Cyprian) to illustrate how the Christian should not yield to idolatrous worship. By now, Calvin is convinced that adoration of the eucharistic elements constitutes idolatry, and he argues that even pretended compliance with it violates the second commandment.[68] In this letter, Calvin abandons the apologetic tone of the 1536 *Institutes* and writes instead even more polemically and with a greater sense of authority. By the time of publication, he has a new title, *sacrarum literarum in ecclesia genevensi professor*, which declares his authoritative position as a reader of holy scripture in Geneva beginning in September 1536.[69] But beyond this official designation, Calvin appears to have an increased awareness of a divine vocation. This is especially evident near the end of his letter, where he presents himself as a divine spokesperson: "The advice that you sought you have from me, or rather from the Lord, through my hand."[70]

During the rest of 1536 and into 1538, Calvin's activity as a spokesperson for God and the church at Geneva increases: he gives two responses at the Lausanne disputation (October 1536), participates in the congregations of pastors in Geneva, is himself called as a pastor (end of 1536), and writes a catechism for the Genevan church.[71] In the same period of time, however, controversy surrounding his authority also mounts, resulting initially in doctrinal victories in the Caroli affair (1537) and the colloquy at Bern (1537).[72] Nevertheless, Calvin's authority in Geneva remains a matter of dispute, and, eventually, Calvin and Guillaume Farel are dismissed from their posts and driven from the city. After the failure of attempts at reconciliation, the two men settle briefly in Basel.

On the basis of Calvin's correspondence from this time, Ganoczy has argued that he experienced sincere doubt about his call to ministry but that he later regained a deepened sense of confidence in his vocation.[73] One can detect something of Calvin's utter trust in his divine calling in the response that he wrote from Strasbourg in the summer of 1539 to Jacopo Sadoleto's letter to the Genevans.[74] Calvin begins his response by insisting that he has a legitimate vocation and that his activity among the Genevans proceeded from this calling. He claims that Sadoleto has called this vocation into question and that he writes for this reason to defend both the divine authority of his vocation and his role as a pastor to the Genevans. It thus appears that Calvin's perplexity as to the origin of his call to ministry was, however intense, of short duration. At least by August 1539— he was now a minister in Strasbourg—he seems to have resolved the crisis. Even though he continued to experience periods of deep discouragement and met with profound external conflict, he no longer questioned the divine origin of his call to ministry.

In Strasbourg Calvin was involved in various aspects of parish ministry. He continued his exegetical work, lecturing first of all on the Gospel of John and then on the Pauline epistles, beginning with 1 Corinthians.[75] In August 1539 he finished his first biblical commentary, on Paul's epistle to the Romans. The same month saw the publication of the second Latin edition of the *Institutes*, which he then began translating into French. According to Ganoczy, it was in Strasbourg that Calvin "attained full maturity" as a reformer. Having undergone his first and apparently only crisis concerning his pastoral vocation, he had attained a conviction of his own calling, the legitimacy of which he was now prepared to defend. Ganoczy's examination of the correspondence with du Tillet and the *Reply to Sadoleto* suggests that in these texts Calvin is at "the end of his spiritual transformation, when he becomes fully aware of his pastoral and reformist calling."[76]

On Dry Land: The 1539 Institutes

Assuming that Calvin has now indeed arrived at his mature theological position, what is this position, and how does it affect his understanding of faith? By tracing first some of the general changes in the second Latin edition of the *Institutes*, and then focusing on the changes to the discussion of faith in particular, one can determine that Calvin's views have indeed broadened. He expands his understanding of theology by developing the ideas about God and God's providential activity that we found already expressed in 1536 in his discussion of the first article of the Creed. In 1539 Calvin's understanding of the divine activity takes on a distinctly twofold character, so that the idea of a *duplex cognitio Domini* begins to function as a theological principle. In addition, the second edition bears witness to an even greater preoccupation with the question of knowledge, which Calvin now explores not only from the angle of what is needful to know but also from the perspective of how saving knowledge is possible. This broadening of perspective is evident in the formal and structural changes in the second edition of the *Institutes*, in two important substantive changes in the discussion of knowledge of God and the nature of divine activity, and in a more precise definition of faith.

The 1539 *Institutes* is three times longer than the first edition, consisting now of seventeen chapters instead of six.[77] It begins with a new preface to the reader, followed by the slightly revised dedicatory letter to Francis I. Calvin modifies the opening sentence of the text itself so that instead of "nearly the entire sum of sacred doctrine" the subject of the sentence is now "nearly all the wisdom that we possess, that is to say, true and sound wisdom" that consists of the two parts, knowledge of God and of ourselves.[78] He also composes two entirely new chapters, corresponding to each of these parts. The discussion of the law and the Decalogue now appears in chapter 3 and the discussion of faith, the Trinity, and the Apostles' Creed in chapter 4. This section contains much new material, especially in the discussion of faith. Chapter 5 offers a new discussion of penance, formed with some material carried over from the chapter in 1536 dealing with the so-called five false sacraments. Chapter 6 discusses justification by faith and the merit of works. Chapter 7, also a new chapter, deals with the similarity and difference between the Old and New Testament. Chapter 8 treats the topics of predestination and providence. The discussion of prayer and the exposition of the Lord's Prayer appear in chapter 9, which is followed by three chapters on the topics of the sacraments, baptism, and the eucharist. For these chapters Calvin draws on the material in chapters 3–4 in 1536, expanding the discussion to reflect the ongoing polemical battles over these topics. Chapters 13–15 treat Christian freedom, ecclesiastical power, and political administration. The remaining material on the five false sacraments follows in chapter 16, and the work closes with a new final chapter on the life of a Christian.

A brief word about Calvin's editorial process is in order. In revising his earlier material, Calvin usually did not rewrite passages but only, as he says in the preface to the 1559 edition, enriched the earlier discussions with some additions. It will hardly be surprising to anyone who has undertaken revision of his or her own work that Calvin also seemed loathe to throw anything out. He sometimes shifted entire discussions to different locations, but even in the extensive reorganization undertaken for the final edition in 1559 his earlier lines of argumentation on particular topics remain largely intact. This conservative editorial process notwithstanding, his views did not remain static. Indeed, the increasingly extensive expansions and shifting of material imply that Calvin's views were constantly unfolding and that his perspective, though not fundamentally changing, was broadening. It would be impossible to identify all the impulses—polemical, exegetical, pastoral—that led Calvin to restructure and augment earlier discussions. Even so, it remains true that he perceived a need to clarify and expand his previous work in light of new information, challenges, and experiences. As he strove to make his summary of Christian faith more comprehensive, his views on particular topics unfolded in ways that revealed, over time, important shifts in emphasis, if not in ultimate meaning. Furthermore, the reordering of material, especially in 1559, itself does not indicate that Calvin reversed earlier positions. Still, he must have assumed that certain discussions simply made better sense somewhere else and, in moving material around, ensured that these discussions were read in other contexts. This understanding of the expansions and reorganization of material as signs that Calvin's views were expanding and his perspective broadening is supported also by the citation from Augustine that appeared first in the preface to the 1543 edition: "I count myself one of the number of those who write as they learn and learn as they write."[79] Calvin apparently considered his revisions a way toward learning about his subject, and it is my contention, to be borne out hereafter, that this learning entailed a broader, deeper, and more comprehensive understanding of the doctrine of faith than that set forth in 1536.

A new title recalls the bold claims of the title of the first edition and declares the more comprehensive scope of this edition: *Institutes of the Christian Religion, now truly corresponding to its title*. But it is not simply the amount of material that makes this second edition more complete. I showed earlier that even the 1536 edition was not well suited to instruct the common believer in the evangelical faith. This expanded edition, also in Latin, could hardly be expected to be a more adequate catechism for the simple person. Besides, Calvin had already published a small catechism in both Latin and in French while he was in Geneva. In addition, even though the Dedicatory Epistle remains, the sheer bulk of this edition makes it a less likely defense of the core of evangelical teaching, the free forgiveness of sins through faith in Christ. This is not to say that Calvin has abandoned the instructional and apologetic aspects of the 1536 edition. But he does have a slightly different purpose and a new audience in mind.[80] He now conceives of his work as a hermeneutical tool for ministers, that is, as a guide for studying scripture, as he says expressly in his new preface:

> Moreover, it has been my purpose in this labor to prepare and instruct candidates in sacred theology for the reading of the divine word. . . . for I believe I have embraced the sum of religion in all its parts, and have arranged it in such an order, that if anyone rightly grasps it, it will not be difficult for him to determine what he ought especially to seek in scripture, and to what end he ought to relate its contents.[81]

As Wendel has pointed out, even though this Latin preface did not appear in the French editions of the *Institutes* until 1560, the French preface to the 1541 edition also expressed the idea of the *Institutes* as a hermeneutical tool.[82]

The explicit linking of the *Institutes* with the interpretation of scripture is an important development for our consideration of Calvin's theology, for it signals one way that he attained to a greater clarity about the nature of theology (or at least the purpose of his *Institutes*) between 1536 and 1539. This greater clarity was at least in part a result of his exegetical activity. By the time of the second edition, Calvin had been lecturing on scripture and preaching for two and a half years. His early interest in the question of the proper interpretation of scripture, described in the dedication to his Romans commentary (1540), had been heightened by the actual experience of having had to explain, interpret, and preach; he now understands theology to have at least in part a hermeneutical dimension.[83] The *Institutes* is no longer merely a summary of what can be found in scripture but rather a methodological guide for the study of the word.

Related to the clarity of purpose expressed here and carried through all later editions of the *Institutes*, a certain coherence in theological substance begins to manifest itself in 1539. Many scholars have insisted on the foundational character of this edition for Calvin's theological program. They have likewise perceived the importance of his exegetical activity and his reading of the church fathers for this development.[84] For example, Peter Barth, seeing the 1539 edition as well as the Romans commentary as the mature result of Calvin's labors on Romans, argues that the 1539 edition "proceeds upon the fundamental theological lines which were to be followed in all subsequent editions of the *Institutes*."[85] I take these "fundamental theological lines" to be certain key elements of Calvin's thought that were perhaps present in 1536 but that attained increased prominence in 1539. Foremost among these, and the most significant for my consideration of Calvin's idea of theology, his understanding of God, and his view of faith, is the greatly expanded concern with knowledge.[86] As I have shown, knowledge was already a theme in the 1536 *Institutes*, yet Calvin greatly expands this theme in 1539 and increases its prominence. As discussed earlier, he modifies the opening line of the *Institutes* to underscore the centrality of the mutually related knowledge of God and knowledge of self, and he devotes two chapters entirely to this subject.[87] In Calvin's discussion in the first chapter it is possible to trace his attempts to clarify the nature of knowing, his increased concern with *how* humans know God, and, with respect to the content of that knowledge, a heightened interest in knowledge of God's providential activity.

The first chapter shows Calvin's concern with knowing expanding in three areas.[88] The first is the order of knowing. Here he points to the mutual relationship of knowledge of God and knowledge of self, arguing that true self-knowledge requires a corresponding sense of God's glorious nature, while a complete sense of God's majesty is possible only when humans have been thoroughly convinced of their own lowliness.[89] This argument also indicates the greater prominence of the theme of glory of God (and, correspondingly, the humiliation of human beings) in this edition. The second area of development pertains to the perceptual quality of knowledge. Throughout this discussion, Calvin uses the language of perception to characterize the kind of knowledge with which he is concerned.[90] Knowing God and self properly is a matter of "seeing" clearly. The fundamental human problem, according to Calvin, is that human beings fail to see themselves in proper perspective. Humans are deluded about themselves, their abilities, and their righteousness; their vision is impaired.[91] Thus we see the same negative judgment of physical visual experience that we saw in 1536. Yet at the same time, Calvin seems unable to talk about knowing God and self without using visual metaphors. While maintaining his ambiguous attitude toward the physical sense of sight, Calvin suggests that there is also a kind of spiritual vision or inner eye that is directed not only toward external appearances but essentially toward a higher, spiritual reality—toward Christ. Finally, and most important, is the existential or practical character of knowledge. Calvin conceives of the human problem cognitively or noetically, but the kind of knowledge that he claims ought to be gained is not bare cognition, nor is it knowledge of God *in se*. Rather, it is a more intimate familiarity with God, a knowledge of who God is toward human beings. Such knowledge inspires humans to right worship and hope of a future life, since humans can see that the benefits it promises are not fully bestowed in this life. Dowey notes that many scholars have spoken of the "practicality" or "utility" of this kind of knowledge, indicating therewith its nonspeculative character as well as its impact on the whole human person, not just on the intellect. Dowey suggests the adjective "existential," meaning "knowledge that determines the existence of the knower."[92] Calvin calls this a special or unique knowledge of God and says that it issues in an affection of piety (*pietatis affectus*).[93] It is, according to Calvin, not just a function of the intellect but also bears fruit in the heart.[94] In other words, proper knowledge of God affects and involves the entire human person.

In addition to these reflections on the nature of knowing, the question of how humans know God is a focus of concern in Calvin's essentially new first chapter. All in all, he is less interested in *what* humans should know about God and themselves than he was in the 1536 edition.[95] There he listed four things necessary to know about God, then moved quickly through the need to know that Adam's sin affected all subsequent generations, and came promptly to the discussion of the law. In 1539, however, the question of *how* humans gain knowledge of God in the first place absorbs his attention. To explore this topic further, he introduces three possible means for attaining knowledge of God: an inner religious awareness, the external witness of creation, and, finally, the special revelation of scripture.

In his considerations of how human beings attain knowledge of God, Calvin first suggests the sense of divinity (*divinitatis sensus; sentiment de divinité*) and the seed of religion (*religionis semen; semence de religion*) as deep-seated impulses to knowledge of God internal to the human subject. The phenomenon of idolatry— the inevitable result of deluded corruption of this religious impulse—confirms the existence, universality, and ineffaceability of this inner awareness.[96] The fact that the impious themselves manifest a fear of God's wrath, vengeance, and judgment is proof for Calvin that all people have some inner conception of God and hence that religion is no arbitrary invention externally imposed on humans against their will. However, the fearful recognition of God that issues in idolatry and further self-delusion is diametrically opposed in Calvin's mind to the proper, pious knowledge of God to which the internal witness *ought* to give rise. Calvin goes on to consider briefly the kind of response that this awareness of God should produce. People ought to be led by this internal testimony not only to fear and revere God but also to seek in God all good and to respond in thankful acknowledgment. However, he explains, the seed of religion has been so corrupted that it now only produces bad fruit, which is of two sorts: false worship or a recognition of God motivated by slavish or forced fear. Closing his reflections on the internal witness to God, Calvin once again contrasts this twofold corruption with the special knowledge of God, which he designates as an affection of piety, that is aroused in the hearts of the faithful. In contrast to the idolater, the faithful heart does not dream up any god it chooses but rather remains content with God's own self-revelation. Relying on God's will rather than on its own delusions, the pious mind would be led to recognize God's guiding and protecting providence over all things, to see God as the author of all goodness, as both Lord and father, as righteous judge, and to act out of love in accordance with God's will.[97]

Second, Calvin extols creation's witness to all that is needful for humans to know about God and then condemns humanity's failure to comprehend this testimony. As with the internal witness, the knowledge of God "engraved on each of his works" is a revelation accommodated to finite human capacity. Once again, the language of perception is prominent: "First of all, wherever one casts the eyes, there is no spot in the universe wherein one cannot discern some sparks of his glory." Similarly, with reference to what is said by "the author of the letter to the Hebrews," Calvin says that the universe is a mirror in which one contemplates the invisible God.[98] By contemplating the manifestations of divine power in nature, human beings ought to be led to knowledge of God's eternity, God's goodness in preserving creation, and God's love, shown in God's bestowing mercy on every creature. God's power is also abundantly displayed in the course of events, especially in the administration of human society, which points to God's wisdom. And yet, just like the internal witness to God, this external testimony, so clear in itself, is in vain.[99] Humans contemplate the works of creation without considering their author; they consider the course of events and conclude that all is driven by blind fortune. The fault of this dullness is within us, Calvin claims. And so the witness of creation, like the inner testimony, cannot lead to true knowledge of God but serves only to render humans inexcusable.[100]

Third, having asserted the inability of fallen human beings to gain proper knowledge of God through creation, the arts and sciences, or God's providential governance of affairs, Calvin turns to the only effective remedy for humans blinded by sin: the word.[101] The seed of religion, the sense of divinity, and the witness of nature and history were all accommodations to human finitude. But humans, according to Calvin, are not only finite but also fallen. As fallen, they cannot gain proper knowledge of God from these other means. However, in the divine word, first communicated to the patriarchs (of whom Calvin explicitly lists Adam, Noah, and Abraham) in oracles, visions, and human work and ministry and eventually recorded as scripture for posterity (a singular testimony to divine providence), God provided a "special school" for God's children. Scripture is thus the particular and more certain source of knowledge of God, given the situation of human fallenness.

Calvin follows this with a long defense of the authority of scripture over the church.[102] The authority of scripture, he argues, comes from God, not from the church. The inner illumination of the Spirit authenticates authoritative interpretation; apart from this activity of the Spirit, scripture can be distorted by human judgment. As I have shown, this was precisely the problem with the extrascriptural testimony: humans always judged and continue to judge it from their own fallen perspective. With scripture this should not happen, according to Calvin, since word and Spirit are united. God as Holy Spirit works to seal the objective witness of scripture on human hearts, so that the knowledge of God attained thereby is sure and certain, conveying a witness to God that is identical to that in creation and aims toward the same goal.

Guided by his concern for how human beings attain proper knowledge of God, Calvin thus moves in this new first chapter along three avenues leading to that goal, two of which, he determines, are dead ends. It is only God's word, now expressed in written form in scripture and sealed by the Spirit on the human heart, that provides the testimony sufficient to override human judgment and lead fallen human beings to proper knowledge of God.[103] However, despite the thoroughness of this investigation, it is still clear that the question of how God is known has not yet been fully answered. First, one notices that Calvin struggles very hard to defend the authority of scripture; this raises one's suspicions that the knowledge of God provided in scripture is not as objectively clear as Calvin hopes it is. Or, even if it is objectively clear, one's impression that there is still something lacking in the epistemological scheme is confirmed by his concluding sentence to chapter 1. Here he asserts that faith in Christ is also necessary in order for this witness to be grasped. Calvin thus concludes chapter 1 by pointing ahead to the discussion of faith yet to come:

> For since the Lord does not properly show himself for intimate contemplation except in the face of his Christ, which cannot be gazed upon except with the eyes of faith, that which remains to be said about the knowledge of God is put off to that place where the perception of faith [*fidei intelligentia*] will be treated.[104]

This closing statement indicates that the problem of knowledge has not yet been fully resolved and, furthermore, that it cannot be fully resolved merely by asserting the authority of scripture. With his discussion of biblical authority, Calvin has only begun to travel down the avenue of God's word. Until he has arrived at the point for discussing Jesus Christ (the word made flesh) and faith's apprehension of this word, Calvin's discussion of the knowledge of God remains incomplete.

Even though he pays the greatest attention to how humans know God, Calvin continues to be concerned with what they ought to know about God, a theme that, as in 1536, receives treatment in various parts of the text. With respect to this issue, I note in particular a heightened sensitivity to God's providential care and an expanded interest in God's activity apart from redemption. For example, I have already shown that in chapter 1 Calvin is interested in a knowledge of God as the author of all goodness, benevolent creator and sustainer, righteous judge, and loving father. These themes, some of which Calvin had mentioned briefly at the beginning of the 1536 edition, receive more detailed treatment in 1539. Calvin underscores their importance by presenting them as defining characteristics of true worship and religion. Of particular note is the fact that in chapter 1 Calvin refers twice to Heb. 11:3, that the world is a theater of invisible things. The first time Calvin makes the point that the world is a mirror for contemplating God.[105] Yet, as I have shown, he goes on to argue that fallen human beings cannot make positive use of creation's witness. However, in the second mention of the verse, Calvin ascribes to *faith* the power of restoring this lost vision of God:

> For this reason, the apostle, in that very passage where he calls the world the images of things invisible, adds that through faith we understand that they have been fashioned by God's word. He means by this that the invisible divinity is made manifest in such spectacles but that we have not the eyes to see this unless they be illumined by the inner revelation of God through faith.[106]

Through faith, godly eyes have the ability to know and see God's goodness through the contemplation of God's works.

Another example of Calvin's heightened sensitivity to providence is found in his discussion of the first article of the Creed, where in 1536 he had discussed God's providence in just a few sentences. In 1539 he prefaces this short discussion with a consideration of how believing in God the Father is to have God for one's own, as a loving father. He then asserts that this is to attribute to God an active and effective omnipotence, by which God regulates all things. He mentions this only in passing, telling his readers that he will take the topic of God's providence up later. However, he also links this to the discussion of faith just finished by declaring that faith arms itself with a double consolation from consideration of God's omnipotence, a topic that he will treat at greater length in chapter 8.[107] Calvin then offers a longer reflection on the words "creator of heaven and earth," in which he presents, once again referring to Heb. 11:3, in some detail the view that it is through faith that human beings recognize God as the creator and perpetual governor of the world.[108]

Finally, in addition to the treatment of providence in chapter 1 and under the first article of the Creed, Calvin has a new discussion of this topic in chapter 8. Here he treats first the doctrine of predestination, which leads him into a discussion of God's governance of all things. Calvin's main concern in this latter discussion is to distinguish God's special and deliberate foreordination of every event from the confused and mixed sort of governance that some call universal providence.[109] He distinguishes providence from his view of the Stoic understanding of fate by arguing that God does not act according to necessity.[110] From the human perspective events appear to be fortuitous, though they are not. This does not mean that human beings should not act, for example, to preserve their lives, since, Calvin writes, "he who has set the limits to our life has entrusted to us its care."[111] Calvin sets forth his views in a polemical tone; even in the section where he describes the comfort that the doctrine of special providence affords believers, one still has the sense that this element of knowledge about God is one that Calvin perceives to be under attack. In this chapter he identifies at least four opponents. He rejects the deterministic view that he attributes to opponents that he calls Stoics and the view of those unnamed opponents who, in the interest of preserving human freedom, imagine a bare foreknowledge or leave to God a confused governance that does not extend to every event. He also engages in polemic against those he calls Epicureans, who imagine God to be indulging himself in idleness.[112]

In addition, he seeks to refute the view that if all has been already decreed by God, then there is no point to any action whatever.

These considerations of Calvin's expansions of particular themes in the 1539 *Institutes* suggest that Calvin has broadened the soteriological perspective that governed the 1536 edition. While the question of human salvation still looms large, it no longer drives the entire presentation. Instead, we find at least three significant substantive developments that suggest that, while not at all diminishing the significance of this question, Calvin now conceives of it in a broader context. The first development I have traced is his expanded concern for epistemology, expressed particularly in his interest in not merely what humans know about God but also how knowledge of God is possible and what kind of knowledge this is. Even though Calvin now construes the human problem epistemologically and expresses it largely in perceptual imagery, it does not seem that the correction of human blindness is his final concern. Instead, the discussion of knowledge serves to expand the idea briefly raised in the Dedicatory Epistle in 1536 that the ultimate issue at stake is something larger than human salvation; namely, the glory of God. Hence, second, along with this heightened interest in epistemology, we find renewed emphasis on the majesty and glory of God. As noted earlier, this was already a theme in 1536, and as early as the 1537 catechism Calvin had asserted glorification of the divine majesty to be the very telos of all creation.[113] In 1539 the question of God's glory increases in prominence and receives more detailed reflection.[114] For example, chapter 1 is really an extended meditation on the majesty of God. In my discussion of Calvin's treatment of the first article of the Creed and of providence in chapter 8 I have shown his concern to defend the doctrine of providence extending to the governance of all things. To deny providence is to undermine the divine omnipotence, with the result that human beings will be disinclined to worship God. Finally, compared to the 1536 edition, he pays greater attention here to God's providential activity.[115] As early as his preface to Olivétan's French Bible, written in Basel in 1535, Calvin had extolled the divine majesty and wisdom engraved on the entire created order and evident in the biblical history.[116] And yet, as I have shown, the themes of creation and providence did not figure prominently in the 1536 *Institutes*. In part Calvin's inclusion of the topic of providence in 1539 derives from Bucer's suggestion that he do so.[117] Moreover, he may have been influenced by other evangelical contemporaries' treatment of this theme.[118] Perhaps his regard for this topic also reflects the heightened sensitivity to divine providence that arose as a result of his vocational struggles. In any case, the divine activity is now explicitly construed on a much larger scale: Calvin places God's redemptive activity in the broader context of God's ongoing providential activity.

These developments suggest that the evolution in Calvin's thought between 1536 and 1539 involved the formulation of a distinction both within the divine activity as revealed in scripture and, correspondingly, in the way that human beings apprehend God's acts toward them: a distinction between God's providential activity, which, for Calvin, is really an extension of God's creative activity, and God's redemptive activity, which, for Calvin, relates to the restoration of a fallen creation. Throughout the rest of his career Calvin continued to work with this distinction. In the final edition of the *Institutes*, Calvin refers explicitly to a twofold knowledge of God, knowledge of God as redeemer and knowledge of God as creator. Regardless of whether one agrees with the idea that the twofold knowledge forms the organizational principle of the 1559 edition, the concept still remains an important and central feature of Calvin's presentation of the Christian faith, and its influence can be discerned as early as the 1539 edition.[119]

Since for Calvin knowledge of God is knowledge of God's acts *pro nobis*, proper knowledge of God includes knowledge of both types of activity and reflects a corresponding distinction in human apprehension of God's redemptive and creative/providential work. Scripture provides fallen human beings with information about both realms. On the one hand, scripture confirms what could be known about God through the internal and external testimony to the creator if human beings had eyes to see it. On the other hand, fallen human beings cannot have complete knowledge of God without faith in Christ, and scripture instructs concerning God's saving work in Christ as well. In both cases, the objective witness of scripture alone is not sufficient; in order to grasp both aspects of knowledge of God provided in the word, one needs the inner illumination of the Spirit.

In order to trace Calvin's discussions of this second type of knowledge, I turn now to his treatment of the special discernment of faith, to which he directed his readers at the end of chapter 1. It is clear that he has broadened the soteriological perspective of the 1536 edition of the *Institutes* so that the question of human salvation no longer drives the discussion but is set within the larger context of the fullness of the divine activity. Yet inasmuch as faith in Christ provides the ultimate solution to the problem of knowledge of God, the christological orientation of the earlier edition is maintained.

In the introduction to his translation of the 1536 edition of the *Institutes*, Ford Lewis Battles remarks that the chapter on faith "was the chief casualty of the later editions." He reasons that "the centrality, existentially speaking, of faith to Calvin's whole religious view, demanded more than a mere reliance on an ancient and post-scriptural epitome of evangelical teaching, such as the Apostles' Creed."[120] Indeed, in 1539 Calvin greatly expanded his discussion of the subject of faith and treated it in a separate chapter, though it still preceded the exposition of the Creed, which, prefaced by the discussion of the Trinity, followed in chapter 5. Within the discussion of faith itself, there are many new additions. Among these are more detailed polemical responses to the scholastic distinctions (between formed and unformed faith and between implicit and explicit faith); extensive reflections on faith's relationship to certainty, doubt, and fear; broader biblical references and allusions; and, above all, a new formal definition of faith, along with an explication of it. In considering some of these additions, one can see how several of the developments I traced earlier have left their impression on Calvin's understanding of faith.

Calvin enriches his opening comments on faith by exploring what sort of faith he means in much more detail. He refers explicitly to the distinction between unformed and formed faith, which he designates as absurd. He also expands his explication of the two broad types of faith. The first category includes people who simply assent to the truth of the gospel history as well as those whose belief does not penetrate to the heart. These, Calvin asserts, like Simon Magus (Acts 8) and the seeds sown on the rocky soil in the Gospel parable, hold God's word to be a certain oracle and appear to show such obedience to it that they convince others and themselves that they show true piety. Far superior is true faith, which aims at and rests on the word, in which it both perceives and contemplates God's benevolent will toward humans. His primary authority continues to be the apostle Paul: "We recognize and proclaim with Paul only one faith among the pious."[121] And yet Calvin is also more attentive here to the fact that there are diverse meanings of the word "faith" in scripture, as his discussions seeking to fit these to his definition attest.

At this point Calvin introduces something completely new into the discussion: a distinction within what can be known about God from God's word. Faith, Calvin claims, does not rest on all aspects of God's will revealed in the word; some words of God shake and threaten faith. Faith finds its support only in God's benevolence or mercy. Calvin returns to this issue later. For now, this line of reasoning leads him directly to the most significant change in the 1539 edition; namely, the formulation of a definition of faith that he carries unchanged through the remaining editions of the *Institutes*: "Now we shall possess a right definition of faith if we say that faith is a firm and certain knowledge of the divine benevolence toward us, which, founded on the truth of the free promise in Christ, is both revealed to our minds and sealed on our hearts through the Holy Spirit."[122] The rest of the discussion, nearly all of it new in 1539, treats in greater detail individual elements of the definition. I will consider these elements in turn, referring on occasion to other parts of chapter 4 where they appear.

Calvin considers first the characterization of faith as knowledge and how this accords with other ways of knowing. He distinguishes the knowledge of faith from ordinary sense perception in language that recalls the passages I examined from 1536, specifically those discussions of Heb. 11:1. Citing Eph. 3:18, "to comprehend what is the breadth, length, depth and height, and to know the love of Christ, which surpasses knowledge," he endeavors to show how "this kind of knowledge is loftier than all understanding."[123] He then offers a scriptural basis for understanding faith as knowledge. He claims on Paul's authority that faith is like knowledge in that it grasps the secrets of the divine will that God has revealed (Col. 1:26).[124] Yet the knowledge of faith appears to be distinguished from ordinary knowledge first of all by the immutable and infinite nature of its object, the divine word. A second distinction lies in how this object is apprehended. Faith, Calvin remarks, is often called recognition (*agnitio*).[125] John, however, calls faith *scientia*; Calvin grants this but, it appears, with a Pauline qualification. He wants to make sure that his readers understand that this does not mean that faith is a bare assent to propositions demonstrated rationally. Faith is not only a matter of the intellect. So faith is also different from ordinary knowledge in that the divine truths remain incomprehensible to the human intellect and thus "unseen" (see 2 Cor. 5:6). Faith's task is to persuade humans that those infinite things that the finite human mind cannot fully comprehend are indeed true and reliable. Thus, he concludes, "the knowledge of faith consists in assurance [*certitudine*] rather than in comprehension [*apprehensione*]."[126]

Specifying faith's knowledge as assurance rather than as comprehension, Calvin also conceives of knowing as a kind of seeing, resorting repeatedly to perceptual language to characterize the knowledge of faith. For instance, he compares the word to a mirror "in which faith may fix its gaze [*intueatur*] and contemplate God."[127] The view is at first cloudy or obscure, but the object is nonetheless intelligible:

> [As soon as] the least drop of faith has been instilled in our minds, already we begin to contemplate the face of God peaceful and calm and graceful toward us. Certainly we see it far off, but with a certain intuition, so that we know that we are not hallucinating at all. How much we then advance (as it is fitting for us to advance), with steady progress we come more clearly and certainly into the view of him.[128]

While distinguishing the knowledge of faith from ordinary vision, Calvin speaks of faith as a spiritual capacity to see things illumined by the Holy Spirit.[129] Recall that at the end of chapter 1 he referred to faith as an eye.

In calling faith "knowledge" Calvin is moving away from the terminology of trust or confidence that, as I showed, characterized his position in 1536–1537.[130] Yet while he favors the language of knowledge over that of trust or confidence, he does not eliminate faith's fiducial character. In part, Calvin employs noetic terminology to underscore the certainty of faith and therewith faith's confidence. Nonetheless, citing Paul (Eph. 3:12), he will not equate *fiducia* and *fides*. In this verse, confidence is derived from faith; the link between the two is so close that Calvin acknowledges that "the word faith is often used for *fiducia*."[131] Strictly speaking, however, *fiducia* is a characteristic of faith as knowledge. The fiducial nature of faith is expressed, according to Calvin, in the idea that the knowledge of faith is firm and certain, a notion that he claims is attested broadly in scripture. Faith's confidence constitutes an important element in Calvin's understanding of faith's knowledge, even though faith is no longer synonymous with trust, as it was in 1536.[132] He criticizes medieval understandings of faith for neglecting confidence and, at one point, says that confidence of the heart is the principal element in faith.[133] One must ask first how Calvin perceives the fiducial element in faith and then, granted the centrality of this element, why he speaks of faith as knowledge rather than trust.

For Calvin, human beings are confident about things that repeated experience has demonstrated are reliable. The question is, how can human beings have such experience of heavenly wisdom and mysteries—things that the mind cannot comprehend, which are therefore far off and unseen? The answer lies in the peculiar knowledge of faith, in the characteristics that distinguish it from ordinary knowledge that I noted earlier: the uniqueness of faith's object and the special mode of faith's apprehension of this object. Like ordinary knowledge, this special kind of knowledge is based on actual, subjective experience of its object. Calvin writes, "Here is the chief hinge on which faith turns: that we do not regard the promises of mercy that God offers as true only outside ourselves, but not at all in us; rather that we make them ours by inwardly embracing them."[134] Believers have firsthand experience of the divine benevolence and are therefore absolutely certain of their salvation. Indeed, given the immutability and infinite nature of the divine promise of mercy and the power of the Spirit revealing this to their minds and sealing it on their hearts, they are *more* certain of the things known by faith than they could be of anything known ordinarily. So while the knowledge of faith, unlike ordinary knowledge, does not rest on rational demonstration or physical sense perception,[135] because of the immutable nature of its object and because it is effected by the Spirit, such knowledge is characterized by a higher degree of certainty. Faith is, as Dowey has said, a "suprarational knowledge" through which the mind achieves a "supernatural certainty of personal salvation."[136] Faith and confidence are thus distinguished without being separated.[137]

Granted the importance of faith's firm and certain character and given also that faith inevitably leads to *fiducia*, why is it that Calvin identifies faith explicitly as knowledge? In this shift in terminology from *fiducia* to *cognitio* one can detect the enormous impact that Calvin's fascination with the problem of knowledge was having on his theology. The fundamental human problem, according to Calvin, appears to be not misdirected trust but rather false knowledge of God and self.[138] Hence faith is not essentially *fiducia* but rather proper knowledge. However, it should be clear that, in defining faith as knowledge and distinguishing it from trust, Calvin is not adopting a purely intellectualistic notion of faith.[139] Rather, he rejects such a view, which he equates with the scholastic implicit faith. Instead, he is expanding the definition of knowledge and working within, as Olivier Millet has shown, the rhetorical tradition of Lorenzo Valla and Guillaume Budé, mediated by Bucer and Melanchthon.[140] As I showed earlier, knowledge, for Calvin, involves the whole human being; true knowledge is not merely a matter of the intellect but also of the will. For this reason the knowledge of faith consists of two elements: the Spirit both reveals the object of faith to the mind *and* seals it upon the heart. Faith as knowledge, Calvin says, is higher and deeper than understanding; he might just as easily have said that it is higher and deeper than the will. Yet Calvin refuses to reduce faith to trust because he would thereby forfeit the cognitive element. He understands knowledge to pertain to the entire human soul, which he claims is fallen in both its parts (understanding and will). He therefore finds in knowledge a concept that is comprehensive enough to capture the whole character of faith.[141] Moreover, he seems to find the idea of faith as knowledge to have a broader biblical basis, as is indicated in his proof texts from Paul and the Johannine writings.

Having emphasized the full assurance and certainty of faith, Calvin must now respond to the charge that his definition of faith leaves no room for the experiences of doubt, temptation, and fear, all of which are widely recognized in scripture and verified empirically. He begins by making a distinction between the flesh and the spirit, thereby indicating a connection between the strength of faith and the process of sanctification. Believers, according to Calvin, feel in themselves a division between spirit, the already regenerated elements of their nature, and flesh, those remaining vestiges of fallenness and sin. In the lifelong process of sanctification, believers experience conflicts as a result of this division. Consequently, faith, which is conceived inwardly, is subject to attack from without in the form of doubt, temptation, and fear. Faith does not yet reign perfectly in the whole human being, but where it does rule, its power cannot be shaken. Faith arms itself with the immutable word of God and is ever confident in God's promise of mercy. These external attacks sometimes work to strengthen faith's hold on the word by forcing the believer to seek refuge in God, thereby displaying the certainty of faith's confidence. Moreover, these experiences remind believers that they are not yet completely regenerate, thus encouraging them to "shake off the sluggishness of their flesh."[142] These tensions between certainty and doubt and confidence and fear signal Calvin's recognition of faith's present imperfection. Yet he also maintains that true faith could never succumb to doubt, temptation, or fear.[143] His unwillingness to admit this underscores the fact that faith's certainty, however closely the growth of faith might be tied to the process of sanctification, does not rest on this process but rests rather in the gratuitous promise of mercy, the decree of justification.

Therefore these considerations of the imperfection of faith and the process of sanctification should not suggest that Calvin has strayed from the principle of the free forgiveness of sins through faith in Christ. He is confident that true faith, "even the tiniest drop," rests firmly in the clear knowledge of the salvation wrought by Christ. Though faith may not yet reign perfectly over the whole human being, even these small beginnings are sufficient for salvation. As I showed earlier, for Calvin the knowledge of faith involves actual subjective experience of this fact; that is, it is revealed to the mind and sealed on the heart by the Holy Spirit. This experience is so certain that nothing can ultimately shake it. Therefore he refutes the scholastic notion that because believers are not yet holy they can only have conjectural certainty about salvation. He argues further that the purity of life toward which the faithful strive does not in any way merit God's favor. If merit were required, doubt would return and no certainty would remain.[144]

Underlying the lengthy discussions of doubt, temptation, and fear and the repeated emphasis on certainty is the same soteriological concern that we saw in the 1536 edition. The particular trials afflicting faith are all portrayed as calling the promise of salvation into question. The certainty that the believer possesses is certainty of one's own salvation in Christ. Thus in Calvin's definition "divine benevolence" refers primarily to God's redemptive activity: to God's promise of free forgiveness of sins and eternal life through Christ.[145] In fact, at times it appears almost to be restricted to this. At one point, he writes that "the chief assurance of faith lies in the expectation of the life to come." He goes on to say that, of course, the divine benevolence is the source of every good, not just eternal salvation. Likewise, faith is certain that God is true in all things. Yet it looks particularly to the promise of mercy, that is, the promise of salvation, the gospel. The gospel alone, not God's law, commandments, or precepts, offers a "sufficiently firm testimony of God's benevolence."[146]

We see again what Calvin mentioned briefly at the beginning of his discussion of faith; namely, the idea that faith does not have equal regard for every word of God but looks particularly, perhaps exclusively, to God's benevolent word, the promise given in Jesus Christ. While never denying that the Christian must believe all of scripture, Calvin nonetheless maintains that only a part of scripture is the object of faith proper.[147] The law, for example, cannot be the object of a faith that makes one certain of one's salvation, for the law throws responsibility back on the human being.[148] This means that certain elements of knowledge of God, for example, God as judge, and presumably also God as creator and providential governor of the world, are not the object of faith as it is here described, for these are divine activities that are distinct from the reconciling activity proclaimed in the gospel. Calvin writes:

> Therefore, when we say that faith must rest upon a freely given promise, we do not deny that believers embrace and grasp the word of God in every respect: but we point out the promise of mercy as the proper goal of faith. As on the one hand believers ought to recognize God to be the Judge and Avenger of wicked deeds, yet on the other hand they properly contemplate his kindness, since he is so described to them as to be considered one who is kind, and merciful, far from anger and of great goodness, sweet to all, pouring out his mercy on all his works.[149]

As I will show, at least one opponent charged that Calvin did not successfully maintain the unity of God's word in making this distinction in divine revelation.

Calvin's distinction reflects his nascent understanding of the twofold character of the divine activity as perceived by fallen humans. Augmenting his earlier emphasis on God's redemptive activity with heightened attention to God's glory and providential activity, Calvin needs to specify more precisely how the knowledge of God that is faith relates to all that can be known about God from God's word. In the discussion of faith, he achieves this by speaking of faith's "proper goal" and believers' proper contemplation. The person of faith believes every word of God is true but relies only on God's word of mercy in Christ; by extension, this person believes the divine activity apart from redemption but rests only in God the redeemer. Faith in its strictest sense then is saving knowledge of God and as such provides entrance into knowledge of the broader divine activity. It now becomes clear that fallen human beings must grasp revelation in a particular order: knowledge of God the redeemer precedes knowledge of God the creator. Moreover, knowledge of God the redeemer not only has logical priority but is also the ground or the condition for the possibility of all other knowledge of God; all true knowledge of God is through knowledge of God's saving activity in Christ.

This resolution of the issue of how humans know God leaves unanswered the question of faith's relationship to the divine activity apart from redemption in Christ. Is this knowledge of the broader divine activity also "faith"? Calvin's concern to specify the faith that saves leads one to wonder if one can speak at all meaningfully about faith—in its proper sense—in God the creator. That Calvin assumes some relationship between faith and the divine activity apart from redemption is beyond dispute. As I showed earlier, he says that knowledge of God's providence confirms faith, that faith as certainty of one's salvation is doubly confirmed from consideration of God's omnipotence.[150] The fact that he defines faith as knowledge itself establishes a crucial link between the ideas expressed earlier in the *Institutes* and the knowledge of faith. However, it is impossible to specify this relationship exactly and, on the basis of the apparent restriction of the proper goal of faith to God's word of mercy, it appears unlikely, at least in 1539, that one could speak of true faith with respect to any divine activity apart from redemption. In 1539 Calvin's broadening of the soteriological perspective that governed his 1536 edition has apparently not yet extended to his discussion of faith, in which, in response perhaps to his expansion of nonsoteriological themes, he paints a portrait of faith that emphasizes faith's saving activity to the virtual exclusion of faith as firm and certain knowledge and assurance of God's creative and providential activity.

There are, in my view, two factors contributing to this disjunction. First, Calvin's discussion of faith in 1539 continues to be fundamentally Pauline. Nearly all the significant biblical texts in chapter 4 are from New Testament writings that Calvin thought to be from the hand of Paul.[151] Moreover, the distinctly Pauline themes of faith in Christ, certainty, the imperfection of faith, justification, and eternal life dominate the discussion. In his endeavor to do away with the highly fluid medieval terminology about faith, which he felt was humanly devised, Calvin sought and found in his reading of the apostle Paul a biblical way of speaking about faith. In addition to drawing on Paul's vocabulary, he also adopted a distinctly Pauline emphasis on soteriology. Second, I believe that in 1539 Calvin was just starting to integrate his expanding interest in the full scope of the divine activity into his theology. He was just beginning to augment the soteriological perspective that governed the first edition of the *Institutes* by incorporating ideas about God's creative and providential activity that he found in scripture, saw expressed in the Creed, and felt confirmed in his own experience. Related to this broadened perspective on the divine activity is the growing concern for the problem of knowledge that Calvin brought into this edition. In the section on faith, the expanded concern for knowledge is clearly evident, but there are virtually no traces of the heightened sensitivity to God's providential activity. Nonetheless, recall that in each of the three places that this interest in God's providential activity manifests itself (chapter 1, the end of chapter 4, and chapter 8), Calvin speaks of faith in relation to providence.

Before turning from the 1539 *Institutes*, a few concluding observations will provide a bridge to my consideration of the subsequent editions. The seeds for the idea of a twofold knowledge of God are implicit in the sections where Calvin explores God's providential activity; the idea continues to develop and becomes important and explicit in the 1559 edition. In addition, the notion of a twofold knowledge of God also left its impression on those parts of chapter 4 where Calvin makes a distinction in special revelation, though the distinction between God's word of mercy and God's word of judgment does not exactly parallel the distinction between God's redemptive and providential or creative activity. More obvious marks were left by the heightened interest in epistemology. This concern clearly made its presence felt in chapter 4 on faith, where Calvin identifies faith as knowledge and spends pages explicating what kind of knowledge this is. Faith is, for Calvin, the solution to the problem of knowing raised in chapters 1 and 2. Through the eyes of faith, fallen human beings can once again contemplate God as revealed in the face of Christ. And though Calvin intimates that eyes healed by faith can contemplate God's revelation in the world, he does not treat this theme at all in the discussion of faith itself.

Thus Calvin's formal definition of faith in 1539 reflects something of the important development that his thought as a whole has undergone since the first edition of the *Institutes*. And while one cannot yet answer the question about the relationship between faith and God the creator, one can expect that inasmuch as the concept of a twofold knowledge of God continued to develop, Calvin's ideas about the knowledge of God that is faith also were to evolve. This is indeed the case. As with the formation of his present views on faith, Calvin's reading of scripture played an important role in this evolution, reflecting his eventual move to a view of faith that, like the knowledge of God, is twofold. Calvin's exegetical work on Paul throughout the 1540s allowed him to refine and sharpen the themes already expressed in 1539, where the discussion of faith clearly reflects Calvin's recent work on Romans and the Gospel of John. Though, of course, it is impossible to establish how the lectures on scripture themselves influenced the views in the 1539 *Institutes*, chapters 2 and 3 will suggest ways that his lectures might have contributed to his discussion of faith by showing how the themes emphasized in the 1539 *Institutes* emerge also in his later commentaries. In the 1550s, however, Calvin began lecturing and writing commentaries on the Old Testament works. The Old Testament texts, particularly Genesis, the Psalms, Isaiah, and Job, intensified for Calvin the themes of the hiddenness of God, the perception of providence, and the confusion of history, issues that have more to do with the divine activity apart from specific redemption in Christ. Pondering these and similar issues, Calvin began to relate his understanding of faith to them. As I will show in chapters 4 and 5, the fruits of this reflection are apparent in the understanding of faith expressed in the 1559 *Institutes*.

As the final stage of preparation for my consideration of the exegetical influences on Calvin's views on faith, the concluding section of this chapter will outline the development of his discussion of faith in the subsequent editions of the *Institutes*, up through the penultimate Latin edition of 1554.

The Quest for Certainty

In September 1541 Calvin returns to Geneva, where, contrary to his initial expectations, he is to remain for the rest of his life. While attending to all the responsibilities of his position as pastor, he continues to work on his *Institutes*, publishing three revised Latin editions and French translations of each of these, many of which will be reprinted numerous times.[152] In all the remaining editions prior to the final edition of 1559, the discussion of faith follows the order first established in 1539. In the third (1543) and again in the fourth (1550) Latin editions, Calvin expands the discussion of faith slightly in order to respond to polemical challenges raised against the argument set forth in 1539. There are two major issues addressed in these editions: first, the challenge to the certainty that Calvin claimed for faith and, second, a criticism of the distinction that he had made within special revelation when he argued that faith looks especially to God's promise. In responding to these criticisms, Calvin refines and sharpens the line of argumentation from 1539. In addition, I will consider briefly two minor changes that he made in his treatment of Heb. 11:1.

In formulating his views on the certainty of faith in 1539 Calvin insisted that faith involved an absolute certainty of God's benevolence and, in particular, subjective certainty of one's own salvation. The dominance of this theme has led Schützeichel, the author of the most detailed investigation into Calvin's concept of faith, to argue that the description of certainty is the core of Calvin's discussion of faith.[153] Schützeichel also demonstrates how Calvin's arguments for the certainty of faith need to be understood in the context of medieval scholastic debates about the certainty of grace.[154] Medieval theologians such as Alexander of Hales, Bonaventure, Albert the Great, Thomas Aquinas, and Gabriel Biel agreed that one could know for certain that one was in a state of grace only through a special revelation, as was the case, for example, with the apostle Paul. All denied any certainty on the grounds of speculative knowledge but affirmed a conjectural certainty based on particular experiences or signs. Therefore, because God is ultimately inscrutable, no one can be sure of having received the gift of *gratia gratum faciens* or *caritas* unless through a special and exceedingly rare revelation. As Schützeichel points out, medieval theologians tended to be most concerned with grace as a divinely infused gift. Moreover, their primary concern was not whether God was gracious but rather whether the individual possessed this inner gift of grace. Maintaining a merely conjectural certainty, a kind of hope, of having received the gift of grace did not, for them, undermine the reality of God's disposition of grace toward humans.[155] One could affirm this and hope that it would extend to one's self.

With the medieval tradition, Calvin rejected the speculative certainty of faith, but in contrast he also denied conjectural certainty and extended to all believers the subjective certainty that comes from revelation. This revelation is a disclosure of God's nature, which, for Calvin, is not an abstract knowledge of God *in se* but rather a revelation of who God is *erga nos*. Reversing the priorities of the preceding tradition, Calvin focused on grace not as a divinely infused gift but as a divine disposition, as God *erga nos*. For Calvin, the revelation of God's benevolence— God's gracious disposition—comes through the Holy Spirit and is subjectively appropriated as the Spirit "seals" this knowledge of God on the individual human mind and heart. As Schützeichel summarizes, the true believer individualizes the truth of the gospel and refers the promises of God to himself.[156] So, for Calvin, there can be no question of whether one has received the "gift" of grace, for, in his view, the revelation of God's grace ineluctably leads to the personal, individual appropriation of it. Likewise, one cannot be certain of God's graceful benevolence toward humans while only hoping that this grace extends to one's self. If faith is firm and certain knowledge of God's benevolence, then, for Calvin, it includes certainty of one's own salvation. Faith does not merely hope for eternal life but is fully assured of it.[157]

Related to Calvin's transformation of the medieval concept of and teaching on grace and the certainty of grace is his revision of the scholastic tradition's understanding of the role of doubt and the place of fear. His frequent accusations

that the scholastics (especially in their understanding of *conjectura moralis*) mix faith and doubt are not exactly accurate, for many medieval theologians also held that doubt contradicts faith.[158] Moreover, his understanding of different types of fear (a slavish, forced fear that results from the perversion of the religious impulse; a fear of divine wrath that forces the believer to seek refuge in the word or strive toward mortification of the flesh) also has medieval roots.[159] Yet in contrast to scholastic theology Calvin holds that while doubt, temptation, and fear assail faith they can never destroy faith's certainty of salvation. The rejection of the subjective certainty of salvation by the sixth session of the Council of Trent (January 1547) is indicative of the resistance with which this understanding of doubt and certainty was met in the middle third of the sixteenth century. It is significant that his attempts to specify his views in the subsequent revisions to the *Institutes* as well as in his response to the Council of Trent in 1548 rely heavily on Pauline proof texts.[160]

In the four additions made to the discussion of faith in 1543 Calvin continues to insist on, underscore, and expand the theme of certainty. There are probably several reasons why he added to the discussion. One section is clearly a polemical response to a position that he considers inadequate; in addition, perhaps the issue of certainty and the reality of doubt had become an even more pressing pastoral as well as polemical concern. Finally, all the new sections reveal the influence of Paul, suggesting the importance of Paul's views for Calvin's presentation of faith.

The first addition expands on one of Calvin's favorite proof texts for the certainty of faith, Eph. 3:12.[161] In 1539 Calvin had cited this passage to demonstrate that *fides* and *fiducia* are two distinct yet closely related concepts. In 1543 he inserted two sentences into this discussion: "With these words [Paul] shows clearly that there is no right faith except when we dare to stand in God's sight with tranquil hearts. This boldness arises only out of a sure confidence in divine benevolence and salvation."[162] These sentences underscore the subjective assurance of faith and the certainty of salvation that this entails.

The second addition attempts to spell out in more detail the relationship between faith and unbelief (*incredulitas*).[163] Picking up on Paul's reference in Eph. 6:16 to the "shield of faith," Calvin employs lively battle imagery to depict faith as a strong soldier assailed from without but never mortally wounded within. He also draws on the example of David in Ps. 23:4 and cites approvingly a statement from Augustine that faith dwelling in the heart casts aside the devices hurled at it by the devil. Calvin thus tries to provide analogies for the coexistence of a firm and certain faith with doubt and temptation.

The third expansion appears immediately after this, when Calvin reflects on the positive effects of such affliction. The first benefit arises when believers consider examples of the divine wrath being executed on the ungodly. In 1539 Calvin referred to 1 Cor. 10:1–13 to support his argument that fear of the divine wrath shakes off the sluggishness of the flesh, restrains presumptuous overconfidence, and is therefore beneficial. In 1543 he reflects further on these themes, perhaps conflating Paul's discussion in 1 Corinthians 10 with his statements in Rom. 11:17–24. Both these passages threaten Calvin's idea of certainty, for in both Paul warns his audience that they might through their pride be cut off from God, just as many of the Jews were. Calvin cautions that Paul is addressing hypocrites, who only appear to have faith, as well as believers. Also, he says, Paul is not talking to individuals, but rather making an example of the Jews and Gentiles to explain that hypocrites might appear even among the Gentiles. At the end, however, he allows that someone might understand this example to apply to the elect, and in this case Paul's exhortations would serve to curb arrogance, but they would not so "dishearten the conscience with fear that it cannot rest with full assurance in God's mercy."[164]

Returning to the line of argumentation from 1539, Calvin discusses how believers can "be afraid" and still posses "surest consolation." Paul's statement to work out salvation in fear and trembling (Phil. 2:12) as well as statements from the Psalms and Proverbs teach that faith is always joined with reverent fear arising from the sense of God's holiness and human ruin. This kind of fear makes humans cautious but does not cause them to fall; a second benefit of affliction is that it makes believers more certain in the Lord. In 1543 Calvin appends to this a long, polemical response to unnamed "half-papists" who he says advance the view that as long as human beings look to Christ, they are confident, but when they consider their own unworthiness, they necessarily waver.[165] Thus, Calvin claims, they hold that unbelief and good hope reign alternately in the human mind. He vehemently rejects this view, citing Rom. 8:10 and arguing that because of the union they share with Christ, believers are certain that salvation is theirs. He ends with a long quotation from Bernard of Clairvaux.[166] David Willis notes that underlying Calvin's refutation is an understanding of believers' knowledge of self that is fundamentally different from that he attributes to his opponents. Because of their inseparable union with Christ, believers cannot consider themselves or their unworthiness apart from Christ: "the only selves they even have to consider, in fact, is that of persons who participate in Christ himself and therefore in his benefits."[167] In short, the opponents' anthropological assumptions seek to undermine the important distinction between reverent and servile fear and threaten the proper understanding of faith's certainty.

The additions to the discussion of faith in 1543 reveal Calvin's ever-present concern with and his ongoing attempt to specify the certainty of faith; as I will show, this concern also underlies the major addition to the section on faith in 1550. However, before taking up that issue, it is worth mentioning two seemingly minor changes in 1545 and 1550 in Calvin's treatment of Heb. 11:1. The Latin edition of 1545 was a virtually unmodified reissue of the 1543 edition.[168] Yet Calvin did add a brief clarification (indicated by small capitals below) qualifying his earlier statement that Heb. 11:1 represents a definition of faith and in 1550 added two other short phrases (indicated in italics):

> Therefore we have adopted this definition, which nevertheless does not differ at all from that DEFINITION OR RATHER DESCRIPTION of the apostle, *which he applies to his discourse*, where he teaches that faith is the substance of things to be hoped for, the indication of things not appearing. Now, by the word "hypostasis," which he uses, he means a sort of support upon which the godly mind may lean and rest. It is as if he were to say that faith itself is a sure and secure possession of

those things that God has promised us, *unless someone prefers to understand "hypostasis" as confidence. This does not displease me, although I accept what is more commonly received.*[169]

Though Calvin's interpretation of Heb. 11:1 will be taken up in more detail in chapter 3, I note for the present that in 1545 Calvin is cautious about designating Heb. 11:1 a definition of faith and that while he maintains the images of *fulcrum* and *possessio* he introduces the word *fiducia* in 1550. Moreover, beginning with the 1539 edition, Calvin treats the passage as one that he must prove does not conflict with his definition of faith, which, as I have shown, relies heavily on Pauline proof texts. Calvin's discussion treats Heb. 11:1 as being of apostolic authorship but no longer explicitly links it to the apostle Paul.[170]

It is hard to determine what combination of polemical challenges, pastoral concerns, and exegetical insights worked together to inspire the additions I have traced. In contrast to these general influences, the one major addition to the discussion in 1550 derives from a particular impulse. In 1542 a canon in Utrecht, Albert Pighius (1490–1542), had attacked Calvin's definition of faith in the 1539 *Institutes*.[171] In 1550 Calvin added a new paragraph in which he refutes Pighius's criticism of the distinction that Calvin had introduced into special revelation.[172] Calvin complains that Pighius and others had unjustly charged him with denying that faith has regard to all parts of God's word. To clarify his position, Calvin makes two points, both of which reiterate earlier statements. The first reaffirms that faith's stability depends solely on the freely given promise; the second underscores the need for faith to join believers to Christ in order to reconcile them to God. Reliance on the promise and engrafting into Christ are *the* characteristics that distinguish true faith from all pretenders, for it is faith in God's mercy that is salvific. Calvin goes so far as to say that the very purpose of discussing faith is that "we may grasp the way of salvation." How, he asks, can there be a saving faith (*fides salvifica*), without it engrafting us into the body of Christ? Calvin thus retains and sharpens the distinction in revelation, introducing the term "saving faith" as a kind of shorthand for his definition.

As with each addition in 1543, Calvin quotes Paul as an authority for his position, in this case citing Paul's statement in Rom. 10:8 that the gospel is the word of faith to legitimate the privileged status of God's word of mercy, the promise, the gospel. Along with the Pauline proof texts, Calvin also appropriates distinctly Pauline themes into his discussion of faith. In particular, he embraces Paul's concern for soteriology and finds in him an emphasis on certainty. These not only form the basis of Calvin's definition of faith but also serve to sharpen and refine it. Pushed to clarify his definition, Calvin underscores the centrality of these two themes until finally faith, stripped to its bare essentials, appears to consist of certainty of salvation. The subtle changes that I have traced in the 1543 and 1550 editions of the *Institutes* suggest the profound influence that Calvin's reading of Paul exercised on his views on faith. In seeking out the exegetical underpinnings of Calvin's views, I will attempt to discern not only which Pauline passages and themes shaped the discussion of faith in the *Institutes* but also how Calvin's own theological assumptions about faith shaped his reading of Paul.

Conclusion

The view of faith in the 1536 *Institutes* expresses the dominant soteriological and christocentric orientation of the entire work. Calvin's view of faith particularly illustrates these two tendencies in his concern to understand faith as that which gratuitously renders one acceptable to God. In presenting his view, Calvin takes his scriptural bearings from Paul, especially from Romans and Hebrews. He collapses the different types of faith that he inherited from his medieval predecessors into two broad forms, one of which he denies is properly called faith and the other of which he designates as trust, persuasion, or conviction of mind. In the years between the writing of the first and second Latin editions of the *Institutes*, Calvin's theological views expanded, and he began to speak of the divine activity in broader terms. The 1539 *Institutes* testifies to his expanded concern for the problem of knowledge and shows him beginning to distinguish between God's specifically redemptive activity and God's activity as creator and providential sustainer of the world. These two developments, an expanded awareness of the divine activity and an increased appreciation for knowledge, led to several important changes in the 1539 *Institutes*. With respect to the view of faith in particular, the results of Calvin's reflections on knowledge are evident. The influence of the expanded awareness of the divine activity is visible as well in the distinction that he made when he specified that faith looks properly only to one part of God's word, namely, God's promise of grace. Between 1536 and 1539, Calvin's understanding of faith evolved from a view of it as fundamentally *fiducia* to an expanded definition of it as knowledge—a knowledge that, nonetheless, contains a fiducial element. Yet in one respect the actual role of faith in his theology did not change all that much. Faith, for Calvin in all the editions of the *Institutes* that I have surveyed, is still primarily concerned with matters of justification and salvation, with God's redemptive activity rather than with God's providential activity. As such, its location in chapter 4 serves both to answer the question about knowledge of God raised in chapters 1–2 and to introduce the entire ensuing discussion. Hence, the soteriological focus, though broadened, still shapes the structure of the work, with faith as the answer to the soteriological and epistemological dilemma raised and detailed in the preceding chapters. In the next chapter, I will explore the exegetical basis for this view of faith as primarily "saving faith" as I consider how Calvin's exegesis of Paul shaped and reinforced his understanding of the relationship between faith, on the one hand, and justification and salvation, certainty and doubt, and Christ as the object of faith, on the other.

2

The Just Shall Live by Faith

How did Calvin's interpretation of the Bible not only reflect and reinforce but also transform his understanding of faith? The first stage in the investigation of this question focuses on his exegesis of the Pauline epistles, especially Romans, in order to sketch the outlines of his reading of Paul and begin to establish the fundamentally Pauline shape of his understanding of faith. I will show how and where Calvin finds in Paul support for his views on the certainty of faith, the perceptual nature of faith, and faith as knowledge. In addition, I will show that Calvin's interpretation of the Pauline view of justification, the law, and the fundamental human problem provides the primary contours for his definition of faith. Determining the important exegetical underpinnings of the view of faith expressed in the *Institutes* provides insight into the scriptural background for Calvin's definition of faith as knowledge, his distinction between *fides* and *fiducia*, and his restriction of the proper object of faith to God's word of mercy.

In general, Calvin's exegetical work on Paul from the late 1530s to the early 1550s reinforces his emphasis on "saving faith," that is, faith by which sinners are justified and receive salvation—the faith by which the "just" obtain life. As I have shown, this emphasis dominates his discussion of faith in the *Institutes*. Subsequent chapters will show that it governs his interpretation of faith in other parts of the Bible as well. However, attention to the exegetical works also indicates where Calvin's primary understanding of faith runs into difficulties as he encounters passages that challenge this understanding. His exegesis of these passages often reveals his deepest theological assumptions about the nature, object, and certainty of faith, as he struggles to reconcile his emphasis on a saving faith gleaned from Paul with the alternatives presented in the text. In this chapter, I will show how Calvin's exegesis of two passages from Paul lead him to broaden his discussion of faith's activity beyond the explicitly soteriological context that usually governs his interpretation of Paul's epistles.

The approach taken here has both chronological and theological justification. By beginning with Calvin's first commentary, the Romans commentary of 1540, and considering subsequently his exegesis of the remaining Pauline corpus, I am following the rough chronological order in which Calvin published his commentaries.[1] The commentary on Hebrews appeared in 1549, when Calvin had already published commentaries on Romans (1540), 1 Corinthians (1546), 2 Corinthians (French, 1547; Latin, 1548), the four epistles to Galatians, Ephesians, Philippians, and Colossians (1548), and 1 and 2 Timothy (1548). Commentaries on Titus and 1 and 2 Thessalonians appeared in 1550; the commentary on Philemon appeared for the first time in the collected edition of 1551, which, incidently, included the commentary on Hebrews.[2] The commentary on John was not published until 1553.

Although Calvin lectured on the Fourth Gospel at the school in Strasbourg, he did not treat it or any other book in a commentary until he had nearly finished his commentaries on Paul's epistles. This precedence granted to the Pauline epistles suggests the eminent theological value that Calvin placed on them. Indeed, Benoit Girardin, Ganoczy, and David C. Steinmetz have confirmed the centrality of Paul for Calvin's theology, especially Paul read in light of a Lutheran understanding of justification.[3] The two latter scholars have also indicated the relative independence that Calvin exercised vis-à-vis his theological predecessors, including the apostle. My consideration of the Pauline character of Calvin's understanding of faith will corroborate these findings, demonstrating that the doctrine of faith represents a particularly intriguing example of how Calvin interprets and reinterprets Pauline themes.[4]

The Commentary on Romans (1540, 1551, 1556)

If the sixteenth century was, as T. H. L. Parker has claimed, "above all things, the age of the Bible," it was moreover, as Parker's subsequent research has demonstrated, the age of the commentary on Romans.[5] Steinmetz calculates that more than seventy sixteenth-century theologians commented on this epistle.[6] This popularity needs to be understood first in the context of a renewed interest in the apostle Paul among Renaissance and Christian humanists in the latter fifteenth and early sixteenth centuries.[7] Paul was esteemed by Lorenzo Valla for his rhetorical prowess, by Marsilio Ficino for his sublime knowledge of heavenly mysteries, by Faber Stapulensis for his interpretation of the Old Testament, and by Erasmus for offering a *summa* of theology.[8] In addition to holding Paul in highest esteem, these humanists and their contemporaries crafted and employed new grammatical and hermeneutical tools to unlock the meaning of his letters. They thus prepared for and incited the explosion of interest in Paul, especially in Paul's epistle to the Romans, among subsequent interpreters, and especially those adherents of the Wittenberg theology inspired by Martin Luther.

Of course, this was not the first time that Paul or his letter to the Romans had been so highly regarded or that the proper interpretation of Paul had been such an important, urgent, and even controversial matter.[9] From the acknowledgment by the author of 2 Peter that there are some things in Paul's letters that are hard to understand (2 Pet. 3:16), to Marcion, to Augustine and the Pelagians, to William of St. Thierry and Peter Abelard, the history of Pauline interpretation bears witness to the problematic nature of these writings. Sixteenth-century interpreters, equipped with new grammatical and hermeneutical devices, did not read Paul in isolation from this turbulent past. Frequently they sought guidance from earlier authorities; even when they did not, their interpretations still betrayed the influence of prior exegetical questions and decisions. Even an exegete such as Calvin, whose professed goal was simply to unfold the mind of the biblical writer, is, in the words of Steinmetz, "part of a long theological discussion over the meaning of Paul, a discussion which he did not initiate and to which he feels himself obliged to respond."[10] Hence the popularity of Romans among Roman Catholic and evangelical commentators in the sixteenth century reflects not only the esteem and insights of the more recent humanists and the enthusiasm of the evangelical movements but also the important status of the writings of Paul and this text in particular in the Western exegetical tradition.

Calvin wrote his commentary on Romans while he was in Strasbourg and published it in 1540. He revised and expanded it in 1551 and 1556. In his prefatory summary, which underwent only minor changes in subsequent editions, he asserted the particular significance of this epistle, echoing a general assumption of much of the previous Western exegetical tradition: "If we have gained a true understanding of this Epistle, we have an open door to all the most profound treasures of Scripture."[11] For Calvin, these treasures appear to be concentrated in chapters 1–5, which, he says, set forth the main subject of the epistle: namely, that human beings are justified by faith. According to Calvin, Paul's most extensive treatment of this topic begins toward the end of Romans 3 and continues through Romans 4 in the example of Abraham, a discussion in which, he maintains, the greatest treasure of Romans is to be found. Because Calvin designates justification by *faith* as the main subject of Romans and because he sees this theme receiving its most extended treatment in Rom. 3:21 to the end of Romans 4, this section provides a fruitful field for inquiry.

In Rom. 3:21–4:25, Paul handles explicitly the question of acceptance before God, which leads him to discuss righteousness and justification. This discussion itself supports his additional concern to proclaim salvation in Christ.[12] He has just dramatically depicted a universally dismal human situation, concluding that all human beings are in bondage to the enslaving power of sin (Rom. 3:9). In Rom. 3:21–31, Paul asserts the sufficiency of faith in Christ for salvation for all human beings. He argues, on the one hand, that God's righteousness is distinct from the law, yet, on the other hand, that since the law and the prophets bear witness to it, it is not inconsistent with the law. God's righteousness, in this context, refers to God's faithfulness and to God's saving activity. Paul claims that this righteousness has been manifested not in the law but in Jesus Christ, to whom, nonetheless, the law and the prophets attest.[13] Faith in Jesus Christ, which is independent of the works of the Jewish law, is for both Jews and Gentiles the means by which a sinful human being embraces God's faithfulness and is established in God's favor. In chapter 4, Paul employs the example of Abraham to underscore and expand his theme. He first stresses the distinction between faith and the works of the law. Faith is not a work, not something of which Abraham could boast, but rather a reliance on or trust in God's faithfulness to save.[14] Such reliance or trust is itself counted as human righteousness before God. Moreover, the example of Abraham illustrates the antiquity of the way of faith and leads Paul to claim that Abraham is the father of all who come to God's righteousness through faith, whether they are Jews or Gentiles.

Paul's emphasis on Jesus Christ (evident especially in Rom. 3:22, 3:24, and 3:26) and his focus on soteriology provide the context for Calvin's discussion and shape the view of faith that emerges there. Determining how Calvin moves within this context is no easy task. Paul's argument is difficult, and Calvin's understanding of the argument is no less complex. Yet this determination is necessary if one is to see why Calvin's understanding of faith takes the shape that it does. Calvin understands the main theme of the passage (and the whole epistle) to be justification by faith in Christ.[15] In following Paul and distinguishing sharply between faith and other alleged means of salvation he thus defines faith, fundamentally, in terms of its relationship to the themes of the law and justification.

Calvin's Interpretation of Romans 3:21–4:25 in 1540

Calvin's treatment of the theme of law centers on explaining "law" in light of Paul's claims that God's righteousness is distinct from but not inconsistent with the law. Like many previous and contemporary exegetes, Calvin distinguishes different senses of the word "law" in order to accomplish this; however, he explicitly or implicitly rejects certain traditional designations, for example, natural law, moral law, ceremonial law, Old Testament law. Instead, he advances both a narrow, negative understanding of the law as works and a broad, more positive understanding of the law as teaching and the promises. This distinction is essential for the discussions of faith in this passage and in general, since, as I will show, Calvin defines faith in opposition to the narrow, negative understanding of law.

Calvin understands Paul's allegation in Rom. 3:21 that "the righteousness of God has been manifested apart from the law" as a complete rejection of the law as a means of revealing righteousness, referring law in this instance to works of all kinds. He takes "apart from the law" to mean "without the assistance of the law" and contends, as he had implied in his exegesis of the previous verse, that "law" in this context refers to works.[16] His exegesis of the rest of Romans 3 shows him radically excluding works of every kind from justification. He argues against earlier and contemporary exegetes who restrict "law" in this passage to the ceremonial law.[17] For Calvin, such a restriction blurs the distinction between works and faith by allowing the so-called moral law a place in obtaining righteousness. He applies Paul's exclusion of human boasting in Rom. 3:27 to the contemporary concepts of congruous and condign merit and declares that both are destroyed by Paul's argument.[18] He thus includes even works of supposed religious significance in the "law." Discussing Rom. 3:28, where Paul says that justification is by faith apart from the works of the law, Calvin addresses the challenge posed by James 2:24. This verse claims that one is justified by works and not by faith alone.[19] Calvin tries to harmonize the apparent contradiction by saying that James is talking not about the imputation of righteousness but rather about the declaration of righteousness; that is, that one who has been justified bears witness to this justification in works.[20] Because James is talking about a righteousness that flows from the righteousness of faith, his statement about works does not imply, according to Calvin, that works contribute to justification.

In discussing Paul's statements about how the law supports or confirms the righteousness of God or of faith, Calvin talks about the law in a different, more positive sense. Still, he maintains that justification is not based on the law or works. This can be seen in his interpretation of the second half of Rom. 3:21 but in more detail in his interpretation of Paul's statement in Rom. 3:31 that the law is established through faith.[21] Calvin bolsters this view by drawing on the declaration of Jesus in Matt. 5:17 ("I came not to destroy [the law and the prophets], but to fulfil"). Here he adopts a broader interpretation of the law, arguing that to limit the law only to a righteousness of works is to have a false view of the law. Since the law also contains the promises, and since it indeed proclaims and demands righteousness, the whole law, both moral and ceremonial, is confirmed and established by faith. Moreover, Calvin demonstrates how the law properly leads to Christ: the moral law proclaims what is right, but, due to human blindness and sin, it does this in vain. Yet since the law thus makes a person aware of iniquity it leads to Christ; faith then confirms and establishes the law.[22] Finally, even though the law is not the basis of justification, in justification the exact righteousness of the law is imputed to human beings. Moreover, in the process of sanctification human hearts are formed to the law.[23]

Calvin's statements about the law are nuanced and complex. He does not understand Paul to be using the word univocally. In Rom. 3:21 alone Calvin equates the law with works in the first clause and with scripture—Mosaic teaching and the prophets—in the second. He says that it is not legitimate to make a distinction between the moral and ceremonial law to explain Rom. 3:20–21, a view he reiterates in his comments on Rom. 3:27 in 1551 and Rom. 3:28 in 1556. Yet this does not mean that he absolutely rejects this distinction. He invokes it in his interpretation of Rom. 3:31 to show that the moral and ceremonial aspects are both established by justification by faith but in different ways. For Calvin, the important distinction is not between the ceremonial law (abolished) and the moral law (upheld and confirmed). Rather, the key to Paul's apparently contradictory statements lies in a narrow view of the whole law as works (abolished) and a broader view of the whole law as expression of the will of God and therefore containing the promises (established).

It is important to note in advance that the understanding of faith that Calvin sets forth is developed in opposition to the more narrow, negatively assessed understanding of the law. But before investigating this issue, one must consider the roots of this dual assessment of the law. The variations in meaning and assessment of the law arise from the fact that Calvin defines the law in terms of its relationship to righteousness or justification. When the question of obtaining righteousness or justification is at stake, his narrowest definition and harshest evaluation of the law emerge. This dynamic, of course, follows Paul's own dual attitude toward the law in this passage; like Paul, Calvin wishes to limit the role of the law in (or even exclude it entirely from) soteriology. However, his particular interpretation of Paul's understanding of righteousness and justification underlies the picture of the law just described. And since Calvin acknowledges, as he did with the law, different senses in which these terms are used, I need to consider next the primary meaning of these terms as he interprets them in this passage.

Already in Rom. 3:21 Calvin admits that the phrase "righteousness of God" can be understood in two different senses, both of which he accepts: a righteousness that can stand in the presence of God or a righteousness that God confers in mercy.[24] Calvin usually interprets the phrase as an objective rather than a subjective genitive. Righteousness so understood is a status obtained through faith and not a divine attribute. Throughout his exegesis of this passage Calvin uses the expression "righteousness of God" interchangeably with the phrases "the righteousness of faith" and "the righteousness of Christ"; he thereby presents Paul's understanding of righteousness as clear and univocal. He is most concerned to stress that this righteousness of faith apart from the law is an imputed righteousness that includes the complete, unmerited remission of sin and the gift of eternal life.[25] Righteousness is applied to human beings as a relational term having to do with the status of the human being *coram deo*. Justification is the act by which a sinful human being, though not actually righteous, is not considered by God as he is in himself but rather is viewed as righteous on the grounds of Christ's righteousness.[26] Calvin offers a succinct statement of his position in his comments on Rom. 3:22, where Paul repeats the phrase "the righteousness of God."[27] There Calvin stresses the following points: first, justification refers not to human but to divine judgment. Second, Christ's assistance in justification is necessary, because Christ alone can make sinful humans just by transferring his own righteousness to them. Sometimes Calvin uses, as he does here, the language of participation to express this transfer; at other points he describes this as being clothed with the righteousness of Christ.[28] What is significant is that this transference, for Calvin, means that the righteousness of faith and the righteousness of Christ are identical. It is interesting that Calvin uses an Aristotelian scheme of causes to describe this process, stating that the efficient cause of justification is the mercy of God, the material cause is Christ, and the formal or instrumental cause is the word with faith.[29]

This understanding of righteousness and justification emerges as the dominant one in Calvin's exegesis of this passage and is, moreover, the normative meaning for Calvin. It reflects how he takes his bearings from Paul's soteriological concern and casts that concern in light of sixteenth-century theological debates. Like other evangelical reformers, Calvin is concerned to define the righteousness by which human beings are saved in such a way as to exclude human merit completely. In order to safeguard justification as solely a work of divine grace, he rejects the typically medieval, even Augustinian notion that the justification that leads to salvation is both a counting righteous and an actual making righteous. Although he uses the language of participation and the Aristotelian notion of causes, he clearly makes justification as forgiveness of sin and the imputation of Christ's righteousness the sole ground for salvation, thereby virtually collapsing justification and salvation.[30] That Calvin takes Paul's meaning to be the most proper and appropriate is evident in the negative contrast he makes between his Pauline view and a righteousness of the law, that is, meritorious works. Moreover, in discussing Rom. 3:28 and 4:3, he opposes his Pauline view to the meaning of the word "righteousness" in James. According to Calvin, these alternative views either misunderstand the soteriological dilemma, focused through the lens of Paul on the question of justification, or are simply not concerned with the issue of justification at all.

Paul's quotation of Ps. 32:1 ("Blessed are they whose iniquities are forgiven and whose sins are covered; Blessed is the man to whom God does not impute sin") in Rom. 4:6 provides the occasion for Calvin to confront two challenges to his view that the imputed righteousness of Christ alone apart from any works is determinative for salvation. First, Calvin refutes the scholastic doctrine that in justification the fault of sin is forgiven but the punishment remains and hence penance is required.[31] David's statement, Calvin claims, declares both that sins are removed from God's sight and that they are not imputed; the forgiveness in justification is complete, and (as Calvin adds in 1551) this free righteousness continues to be imputed throughout one's life. Second, Calvin underscores his position that works, however righteous, cannot justify, in a discussion of Ps. 106:30–31, a text not quoted by Paul. These verses praise the priest Phinehas for a deed described in Num. 25:6–9. Steinmetz points out the difficulty that Phinehas created for certain sixteenth-century interpreters, since Ps. 106:31 praises Phinehas's action and declares that it "has been reckoned to him as righteousness from generation to generation for ever."[32] Moreover, Numbers 25:10–13 relates that Phinehas received a covenant of peace and perpetual priesthood because of his deed. Calvin's solution to the obvious difficulty that these passages present is to insist that Phinehas must have been first justified by faith in order for his deed to have been accounted righteous.[33] Without the righteousness of faith, no work would be counted just. There is a righteousness of works, but it is an effect of the righteousness of faith, which alone justifies. Using Luther's familiar image, Calvin argues that the relationship between the two is like the fruit from the tree.[34] But he insists repeatedly that it is one thing to be reckoned righteous through faith, which is justification and the cause of salvation, and another to perform righteous deeds that, though in accordance with God's law, contribute in no way to justification and, thus, to salvation.

It is in the context of these understandings of the law and justification and the question of salvation underlying them that Calvin formulates his understanding of faith. As I will show later, this "Pauline" understanding of faith functions, as do the "Pauline" understanding of law and justification, as the normative meaning for Calvin. The view of faith is, not surprisingly, nearly identical to the view I have shown him developing over the course of revising his *Institutes*. In fact, in his comments on Rom. 4:14 he advances a definition of faith as "certain knowledge" that has obvious similarities to the formal definition of faith in the 1539 *Institutes*:

> The apostle teaches that faith will perish if the soul does not rest securely in the goodness of God. Therefore, faith is not the mere recognition [*nuda agnitio*] of God or his truth, nor is it even the simple persuasion that God exists and that his word is truth, but a certain knowledge of the divine mercy conceived from the gospel, which brings peace of conscience before God and rest.[35]

And yet the exegetical context combined with contemporary questions about works and faith lead Calvin to focus on two themes in particular. First, he upholds the principle of faith alone and refines this concept by repeatedly insisting that the faith that alone justifies is in no way a meritorious virtue. Second, he occupies himself extensively with the issue of certainty and, to a lesser extent, the matter of perception.

In chapter 4 Paul employs the example of Abraham in Gen. 15:6 to demonstrate that Abraham's faith is not a work of the law. He argues that Abraham's faith precedes the law and therefore all who follow the example of Abraham's faith, whether they are circumcised or not, will be reckoned righteous. Calvin introduces the language of merit into this discussion and elaborates on his ideas on the instrumental and nonmeritorious character of faith that he had advanced in his comments on Rom. 3:22 and 3:27. His interest is not so much to argue that all who follow Abraham's example will be saved as it is to prove that faith is not a meritorious virtue. Faith is not something that Abraham "does" that is rewarded with righteousness. To demonstrate this, Calvin "completes" Paul's argument in Rom. 4:2 by linking boasting on the basis of works to merit. He says that Paul's statement "For if Abraham was justified by works, then he has something by which to boast, but not before God" ought to be rendered as "If Abraham was justified by works, he can boast in his own merit, but he does not have any reason to boast before God, therefore he was not justified by works."[36] Then, under Rom. 4:3, Calvin adds that what Abraham brings before God provides no grounds for boasting "because he brings nothing of his own except the recognition of misery which seeks mercy."[37] This corresponds to the character of faith specified earlier, in the comments on Rom. 3:27: since righteousness, he argues, is based on faith alone, "there is nothing that we can claim for ourselves, for faith receives all from God, and brings nothing but a humble confession of want."[38] Abraham does not boast because the faith by which he is justified is not a work of meritorious virtue.

Seeking to counter patristic, medieval, and sixteenth-century interpreters who viewed Abraham's faith as a work or a meritorious act, Calvin argues that the faith believers are to imitate is far removed from merit.[39] His argument reflects his narrow understanding of the law as works altogether and reveals again his concern to exclude works, even those assisted or initiated by grace, from salvation or justification by faith. The understanding of faith that Calvin sets forth is thus advanced in opposition to the more narrow, negatively assessed understanding of the law that we saw earlier. Moreover, this view of faith reflects the soteriological context of the passage: faith understood as something distinct from works is the faith that justifies and is the basis for salvation.

Further indication of the particular soteriological concern shaping the understanding of faith lies in Calvin's elaboration of the theme of certainty.[40] He expounds this theme in this passage especially in his discussion of Rom. 4:14–17. Paul has just said in Rom. 4:13 that the promise to Abraham was not through the law but through the righteousness of faith. In the next four verses he argues that if the true heirs of Abraham are those who are of the law, then both faith and the promise are made void. Since the law works wrath, then the inheritance must come through faith, and this alone makes the promise sure for all the heirs. He then goes on in Rom. 4:18–22 to describe the strength of Abraham's faith: Abraham looked only to the promise of God and did not consider the obstacles that his advanced age and that of Sarah presented.

Calvin begins his exegesis of this section with the wish that his adversaries would attend to Paul's reasoning in Rom. 4:14, for therein lies the source of controversy between Calvin and his undesignated opponents.[41] The issue at stake is the certainty of faith.[42] Calvin writes that Paul assumes that full assurance of mind is necessary to receive God's favor effectively. If the inheritance (salvation) depends on the law, then human consciences would have no certainty, and human beings would be driven to despair. He sums up this argument as follows in his comments on Rom. 4:16:

> If the inheritance of salvation comes through works, then faith in it will collapse and the promise of it be abrogated. But both faith and the promise ought to be certain. Therefore it [the inheritance] comes to us through faith so that it might be secured, being established on the goodness of God alone.

Looking forward to Paul's characterization of the strength of Abraham's faith in the verses to come, Calvin continues: "See that the apostle calls hesitancy and doubt 'unbelief,' by which faith is abolished and the promise abrogated. And this, however, is the doubt which the schoolmen call 'moral conjecture' and substitute for faith, as if this pleased God."[43]

Given this stress on the certain character of faith, it is noteworthy that in his treatment of Abraham's response to God's promise Calvin creates room for the imperfection of faith and the reality of doubt even where his translation of Paul appears to shut this out. In Calvin's translation, Paul claims that Abraham, without being weakened in faith, did not consider his own body but was rather strengthened in faith (Rom. 4:19–20).[44] This, however, might create such distance between Abraham and the ordinary believer that Abraham's example would become unattainable. While maintaining Abraham's exemplary character and contrasting his faith with that of believers, Calvin also presents Abraham as questioning and tempted by doubt. In demonstrating how an uncertain situation can become an occasion for even greater faith, Abraham thus exemplifies a more realistic and attainable standard.

Calvin first creates a link between Abraham and the concerns of evangelical believers by focusing on the temptation to doubt that Abraham faced. In his comments on Rom. 4:19, Calvin observes that, contrary to what Paul says, Abraham did in fact consider his body. Scripture elsewhere points out that Abraham asked how a one-hundred-year-old man and a woman of ninety could become parents (Gen. 17:17). Abraham, however, laid these considerations aside; he looked away from all that was opposed to the fulfillment of the promise. Calvin admits that the fact that Abraham confronted these challenges without being weakened in faith contrasts with the vacillation to which the faith of believers is often subject. Faith, he claims, has a twofold weakness: "one which by succumbing to the temptations of adversity makes us fall from the power of God; the other which arises from imperfection." He underscores the fact that the faithful are continually involved in conflict with ignorance and doubt. Even though these are so severe as to cause believers perhaps to lose confidence in God's power, true faith, though imperfect, will triumph and become stronger: "in this conflict their faith is often severely shaken and distressed, but it finally emerges victorious, so that in weakness itself they may be said [to have the] greatest strength."[45] Hence victory belongs even to those who, in contrast to Abraham, face their tribulations with weak and imperfect faith.

Having assured his readers that trials and conflicts are both necessary and beneficial and that faith's victory is assured, Calvin encourages them to imitate Abraham's example for dealing with adverse circumstances. Yes, Abraham questions. But instead of succumbing to doubt, he turns his questioning to a positive end. His attitude distinguishes his questioning from, for example, Sarah's similar reaction to the news of progeny (Gen. 18:10–15). Abraham inquired, Calvin says, but not with incredulity. Rather, like the Virgin Mary, he was led from his inquiry to wonder and then to praise.[46] Hence it appears that Abraham's faith in God was certain so that he was able to inquire in such a way as to be led to fuller assurance. Sarah, in contrast, provides a negative example; she laughs and thereby exhibits her total lack of faith. Calvin then tells his readers that all are in the same position as Abraham, insofar as the circumstances of their lives appear to contradict the reality of God's promises. They must close their eyes to the corruption, mortality, evidences of sin, and signs of God's wrath that surround them and hold fast to the immortality, the righteousness, and divine benevolence that is promised to them.[47]

In his descriptions of Abraham's unwavering faith and pious questioning, Calvin seems to acknowledge that believers often find themselves somewhere between the reverent, modest inquiry of Abraham and the incredulity of Sarah. Nonetheless, he also speaks as if Abraham himself was perhaps not so isolated from vacillations. Calvin argues that the phrase in Rom. 4:20, "sed roboratus est fide," implies that Abraham had conquered unbelief by the constancy and firmness of faith.[48] Yet in order for Abraham to have conquered, he must have confronted some uncertainty. The tension between faith and doubt is inevitable, even for one with faith as certain as Abraham's. The strength of his faith apparently lies in his ability not to avoid uncertainty altogether but to conquer it. Though he inquired concerning God's promise, he did so with an attitude not of mockery but rather of wonder. Rising above the temptation to doubt through his pious questioning, Abraham provides the ideal solution to the believer's dilemma.

The theme of perception receives much less attention than that of certainty. The references to the perceptual elements of faith are infrequent and usually express the bias against physical sense perception that we saw especially in the 1536 *Institutes*. This is evident, for example, in Calvin's portrayal of Abraham's faith in God's promise despite all appearances to the contrary as a pattern for the Christian troubled by doubts about God's promise of mercy. Calvin tells his readers that they should close their eyes to themselves and those things around them that contradict God's promise.[49] In addition, faith should disregard challenges to God's power. As noted earlier, Calvin holds that faith is tempted not only with respect to God's merciful promise but also with regard to God's power. He even says that believers might fall away from God's power through trial. He finds that Abraham himself entertains doubt not so much about God's willingness to fulfill the promise but rather about God's ability to do so (Rom. 4:21). In discussing this passage, Calvin says that faith ought to disregard human weakness and look instead to the power of God.[50] The implication is that the conviction of unrighteousness ought not lead to such despair that one reckons that one is too far removed for God to save. So Abraham also shows how faith looks not only to God's mercy but also to God's power, and confirms the notion, which I discussed in the last chapter, that faith as certainty of one's salvation is doubly confirmed from a consideration of God's omnipotence.[51]

In treating these judgments about where faith "looks" it is important to note that it is not to the experience of God's power or even primarily the proclamation of God's power in the word that is the focus of Abraham's faith. Immediately after these considerations of God's power in his comments on Rom. 4:21, Calvin reminds his readers, in his comments on Rom. 4:22, that it was because Abraham accepted the promise of righteousness in faith that he was reckoned righteous. He urges them to maintain and commit to memory "this relation between faith and the word."[52] Though saving faith can be bolstered by these other considerations, its basis is in the word of promise that God speaks.

Finally, one other theme that arises in Calvin's comments demands attention. While this topic does not receive extensive treatment in 1540, it is worth noting since it is an important theme related to faith. Underlying Calvin's attempt to eradicate all confidence in works is the desire to establish God's mercy alone as the ground of justification and salvation and the object of faith.[53] God's promise of mercy toward sinners constitutes the specific element in God's word on which faith rests. While this close linking of faith and God's mercy is not always explicit in Calvin's treatment of this passage, this important, underlying assumption manifests itself in his reading of the soteriological issues at stake in the discussion. To this end, he speaks of the content of Abraham's faith in general terms as a belief that God is kind and merciful and will fulfill the promise that is contrary to appearances. Believers, therefore, can also trust that God will raise them from the death of their sin.[54]

The view of faith that Calvin sets forth on the basis of Paul's argument reflects his understanding of Paul on the law and justification. He finds in Paul's opposition of the righteousness of the law to the righteousness of God through faith in Jesus Christ an opposition between faith and works (especially works of supposed religious significance, or merit) in the matter of justification. He thus fiercely opposes the idea that faith, the instrumental cause of justification and salvation, is a meritorious virtue. Though Paul does not argue explicitly in this passage for the certainty of *faith* per se, Calvin finds this is implied in Paul's depiction of Abraham as fully assured that God was able to fulfill what God had promised.[55] He thus assumes and attributes to Paul the certainty of faith as certainty of salvation and rejects on this basis the scholastic notion of moral conjecture. Nonetheless, in going beyond Paul's use of the Abraham story to acknowledge the weakness of faith and to leave room for pious questioning, Calvin seeks to uphold the steadfastness of faith while also allowing for the real challenges to faith. Finally, he emphasizes faith as contrary to actual appearances; for the most part, faith should disregard the objects of ordinary sense perception and rest in a higher, heavenly realm. At one point, Calvin invites faith to contemplate God's power. However, even this points to the dominant soteriological concern, since faith does this in order to confirm the certainty of salvation. Thus the soteriological context provided by Paul and interpreted by Calvin leads him to speak of faith in strong opposition to works, to collapse the certainty of faith into the certainty of salvation, and to present faith as contrary to all appearances. The interest in salvation also leads Calvin to treat faith in his exegesis of this passage essentially as a *fides qua*. The example of Abraham in chapter 4 illustrates this *fides qua*, and his history is recorded, according to Calvin's comments on Rom. 4:23, to offer a description of the one, unchanging way to obtain righteousness.[56]

Calvin's Interpretation of Rom. 3:21–4:25 in 1551 and 1556

The changes that Calvin made in his exegesis of this passage in the revised editions of 1551 and 1556 generally tend to strengthen the emphasis on faith as "saving faith" and fall into three major categories. First, he makes a more explicit distinction between justification and regeneration (or sanctification). Along with this, he actively promotes an even more clearly forensic notion of justification. Finally, he strengthens the emphasis on certainty and expands the sections that deal with this topic. I will look briefly at each of these and at other less obvious changes that accompany them.[57] Especially in the case of these three major emphases, the impact of the sixth session of the Council of Trent (January 1547) is clearly evident. Calvin's additions to this section of his commentary on Romans echo his 1548 refutation of the Council's canons on justification and its rejection of faith alone and subjective certainty.[58]

In 1540 Calvin had already argued vehemently for the exclusion of all works from justification and rejected any view of a so-called half righteousness. In 1551 and 1556 he strengthens his comments on these matters in at least three places. Discussing Rom. 3:21, Calvin criticizes in 1551 a view, attributed to Augustine and revived by "some modern theorists," that understands the "righteousness of God" to be the free and unmerited grace of regeneration, which nonetheless issues in works that contribute to justification.[59] Calvin rejects this double justification (by faith through the grace of Christ and by the works proceeding from regeneration) and insists that justification rests on remission of sins alone. "Apart from the law" thus excludes the works "that even believers can possess."[60] Discussing Rom. 3:22b–23, Calvin reiterates that there is no such thing as a partial righteousness; if there were, Paul's argument in these verses would lose its force.[61] Finally, in 1556 he rewrites and expands his comments on Rom. 4:16, "that it may be according to grace," in order to distinguish the gift of regeneration from saving grace. From this statement he concludes that "grace does not mean the gift of regeneration but unmerited favor; for as regeneration is never perfect, it would never suffice to appease consciences, nor of itself ratify the promise."[62] Already in 1540 he had assumed a distinction between justification and regeneration; he saw Paul's statements in this passage as applying only to justification.[63] This assumption becomes even more explicit in his comments on Rom. 4:4 in 1556: "The discussion here is not how we are to regulate our life but rather concerns the reason for our salvation."[64] Along with these additions designed to underscore the distinction between justification and regeneration, Calvin also strengthens his denial that faith is a meritorious virtue.[65]

The sharpened distinction between justification and regeneration is paralleled by an increased stress on a forensic idea of justification. Calvin more clearly denounces the notion the righteousness of faith is a quality or substance, an actual rectitude inhering in the human being, and says explicitly that this is a borrowed righteousness.[66] Though he lets stand passages that speak clearly of communion of those justified by faith with Christ, Calvin repeatedly stresses that their righteousness is not what they are in themselves but rather how they are regarded by God.[67] He strives to make even more clear what Paul means by justification and righteousness.[68]

I have already shown that the additions to the *Institutes* demonstrate the increasing importance of the theme of certainty for Calvin in the 1540s and 1550s. This subject receives further, albeit not as extensive, elaboration in revisions to the commentary on Romans as well. In his comments on Rom. 4:14 in the first edition Calvin claimed that Paul assumed beyond all doubt that full assurance of mind is necessary to receive God's favor. In 1551 and 1556, we find this assumption emerging at other points in the text. For example, in refuting at Rom. 3:21 the view that the righteousness of God is the grace of regeneration, Calvin argues that Paul suggests something different from double justification; namely, "that consciences will never be at peace until they rest on the mercy of God alone."[69] Calvin underscores the same theme in discussing Rom. 4:13, which he declared in 1540 was an excellent passage for conferring firm consolation. In 1556 he revises his comments and links them more closely to Paul's argument: "And surely (as Paul will presently add) consciences enjoy true peace only when they feel that they are being freely given what is not their legal right."[70] Finally, Calvin forges a link between Abraham and the theme of certainty of salvation at an earlier point in his comments. Discussing Rom. 4:3 in 1551, he picks up an argument from Melanchthon that Abraham's faith in the promise extended to the whole context; it was not confined to the particular promise of offspring.[71] According to Calvin, those who advocate the narrower interpretation misunderstand what is being said about God's grace; they risk falling into the view that God extended the promise of progeny and then rewarded Abraham for believing it. To counter this potential misunderstanding (and, incidentally, to defend the Pauline exegesis of Gen. 15:6), Calvin declares that the divine grace operates differently: "God bestowed [his grace] to make Abraham more certain both of [God's] adoption and fatherly favor, in which is included eternal salvation through Christ."[72]

In 1540 Calvin discussed the theme of certainty primarily in his comments on Rom. 4:14–22.[73] In later editions he amplifies his earlier statements with short additions in 1556 to Rom. 4:16 and 4:19. In the former case, he rewrites one sentence to underscore his view that Paul assumed the certainty of faith.[74] In his revised paragraph treating the phrase "that it may be according to grace," he argues that Paul confirms the state of uncertainty that results from dependence on works. As just noted, he claims that grace cannot refer to regeneration, which, as it is imperfect, would never appease consciences.[75] Finally, we find new clauses in the section of the comments on Rom. 4:19, where Calvin asserted in 1540 that faith has a double weakness. Earlier he had simply said that the second weakness arises from imperfection. To this he adds: "yet nonetheless does not extinguish faith itself."[76]

In addition to strengthening these three points, Calvin expanded his thinking about faith and God's power in 1556. I have shown that the portrayal of Abraham's full assurance was such as to lead Calvin, already in 1540, to the question not of God's willingness to be merciful but of God's ability to do so, thereby linking faith to God's power. In 1556 he prefaces his original comments on Rom. 4:21 with a more detailed reflection on the importance of rightly honoring the power of God; he discusses how even the most trivial obstacles to God's promise lead humans to degrade God's power. To the end of his comments from 1540 he appends a clarification of what is meant by God's power, on which, he had already said, faith ought to fix its attention: "Faith does not imagine that God can do whatever he wants while in the meantime remaining basking in idleness, but rather locates his power in his continual activity, and applies it in particular to what is effected by [his] word. The hand of God, therefore, is always ready to accomplish what he has spoken."[77] It is important to note here that while faith indeed looks to God's power, it is to God's power as revealed in God's word. It is on the word—in this instance, the promise of salvation—that faith relies, not on the experience of God's power.

Given the attention to Abraham's faith in Romans 4 and in Calvin's comments, it is appropriate to discuss briefly here Calvin's treatment of the figure of Abraham and Abraham's faith in his 1554 commentary on Genesis. In general, his portrayal there of Abraham's faith reflects thematic shifts in emphasis that I will trace in subsequent chapters. In his exegesis of Genesis 12–18, Calvin is concerned not merely with obtaining righteousness (as he is in his exegesis of Romans 3–4) but more broadly with the whole life of faith and with the theme of faith in God's providence. At several points Calvin invokes Paul as the interpretive key to a passage. A premier instance of this is found in the comments on Gen. 15:6, which Calvin does take to be about obtaining righteousness through the free imputation of Christ's righteousness. In his discussion of this topic, he covers many of the same themes addressed in his exegesis of Romans 4, although he does not argue as forcefully against the concept of merit or as explicitly about certainty. Notably, he stresses the perpetual nature of justification by faith, holding that the verse does not relate the beginning of Abraham's justification or his faith but rather describes "how he had been justified though his whole life."[78] Here Calvin seeks to guard against the positions he called in his Romans commentary positions of "half righteousness," which held that faith was just the beginning of justification. Yet however much these soteriological concerns dominate Calvin's comments on this particular verse, they do not determine the larger discussion. The image of Abraham and Abraham's faith gleaned in the exegesis of Romans 3–4 provides an essential key for Calvin's reading of Genesis but does not exhaustively account for the concept of faith set forth in his commentary on Genesis. In fact, his discussion there of Gen. 15:1 points to the further dimension of faith that I will discuss more fully in chapter 4. Writing of God's exhortation not to fear, Calvin remarks: "God exhorts Abram to be of a tranquil mind, but where is a foundation for such security, except when we apprehend by faith that God cares for us and we rest [*recumbimus*] in his providence?"[79] Having discerned the exegetical roots of Calvin's understanding of faith in Paul's Romans, one must go on to complete the picture through consideration of faith in the other Pauline commentaries so that one can begin to see how this Pauline view relates to the other images of faith, such as that in Genesis, that Calvin sets forth in his exegesis of non-Pauline texts.

The various additions in 1551 and 1556 illustrate Calvin's continuing concern to clarify the relationship of works and justification. Moreover, these expansions and clarifications show how the assumption of certainty of faith as the certainty of salvation shapes both Calvin's view of this relationship and his exegesis of these topics in Paul's letter to the Romans. Calvin does not radically revise his position but instead emphasizes and reemphasizes certain key points. He sharpens Paul's soteriological focus and brings into the discussion his own theological assumptions about the relationship of justification and regeneration. In his exegesis of Paul, Calvin discusses the topic of faith primarily from this perspective, speaking of faith as it relates to forgiveness of sin and the imputation of righteousness. Though he can demonstrate an appreciation for nuances in the meaning of the terms "law," "righteousness," and "faith," he defines faith in relationship to particular understandings of the first two terms.[80] Faith has one principal meaning, and this meaning overlaps with the main emphases we saw in the *Institutes*. Faith is the instrumental cause in justification; faith is not a work or a meritorious virtue; faith grasps and rests securely on God's promise of mercy in Christ. Faith relates to God's activity as redeemer.

The Other Pauline Commentaries

Calvin's commentaries on the remaining Pauline epistles contain countless examples of how his exegetical work on Paul reinforced his emphasis on saving faith. Though he recognizes that even Paul can use the word "faith" to designate something other than the faith that justifies and saves, he qualifies such meanings by indicating that faith is being used in a different sense to designate, for example, a partial faith that does not grasp Christ entirely or faith as the summary of Christian doctrine.[81] Far more numerous and detailed, however, are the discussions of faith as the instrumental means of justification and salvation. Apart from Paul's specific discussions of justification by faith, this proper nature of faith is suggested to Calvin by Paul's statements about wisdom, knowledge, assurance, and especially the work of the Holy Spirit. In his treatment of such passages, Calvin formulates and defends an understanding of faith as *certain* knowledge of the divine mercy revealed in the gospel.[82] Relying on a position that he had expressed most fully in his comments on Romans 10, Calvin stresses that this knowledge comes through *hearing* the gospel (God's promise of mercy) and apprehending this word inwardly through the work of the Spirit.[83]

Whenever Calvin discusses faith's saving activity, he inevitably touches on one or more of the themes of certainty, knowledge, or perception. As I have shown, within his discussion of Rom. 3:21–4:25, Calvin advances a definition of faith as knowledge in his comments on Rom. 4:14. He also elaborates the implications of the certainty of faith in some detail in the discussion of the subsequent verses. Finally, he provides some insight into the relationship between faith and perception in his exegesis of Rom. 4:18–21. Both the exegetical context and contemporary debates about the role of works in justification and salvation lead Calvin to focus his discussion on the issue of certainty. In so doing he covers all the essential elements of faith's certain character. He elaborates the certainty of faith from various perspectives: he distinguishes sharply between faith and works with respect to justification; stresses that faith is a divine work; emphasizes the certainty of faith's object (Christ, the gospel, the promise); and includes in faith's certainty the certainty of salvation and eternal life.

Nonetheless, he also allows for faith's weakness and imperfection, so that increase and progress in faith are not incompatible with its certainty. He underscores the emphasis on certainty with the additions to this section in 1551 and 1556. Passages elsewhere in Romans and in the other Pauline epistles allow him to pursue these aspects of faith, certainty, and their implications in greater detail; however, they add little or nothing that is substantive to the view he sets forth on the basis of this passage.[84] It is otherwise, however, with respect to the theme of perception and, to some extent, that of knowledge. These themes receive more detailed treatment at other points in the commentaries on Paul. In particular, Calvin's comments on 1 Cor. 2:10–16 (1546) and Eph. 1:13 and 3:12 (1548) provide insight into his designation of faith as knowledge; and his comments on 1 Cor. 13:12–13 (1546) and 2 Cor. 5:6–7 (1547/1548) are foundational for his understanding of the perception of faith.

Faith as Knowledge: Calvin's Interpretation of 1 Cor. 2:10–16 (1546), Eph. 1:13, and Eph. 3:12 (1548)

While one can determine to some extent passages that Calvin relies on to support his view of faith's certain character, it is extremely difficult to isolate precisely the exegetical underpinnings in Paul of the idea of faith as knowledge. Unlike the authors of the Gospel of John or the first Johannine epistle, Paul does not directly identify faith as knowledge.[85] However, Calvin assumes this connection in Paul and finds it especially in Eph. 3:18–19, a passage that he cites in the 1539 *Institutes* to support the idea of faith as knowledge.[86] Another instance is in Gal. 1:8, where Calvin finds that Paul not only demonstrates his confidence in the gospel but also defines exactly what the gospel is. This leads Calvin to engage in polemic against the notion of implicit faith and to assert that there is no faith where there is no knowledge.[87] He also derives the idea of faith as knowledge more indirectly from passages such as Romans 1, where, to his mind, Paul defines the human condition in terms of blindness and false knowledge of God.[88] The fact that the remedy that Paul proposes is faith implies for Calvin that faith has something to do with the restoration of knowledge, illumination, and proper perception. Moreover, Paul frequently urges knowledge and wisdom in his letters; Calvin understands many of these passages as speaking about faith. A characteristic example is in the exegesis of Eph. 1:17–18, in which Paul prays that the spirit of wisdom and revelation in the knowledge of God be granted to the Ephesians and that the eyes of their understanding be enlightened. Calvin interprets this to be about the increase of faith.[89]

Calvin's exegesis of 1 Cor. 2:10–16 explores the theme of faith as knowledge overcoming the situation of blindness and ignorance. This passage also demonstrates how closely he links knowledge to the perception and certainty of faith. In discussing the verses leading up to this section (1 Cor. 1:18–2:9), Calvin underscores Paul's contrast between human and divine wisdom. He develops the idea of the gospel as wisdom that transcends the perspicacity of the human intellect and does not depend on human esteem for its authority. Because of human blindness, God's wisdom manifest in the theater of creation provides a slight taste of divinity that serves only to render human beings inexcusable.[90] Furthermore, the hidden things of God are completely inaccessible to human understanding. First Cor. 2: 10 declares that these hidden and inaccessible promises have been revealed to humans by the Spirit, which, Calvin says, honors believers with a special illumination. The comments on the next verse make clear that this illumination involves a revelation of the gospel. Calvin's own particular brand of soteriological concern emerges in the content that he ascribes to this revelation. In 1 Cor. 2:9 Paul refers to a passage from Isaiah (64:4) that extols the "things which God has prepared for those who love him." Paul himself speaks only in *general* terms about knowing what God has given us, designating them "spiritual things" (*spiritualia*) in 1 Cor. 2: 13. Calvin, however, provides a specific content. He renders the last phrase in 1 Cor. 2:12 ("that we might understand the gifts bestowed on us by God") "so that we may know those things that are given to us by Christ." He then lists specifically the following blessings obtained through Christ's death and resurrection: reconciliation with God, remission of sins, adoption to the hope of eternal life, sanctification, regeneration, and new life for God.[91]

God's goodness, Calvin claims, is especially manifest in the way that God makes humanity's defect (blindness and ignorance) work to its advantage: the greater the bluntness of the human intellect in grasping these hidden things, the greater is the certainty of faith, which rests on divine revelation. Calvin finds that Paul's analogy in 1 Cor. 2:11–12 has some limitations. Nonetheless, he judges that it confirms both that the Spirit's illumination is the only way for blind humans to grasp the wisdom of the gospel and that those who have the Spirit's testimony "have an assurance as firm and solid, as if they felt with their hands what they believe, for the Spirit is a faithful and indubitable witness."[92] These considerations lead him to refute the scholastic doctrine of moral conjecture and assert that by this testimony the elect have certainty of salvation. He then declares the nature of faith to be "that the conscience has from the Holy Spirit a sure testimony of God's benevolence toward it, [and] resting on this, it does not hesitate to invoke God as father." He claims that Paul uses the word "knowledge" (*scientia*) in 1 Cor. 2:12 "to express better the security of confidence."[93]

In these comments the assumptions about faith and the human condition that Calvin derives from Paul's epistle to the Romans help him develop the idea of faith as knowledge in a passage in which Paul does not even mention the word "faith." Calvin equates the wisdom of which Paul speaks with the gospel that Paul says earlier (1 Cor. 2:1–5) that he proclaimed to the Corinthians. If the gospel is wisdom about salvation in Christ too lofty to be grasped by natural mental capacity, then faith, as the instrumental means of justification, is the special way of knowing that apprehends this saving wisdom. Because faith rests on revelation and because one who has faith has the Spirit of God (1 Cor. 2:12), the salvation known by faith is certain and is known certainly.[94]

At times the distinction between faith as knowledge and the certainty of faith can be particularly elusive. For example, as I showed, in his exegesis of 1 Cor. 2: 12 Calvin claims that Paul uses the word "know" to express the assurance of confidence more fully. However, Calvin's comments on Eph. 1:13 and 3:12 illustrate how he distinguishes between knowledge and certainty while continuing to view them as inseparable elements of faith; there he establishes a difference between faith and confidence, arguing that faith is characterized by but not reduced to an attitude of certainty.

Calvin reads Eph. 1:13 first of all as a proof text for certainty, since in it, as in 1 Cor. 2:12, Paul discusses the work of the Holy Spirit in the elect. Paul's reference to the sealing activity of the Spirit reaffirms for Calvin that the foundation of believers' conviction about the word of God, their own salvation, and religion in general is firm and certain—which it would not be if it consisted of human wisdom or philosophical arguments.[95] However, this verse also presents a difficulty in its statement that the Ephesians were sealed in Christ with the Holy Spirit *after* they had believed. This would suggest that faith precedes the sealing and might lead to a separation between faith and certainty. Calvin resolves this difficulty by distinguishing two operations of the Spirit in faith, which correspond to two parts of which faith consists: the Spirit enlightens the mind (*mentes*) and confirms the heart (*animos*). "The commencement of faith is knowledge; the completion of it is a fixed and steady conviction that admits no opposing doubt."[96]

Calvin's desire to distinguish but not separate faith as knowledge and the certainty of faith is also evident in his treatment of Eph. 3:12. As I showed in the last chapter, he argued, on the basis of this passage, in the 1539 *Institutes* for a distinction between *fides* and *fiducia*; in 1543 he expanded this discussion in order to use the passage to support the certainty of faith. In the commentary, this latter concern dominates. Calvin wants to establish the inseparability of faith and confidence; the "papists," he claims, might learn the proper meaning of faith from this passage, if they were not preoccupied with false opinions. He takes Paul's designation of faith as the "faith of Christ" to mean that "everything that faith ought to contemplate is exhibited to us in Christ." Faith is not empty or confused knowledge but rather knowledge of Christ's power and offices; it is knowledge directed toward Christ for the purpose of seeking God. This knowledge gives rise to confidence, which in turn produces boldness.[97] Having thus distinguished faith as knowledge of Christ from confidence, Calvin argues that the two cannot be separated any more that heat and light can be taken away from the sun. True faith cannot exist without confidence, though the measure of confidence will vary in accordance to the degree of faith, that is, knowledge. This confidence includes reliance on Christ as mediator, rest in the paternal love of God, and certainty of salvation.[98] Calvin concludes his comments on this verse by citing James 1:6–7 to refute the view that believers should hesitate in prayer.

These passages confirm that, although the question of the certainty of faith was an extremely pressing polemical concern, Calvin did not view certainty as the essence of faith. He saw faith as inseparable from but not reduced to an attitude of confidence or certainty.[99] Calvin's reading of Paul led him to affirm that faith is essentially knowledge, although this was not because Paul himself explicitly advanced this view but rather because of the way that Calvin interpreted Paul's assessment of the effects of the Fall and his concern with heavenly wisdom. Any firm distinction between knowledge and certainty is difficult to maintain, since for Calvin the knowledge of faith is itself certain because its object, variously described as Christ, the wisdom of the gospel, the promise of salvation, mercy, or adoption, is, on the one hand, itself divine, and, on the other, divinely revealed and confirmed.[100] Yet faith as confidence or certainty alone would not be sufficient to respond to the human problem understood as ignorance and blindness.

Faith as knowledge is shaped by the soteriological context that emerges from and is confirmed by Calvin's reading of Paul. In elaborating this theme, Calvin sometimes uses the Paul of Romans to interpret Paul elsewhere. Each of the passages where he does so is typical in showing that this knowledge is restricted to a knowledge of God's redemptive activity in Christ. Calvin's translation of 1 Cor. 2:12 focuses the verse on the salvation won by Christ; the spiritual things of which Paul speaks in 1 Cor. 2:13 are equated with the gospel and not presumed to be other mysteries.[101] Moreover, Calvin does not seem to notice that Paul nowhere mentions the theme of divine adoption in 1 Cor. 2:12. Calvin says that the faith spoken of in the second half of Eph. 1:13 is clearly directed toward the "word of truth, the gospel of your salvation" mentioned earlier in the verse. And the "faith of Christ" in Eph. 3:12 restricts the contemplation of faith to those things exhibited in Christ. Finally, as I have shown, it is Calvin's view that the confidence associated with faith is, like knowledge, directed at God's redemptive activity. It is confidence in the promises of God apprehended by faith—confidence in Jesus Christ and the salvation offered in him.

Faith and Perception: Calvin's Interpretation of 1 Cor. 13:12–13 (1546) and 2 Cor. 5:6–7 (1547/8)

Inasmuch as Calvin presents the human problem in terms of ignorance and blindness, the theme of knowledge is also closely connected with the theme of perception. His interpretation of two passages, 1 Cor. 13:12–13 and 2 Cor. 5:6–7, shapes his views on the relationship between faith and perception. A grasp of this fundamental position is especially necessary in order to clarify in the next chapter how Calvin treats this theme in his comments on Hebrews 11 and John and to prepare for my consideration of the perception of faith in his Psalms commentary.

In his exegesis of 1 Corinthians 13 Calvin finds Paul to be using faith in two different senses. He argues that in 1 Cor. 13:2, as well as in 12:9, Paul is speaking of a special faith (*fides particularis*), a faith of miracles, which may exist in a person apart from the Spirit of sanctification and, presumably, apart from love. He does not say that Paul is using the word "faith" improperly, nor does he say that such a faith would not save. However, he implies at least the latter through various comments and strategies. He is careful to acknowledge here that the word "faith" can be used in different senses. He insists that this verse cannot be used to undermine the excellence of faith: Paul "restricts" faith in this case to miracles, hence this is a "special" faith that "does not apprehend a whole Christ but simply his power in working miracles." Finally, Calvin ascribes such a faith to Judas, who was undeniably reprobate.[102] Presumably, the reason why this special faith could not save is not because it lacks love but because it fails to grasp Christ properly. In contrast, the faith mentioned in 1 Cor. 13:13 has a broader meaning: "the knowledge of God and of the divine will that we obtain through the ministry of the church, or, if you prefer, faith universal and understood in the strict sense."[103] In his remaining comments on this verse, Calvin argues that Paul's declaration that love is superior to faith—which holds only in certain respects—does not entail the conclusion that it is love and not faith that justifies.[104] What is important for my purposes is that Calvin links the faith that justifies in 1 Cor. 13:13 with Paul's statements about knowledge and vision of God in 13:9–12.

According to Calvin, 1 Cor. 13:9 ("we know in part and we prophesy in part") does not refer to the fact that believers make progress in knowledge and prophecy, although this is true. Rather, Paul means that believers have knowledge and prophecy because of their present imperfection; someday, however, these will no longer be necessary. Paul expresses this idea in 1 Cor. 13:12 through the analogy of seeing obscurely through a glass or mirror (*per speculum in aenigmate*). The "glass" refers for Calvin to those means by which the invisible God has disclosed God's self: the total structure of the world, and, more properly in the context of this discussion, the ministry of the word and the instruments required for carrying out this ministry.[105] At present, believers contemplate the image of God "in the word, the sacraments, and the whole service of the church." Later, however, they will have a more distinct vision of God "face to face." Calvin confirms this by citing 2 Cor. 5:7: "as long as we dwell in the body we are absent from the Lord, for we walk by faith and not by sight." Faith now "beholds God as absent," but later "it will behold him as near and before [its] eyes."[106] Calvin rejects the view that this line of reasoning implies that the knowledge of God, that is, faith, derived from the word is confused, perplexed, or dark. The knowledge that is faith is certain, but when compared with the full vision of God to come it is designated "obscure."[107]

In his interpretation of this passage Calvin contrasts faith as knowledge of God through the word with the full vision of God on the last day. Yet he also portrays faith as a kind of perception, since it is faith that now beholds God's image in the word. There is thus both a disjunction and continuity between the present world and the realm to come. On the one hand, he suggests that faith as knowledge in the present world will give way to a completely different mode of apprehension (i.e., sight) in the world to come: knowledge in the present, seeing in the future. On the other hand, faith already has a kind of obscure "vision" in the present that will be completed by the full vision of God.

Calvin's exegesis of 2 Cor. 5:6–7 strengthens the opposition between faith and sight (*aspectus*) but also the idea of faith as a kind of perception.[108] Just as he used 2 Cor. 5:7 to shed meaning on 1 Cor. 13:12–13, Calvin quotes 1 Cor. 13:12 twice in his interpretation of this passage. The first time is in his comments on 2 Cor. 5:6, where he uses the idea of a future face-to-face vision of God to confirm the view that God is not openly seen by believers in the present world. God is always present with believers, but to the extent that they will apprehend God more openly and clearly in the future kingdom, Paul is correct in saying that believers are now absent from God (or, conversely, that God is absent from them). The subsequent discussion under 2 Cor. 5:7 adds a nuance not found in the comments on the passage from 1 Corinthians. Here faith is not only opposed to the future vision of God, when the elect will behold God "face to face," but also to present visual perception: "faith is opposed to sight because it grasps those things that are hidden from human perception [*ab hominum sensu abscondita*]."[109] Believers often appear even to themselves to be dead and forsaken by God, so they must now hope for the life in God, which is hidden yet perceived by faith. Calvin refers to Rom. 8:24 to underscore the hiddenness of the objects of hope; he then paraphrases Heb. 11:1 to support the view that faith is the very manifestation of these things that do not appear to sight. He concludes his comments by referring again to 1 Cor. 13:12 to stress the idea of faith as a unique mode of perception: "It is not surprising therefore if the apostle says that we do not yet come into possession of sight as long as we walk by faith. For we see, but in a mirror and obscurely, that is, in the place of the reality we rest on the word [*in verbo acquiescimus*]."[110]

Calvin's exegesis of these two passages from Paul's epistles to the Corinthians illustrates more fully an important dimension of Calvin's understanding of faith: faith as a kind of perception that looks beyond or even away from the objects presented to the physical senses and apprehends in a preliminary and proleptic fashion the full vision of God that the elect will someday enjoy. Obviously, this image of faith reflects traditional understandings of Hebrews 11. However, it is noteworthy that Calvin develops this view in his exegesis of texts that he considered, in contradistinction to Hebrews, to be authentically Pauline. From his reading of Paul, and perhaps in light of traditional imagery of faith as an eye, Calvin develops both a positive and a negative assessment of the relationship between faith and perception of things in this world. Frequently he presents the vision of faith in contrast to both the physical perception in this world or the clear vision of God "face to face" that is to come.[111] These views inform and reinforce the bias against physical sense perception that, as I have shown, is not only expressed in the *Institutes* but also applied to the example of Abraham in Calvin's exegesis of Romans 4. However, the passages also contribute to a notion of faith as a kind of perception in this realm: faith "sees" the image of God in the word, the sacraments, the ministrations of the church, and perhaps even in the structure of the world. However, Calvin only suggests and does not explore this option.[112] His reticence about the topic here should not diminish the significance of these means, especially the sacraments, as visible aids for a faith that experiences God's redemptive hand at work in them.[113]

Calvin's exegesis of the passages considered in this section demonstrates once again the interrelatedness of the themes of knowledge, certainty, and perception in the idea of faith that he sets forth on the basis of his reading of Paul. He clearly approaches the Pauline texts with an interest in these issues and an assumption that it is in the reality of faith that they combine to answer the fundamental human problem: ignorance and blindness. The Pauline texts speak to these themes and allow him to develop them further. The result is, first, a multifaceted notion of faith. From this reading, Calvin derives not only proof texts for faith's certainty but also images of the noetic character of faith and of faith as a kind of perception. His understanding of these various aspects is quite fluid. Though he distinguishes, for example, between the noetic element and the certainty of faith in his exegesis of Eph. 1:13 and 3:12, most often these so imply one another that they virtually collapse. This is clear, for example, in his interpretation of 1 Cor. 2:12. Similarly, the idea of "illumination" by the Holy Spirit into the wisdom of the gospel—the benefits wrought by Christ's death and resurrection—implies both faith as knowledge that grasps this heavenly wisdom and faith as a perception that sees the spiritual realities it conveys. Finally, even faith's perception expresses its certainty; though it is not yet actual sight, the fact that it rests in things hidden to the physical sense of sight and beyond the ordinary rational capacity makes it more certain than common empirical experience.

Second, it is significant that shaping this complex notion of faith is the question of soteriology, narrowed in Calvin's view to the issue of justification by faith alone. Calvin's Pauline notion of faith consists in a knowledge of God's benevolence not in general but specifically made known in the incarnate Christ. It offers a vision of Christ's saving benefits (forgiveness of sins and eternal life) in spite of apparent evidence to the contrary in the present rather than a view of God's general activity in the world. Faith rests on God's redemptive work made known in the word and not on the works of God manifest to empirical experience and physical sense perception. Faith is itself a divine work—the instrumental cause of justification—and not a human work deserving reward.

Broadening the Soteriological Perspective

The issues and questions connected with individual salvation dominate Calvin's commentaries on the Pauline epistles, and, as I have shown, these soteriological concerns shape the view of faith that he sets forth on the basis of his reading of Paul. However, at times the focus on the question of salvation yields to other, broader concerns, for example, God's just governance of the world and history.[114] In Calvin's treatment of the two exemplary passages to be discussed hereafter, one can detect a definite shift in emphasis that is having an impact on the view of faith that he is developing. Underlying his exegesis of 2 Thess. 1:5–12 and Phil. 4:4–7 is not so much the concern with the question of salvation from a situation characterized by blindness and ignorance, or with the process of regeneration. To be sure, discussions about faith's role in overcoming pangs of conscience and combatting the ever-present reality of sin are frequent in the Pauline commentaries, especially in the passages where Paul raises up the theme of spiritual warfare.[115] A prominent example of this is found in Eph. 6:10–20, which puts forth (in 6:16) the important image of faith as a shield.[116] Yet 2 Thess. 1:5–12 and Phil. 4:4–7 suggest to Calvin a related but different problem; namely, the problem of the confusion of history: the prosperity of the wicked and the persecution of the godly. This shift in perspective leads him to discuss faith from a different angle, not from the standpoint of faith's role in justification, in overcoming doubt about salvation, or in persevering amid pangs of conscience. Instead, he treats faith in the face of tribulation occasioned by the inscrutability of divine providence. As a result of this specific challenge, the perceptual qualities of faith in particular become more nuanced and the refuge to which faith flees takes on a new character.

Paul prefaces his apocalyptic discussion in 2 Thessalonians 2 by commending in chapter 1 his audience's patience and faith in the face of affliction. He claims in 2 Thess. 1:5 that the present persecutions and afflictions of the Thessalonians are evidence of God's righteous judgment, by which they are deemed worthy of suffering for the kingdom of God. In 1:6–7, the author adds that it is just also for God to afflict their persecutors and to give rest to the Thessalonians. This recompense, however, lies in the future, as 1:7–10 makes clear. When Jesus returns with his angels, vengeance will be taken on those who do not know God or obey the gospel (2 Thess. 1:8), and Jesus will be glorified and admired in those who have believed the testimony borne to them (2 Thess. 1:10). Second Thess. 1:11–12 express the author's prayer that God might reckon the Thessalonians worthy of this calling and fulfil the work of faith with power.

In Calvin's view, the problem the passage raises is that the Thessalonians are suffering for the gospel while their persecutors remain exempt from judgment. He commends, along with Paul, the Thessalonians' faith and the patience to which it gives birth; it is their faith in God's promises that sustains them in their trials.[117] Rejecting without detailing earlier interpretations of 2 Thess. 1:5, Calvin says that the meaning is that "the injuries and persecutions, which the innocent and godly sustain from the cruel and wicked, demonstrate, as in a mirror, that God will judge the world."[118] This remarkable logic reveals Calvin's deepest assumptions about God's sovereignty over history. He observes (with Paul) the fact that God at present spares the wicked and overlooks the injuries they inflict on the godly. He combines this observation with the assumption, derived from 2 Thess. 1:6 ("it is just for God to afflict those who crush you"), that God is the just judge of the world. Together these lead to his conclusion that God will some day restore order. Hence, "the present disorder is a demonstration of the judgment that does not yet appear."[119] The confusion of history does not undermine but rather evidences divine sovereignty!

How does faith sustain believers amid these special trials? The allusion to the language of Heb. 11:1 in the passage just quoted makes the point that Calvin derives, as I have shown, from such passages as 1 Cor. 13:12 and 2 Cor. 5:6–7: faith rests on a future reality not perceptible to carnal sense or ordinary intelligence. Yet this future reality is in a way mediated by immediate sense perception, since the present disorder and God's refraining from exercising the office of judge themselves become tokens of future judgment. Nonetheless, faith does not remain fixed on these present realities. By not restoring order completely in the present, God raises the minds of the godly above the world, where they contemplate God's righteous but future judgment.[120] In his exegesis of 2 Thess. 1:7–10, Calvin underscores the distinction between the present confusion and affliction and the future manifestation of justice, the contemplation of which is the source of strength in the present trial. In 1556 he adds to his comments on 2 Thess. 1:10 the following conclusion to Paul's statement about the future restoration of the godly: "the godly should pursue the brief journey of this earthly life as if with closed eyes, always having their minds intent on the future manifestation of Christ's kingdom."[121] Calvin deals cautiously with the mention in 2 Thess. 1:11 of "accounting worthy" and the "work of faith": these expressions do not imply that the perfecting of faith rests on anything but divine grace. God, says Calvin, has already accounted those who have faith worthy, and the import of the prayer is that God "may complete [*absolvit*] the building of faith that he has begun."[122]

Despite this familiar insistence that faith from beginning to end is a divine work and that salvation is not based on human merit, the problem that is uppermost in Calvin's mind is not the individual's doubt about salvation or fear that God will not be merciful. Rather, the specific trial that the confusion of history occasions is the fear that God is not affected by calamities or, perhaps worse, that God has no control over events. In his comments on 2 Thess. 1:5, Calvin opposes his reading of the verse—that the persecution of the godly by the wicked shows, as in a mirror, God's future judgment—to "that profane opinion, which we are accustomed to entertain whenever it goes badly with the good and well with the wicked. For we think that the world revolves by mere chance and we leave God no control."[123] He quotes observations from Solomon (Ecc. 9:3), Ovid, David (Ps. 73:1–12), and Dionysius the Younger as examples of this notion.[124] But this conclusion is faulty, he argues, because it is based on "carnal sense" and does not take into account the judgment that does not yet appear. Similarly, in the comments on 2 Thess. 1:7, Calvin points out that faith ought to consider the end of Jesus' return, namely, to exercise judgment. The vivid description of Jesus' return in 2 Thess. 1:8–10 ought to convince the godly of God's care. "For the chief reason for grief and distress is this—that we think that God is but lightly touched by our calamities."[125] Once again, David provides an illustration of this sentiment.

In light of this specific trial occasioned by the confusion of history, Calvin treats not the origin but the perfecting of faith. Moreover, he treats this not in response to trials calling salvation and with that God's mercy into question, as he does in a sermon on 2 Thess. 1:6–10 that was published in 1548.[126] Rather he poses faith as an answer to challenges and affronts to God's justice and power. In the face of these challenges, he calls believers to contemplate God's righteous judgment and the forthcoming ruin of the wicked, though he warns his readers not to be carried away by inordinate desire for vengeance. Still, as noted earlier, the soteriological element is not completely absent; in the 1556 addition to 2 Thess. 1:10 Calvin reminds his readers that the reason that Paul mentions Christ's future manifestation and coming to power is to spur the Thessalonians to leap forward in hope to the resurrection that is at present hidden.[127] But clearly there is a shift of emphasis, and with that, a shift in the orientation of faith. Not simply resting in the benefits of Christ the Redeemer, faith looks particularly to God's righteous judgment to correct the faulty conclusion of the flesh concerning God's providential governance of events.

Faith in the process of being perfected is still primarily future oriented and clearly opposed to carnal sense perception. Nonetheless, the evaluation of the perception of present events is not entirely negative. Present persecutions become "mirrors" of future rectification. Though believers are to close their eyes to the present confusion, the partial nature of judgment exercised in the present is itself a spur to look to the future and not remain fixed in the earthly realm. This perspective is carried through in Calvin's comments on the subsequent chapter. In his exegesis of 2 Thess. 2:3 ("that day shall not come"), he cites historical examples that confirm Paul's prophecy, concluding that "we see with our own eyes that this memorable prediction of Paul has been confirmed by the event."[128] Similarly, in the comments on 2 Thess. 2:13, Calvin suggests that the reprobate themselves are mirrors for considering God's mercy, since the godly do not perish with them.[129]

Calvin's exegesis of Phil. 4:4–7 offers a slightly different remedy to the problems raised by the confusion of history. Instead of urging his readers to look away from the world into the future, he stresses the need to rest securely in God's providence in this realm. Here the present realm becomes more than a mere stepping-stone to a new, higher perspective. By reflecting on the fact that God is present with them in this realm, believers learn to make sense of their confused situation.

In these four verses Paul urges the recipients of his letter to rejoice in the Lord, to make their moderation (*moderatio*) visible to all people, not to be caught up in cares, and to pray with thanksgiving (Phil. 4:4–6). He declares that the Lord is near (Phil. 4:5) and promises them that the peace of God will hold their minds in Christ Jesus (Phil. 4:7). Because this passage is so short and its statements, in isolation from the context, might appear quite general, it is helpful to consider briefly the discussion preceding them: the warning against dogs and evil workers (Phil. 3:2) and the recommendation of the author's example for imitation. In this discussion, Paul stresses the value of knowing Christ, contrasts the righteousness of faith and the righteousness of the law as paths to Christ (Phil. 3:9), and urges his audience to follow him in striving toward the prize of God's calling in Christ Jesus (Phil. 3:14). After this, Paul contrasts the heavenly conversation of his audience with the earthly-minded and belly-oriented behavior of the enemies of Christ's cross (Phil. 3:18–21). In light of this situation, the letter exhorts its readers to stand fast in the Lord (Phil. 4:1).

Calvin understands the exhortations in Phil. 4:4–7 as a response not to a dispute about justification by faith but rather to the enemies internal to the church who think only of themselves. These enemies are pastors who seek their own interests at the expense of the gospel. Calvin says that they urged circumcision, not, however, because of zeal for the law but rather to curry human favor and lead lives free from annoyance. Seeing the rage kindled against true preachers of the gospel, like Paul, these impostors compromised the gospel so as not to have this rage turned against themselves. In Calvin's view, Paul reminds his audience that their citizenship is in heaven and stirs them up to look to heaven and seek Christ there.[130] The exhortations in Philippians 4 encourage the Philippians to continue (like Paul) in their steadfast resistance. Calvin finds the command to rejoice (Phil. 4:4) is especially suited to the situation of the Philippians. Somewhat suddenly, this situation appears much more precarious than it had before, and Calvin is concerned to urge stability amid these uncertainties. Perhaps he is thinking not only of the internal disorder that he had described in his comments on Philippians 3 but also of more widespread persecutions and afflictions to which the early church was subject. In any case, he observes that in this exceedingly troubled situation, with dangers threatening on every side, they ought to be especially encouraged by these words from Paul, who himself was in prison "in the very heat of persecution and, in short, apprehensions of death," yet not only rejoiced but also encouraged others to do so.[131] Calvin's concern with the ability to persevere in the face of persecution extends into his interpretation of Phil. 4:5. Though he admits that the exhortation to *moderatio* can be understood to mean that the Philippians should act with equity toward others, he much prefers an alternative meaning. Paul is exhorting his audience "to endure all things with equanimity." Calvin adds in 1556 that in the face of "injuries and inconveniences" Paul urges them to act peaceably and exercise self-control.[132]

According to Calvin, Paul's statement in Phil. 4:5, "the Lord is near," anticipates an objection raised by carnal sense to this reaction to persecution. Calvin argues that the moderate endurance of afflictions incites the ungodly to greater rage. This might lead the godly to conclude—in agreement with the proverbs "We must howl when among wolves" and "Those who act like sheep will quickly be devoured by wolves"—to return violence with violence.[133] Paul's statement, however, prevents this inference by opposing confidence in divine providence to these considerations. By declaring that the Lord is near, Paul intimates that God's power and goodness will overcome the wicked. Moreover, in Calvin's view, this teaches that it is precisely the ignorance of providence that causes impatience and throws the godly into confusion; they become disheartened because they fail to recognize that the Lord cares for them. The only remedy is to repose "completely in his providence, knowing that we are not exposed either to the rashness of fortune or the caprice of the ungodly but that we are governed by God's fatherly care."[134] Calvin points out that, though "the Lord is near" can also refer to God's impending judgment, this is not the meaning of the phrase here. In this context, it means that God is ready to assist his own people (*ad opem suis ferendam*), and it is used, according to Calvin, in this sense also in Ps. 145:18. Thus he directs his readers' attention to God's present care rather than God's future judgment and urges them to gain strength from God's presence with them.

Through the exercise of prayer, which is mentioned in Phil. 4:6, the godly lean on the present Lord and attain consolation. However, though their attention is directed more toward the present than toward the future, they nonetheless rely not on visible or tangible realities but rather on the word. Calvin acknowledges that "those who look hither and thither to the vain comforts of the world may appear to be in some degree relieved." But the only certain refuge (*certus portus*) is to rest on the Lord.[135] Similarly, the peace in Phil. 4:7 is designated as God's because "it does not depend on a present view of things, nor does it give way to the world's various changes, but is founded on the firm and immutable word of God." This peace surpasses, Calvin says "all understanding or sense," since it is, as I have just shown, not at all the result of the human mind's inference from the behavior of the wicked.[136] It is the word alone, whether of God's future judgment or present providence, sealed inwardly by the Spirit, that enables the believer to stand firm amid the confusion of history.

A brief contrast with Calvin's interpretation of one other passage helps accentuate the distinctiveness of the perspective that his interpretations of these two passages evidence. In his interpretation of a similar set of exhortations in 1 Thess. 5:16–18, he summarizes his interpretation of Phil. 4:4–6 and notes that Paul urges repose in God's providence, prayer, and thanksgiving as remedies for "grief, sorrow, anxiety, and fear." He says that in 1 Thessalonians Paul presents the same order of exhortations (rejoice, prayer, give thanks) but in fewer words.[137] However, in his comments Calvin grounds the joy not in the recognition of God's presence and ongoing care for believers but rather in consideration of the benefits conferred by Christ. He designates as ungrateful a person who does not value the righteousness of Christ and eternal life enough to be able to rejoice in the midst of sorrow and cautions against impatience, which undermines thanksgiving. He stresses that it is God's disposition in Christ that not only occasions thanksgiving amid afflictions but also turns everything that happens to believers' advantage. Therefore, he concludes, the special remedy for impatience is "to turn our eyes from beholding present evils that torment us, and to direct them to a different consideration: how God stands affected toward us in Christ."[138]

As was the case with Phil. 4:4–7, the evils and afflictions that are the source of impatience are not specified. Yet if one glances back at Calvin's interpretation of earlier chapters of the letter, it appears likely that the difficulty that these urgings to consider Christ address is not the confusion of history but rather excessive sorrow arising over the death of loved ones. Though Paul mentions persecutions in 1 Thess. 3:1–5, Calvin does not understand this to be the major issue confronting the Thessalonians, probably because Paul rejoices in 1 Thess. 3:6–7 over Timothy's report of their faith and love. Calvin understands these verses as an exhortation to perseverance but does not dwell on the need for it. More problematic, however, are hints that some of the Thessalonians, through their excessive grief, betray that the persuasion of the resurrection is not sufficiently fixed in their minds. In his comments on 1 Thess. 4:13–15, Calvin first says that he does not think that the situation among the Thessalonians had deteriorated as far as it had in Corinth, where "profane men" had torn up the hope of the resurrection. Still, there appears to be some uncertainty, since some imagined that only those alive at the time of Christ's return would be raised. Paul corrects this misconception. In discussing Paul's comments, Calvin stresses the need for Christians to bridle their grief through hope in the resurrection.[139]

It appears that it is this problem, and not the confusion of history or even the approaching day of the Lord mentioned in 1 Thess. 5:3, that underlies Calvin's interpretation of 1 Thess. 5:16–18. He begins his comments on 5:16 by referring the command to rejoice "to moderation of spirit, when the mind keeps itself in calmness under adversity and does not give rein to grief." He thus combines the understanding of moderation from his comments on Phil. 4:5 with the present interest in restraining undue grief. He also remarks that recognition of and meditation on Christ's benefits should "overcome all sorrow" and concludes that "if we consider what Christ has conferred on us there will be no grief so bitter as not to be alleviated and give way to spiritual joy." Finally, as I have shown, he chastises the person who cannot rejoice in the midst of sorrow.[140]

These considerations should not suggest that the problem of confusion of history was one of which Calvin was unaware until his commentary on Philippians in 1548, where mention of it appears not only in the commentary itself but also in the dedicatory epistle to the volume containing the commentaries on Galatians, Ephesians, Philippians, and Colossians. Concern with this problem is evident also in the 1540 Romans commentary.[141] Nevertheless, this idea receives little explicit attention in the commentaries on Paul. Yet where this theme does emerge, it implies changes for the shape of Calvin's understanding of faith. Consideration of this particular problem leads him to emphasize the perceptual character of faith, which directs its attention to the future restoration of order in God's judgment. Or it brings him to focus on God's present providential activity, revealed in the word. He can sometimes even treat past and current events, when viewed through the lens of the word about God's justice and providence, as mirrors of these attributes. These passages add to the complexity of Calvin's Pauline understanding of faith by providing him with a context for reflecting on faith that is not shaped primarily by soteriological concerns. They suggest at least the possibility of talking about faith apart from the immediate question of justification or even sanctification. In these contexts Calvin speaks about the relation of faith to God's creative and providential activity as well as to God's redemptive activity. Such instances point to a broadening of the Pauline perspective that, as I will show in chapter 4, is pressed farther in Calvin's commentary on the Psalms.

Conclusion

The view of faith that Calvin sets forth in his commentaries on the Pauline epistles is multifaceted but nonetheless focused clearly on the question of salvation and even more particularly on the question of *how* fallen human beings obtain new life. The answer that Calvin finds in his exegesis of Paul is that the just shall live by faith. His commentaries on Paul thus reinforce the understanding of faith in Christ as the instrumental cause of justification. Faith, as the means of justification, is sharply distinguished from works and love and is tied but not reduced to an attitude of trust or confidence. Moreover, faith is portrayed as a kind of perception but is definitely not to be confused with physical sight. Faith is not sight but comes through hearing; it rests on God's word of mercy in the gospel and so furnishes the remedy to the problem of ignorance and blindness, in the face of which human beings are both helpless and without excuse. Faith provides saving knowledge of God's redemptive work in Christ, certainty in the word proclaiming this redemption, and a new perception that rises above carnal sense to grasp through the eye of faith the promised redemption that remains hidden to the eye of the flesh.

The point of this investigation was to establish that the view of faith that Calvin advances and reinforces in the *Institutes* is fundamentally Pauline. But in considering his exegesis of Paul, only half the task is done. For although this view of faith, both its content and the context in which it is discussed, corresponds to

Calvin's understanding of faith in the *Institutes*, it has not yet been shown that Paul's is the dominating biblical perspective shaping Calvin's understanding of faith. It has only been shown that Calvin finds in Paul the same elements that he expresses in the *Institutes*: an interest in faith as *fides qua*, an ever-increasing preoccupation with the certainty of faith, a sense of general opposition between faith and sight, an understanding of faith as knowledge that apprehends heavenly wisdom. The next step is to determine which of these emphases are distinctively Pauline or whether they are simply views that Calvin finds universally expressed in scripture. One must then see whether the distinctively Pauline themes, if any, are indeed the dominating ones for Calvin's understanding of faith. To take this next step, I need to consider Calvin's exegesis of non-Pauline texts and especially how he treats the theme of faith in them.

As I will show in the next chapters, the view of saving faith that Calvin sets forth in his exegesis of Paul functions as a lens though which he views other scriptural passages about faith. His reiteration of familiar Pauline themes and particularly his correction of other passages in light of his Pauline view demonstrates the normative status of the view of faith that he finds in Paul. Sometimes reinforcing, sometimes challenging his Pauline presuppositions, other passages not only maintain the Pauline perspective but also contribute to the broadening of it that, as I have shown, was already beginning to happen in Calvin's interpretation of Paul.

3

From Faith to Faith

To explore how Calvin's commentaries on New Testament texts not from the hand of Paul reflect both his Pauline assumptions and his reinterpretation of Pauline themes, I will consider his treatment of selected biblical passages in his commentaries on Hebrews (1549), James (1551), 1 John (1551), and the Gospel of John (1553). Not only does each of these biblical writings have faith as one of its prominent themes, but also Calvin treats passages from each of them in his discussion of faith in the *Institutes*. Most important, however, these commentaries provide instructive examples of how the view of faith that Calvin brings to expression in his Pauline commentaries functions as a guide and norm for reading other biblical texts about this topic. Calvin's Pauline assumptions underlie his interpretation and contribute to the resolution of exegetical or polemical difficulties these texts present. Often his Pauline understanding functions as a lens for reading and correcting other statements about faith. Sometimes, however, a particular text leads him to expand his view of faith and thus to reinterpret Paul in this new light. The discussion will trace some of these developments and show which texts Calvin finds problematic and which texts allow him to explore the theme of faith from different perspectives.

It would be simplistic and incorrect to assume that Calvin did not reckon with the challenges that the selected passages raise prior to his attention to the text in the commentary or that they had no influence on his understanding of faith prior to that time. Rather, as I have shown already in my discussion of the Romans commentary, Calvin addressed the difficulty posed by James 2 long before he actually wrote the commentary on James. Moreover, he attended to other New Testament passages about faith (for example, Hebrews 11) in the early editions of the *Institutes*. Nonetheless, consideration of Calvin's exegesis of the these passages shows more clearly how the Pauline perspective dominated his reading of other New Testament texts on faith and, in subtle ways, was in turn shaped by them.

The Commentary on Hebrews (1549)

As noted earlier, Calvin treats Hebrews as a Pauline writing in the 1536 edition of the *Institutes* but later distances himself from this view. From the 1539 edition on, he locates his discussion of Heb. 11:1 near the end of the section of faith and argues that the view of faith expressed there is completely consistent with the idea, described in detail in the preceding discussion, of faith as firm and certain knowledge. One of the rare modifications to the 1545 edition of the *Institutes* appears to qualify Calvin's earlier statement that Heb. 11:1 was a "definition" of faith. By the time he publishes his commentary on Hebrews four years later, he explicitly denies both Pauline authorship and that Heb. 11:1 offers a full definition of faith.[1] Nonetheless, at various points in the epistle to the Hebrews, and especially in Heb. 11:1, he finds opportunity to confirm his Pauline assumptions about faith. The text of Hebrews raises familiar themes but at the same time views them from a different perspective. The text focuses on Christ, yet it does not make specific reference to Christ as the object of faith; in fact, of thirty-two appearances of the substantive *pistis* only one appears with an object (Heb. 6:1), and the object is God, not Christ.[2] Hebrews stresses the confident, certain, and steadfast character of faith, though it emphasizes this primarily as perseverance incorporating hope and patience rather than a guaranteed means of salvation distinct from the works of the Torah. Naturally the close link between faith, hope, and patience is something that Calvin finds in Paul's theology as well, for example, in Rom. 8:24–25.[3] Nonetheless, in Hebrews hope and patience constitute the essence of faith (compare Heb. 6:11–12 and 10:22; 10:36–39 and 12:1), whereas in Paul they are fruits of tribulation (Rom. 5:3–5) and distinct, though not separate, from faith (Gal. 5:5; 2 Thess. 1:4).[4] Also like Paul, Hebrews underscores the relationship between faith and the word. However, Hebrews presents faith as the necessary precondition for receiving the word (Heb. 4:2) rather than as itself originating through preaching (Rom. 10:17).[5] Finally, Hebrews advances a statement of the perceptual nature of faith that is no less cryptic than it is significant.

In general, Calvin does not perceive Hebrews, or potential readings of it, as challenging openly his presuppositions about faith. For the most part his exegesis evidences an easy, almost unconscious harmonization; he simply fills in the gaps with Pauline content. For example, despite the lack of explicit reference to Christ as the object of faith, Calvin nonetheless finds that the text confirms this point.[6] Similarly, he interprets verses about the word and faith in a Pauline light. He understands Heb. 4:2 to speak of the calling of God, that is, the origin of faith, and to make the Pauline point that the word is effective only in the elect, whose faith it precedes.[7] He refers the word of God as a two-edged sword in Heb. 4:12 to the summoning of guilty consciences before the divine tribunal.[8] The Pauline perspective emerges for the most part to help Calvin clarify obscurities.

Yet Calvin's treatment of faith in Hebrews is not always a matter of invoking Paul to illuminate the meaning of a passage. Rather, while the distinct emphases of the text do not, for Calvin, openly conflict with the Pauline view, they nonetheless broaden his perspective by allowing him to develop new but related themes with respect to faith. Calvin's exegesis of two chapters, Hebrews 6 and 11, illustrates both the harmonization with Paul and the development of independent aspects.

Calvin's Exegesis of Hebrews 6

Hebrews 6 seeks to prepare for the exposition of the text's main theme in Heb. 7: 1–10:18; namely, Jesus Christ's high priesthood.[9] The first two verses declare the author's intention to skip over the beginning tenets of doctrine and press forward to perfection. This is followed by a warning against falling away, since a return from apostasy is impossible (Heb. 6:4–8). After this admonition, the author calms and encourages the readers (Heb. 6:9–10) and urges them to press on, imitating Abraham, in patient expectation of God's reliable promise (Heb. 6:11–20). The passage leads Calvin to discuss three distinct degrees of faith: a faith that can be left behind (Heb. 6:1–2), a faith from which it is possible to fall away (Heb. 6:4–6), and a faith that waits patiently for the fulfillment of the promise (Heb. 6:11–20).

In his comments on Heb. 6:1 Calvin applauds the author's exhortation to leave behind the rudiments of Christianity, for though these are the foundation, "higher doctrine ought to complete the building." Faith is so founded, he declares, "as to rise upward, until by daily progress it be at last completed."[10] However, these rudiments, repentance and faith, hardly seem surpassable. They "include the fullness of the gospel." Moreover, Christ commanded his disciples to teach these two things, and Paul points to his care in teaching them to prove that he had faithfully performed his duty. We ought not to omit but rather "make progress in both through the whole course of our life." Calvin solves the difficulty by pointing to the words "from dead works." This addition shows that the author is speaking of first repentance, "when those who were recently and for the first time converted to faith commenced a new life." In this context, the word "faith" means the articles of faith.[11] Thus the faith that is to be left behind, but not forgotten, appears to be a *fides quae* embraced by converts. It seems, moreover, that the faith that should rise upward and be completed is, in Calvin's exegesis of this verse, also a *fides quae*, to be completed by "higher doctrine." Thus the distinction between justification and sanctification, which we saw in Calvin's interpretation of Romans, provides the solution to the difficulty by allowing him to distinguish between first repentance and lifelong sanctification and between the foundational tenets of faith and its subsequent progress.

The warning in Heb. 6:4–6 against second repentance for apostates was apparently used by heterodox Novatians (ca. 250) to deny pardon to those who had fallen.[12] Calvin acknowledges that it was on the basis of the Novatian exegesis that some in the Western Church denied the authority of Hebrews. The problem lies, according to Calvin, in the interpretation of the words "fall away." This does not mean theft, perjury, murder, drunkenness, or adultery, but rather "refers to a total defection from the gospel, when a sinner offends God not in some one thing but entirely renounces his grace."[13] This, Calvin says, is sin against the Holy Spirit, and a person who falls in this way is excluded from all hope of pardon. The author portrays this danger to believers so that they might guard against going astray.

A consideration of what is forsaken in the act of apostasy not only functions as a commendation of what believers possess but also leads Calvin to the question of whether such a fall is really possible. He takes each of the things mentioned in Heb. 6:4–5 to be a different aspect of knowledge of the gospel, but these could be equally well said to be elements of faith. This is supported not only by the consideration that, for Calvin, faith is essentially knowledge of the gospel, but also by the language that he uses to specify these elements. The elements supposedly forsaken in apostasy include illumination of blindness, reception of Christ's supernatural benefits, spiritual revelation, grasp of the gospel, and a foretaste of future life hid from the perception of the senses.[14] After summarizing these riches, Calvin reminds his readers, on Paul's authority (Rom. 8:24), that the elect cannot lose the pledge of adoption. They have the Spirit of regeneration, renewing them in God's image; by the Spirit they have received a pledge (*arrha*) of future inheritance and have the gospel sealed on their hearts. Calvin's presuppositions about the certainty of faith thus exclude the possibility of apostasy among the elect. However, he goes on to admit a kind of faith among the reprobate, which can be lost:

> But I deny that prevents God from granting the reprobate also some taste of his grace, from irradiating their minds with some sparks of his light, from giving them some perception of his goodness, and from engraving his word on their hearts in some way. Otherwise where would be the temporary faith mentioned in Mark [4: 17]? There is therefore some knowledge [*cognitio*] even in the reprobate, which afterwards vanishes away, either because it did not strike roots sufficiently deep or because it suffocated [and] withered.[15]

Calvin understands the existence of a temporary faith among the reprobate to be a "bridle" for the elect; it should not disturb their peace of conscience but keep them in fear and humility by exercising the flesh.

The faith from which one can fall away is thus not the certain faith of the elect but rather a knowledge of God—perhaps even an accurate knowledge of God—apart from the spiritual gift of regeneration (sanctification). Apparently this insoluble link to new life distinguishes the firm yet ever-growing faith of the elect from the temporary faith among some of the reprobate. Because rebirth is lacking in the latter, the knowledge of God cannot strike firm roots, and a fall from faith is possible; indeed, one would have to say, this fall is inevitable. Calvin characterizes this decline as a gradual regress into self-delusion: the reprobate add sin to sin until they are completely hardened in their hatred of God. He concurs with Heb. 6:6 that one who has fallen so completely never truly feels the repentance necessary to return to God. From this he draws two conclusions: first, that repentance is a divine gift and not a product of the human will. Second, that the fact that a person "rises up again after falling" is proof that the defection was not complete. He thus takes the passage primarily as a commendation of the efficacy of divine grace. The harshness of the warning stimulates believers to continue in repentance, which, Calvin had already informed his readers in the comments on Heb. 6:1, is a lifelong process. His comments reveal a struggle to maintain a balance between the total efficacy of the divine and human responsibility. Though the elect are beyond danger of finally falling away, nevertheless they do fall. This passage reminds them to make good use of the gift of repentance that God makes available to them, so that they would not delay repentance and thereby alienate themselves more and more from God.[16]

In his exegesis of the rest of Hebrews 6, Calvin sets forth a view of true faith as inseparable from hope and patience. There is thus an implicit contrast to the ideas of faith treated in the earlier sections: this is faith as it relies securely on God's word, a *fides qua* rather than a rudimentary *fides quae* that must be transcended. Moreover, it is faith as fully assured, waiting patiently for fulfillment of the promise, a faith that cannot be lost. However, though he establishes essential links between true faith and hope and faith and patience, Calvin nonetheless refuses to collapse these completely.

Calvin understands Heb. 6:11, "we desire that each one of you demonstrate the same zeal for the certainty of hope to the end," as an exhortation to persevere in fixed and certain faith.[17] He translates the word *plerophoria* as certainty (*certitudo*) and argues that the word "hope" is to be taken for faith.[18] This is the second instance (compare Heb. 3:6) where Calvin finds that the author of Hebrews has used hope for faith. According to Calvin, hope expresses the constancy and endurance of faith. For this reason, he claims, when the author exhorts the Jews to perseverance in Heb. 10:23, he speaks of "the confession of our hope" when he really means confession of our faith. Hope nourishes and sustains faith.[19] Therefore, when the author exhorts his readers in Heb. 6:11 to persevere in faith, he uses the word "hope." Moreover, Calvin finds that here the use of the word "hope" instead of "faith" shows how different true faith is from "that general apprehension that the ungodly and devils have in common." These have no good hope because they do not apprehend God's paternal favor in Christ.[20]

Calvin's exegesis of Heb. 6:19 offers another example of the fluidity of the concepts faith and hope in this commentary. This verse describes the hope mentioned in the previous verse as "a sure and steadfast anchor of the soul" that, following the forerunner (*praecursor*) Jesus, enters into "those things within the veil," that is, behind the curtain to the Temple's holy of holies.[21] Calvin says that the likeness is between faith leaning on God's word and an anchor but later stresses "our hope must be fixed on the invisible God" and not on created things.[22] The rope attached to the anchor connecting the ship and the earth is the truth of God, which, unlike rope itself, cannot be broken through the violence of the sea. Calvin concludes, "the power of God to sustain us is wholly different, and so also are the strength of hope [i.e., the anchor] and the firmness of his word." However, he returns to faith in the next sentence, which contains his observations on the part of the verse describing the entrance within the veil: "As we have said, until faith reaches to God, it finds nothing but what is unstable and evanescent; it is hence necessary for it to penetrate even into heaven." According to Calvin, by urging his Jewish readership to penetrate the hidden recesses of the veil, the author intimates that they should pass over the ceremonies and fix their faith in Christ alone. For Calvin's readers, this means that they should direct their faith to Christ in heaven.[23]

Just as true faith is always connected with hope, so closely in fact that sometimes the words can be used interchangeably, so is faith accompanied by patience.

However, for Calvin faith and patience are not the same thing, and so he is careful to distinguish between them. This is especially clear in his comments on Heb. 6: 12–15. He understands the phrase "through faith and patience" in Heb. 6:12 to be a rhetorical figure (hypallage) expressing "a firm faith, which has patience as its companion." Anxious to protect the concept of faith from any connection to merit, Calvin cautions that it is primarily faith, and not patience, that obtains the promises. Nonetheless, the author shows, presumably with the explicit mention of patience, that endurance (*tolerantia*) is "the true evidence of that faith that is not fleeting and vanishing."[24] The point is similar to the one Calvin made about knowledge of God in his comments on Heb. 6:11: true faith is known by its fruits. Moreover, he observes, that the promises were obtained by faith excludes any notion of merit; likewise, that they came by inheritance means that they come only by right of adoption. It is noteworthy also that his earlier discussion of a temporary faith continues to inform his comments.

Having made it clear that fulfillment of the promise is not a reward for patience but rather a gratuitous gift received in faith, Calvin turns to the example of Abraham mentioned in Heb. 6:13–15. According to Calvin, the example of Abraham proves that the grace of God can be received only by embracing the promise by faith and patiently cherishing it "in the bosom of our hearts." However, he does not focus on Abraham's grasping the promise through faith but rather on his patient waiting for its fulfillment. Moreover, Calvin appears to restrict the example to refer to the particular promise of offspring.[25] Abraham's patient expectation of the fulfillment of this specific promise provides a general pattern for the faithful: "We must quietly hope for what he [God] does not yet show to our senses but hides and defers for a long time in order to exercise our endurance [*tolerantia*]."[26] In subtle contrast to the view in Romans 4, Abraham in Hebrews 6 provides the "clearest mirror of faith" not primarily for the beginning of the life of faith but rather for the living of it.

This concern with living the new life of faith underlies each of the three moments that I have traced in Calvin's exegesis of Hebrews 6. Heb. 6:1–2 set the progress of regeneration in motion by calling for a transcendence of the first principles and a striving toward higher truth. The admonition in Heb. 6:4–6 stimulates progress and warns against the false confidence of the flesh, which puts off into the future the repentance that is needed daily. The portrayal of right faith as faith accompanied by hope and patience in Heb. 6:11–20 presents a picture of faith's activity in the process of regeneration. This is faith that has already embraced the promise of adoption and new life and is now waiting patiently for its fulfillment.

Surely a concern with faith not simply as the means of justification but also as the basis of sanctification is an idea that Calvin finds in Paul, especially in Romans 6, a chapter that, according to Calvin, deals explicitly with the newness of life imparted simultaneously with justification.[27] Yet Hebrews 6 offers him an opportunity to develop the relationship between faith and regeneration in relative isolation from the polemical concern for justification. In this context Calvin presents faith as apprehending new life hand in hand with hope and patience. However, though he finds true faith and hope as ever connected, he does not completely collapse hope or patience into faith. His Pauline perspective is evident in the clear preference for the full assurance of the faith of the elect, which is underscored by his translation of the term *plerophoria* as certainty. The allusion to the common knowledge of God that Calvin, as I will show, criticizes especially in his exegesis of James 2 is another indication of how the Pauline categories are not far from his mind.

Despite this repetition of Pauline themes, there are two elements in the view of faith in Hebrews 6 that cannot be easily harmonized with these general Pauline assumptions, and it is curious that Calvin makes no attempt at such a harmonization. First he provides no details on the faith that should be transcended beyond designating it as a *fides quae*. Is this faith "saving"? How does it relate to a mere historical faith, or the general, common knowledge of God? Calvin's lack of interest in these questions suggests that the concern for how faith justifies is not uppermost in his mind as he reads Hebrews, adding weight to the suggestion that the text leads him to focus not on the obtaining of faith (justification) but on the life of faith (regeneration, sanctification). The second curious element is Calvin's rather detailed discussion of a faith among the reprobate, which he never *explicitly* says is not a real faith. All that can be gathered from his comments is that such "faith" lacks the gift of regeneration, which, in his view, is nonetheless always received by faith along with the promise of adoption among the elect.

Calvin's Exegesis of Hebrews 11

In his exegesis of Hebrews 11 Calvin continues the reflection on faith and the life of regeneration that I showed him developing in his comments on Heb. 6:11–20. However, Hebrews 11 seems more problematic from Calvin's perspective. The fact that Hebrews 11:1 was taken by many scholastic theologians as a proper definition of faith, yet makes no mention of Christ or the word, is one difficulty.[28] Moreover, Heb. 11:6 might suggest that the faith that pleases God is to believe that he exists and that he rewards those who seek him. Understood this way, the verse would imply that all the deeds undertaken by faith and catalogued in Heb. 11:2–39 somehow merited God's favor. As I will show, Calvin also finds Heb. 11:3 and 11: 7 to have their own particular problems that require careful clarification. In his resolution of each of the difficulties, his Pauline presuppositions are much more evident and even explicit than in his exegesis of Hebrews 6.

The first problem that Calvin confronts is whether Heb. 11:1, "faith is the substance [*hypostasis, substantia*] of things hoped for, and the evidence [*demonstratio*] of things not seen," offers an exact definition of faith. He denies this and argues that the verse is to be understood in the context of the discussion of patience at the end of the preceding chapter (Heb. 10:36). He treats Heb. 10:36–11:1 as one section and criticizes those who separated this verse from the preceding ones and made it the beginning of the chapter 11.[29] The discussion of this section echoes his comments on Heb. 6:12–15: though the promise of eternal life is certain, since "life is like a race [*instar stadii*]," believers are to proceed toward their future inheritance as toward a goal.[30] For this they need a true, prior faith that has given birth to patience. Hence, according to Calvin, the author makes this statement about faith in Heb. 11:1 to show that this faith includes (*in se continet*) or is joined to (*coniuncta*) patience. That faith is the substance of things hoped for makes, Calvin finds, the same point as Rom. 8:24; namely, that what is hoped for is not seen, and so, he infers, it is to be waited for patiently. Faith thus regards not present things but those that are absent and waited for; it is the "prop or possession on which we plant our foot."[31] Similarly, faith is the "evidence of things not appearing." The things for which faith waits in patience are beyond the reach of human understanding and are not seen or subject to human senses.[32] It is interesting to note that, after this careful circumscription of Heb. 11:1 in the 1549 commentary, in the 1550 *Institutes* Calvin explicitly introduces the word *fiducia* as a possible translation for "hypostasis."

Calvin consciously sets the statement about faith in Heb. 11:1 apart from the discussion of faith in the rest of the chapter. He places this statement in the immediate context of the discussion of the preceding verses and in the larger context of his statements about faith's close connection to hope and patience that he had developed earlier in his commentary on the text. To characterize this particular aspect of faith, namely that it is joined with patience, Calvin drinks more deeply from the Pauline well than he had earlier in the commentary. The Pauline perspective emerges not only in the explicit reference to Rom. 8:24 but also in the implied reference to 2 Cor. 5:7, which underlies his interpretation of this verse: faith is not sight in the present; it grasps unseen objects. Moreover, Calvin says that the hidden things of which faith is the substance and the demonstration are shown to us by the Spirit. This suggests the point of view shown earlier in the example of his comments on 1 Cor. 2:10. Finally, when Calvin specifies exactly what these hidden things that cannot be grasped through ordinary sense perception are, he offers essentially the same list of promises he said in Rom. 4:20 are grasped by those who imitate Abraham's faith: eternal life, a happy resurrection, righteousness, happiness, an abundance of good things, and God's timely deliverance.[33] In specifying the link between faith and patience Calvin's comments not only draw on the perceptual elements of faith that he found in Paul but also hint at his reading of Pauline soteriology.

The opposition between faith and carnal sight is developed further in Calvin's discussion of Heb. 11:24–27, which commends the faith of Moses. He first establishes faith's exclusive reliance on things unseen in his comments on Heb. 11:24–25. He attributes the fact that Moses rejected his adoption, left Pharaoh's house, and returned to his own people to Moses' reliance on the blessing promised to Abraham. There was no visible evidence of this blessing, and the only witness to it was God's promise. Moses "could see nothing [of the blessing] with his eyes. It hence appears that he beheld by faith what was far removed from his sight."[34] Following this, Calvin turns his attention to the claim in Heb. 11:27 that it was as if Moses had seen him who is invisible (*quasi enim invisibilem vidisset*). Calvin notes that this statement appears to be contradicted by the fact that upon leaving Egypt Moses "saw" God in the burning bush. He resolves this difficulty and upholds the opposition between faith and sight by arguing that Moses saw a symbol of God's presence in the vision, yet "he was far from seeing God as he is." Moses' vision did not exempt him from difficulties, and as a result he could sometimes think that God was absent. "In short, God appeared to Moses in such a way as still to leave room for faith." Calvin's argument suggests that had Moses really *seen* the invisible God, he would have had no more need for faith. "We gather from this that the true nature of faith is to set God always before our eyes. Second, that faith beholds higher and more hidden things in God than what our senses can perceive; third, that a view of God alone is sufficient to strengthen our weakness."[35]

Having linked Heb. 11:1 to the preceding discussion and argued that this represents only a partial view of faith, Calvin appears to find faith discussed differently in the rest of Hebrews 11. He introduces his comments on Hebrews 11: 2, "per hanc [fidem] enim testimonium consequuti sunt seniores," by noting a shift in topic. This subject is also one that I have shown in Calvin's interpretation of Paul, namely, "that the fathers obtained salvation and were pleasing to God in no other way than by faith."[36] Calvin does not say explicitly that the author is talking about faith in a different, more complete, or more proper way. Yet it seems that this is so, since from this point on the discussion centers on faith as the means of divine acceptance and salvation, that is, faith's specifically justifying activity, rather than on faith and its relationship to patience.

Calvin's Pauline view of the relationship between works and faith provides the key to his interpretation of the deeds of the Old Testament figures catalogued in this passage. The opening sentence in his comments on Heb. 11:4 on the figure heading up the list, Abel, reiterates the point that he made, for example, when he dealt with Phinehas: "From here on [the author] will explain that however excellent the works of the saints were, it was from faith that they derived their value, their worthiness, and whatever excellence they possessed." Abel's sacrifice was acceptable "because he himself enjoyed God's favor." He found favor with God because his heart had been purified by faith.[37]

Calvin likewise understands the potentially problematic Heb. 11:6 ("but without faith it is impossible to please God, for he that comes to God must believe that he is and that he is a rewarder of those who seek him") in light of this presupposition about works and faith. He acknowledges that the passage is a little obscure and hence proposes a close examination. The first part of the verse, "without faith it is impossible to please God," poses no difficulty; Calvin finds that it confirms his view that access to God is opened by faith. "To believe that God is" means, for Calvin, that the certain knowledge of the true God is deeply rooted in the heart. It does not refer to the belief that there is some god or to faith in an idol.[38] Calvin argues that the final clause does not refer to the merit of works but rather to the fact that faith includes the firm conviction that God is not sought in vain, that believers are assured that salvation and eternal life are to be found in God.[39] He refutes the view that the mention of reward implies that works have a role in obtaining God's favor by asserting a "scriptural" position that echoes his reading of Paul on the role of the law: "Now scripture assigns this as the way of seeking God: that a man, prostrate in himself, overwhelmed by the charge of eternal death, and despairing of himself should flee to Christ as the only asylum of salvation."[40] Together the two clauses of the verse express the two parts of faith that Calvin described in his comments on Eph. 1:13: the first clause urges true knowledge of God, the second clause adds confidence.[41] Calvin thus views the verse through his Pauline lens to clarify the obscurity.

In his exegesis of the rest of the chapter, Calvin deviates somewhat from proclaiming what he views as the author's "main point" (that the fathers pleased God by faith alone) in his comments on Heb. 11:3 and 11:7. These passages raise additional questions concerning faith that Calvin resolves by appealing to Paul.

Hebrews 11:3, a passage that I showed in chapter 1 appears several times in the *Institutes,* not only offers another example of how Calvin uses Paul as a guide for interpretation but also shows how he sometimes expands his perspective beyond what he derives from Paul. In explicating the first clause, "by faith we understand that the world [*saecula*] was made by the word of God," Calvin wants both to affirm this statement and to harmonize it with Paul's statement in that even un-believers know this and therefore are to be condemned for their ingratitude (Rom. 1:19–21). From Rom. 1:21, he notes, it appears that the knowledge that the author of Hebrews ascribes to faith actually exists without faith.[42] To resolve this apparent discrepancy, Calvin argues that the heathen (*gentes*) formed an opinion about God as the creator of the world that was far removed from understanding. Moreover, they did not perceive anything of God's providence but attributed the government of the world to fortune and chance. The godly, in contrast, behold the true God; they are fully persuaded not simply that God created the world but also that God continually preserves it. Calvin notes that they understand the power of the word by which God governs all things and that they perceive, in addition to this power, God's goodness, wisdom, and justice.[43]

Calvin takes the same passage from Romans as the key for the interpretation of the second half of the verse. He criticizes all earlier interpretations and trans-lations of *eis to mē ek phainomenōn,* which he renders *ut non apparentium spectacula fierent* and understands to mean that "we have in this world a conspicuous image of God."[44] This, he finds, is the same truth as that taught in Rom. 1:20 ("for the invisible things of him since the creation of the world are clearly seen, being perceived through the things that are made"), which he paraphrases in his com-ments. He follows Paul's logic and concludes that "the world is elegantly called a 'mirror of divinity,' not that there is sufficient clarity for men to know God from looking at the world, but that [God] has revealed himself to the ungodly so that their ignorance is without excuse."[45]

Calvin thus finds Heb. 11:3 to be making the same point as Paul in Rom. 1: 19–21; namely, that the ungodly derive just enough of an idea of God from the witness of creation as to render them without excuse before the divine tribunal. Here, however, Calvin says that they have only an opinion of some creator god rather than knowledge of the true God; in Rom. 1:20, it is explicitly blindness that prevents creation's witness from being effective. The theme of blindness is surprisingly absent in Calvin's exegesis of Heb. 11:3. Moreover, there is another difference: in his comments on the verse in Hebrews, Calvin claims that there is not sufficient clarity in creation for humans to arrive at true knowledge of God from looking at the world. In his comments on Romans, however, Calvin says several times that the fault is not in creation but in human beings themselves.[46]

Although Calvin brings Paul's discussion of creation's witness to God and human inexcusability to the interpretation of this passage and reads the Hebrews passage through the Pauline lens, nonetheless it seems that he finds a distinct emphasis in Hebrews that is lacking in Rom. 1:19–21. There Paul is condemning the failure to acknowledge God from creation, while Hebrews 11:3 speaks positively of the benefits that faith derives from creation. Indeed, Calvin conceded this difference in his comments on Rom. 1:20 from 1540, after he argued that blindness prevents humans from attaining true knowledge of God from creation: "Hence the apostle [writing] to the Hebrews attributes to faith that light so that [one] can profit truly from the creation of the world."[47] Calvin states this more explicitly at the end of his comments on Hebrews 11:3: "The faithful, moreover, to whom [God] has given eyes, discern sparks of his glory as if glittering in every created thing. The world was no doubt made in order be a theater of the divine glory."[48] Calvin explicitly introduces the point made in the latter sentence back in to his comments on Rom. 1:19 in a 1556 addition.[49]

In discussing Hebrews 11:7 Calvin confronts another possible contradiction to the Pauline view of faith. According to Calvin, the text declares that the Noah's faith moved him to fear, and that fear thus motivated him to construct the ark. This raises a question: how can faith be the cause of fear, Calvin asks, "since it has respect to the promises of grace rather than to the threatenings?" He supports this claim by appealing to Paul's statement in Rom. 10:8 that the gospel is the word of faith.[50] Faith, as I have shown, is certain of God's mercy, but fear implies uncertainty. To resolve the apparent contradiction, Calvin invokes the distinction within special revelation that he used in the *Institutes*. Though faith relies especially on the promises, it embraces every word of God as true. Calvin argues that Christ is the real object of faith but that faith also looks to God's threatenings to be taught to fear and obey God.[51]

The same problem, but in a slightly different form, arises in Heb. 11:26, which says that Moses looked to his divine reward. Calvin's comments on this passage provide insight into how he maintains the view that faith looks properly to God's promise but also regards every word of God as true. The fact that Moses had regard for reward might lead one to conclude, Calvin suggests, that his faith did not rest on God's mercy alone. Once again, Calvin invokes a distinction, this time between faith's role in justification and faith's activity in general:

> [F]aith, as far as righteousness before God is to be sought, does not look on reward but on the gratuitous goodness of God, not on our works but on Christ alone. But faith, apart from the matter of justification, since it extends itself generally to every word of God, has respect to the reward that is promised. Indeed, by faith we embrace whatever God promises: he promises reward to works, and therefore faith lays hold on this. But all this has no place in the matter of free justification, for no reward for works can be hoped for unless the free imputation of righteousness goes before.[52]

Calvin's observation immediately preceding this statement that the question here is not concerning righteousness or the cause of salvation but rather whatever generally belongs to faith might apply to his exegesis of the entire letter to the Hebrews. The specific focus of this book allows Calvin to explore the role of faith not in obtaining but in living a new life. Yet even though the Pauline concern with justification is not central, Calvin's exegesis of Hebrews 6 and 11 shows clearly how his interpretation of Pauline themes not only permeates but also sets the boundaries for these reflections on faith. This shift in emphasis is evident, for example, in the fact that he discusses the *fides particularis* and the role of Abraham differently here from in his commentaries on the Pauline passages that I considered in the last chapter; he links these two now to the theme of *repentance* (sanctification), whereas he had before viewed them in light of his concern with *justification*. Only where there is, from Calvin's perspective, a clear danger of interpreting a passage to support works righteousness does he bring up the topic of faith's justifying activity and his Pauline understanding of the relationship between works and faith. He perceives such a danger to be implied in Heb. 11:2, 4, and 6. He therefore asserts at that point that the fathers pleased God by faith alone: that they were first justified by faith and that it was on the basis of the free justification of their persons that their works were acceptable.

Other examples of how Calvin's Pauline perspective sets the parameters are evident. He underscores the relationship between faith and hope and faith and patience but, following Paul, sees hope and patience as partners of faith. He also finds that Heb. 11:1 makes an important statement about faith and that this, however, is not a full definition but only a partial view. Finally, he invokes Romans 10 and the special distinction within revelation that he had made on the basis of this passage in the 1539 *Institutes* to clarify the true object of the faith of Noah and Moses (Heb. 11:7, 11:26). It is noteworthy that in the response to Pighius appearing in the 1550 *Institutes*, where Calvin needs to defend his distinction within special revelation and his definition of faith as relying especially on God's mercy, he supports his view with reference to the example of Noah in this passage from 1549.[53]

Yet at certain points Calvin appears to test the Pauline boundaries. In his comments on Heb. 6:4, 10:26, and 10:28, he speaks of a faith among the reprobate that consists of some taste of divine grace, some sparks of divine illumination, some perception of divine goodness, and a certain knowledge of God's word engraved on the heart. Though the idea of a "faith" unaccompanied by the spirit of regeneration echoes ideas that he found in Paul, Calvin appears to go beyond these earlier ideas in the commentary on Hebrews. His comments suggest that the reprobate have a certain knowledge of God's redemptive activity that is ineffective not because it is incomplete—as would be the case, presumably, with a faith of miracles—but rather because without the simultaneous gift of regeneration it cannot take root. It is hard to know why Calvin pushes the limits here. In his comments, he asserts that the idea of temporary faith is attested elsewhere in scripture. The case could also be made that Calvin's doctrines of double predestination and special providence underlie this idea of faith: he appears to want to emphasize that the faith of the elect as well as the temporary faith of the reprobate are both God's work. However, even in his exegesis of Romans 9, the *locus biblicus* for Calvin's teaching, he speaks only of God blinding the reprobate, not of God enlightening them. Hence judgment of Calvin's ideas of a faith among the reprobate will have to wait until my analysis of his treatment of this matter in the 1559 *Institutes*.

Calvin's commentary on Hebrews underscores the Pauline opposition between faith and sight, stressing that faith is opposed to the physical sense of visual perception and that the things that it apprehends are beyond carnal sight and un-derstanding; they are unseen and incomprehensible. The detailed attention to faith and hope in the commentary on Hebrews strengthens this opposition. Nonetheless, Calvin also draws on and expands his Pauline notion of faith as having its own unique perception, not merely of the unseen objects of hope but of present reality as well. In his comments on Heb. 11:3 he develops what he had only hinted at in his comments on 1 Cor. 1:21 and 13:12: the visible world is a mirror in which the invisible God can be seen. Though he places this passage clearly in the context of Paul's views in Rom. 1:19–21, Calvin expands the boundaries of Paul's discussion by shifting the focus. Unlike Rom. 1:20, this passage, for Calvin, is not primarily about what human eyes could see if they had not been blinded by the Fall but rather about what eyes purified by faith *can* see. Not simply directing believers beyond the world to the hidden and future objects of hope, faith thus also restores (at least in part) their ability to see in this created realm. As I showed in chapter 1, this aspect of faith appears only in the sections of the *Institutes* treating knowl-edge of God and providence, and not in the section on faith itself.

The Commentary on James (1551)

The most serious challenge to the view of faith that Calvin derives from Paul and to the presuppositions about justification and works that shape this view is ad-vanced in James 2:14–26. We have seen that he addresses this challenge in his exegesis of Rom. 3:28, where he attempts to reconcile the apparently contradictory positions. He had already tackled this problem in the *Institutes* (1539), and he returns to it again in his commentary on James (1551).[54] His exegesis of this passage illustrates how he views other biblical texts about faith through his Pauline lens, presupposing and protecting the theological priority of his Pauline under-standing of faith, righteousness, and works.[55]

The author of James contrasts sharply between faith and works, arguing that a faith without works is a dead thing and cannot save (James 2:14–17). Faith separated from works is equated with a belief that there is a God (James 2:19). Such a faith apart from works is far different from that of Abraham, whose belief was made perfect by the addition of works (James 2:21–23). The author confirms his conclusion that one is justified by works and not by faith alone (James 2:24) by referring further to the example of Rahab from Joshua 21 (James 2:25).

The problem posed is in part the same that Calvin tackled in his excursus on Phinehas in his comments on Rom. 4:6, but James raises the same difficulty more directly and in more detail. The view of faith that James advances in 2:14–17 is quite different from the view Calvin found in Paul; with its explicit rejection of "faith alone" James 2:24 raises, at least in Calvin's view, the challenge of Phinehas to the Pauline idea of justification in a more pointed way. Calvin assumes that scripture cannot contradict scripture and rejects the idea that James proves or is even trying to prove that Abraham was justified (in the Pauline sense) by works. In establishing this position, Calvin presupposes the understandings of faith and justification that he derived from Paul and interprets James's statements in such a way as not to contradict that Pauline position.

Why does James say that faith alone cannot justify, and what does he mean when he says that Abraham's faith was perfected and scripture fulfilled long after the event described in Gen. 15:6? Calvin's answer hinges on two points. He argues that James 2:19 makes clear that the "faith" that James claims cannot justify is a common knowledge of God, which Calvin has already designated as frigid and bare in his comments on 2:14.[56] As a rhetorical concession to his opponents, James is not using faith in its proper sense but is designating as faith that common knowledge of God that his opponents claim can save. James argues that this "faith" is dead, and thus, Calvin concludes, it is not really faith. He has already shut out the possibility that James refers to two different types of faith, arguing that it is illegitimate to use these verses to support a distinction between unformed and formed faith.[57] The debate, therefore, is not about faith but about this common knowledge of God.

Second, Calvin asserts repeatedly—once each in commenting on James 2:20, 2:22, and 2:25 and twice on James 2:21—that the dispute is also not about the *cause* of justification. James is trying to prove his declaration that faith is never without works, not to show how humans are justified before God. Therefore, James uses the word "justify" in a different sense than Paul does. According to Calvin, Paul uses the word "justified" to refer to the gratuitous imputation of righteousness before the tribunal of God, while James uses it to mean the manifestation of righteousness by its effects before human beings.[58] Abraham's faith was perfected not because it had works added to it but because through Abraham's obedience his faith was proved true. That the scripture is said to have been fulfilled means that the faith by which Abraham was justified was true faith since it bore the fruit of obedience. Therefore Calvin can affirm with James 2:24 that one "is not justified by faith alone, that is, by bare and inane knowledge of God" and that one "is justified by works, that is, righteousness is known and proved by its fruits."[59]

Calvin places this passage within the definitions of faith, works, and justification that he derives from Paul. Unlike Luther, who once said that he could find nothing evangelical in James,[60] Calvin finds James agreeing with Paul that common knowledge of God is insufficient for salvation and that justification by faith issues in works of obedience and love, just as a tree bears fruit.[61] Since, according to Calvin, James is not advancing an actual definition of faith (but is trying only to refute the false view of his opponents) and is not discoursing about the cause of justification, what he says about works does not conflict with the Pauline standard. Faith in its primary and proper sense is certain knowledge of God's mercy; a bare and inane knowledge or a faith separated from love cannot be called faith. Calvin thus assumes the priority of his Pauline perspective and views and corrects James through this Pauline lens.

The Commentary on 1 John (1551)

The Johannine writings provide numerous opportunities for Calvin to underscore the characteristics of faith that he discusses in exegeting the Pauline epistles.[62] Like Paul, the authors of the Gospel of John and the first Johannine epistle stress a christocentric faith and a close relationship between faith and love. Moreover, these writings explore the theme of faith and seeing in detail. The question of human salvation is central to all these writings, although, in contrast to Paul, John and 1 John do not deal directly with the Pauline theme of justification by faith. Rather, the epistle and the Gospel focus on knowledge of Christ and of God through Christ's mediation, presenting this as saving knowledge that overcomes the world. Calvin identifies this saving knowledge with faith and views the discussions of knowledge from his Pauline perspective. In his commentary on 1 John this is evident especially in his emphasis that this knowledge is of the remission of sins through Christ alone and in his relation of this knowledge to love as a cause to an effect. The Pauline perspective also emerges in the frequent appeals to Paul's writings to support Calvin's reading of a text, the repeated references to themes of certainty and confidence in the discussions of knowledge, and the attempt, especially in the commentary on the Gospel, to restrict the proper meaning of faith to his Pauline view.

Calvin's interpretation of 1 John hinges on distinction, noted by him for the first time in the "Argumentum," between the epistle's doctrine and its exhortations. "Doctrine" refers to those things apprehended by faith; namely, statements in the epistle that refer to Christ or Christ's work. In Calvin's view, this includes, for example, the testimony to Christ in 1 John 1, the forgiveness of sins proclaimed in 1 John 2:12–14, and the necessity for Christ held up in 1 John 2:22–23. In the "Argumentum" Calvin explicitly praises the epistle's proclamation of "the inestimable grace of divine adoption." Here he also points out that the truths of doctrine are constantly intermingled with the exhortations to holy life, brotherly love, and caution before false teachers.[63] According to Calvin, the author's Christian readers need to confront both the doctrine and the exhortation. The proclamation of the gospel confirms and strengthens their faith.[64] The exhortations remind them that true faith is always accompanied by a new life of repentance.[65] In treating the subject of new life, Calvin argues that the new life does not mean a life free from sin.[66]

Calvin makes the distinction between doctrine and exhortation in order to protect the Pauline doctrine of justification by faith. Without this distinction, the exhortations could be misconstrued, and salvation might be thought to rely on works, that is, on love for others or purity of life.[67] Armed with it, however, Calvin moves through the epistle and sets off the things that belong to the knowledge of faith (doctrine) from faith's effect (a new life characterized by love). He not only distinguishes between doctrine and exhortation and between faith and love but also establishes doctrine as the ground of the exhortation and faith's priority over love. Underlying this concern, of course, is Calvin's continuing polemic against the idea that faith is merely the beginning of justification, a process that includes the gift of *caritas* granted with the *gratia gratum faciens* to complete or "form" faith.[68]

Calvin's concern to protect justification by faith alone, gratuitous divine adoption, the free remission of sins, and the doctrine of imputation by invoking a distinction between doctrine and exhortation has two consequences for the view of faith that emerges in his reading of 1 John. First, it leads him to underscore the noetic character of faith in order to establish subjective certainty. Calvin reads the epistle's statements about knowledge as statements about faith. Second, while aiming to uphold the connection between faith and love, he also strongly reinforces the distinction between them. His exegesis of 1 John 3:1–2 and 3:14–24 demonstrates this twofold effect.

Calvin's Exegesis of 1 John 3:1–2

Implicit throughout Calvin's interpretation of the epistle, the link between knowledge and faith finally becomes explicit in the comments on 1 John 3:6, "whoever sins has not seen him or known him," where Calvin observes: "by seeing [Lat. *affectus*; Fr. *vue*] and knowing [*notitia*] we are to understand no other thing than faith."[69] Elsewhere he simply assumes that statements about knowing should be applied to faith.[70] He also interprets statements about seeing as referring to faith.[71] The epistle's Christocentrism enables him to stress that faith as knowledge is properly knowledge of Christ. He relies on the epistle's close connection between knowledge (faith) and obedience or love to underscore his point that knowledge of God in Christ is efficacious, both producing confidence or certainty and leading to obedience and works of love.[72]

Calvin's discussion of 1 John 3:1–2 illustrates how his reading of Paul provides the context for interpretation of faith as knowledge of God's gratuitous redemption in Christ. Verse 1, "behold what love the Father has given to us, that we should be called the sons of God; the world does not know us because it has not known him," raises up for Calvin the familiar themes of grace and works and the certainty of salvation. The first clause, he finds, amplifies God's favor and declares that God's love is gratuitous in order to kindle the desire for purity. It means that, in accordance with Rom. 12:1 (which Calvin mentions), the greater God's goodness, the greater are the obligations toward God. It also teaches that "the adoption of all the godly is gratuitous and does not depend on any regard for works."[73] The second clause points to one of the greatest challenges to faith; namely that the world does not yet recognize this adoption and therefore persecutes the elect. Therefore, their present state appears to contradict their gratuitous adoption. Nonetheless, Calvin claims, their salvation is safe and sound.[74]

This gratuitous divine adoption that the world does not acknowledge forms the backdrop for Calvin's exegesis of 1 John 3:2, which explores the themes of knowledge, certainty, and perception. His comments on the first part of the verse continue the contrast between faith and "the present view of things." "Now we are the sons of God, and what we shall be does not yet appear" reminds believers of their adoption and withdraws their view from their present condition, which almost overwhelms them with misery and threatens to shake their confidence "in that happiness that as yet lies hid." In the face of their visible state, the apostle urges them to "hold with an undoubting faith to that which does not yet appear"; namely, their future condition, the fruit of their adoption. Though this will be manifested only with the future appearance of Christ, nonetheless the impending glory of believers is guaranteed. The theme of knowledge arises in the subsequent clause "but we know that when he shall appear." Calvin argues that this teaches the same thing that Paul does in Col. 3:3: "your life is hid with Christ; when

Christ, your life, shall appear, then you also will appear with him in glory." Again he directs his readers' faith away from the present and toward the future, arguing that faith can stand only when it looks to the future coming of Christ.[75] The word "know" (*sciendi*) in the verse expresses faith's certainty and distinguishes it from opinion. It signals that believers' knowledge of their future glory is most securely established even though the manifestation of it is yet to come.[76]

It is obvious that this verse also pertains to the perceptual aspect of faith, raising the themes of the future vision of God and believers' present misery. Calvin views these matters squarely through his Pauline lens. Faith, as I have shown, directs itself away from the misery that believers see as characterizing their present condition. Looking toward heaven, faith anticipates a new condition and a new vision of God. Calvin argues that the phrase "we shall be like him" does not mean that in this new state the elect will be equal (*pares*) to Christ, "for there must be some difference between head and members." Rather, the meaning is the same as Paul's in Phil. 3:21: Christ will conform the lowly bodies of the elect to Christ's glorious body. Commenting a little later on the phrase "for we shall see him as he is," Calvin reiterates this point. The future perfection will not be so great as to enable believers by seeing to comprehend all that God is.[77]

This statement raises additional questions about the nature of this vision of God both in the present and in the future, which Calvin resolves by appealing to 1 Cor. 13:12–13 and 2 Cor. 5:6–7. This phrase first prompts him to ask whether the ungodly will be like Christ, since they also will see his glory. Calvin denies this. Believers will see him as a friend (*familiarem*), but the ungodly will be filled with terror and dread. Calvin supports this latter point by quoting Ex. 33:20 ("No man shall see me and live"), implying that humans tainted by sin can only dread God's presence. Yet believers, insofar as the image of God is presently being renewed in them, already "have eyes prepared to see God." However, until they have been stripped of all corruption, even they "will not be able to behold God face to face."[78] Here Calvin indicates the progress of faith, suggesting that sanctification involves a gradual purification of the sense of sight to prepare for that day when faith will no longer be necessary. He argues that the author does not say that there is no seeing of God now, but rather that he agrees with Paul in 1 Cor. 13:12 that we now see obscurely through a mirror. Yet this, Calvin says, is a way of living that Paul elsewhere distinguishes from the seeing of the eye. He then cites Ex. 33:23, which declares that Moses saw the back of God, to prove that God is not now seen as he is but in such a way that humans can comprehend. This line of argumentation maintains the stark contrast between present faith and the present physical sense of sight. "We shall see him as he is" thus indicates a "new and ineffable way of seeing that we do not experience now." Calvin confirms that this new way of seeing is not a present experience by paraphrasing 2 Cor. 5:6–7.[79] Believers perceive God in terms that they can comprehend through faith; their present seeing through the mirror is not a physical seeing. In the process of sanctification, however, their sight is gradually being purged so that one day they will enjoy a vision of God face to face. Yet even this direct seeing has limitations: believers will not comprehend all that God is.

Calvin's exegesis of this passage illustrates once again how Paul's writings are repeatedly held up as the standard and provide the key to proper interpretation. His comments also advance one's understanding of his views on the perception of faith. Moreover, they help to begin to locate more precisely the biblical roots of his designation of faith as knowledge and to see how his concern for certainty shapes his reading of this theme in 1 John. In the 1539 *Institutes* Calvin mentioned 1 John 3:2 as the example of how faith is called *scientia* by John.[80] His reference to the verse is somewhat curious, implying that believers know that they are the children of God. The text itself, however, says that believers know that when Christ will appear they will be like him. Despite this minor discrepancy in what is known, Calvin's designation of faith as knowledge in both places conveys the same message: the noetic character of faith distinguishes faith from opinion and renders it certain. Though the things understood by faith are far off and unseen (compare 2 Cor. 5:6–7, Heb. 11:1), faith "knows" them, that is, is certain of them. As Calvin observes in the *Institutes*, this knowledge consists in assurance (*certitudine*) rather than in comprehension (*apprehensione*).[81]

Calvin's designation of faith as knowledge in his exegesis of 1 John reflects his desire to establish the subjective certainty of the believer living in this realm, undergoing the process of regeneration. The things apprehended by faith are unseen and not empirically verifiable. Yet faith is certain of their veracity, for faith is knowledge and not mere conjecture. The knowledge of faith is constantly progressing throughout the life of the believer and one day will yield to a new and ineffable sight. The knowledge of faith is an obscure way of seeing for the present. Though it is not yet sight, it provides the certainty of things unseen as if they were indeed seen.

Calvin's Interpretation of 1 John 3:14–24

Faith as knowledge provides subjective certainty because it relies on objective divine truth—the gospel, or, as Calvin designates it in 1 John, doctrine. Faith is knowledge, that is, certainty of the gospel concerning Christ. This knowledge, Calvin claims, is efficacious, yielding obedience and love. Yet it does not rely on obedience to the law or its exhibitions of love. Such reliance would undermine certainty, since even believers fall short of perfect obedience to the law. Hence Calvin not only establishes the certainty of faith by designating it as knowledge but also protects the certainty of faith by distinguishing it from and giving it priority over love.

This theme arises repeatedly in this commentary and can be seen especially clearly in Calvin's exegesis of 1 John 3:14–24. In this passage, the author of the epistle praises love of others. It is unclear whether 1 John 3:14 ("we know that we have passed from death to life because we love one another") declares this love to be the cause of knowledge of the transition to new life or, rather, the cause of this new life itself. Such love is modeled on Jesus' sacrificing love and demands compassion toward the less fortunate (1 John 3:16–17). Moreover, the exercise of love in "deed and truth" (1 John 3:18) provides, according to 1 John 3:19, both knowledge that we are in the truth and assurance before God. The chapter ends with a double command to believe in the name of Jesus Christ and love one another (1 John 3:23).

Calvin's specification of the relationship between faith and love in 1 John presupposes his treatment of this topic in 1 Cor. 13, where he argues for the priority of faith over love in justification. Indeed, in his comments on 1 John 2:11, he explicitly mentions the Corinthians passage as the key to interpretation of this relationship.[82] As noted, such arguments reflect Calvin's polemic against the scholastic notion of a faith formed by love, which suggests to him the idea that love, rather than faith, is the cause of justification and salvation. He thus confronts a potential problem raised in 1 John 3:14 by insisting that love is not the cause of salvation but the evidence of regeneration:

> But when the apostle says that it is known by love that we have passed into life, he does not mean that man is his own deliverer, as though he could by loving the brethren rescue himself from death and procure life for himself, for he is not discussing here the cause of salvation. But as love is the special fruit of the Spirit it is also a sure symbol of regeneration. Therefore the apostle reasons from the sign, not from the cause. . . . [I]t would be preposterous for anyone to infer hence that life is obtained by love when love is later in order. The argument [that love obtains life] would be more plausible if love made us more certain of our life; then confidence as to salvation would rest on works. But the solution of this is not difficult. Though faith is confirmed by all the graces of God as aids, yet it ceases not to have its foundation in the mercy of God only. . . . After faith is founded on Christ, some things can be added to assist it; nevertheless, it rests on Christ's grace alone.[83]

Love, as Calvin insists elsewhere, is not the cause of salvation or the regenerate life. Both of these result from faith, which love accompanies as an inseparable aid.

Another indication of the Pauline underpinnings of Calvin's reading of the relationship between faith and love appears in the polemical climate in which he situates the text. He hints several times that the author of 1 John insists so strongly on love in order to counter opponents who allege that a cold and empty knowledge of God—a "faith" unaccompanied by sanctification—suffices for salvation. Calvin thus assumes a polemical situation similar to that confronted by James. An example of this occurs in his comments on 1 John 3:16, which urges imitation of Jesus' sacrificing love. Calvin cautions that this does not mean that believers are equal to Christ, or that their deaths acquire the same virtue or benefit. In the midst of these qualifications, he observes: "Doubtless since it was the apostle's object to beat down the vain boasting of hypocrites, who gloried that they had faith in Christ without brotherly love, by these words he meant that except this zeal prevails in our hearts, we have nothing in common with Christ."[84]

At stake in the relationship between faith and love is, as I have already shown, the issue of certainty. According to Calvin, certainty comes only through faith, which relies on God's mercy. 1 John 1:19–22 potentially challenges this view by suggesting that it is through fulfilling the exhortation to neighborly love (in 1 John 3:14–19) that believers attain knowledge and assurance (1 John 3:19), that they have confidence before God when their heart does not condemn them (1

John 3:21), and that they receive what they ask of God because they keep his commandments (1 John 3:22). Hans-Josef Klauck sketches two main lines of exegesis of this passage. One line of interpretation uses the passage to speak of God's judgment, understanding 1 John 3:20 to mean that if our own heart condemns us, how can we hope to stand before God's judgment, since God, in Calvin's words, "sees much more keenly than we do"? Other interpreters find in the same verse a proclamation of God's mercy: even though our own heart condemn us, God is greater and will forgive. The former interpretation dominates early exegesis of the passage, is picked up by Calvin and the Catholic reformation, and persists among non-Roman interpreters into the nineteenth century. The latter interpretation appears to have its origins in the late Middle Ages, but it receives its most extended and foundational treatment by Luther, whose exegesis continues to influence most modern interpreters.[85] Although Calvin's reading is located within a traditional trajectory, he is concerned to argue that love is not the ground of faith or salvation, for justification is by faith alone.

In his comments on 1 John 3:19, Calvin first addresses the "knowledge" that purportedly arises from love. He argues that neighborly love is evidence that believers are born of God and that God's truth is in them, but cautions that love is not the cause of knowledge, "as though we were to seek from it the certainty of salvation." Love is an accessory or an inferior aid to faith, not its foundation.[86] Similarly, love is not the cause of assurance. In the face of those professing a false faith, the author says that "we will assure our hearts before God" only to show that "faith does not exist without a good conscience."[87] Calvin understands 1 John 3:21 to mean that "the testimony of a right and honest heart" is needed to enter in calm confidence into God's presence. He refers to Eph. 3:12 and Rom. 5:1 to underscore that it is faith that provides such confidence and peace, observing, however, a difference: "Paul shows the cause of confidence but John mentions only an inseparable addition, which necessarily adheres to it, though it be not the cause."[88] That is, Paul discusses faith, whereas John discusses love. Finally, Calvin argues that the causal particle "because" in 1 John 3:22 does not mean that keeping the commandments is the cause of confidence in prayer, attributing this usage to a convention of speech.[89]

Calvin's assumptions about the priority of faith over love and love as a sign but not the cause of confidence before God emerge with particular clarity in his interpretation of 1 John 3:23–24. He refers once again to the accessory nature of love in interpreting the double command to believe in the name of Jesus Christ and to love one another (1 John 3:23). He also explicitly refutes opinions that understand this verse to teach that confidence in prayer derives partly from faith and partly from works. To do this, he reminds his readers that the author is not discussing the cause of confidence. He reiterates this view in his comments on 1 John 3:24 by contrasting the meaning of this verse to Paul's intention in Rom. 8: 15–16. Though both passages declare that the Spirit testifies to believers that they are God's children, there is a difference:

> Paul speaks of the certainty of gratuitous adoption, which the Spirit of God seals on our heart, but John here regards the effects that the Spirit produces while

dwelling in us. [This is just] as Paul himself does, when he says that those are God's children who are led by the Spirit of God [Rom. 8:14], for there also he is speaking of the mortification of the flesh and newness of life.[90]

Calvin thus protects the priority of faith by distinguishing John's discussion of sanctification from Paul's treatment of justification.

The mention of faith in the name of Jesus Christ (1 John 3:23) also gives Calvin a chance to affirm that faith looks exclusively to Christ and that there is no faith without teaching [*doctrina*]. By this last point, which he supports by referring to Rom. 10:14, Calvin appears to mean that to have faith means to embrace the preaching of the gospel.[91] Moreover, it also harkens back to the distinction between doctrine and exhortation that he made in the "Argumentum," suggesting at least that faith is to seek its certainty in the doctrinal proclamations in 1 John and not in the conformity to the epistle's exhortations to love. For Calvin, the faith that the author claims in 1 John 5:4 overcomes the world is a confidence in the preaching about Christ that is so certain that it is rightly called knowledge. Faith is also, as he there declares, the perpetual work of the Holy Spirit.[92] Therefore, faith in this verse is, in accordance with Calvin's Pauline presuppositions, the basis for both free adoption and new life.

Calvin's exegesis of 1 John evidences a harmonization with Paul that is similar to that noted in his commentary on Hebrews. This similarity goes beyond a superficial level and reflects an exegetical challenge comparable to that he found in Hebrews. Whereas his task vis-à-vis Hebrews was to underscore the text's essential link between faith and hope and faith and patience without collapsing faith into one or the other, in his commentary on 1 John he struggles to clarify a similar connection between faith and love.[93] This attempt becomes more pointed with his perception that the errors of opponents that were addressed by the authors of 1 John and of James were the same. As I have shown, Paul, particularly 1 Corinthians 13, comes to the rescue. Calvin relies on Paul to show that faith is accompanied by love as an inseparable addition but that love is not the cause of salvation. Rather, it is faith, primarily understood as knowledge, that is the cause of salvation. Thus 1 John becomes for Calvin a means for developing the idea of faith as knowledge, for specifying the nature of faith's relationship to love, and for advancing his polemic against the concept of *fides caritate formata*.

The Commentary on John (1553)

In his commentary on the Gospel of John, Calvin continues to explore the theme of faith as knowledge and the connection between knowledge and certainty. The Gospel's frequent references to knowing and the occasional linking of knowledge and belief in the same verse provide Calvin with opportunities to speak of faith as knowledge.[94] He identifies faith with knowledge in his comments on John 17:3 and argues in his comments on John 17:8 that in faith there is such certainty that it is justly called knowledge. In at least one other passage Calvin equates the word "see" with knowledge in order to make the case that the text expresses the certainty of faith.[95] It is surprising that on two other occasions Calvin distinguishes belief and knowledge, arguing that knowledge follows the "obedience of faith."[96]

Beyond providing Calvin with these passages about knowing and believing, the Gospel of John also offers him the most extensive meditation on believing that he has yet encountered and in this presents him with a serious exegetical problem.[97] The Gospel contains numerous statements about people believing: the disciples after the miracle at Cana (John 2:11), the multitudes (John 2:23, 7:31, 8:30, 10:42), the Samaritans who have heard about Jesus from the woman he addressed at the well (John 4:39), the royal official from Capernum and his whole household (John 4:53), the witnesses to the resurrection of Lazarus (John 11:45). Yet often the reality that these statements portray differs greatly from the certain knowledge that Calvin understands to be faith. Moreover, the Gospel frequently appears to link this belief to visible, external signs or miracles. This challenges Calvin's Pauline assumptions: that faith is certain knowledge of God's benevolence in Christ; that faith comes from hearing the word and the inner illumination and sealing of the Spirit; and that faith does not rely on carnal sense perception. Ultimately, the Gospel threatens Calvin's view that there is really only one kind of faith and that this faith is certain. To meet this challenge, Calvin qualifies the evangelist's use of the word "believe" in light of his presupposed definition of faith. However, Calvin's exegesis of John also leads him to a modified view of faith: he not only exhibits heightened sensitivity to but also elaborates in greater detail stages of preparation for faith and the increase and decrease in faith as he understands it.

A few examples will illustrate the problems that the statements about believing raise for Calvin and the strategies that he adopts for resolving them. Various passages about people believing in Jesus (John 2:11, 2:23, 4:39–42, 6:14, 7:31, 11:45) raise the problem that people believe either because of the miracles or signs (John 2:11, 2:23, 4:53, 7:31, 11:45) or because of what someone else said about Jesus (John 4:39). Alternatively, those fed with loaves and fishes do not embrace Jesus as God but rather as a prophet (John 6:14), exhibiting the fleetingness of their belief (at least in Calvin's judgment) in that they promptly misuse their knowledge by wanting to make him a king. They have only an earthly understanding of the sign and earthly expectations of Jesus.[98] The insufficiency of this mode of believing, which is based on something "earthly" rather than on Jesus' word, is made clear for Calvin in John 4:39, which says that the Samaritans believed in him on account of the woman's testimony. Yet John 4:41–42 relates that later many more believed in him on account of his word and that even those who first believed because of the woman's testimony now know for themselves that Jesus is the Christ. Calvin argues that the word "believe" is therefore used improperly in 4:39 for what is, in some respects, a beginning of faith, inasmuch as the minds of the Samaritans were only prepared to receive doctrine.[99] In each of the other instances just listed (except for John 6:14, which does not say that the crowds "believed"), Calvin either suggests or says explicitly that the word "believe" is not being used in its proper signification.[100] Instead, he claims, the evangelist is using it to mean that the people were ready to receive Christ's doctrine or that they held him to be a prophet. Calvin allows that in some cases this might actually be a prelude to full faith in Christ, but it is also in danger of leading in the other direction, as it does in the case of those described in John 6:14, who decide to try and make Jesus a king and thus corrupt the knowledge that they have received.[101] In this frequently distrustful and at the very least ambivalent attitude toward this "improper" faith, Calvin distinguishes himself somewhat from earlier and contemporary exegetes such as John Chrysostom, Augustine, Thomas Aquinas, Erasmus, and Martin Bucer, all of whom saw greater continuity between the preparatory stages of faith they found in these passages and full faith in Christ.

At various points in his exegesis of John, Calvin refers to a more proper understanding of faith, usually in explicating passages that he finds suggest believing in Jesus Christ (e.g., John 3:16, 6:29, 6:47, 7:38). Three times he claims that he has already said what it means to believe in Christ, and one of these explicitly designates the comments on John 3 as the locus of this discussion.[102] There are, however, two places in John 3 where Calvin advances something like a definition of faith: in his comments on 3:16 and on 3:33. Neither of these offers a particularly clear statement, and each has its own particular problems. In the first instance, Calvin treats so many issues that it is hard to say exactly which element of his discussion he might have in mind when he later refers the reader to this discussion.[103] If one takes the later comments as a clue, he means that to believe in Christ is to embrace Christ and his significance; to believe is to rely on Christ alone, especially on his death, as the revelation of God's love. Somewhat confusingly, Calvin also calls this an effect of faith: "to receive Christ such as he is offered to us by the Father."[104] These comments bring out the christocentric focus of faith; they also point to Calvin's increasing preoccupation with the mystical union with Christ that faith effects.[105] They thereby indicate a broadening of faith's noetic character. In contrast, the comments on John 3:33 ("But he who receives his [Christ's] testimony has sealed that God is true") refer to belief in the gospel and focus on faith in a strictly noetic sense. Calvin's statement here is rather uncharacteristic, at least for him: "to believe the gospel is nothing else than to subscribe to the oracles of God."[106] Faith, as we know from Paul, springs from hearing (Rom. 10:17) and relies on the word. Yet it is unusual for Calvin to characterize faith as assent and to focus on God rather than on Christ. Perhaps the important observations on John 17:3 represent an adequate synthesis of these two views. Here Calvin stresses that faith is special kind of knowledge. This knowledge is effected by divine illumination; it is saving because through it believers possess God by being engrafted into the body of Christ.[107] Finally, it is noteworthy that a concern for the certainty of salvation underlies both discussions in John 3. Calvin explicitly says that this is the issue in John 3:16; he follows his explanation of belief in the gospel (John 3:33) by making a distinction between faith and both human inventions and doubtful and wavering opinions.

The distinction between improper and correct uses of the word "believe" is the main strategy that Calvin adopts to resolve the challenge presented by the evangelist's attribution of faith to those who, in Calvin's view, base their belief on the miracles or on an understanding of Jesus as a prophet instead of on the word and a knowledge of Jesus as the Christ, the redeemer. Medieval exegetes might account for these degrees of faith by exploiting the various scholastic distinctions of implicit and explicit, unformed and formed, and demons' faith.[108] Often Calvin appears to deny any positive value to this faith in its improper sense. It is interesting, however, that he, like earlier interpreters (although usually not with the same enthusiasm), is willing to admit that this improper use of the term sometimes indicates a preparation for faith proper, as I showed in the example of the Samaritans. Other significant examples of this preparatory disposition to faith are found in the court official with the sick son (John 4:46–53) and the man born blind whose sight Jesus restores (John 9:6–37).[109] In such cases Calvin's evangelical Pauline assumptions emerge in his insistence that the miracles do not occasion faith; rather, reliance on Christ's word and not solely on his works constitutes proper faith.[110]

Other times Calvin finds that the words "believe" and "faith" are used in a not quite proper sense to indicate not just a prelude to faith but increase and progress in already existent faith. In these instances the miracles or signs play a different role: they confirm faith. This view of miracles was quite traditional, and Calvin articulates this traditional view of miracles in his comments on John 2, defining "miracles" as manifestations of divine power "intended for the confirmation and progress of faith."[111] The most prominent examples of this confirmation are the disciples, who, Calvin assumes, simply by virtue of the fact that they were disciples, already had faith in Jesus as the Christ.[112] Calvin thus holds that before Jesus's death and resurrection the disciples, and selected others, recognized the significance of Jesus and embraced him in faith as the Christ. Their faith, like that of post resurrection believers, is the work of the Spirit; Calvin's assumption about this leads him to deny that the statement in John 7:39 that the Spirit was not yet given can be taken absolutely.[113] The increase of their faith signals the growth in faith that is part of the process of regeneration. Because faith increases, Calvin can admit a kind of ignorance even among actual believers.[114]

Calvin's Interpretation of John 20:24–31

According to Calvin's reading, the faith of believers in the Gospel of John does not simply advance and increase but also decreases. The faith exhibited by the disciples and other devoted followers often seems endangered by too much reliance on externals and too little on Christ and the word. For example, Calvin finds that Martha's faith, when she goes to meet Jesus after the death of her brother, is confused and corrupted by her own feelings.[115] He criticizes Philip for having impure eyes of faith when he asks Jesus to show the disciples the Father (John 14:9).[116] He finds it remarkable that, after the discovery of the empty tomb by the women, that Peter and the other disciple ran to the tomb with such zeal—since "there was so little faith, or rather almost no faith at all, both in the disciples and in the women." In the last example (John 20:3) Calvin concludes that it is not possible that they were motivated by piety to seek Christ. And yet, he continues, "some seed of faith remained in their hearts, though suffocated for a time, so that they did not know what they had."[117] This feeling of piety [*sensus pietatis*] represents the secret work of the Spirit. Insofar as Calvin claims that we see it here bearing fruit, it appears that it indeed moved the disciples to seek Christ, though apparently unknowingly.[118] Because this feeling of piety was directed toward Christ, Calvin designates it "faith," admitting, however, that even he is using the word improperly![119] Yet as much as he attributes an already existent, if presently choked, faith to the disciples, since they were at that time ignorant of Christ's resurrection, Calvin also compares their return to true and sincere faith to a rebirth.

The narrative about "doubting Thomas" (John 20:24–31) allows Calvin to explore the themes of regress and increase in faith and the relationship of externals and the physical senses to this process. Told by the other disciples that they have seen the Lord, Thomas insists that he will not believe until he not only sees Jesus but also touches his wounds (John 20:25). When Jesus appears and indulges Thomas's obstinacy, Thomas confesses his faith in the exclamation "My Lord and my God!" (John 20:28). However, Jesus rebukes Thomas for basing his faith on sight, and declares that those who believe without seeing are blessed (John 20:29).

At first glance the words of Jesus in John 20:29 might seem to vindicate the "proper" definition of faith that Calvin has maintained throughout his commentary. However, he appears to suspect that some will find the evangelist to be saying that Thomas believes because he sees (and perhaps touches) the resurrected Jesus. According to this interpretation, believing through seeing is not as laudatory as believing without seeing. Nevertheless, such belief is still faith. Calvin rejects both of these notions. First, he argues that Thomas's sudden exclamation in John 20: 25 is evidence that his faith had not been wholly extinguished. Thus it appears that we have a case of already existent faith confirmed by sensory experience. This is indeed what Calvin argues: Thomas does not remain on the level of physical sense perception but rests his recovered faith elsewhere. Calvin views the physical encounter with Jesus as a kind of chastisement that removes obstructions and allows the seed of faith to spring up again.[120] He admits that this method is extraordinary: "[Thomas] needed to be dragged violently to faith by the experience of the senses, which is entirely inconsistent with the nature of faith." Still, this does not mean that Thomas believes because he sees; rather, he remembers "the doctrine that he had nearly forgotten."[121] Thus, Thomas, according to Calvin, believes not because he sees but because he recalls the word. Moreover, Calvin denies that a faith based on sight is faith, and in his refutation he marshals all the evidence from Paul and Hebrews that he can. Faith believes things hidden to human senses; though it has its own sight, this is not confined to the world. He refers to Heb. 11:1 and 2 Cor. 5:7 and compares faith to a anchor fixed in heaven, an analogy he had developed in the commentary on Heb. 6:19.

> Here Christ commends faith on this account: acquiescing in the simple word, it does not depend at all on carnal sense or reason. He therefore embraces the force and nature of faith in a brief definition; namely, that it does not remain on [the level of] immediate sight but penetrates to heaven in order to believe those things that are hidden from human sense. And, indeed, we ought to give this honor to God, that we hold his truth to be *autopistos*. Certainly faith has its own sight, but one that does not at all remain in the world and earthly objects. This is why it is called a demonstration of things invisible and not appearing [Heb. 11:1]. Furthermore, Paul, opposing it to sight [2 Cor. 5: 7] means that it does not cling to the consideration of the state of present things and does not look around at things appearing in the world, but it depends on the mouth of God and, relying on the word of God, it rises above the whole world, so as to fix its anchor in heaven.

The chief point is that there is no right faith except that which, founded on the word of God, rises to the invisible kingdom of God, so that it is higher than all human apprehension.[122]

His crowning blow comes in his exegesis of John 20:31, which he understands to be asserting that the miracles recorded in the Gospel were written to awaken faith. After carefully stating once again his position on miracles, Calvin concludes: "Therefore, the meaning of the words is that these things have been written so that we might believe, to the extent that faith can be aided by signs."[123]

To a great extent, the Gospel of John confirms the understanding of faith expressed in the editions of the *Institutes* and the Pauline commentaries that I have considered. Like the Pauline epistles, the Gospel is intensely christocentric and focused on the question of soteriology, though it conceives this latter issue somewhat differently than Paul. Moreover, though its rich imagery of knowledge, light, and sight it allows Calvin to underscore important themes that he has already developed in these other writings. However, the major difficulties that the Gospel of John presents for Calvin's understanding of faith are its broader conception of levels, stages, or types of faith and the complex picture of the role of miracles, signs, and external sense perception in arriving at faith. Calvin meets this challenge by insisting on the following principles, all of which, as I have shown, are furnished in his interpretation of Paul: 1) *Faith comes through hearing*. Calvin rejects the view that miracles effect faith, arguing at several points that miracles have a twofold use: to prepare for faith and to confirm already existent faith.[124] 2) *Faith is not sight*. Calvin evidences the same suspicion toward the physical sense of sight that I have already shown and thus rejects the view that Thomas believes because he has seen. Yet Calvin also continues to employ visual imagery to describe the activity of faith.[125] 3) *Faith is certain*. Calvin designates as improper uses of the word "believe" any that do not present faith as knowledge of Jesus as the Christ. The preparatory stages of faith, based on miracles, testimony, and even the teaching of Christ regarded as a prophet are thus not certain; then again, however, they are also not really faith. Calvin allows for true faith to grow, fall back, and be mingled with confused feelings of the flesh, but he argues that there is always a seed of faith or piety that can never be choked. Even the disciples in the period when they were ignorant of Christ's resurrection were sustained by this seed of faith, almost unknowingly, through an unimaginably challenging trial. In his comments on John 8:32 ("You will know the truth") Calvin admits that this experience is in some way common to all believers: "Thus believers, until they have been fully confirmed, are in some way ignorant of what they know. Yet this is not so tiny or obscure a knowledge of faith as not to be efficacious for salvation."[126]

Conclusion

Erich Grässer observes that the central theme for Paul's idea of faith is the origin (*Entstehen*) rather than the preservation (*Bewahrung*) or increase (*Mehrung*) of faith. This concern as central distinguishes Paul's writings, along with Colossians and Ephesians, from other New Testament texts that speak of faith in a paranetical context.[127] This includes Hebrews, which speaks of faith only in the paranetical sections that urge perseverance and steadfastness, as well as texts that fight against a general weakness of faith, such as James, or for a proper faith in the face of heresy, such as 1 John.[128] Written years after the Pauline epistles, these texts addressed a different situation, one that called for perseverance and for a faith over the long haul. The Pauline walking by faith had taken on marathon proportions. The Gospel of John, though it shares with the Pauline writings a "thoroughly reflective explication of christological faith,"[129] was also written for this later situation. While clearly concerned with the question of the origin of faith, the Gospel's main interest is to establish the firm ground of faith in Christ precisely to foster the community's endurance.

The ideas of faith in Hebrews, James, 1 John, and the Gospel of John reflect the changes in the early Christian church from the time of the Pauline mission. Unaware of the possible historical reasons for these developments, Calvin nevertheless perceives the shifts in emphasis and views them through his Pauline lenses. He protects the distinctiveness of the faith that justifies and gives priority to faith's role in securing salvation by embracing God's gratuitous adoption. He assumes that this is the primary meaning of faith and that justification is faith's primary activity. But faith is the ground not only of free justification but also of sanctification. Faith is just as foundational to living the life of regeneration (sanctification) as it is in embracing the promise of new life (justification). Yet it is the sole ground for justification, while in sanctification it has companions: love, hope, patience.

Calvin's understanding of the Pauline idea of justification by faith, that is, salvation on the basis of an imputed righteousness rather than an actual righteousness acquired in the process of sanctification, determines the categories for his reading of faith in the non-Pauline New Testament texts in several ways. First, in dealing with the need to persevere in the true faith, expressed especially in Hebrews, James, and 1 John, he develops the relationship between faith and love, faith and hope, and faith and patience. Yet he maintains the distinctiveness of faith as the sole ground of salvation and the source of sanctification by viewing love, hope, and patience as companions and inseparable aids. These, he intimates repeatedly, testify to righteousness before human beings but are not the cause of righteousness before God. Second, the Johannine writings provide Calvin with an explicit vocabulary for faith as knowledge. In his treatment of this theme in 1 John and the Gospel, as I have shown, knowledge appeals to him not primarily for its noetic character but because it implies certainty. Thus the category of knowledge does not push Calvin in the direction of an intellectualistic view of faith. Rather, it is a means for him to underscore ideas central to his Pauline view: the firm and certain character of faith and the believer's subjective and personal assurance of God's promise of mercy. Finally, Calvin views the issue of perception through this concern for certainty. He continues to wield the distinction between faith and sight, especially in Hebrews and John, to mitigate the challenges to faith presented by the world of experience. Faith does not rely on things apprehended by ordinary sense perception but on the hidden, future life. It has a way of seeing, but this is distinct from physical sense perception. For the most part, faith directs its view forward and upward, away from all that is in the world and toward the coming manifestation of Christ. Calvin's development of a seeing of the present world by faith in his comments on Heb. 11:3 constitute an important exception to this general view.

While Calvin's commentaries on Hebrews, 1 John, and the Gospel of John uphold his Pauline understanding of faith, they also enrich this understanding by allowing him to focus primarily on faith's role in the living of new life. In other words, they provide him with the opportunity to dwell on the preservation and increase as well as the loss of faith in greater detail. He can focus on faith's relationship to the law understood in its broad sense instead of in the narrow and negative sense that we saw determined the understanding of faith in Rom. 3:21–4:25. These texts lead him from faith as the ground of justification to faith as the ground of sanctification. Still, these commentaries, with the possible exception of the comments on Heb. 11:3, preserve faith's soteriological focus. Though they explore the role of faith in sanctification in greater detail, they still treat faith in its relationship to God's redemptive activity. It is in his commentary on the Psalms that Calvin pursues the idea raised in Heb. 11:3: faith and God's creative and providential activity.

4

Providential Faith

Earlier I showed that one of Calvin's main concerns in his discussion of providence in the 1539 *Institutes* is to defend the idea of God's particular and special guidance of all changes in nature and events in history. Carnal sense, he argues, can perceive and contemplate "a general preserving or governing activity." Faith, however, "ought to penetrate more deeply" and perceive not some universal guidance of the world but God's sustenance, nourishment, and care for "everything he has made, even to the least sparrow."[1] Over the next two decades, perceiving the doctrine of God's special or particular providence to be increasingly under attack, Calvin continues his vigorous defense in various polemical writings: in his tracts against the Libertines and astrology, as well as in his defense of predestination and providence in responses to Giorgio Siculo and Pighius (1552) and Sebastian Castellio (1558).[2] He frequently links the views of his opponents to particular philosophical positions: a too great appreciation for Aristotelian secondary causes, the "Epicurean" notions of an idle god and governance by chance, Stoic determinism or naturalism, and a similar determinism leading to Libertine antinomianism.[3] Susan Schreiner has argued that Calvin's thinking about providence unfolds in these polemics but undergoes no fundamental changes.[4] Hence these writings indicate the central problematic of providence and contribute greatly to our understanding of Calvin's discussion of the topic in the *Institutes*. Yet with respect to the question of the relationship between faith and providence, their testimony is not especially illuminating. They only assert that the understanding of providence is not by reason but by faith; they do not tell us much about the character of this faith.

The significance of the Psalms for Calvin's own faith, explicitly recognized by him in his introduction to his commentary (1557), has been noted repeatedly by biographers and students of Calvin's thought.[5] Beyond this, Bohatec and Schreiner have indicated the special importance of the Psalms for Calvin's understanding of providence.[6] Bohatec speaks of "providential faith" (*Vorsehungsglaube*) and in his two discussions dealing particularly with the nature rather than the content of this faith, his primary source is Calvin's commentary on the Psalms.[7] Building on these insights, this chapter will show that the Psalms were significant not only for Calvin's own faith but for his idea of faith; in shaping his views on providence the Psalms also influenced his understanding of faith. In his commentary on the Psalms Calvin develops the link between faith and providence that he indicated in the 1539 *Institutes* and in his comments on 2 Thess. 1:5–10 and Phil. 4:4–7 and that he hinted at in his comments on Heb. 11:3 and, remotely, in his comments on 1 Cor. 1:21 and 13:12. The notion of providential faith is evident in his other commentaries on Old Testament writings, in particular his commentary on Genesis (1554) and in his commentary on Isaiah (1551; 1559). However, the special biographical and theological importance of the Psalms for Calvin and his doctrine of providence, as well the unparalleled significance of the Psalms in the history of Christian spirituality, justify a particular focus on this commentary.

While Calvin continues in this commentary his polemic against those who deny a particular or special providence, he also repeatedly runs up against the problem that humans do not recognize special providence because they cannot see it.[8] This leads him to focus on the problem of the perception of providence, on the clarity of its manifestation of God's glory and the conditions for the reception of this testimony. In the commentary, Calvin is most concerned with *how* human beings perceive God's providential activity. He not only tells his readers that this "how" is faith but also teaches them what kind of faith this is. Faith in Calvin's commentary on the Psalms is primarily a kind of perception that corrects the noetic effect of sin and enables believers to recognize God's fatherly benevolence not only in God's redemptive work in Jesus Christ but especially in God's providential care of creation and history. It is this latter testimony to God's goodness that receives the greatest attention in Calvin's treatment of the Psalms. He speaks about faith in God's providence to indicate an apprehension of and trust in God's promise of sustaining care that is distinct but never separated from knowledge of God's promise of salvation in Jesus Christ.

To see how Calvin articulates the link between faith and providence, I will consider his exegesis of ten psalms, each of which leads him to view the relationship of faith and providence from a different angle. Taken together, these pieces make up a composite picture that, if not exhaustive in its presentation of Calvin's every reference, is at least a faithful and comprehensive portrayal of his major insights and themes. These examples not only show where and how the themes of faith and providence emerge but also express the character of faith in God's providence: its object, its particular strengths and weaknesses, its peculiar trials, its function in the life of the believer, and, last but not least, its relationship to saving faith in Jesus Christ.

The investigation proceeds along the lines of a general distinction observed by Calvin himself. In his comments, he frequently distinguishes two realms that are the objects of God's providential care: the natural created (but now also fallen) order and the realm of human affairs, that is, history. Because, as I will show, Calvin contrasts the realms of nature and history in terms of their stability and their revelatory power, providential faith, though embracing God's activity in both realms, attends to each realm in a slightly different fashion. For this reason, I will consider first Psalms 19, 29, 33, 46, and 104, which deal primarily with the relationship between faith and creation (the natural order) and then, in the following section, turn to Psalms 8, 23, 48, 9, and 73, which allow us to explore the relationship between faith and history. It is important to note that, despite the grounding in Calvin's own thought, this distinction is a heuristic one.[9] Although he generally recognizes a difference between the order of nature and human affairs or "what we ourselves experience," the boundaries between these two realms are extremely fluid and appear to collapse entirely when, for example, a natural disaster (an instance of God's providence over creation) is perceived as a judgment on the ungodly or sin (an instance of God's providence over history). Moreover, within the realm of history Calvin distinguishes further between God's activity over human affairs in general and that activity specifically directed at the church or the elect. As the discussion will show, the distinctions that Calvin makes in the divine providential activity are relative rather than absolute. Moreover, they are perspectival, reflecting his concern for how fallen human beings perceive God's providence through faith.

Faith and Creation

The shift in focus from immediate soteriological concerns to the themes of creation and providence in Calvin's Psalms commentary leads one to ask about the Pauline character of Calvin's idea of faith. The five psalms studied in this section offer instructive insight into the relationship of Calvin's soteriologically focused, Pauline understanding of faith with the creation-providence centered idea of faith that dominates in this commentary. As Calvin endeavors to explicate more fully a distinct dimension of faith and faith's activity, he further expands his Pauline view, extending it beyond its typically soteriological boundaries.

Calvin's Exegesis of Psalm 19: The Pauline Starting Point

The exegetical tradition read Psalm 19 as a unity, frequently relating the two parts—praising God's works in creation and in the Torah—around one common theme.[10] Calvin views the psalm from the question of knowledge of God and treats the two parts as offering two different sources for this knowledge. In his exegesis, his essentially Pauline solution to the relationship of these two sources emerges. Underlying this discussion is his understanding of Romans 1. But in order to apply Paul's argument for the failure of nature's witness to God in Rom. 1:18–23 to the exaltation of the heavens, the sun, and the law in Psalm 19, Calvin must adopt broad definitions of both the heavens and the law. He therefore distinguishes between God's works in the natural order, which manifest God's glory, and God's word, that is, the law broadly construed, which offers fallen human beings a clearer testimony to God. His reliance on Paul to specify the relationship between the two ultimately leads him to diminish the power of nature's witness. Consequently, in treating the theme "faith," Calvin stresses faith's link to the word of promise.

The priority of word over works is evident from the beginning of Calvin's comments. He opens by noting that this psalm treats God's glory revealed in God's works and then the knowledge of God more clearly revealed in the word.[11] God's works are the subject of the first half of the psalm since, he argues, the figure of the "heavens" represents by synecdoche the entire created order. His view that the manifestation of God's glory in this created order utterly fails does not become fully explicit until Ps. 19:7, the beginning of the discussion of the law. Until that point, Calvin speaks of nature as a powerful proof of God's providence, a witness to God's creation of the universe equal to that of scripture.[12] The heavens are a clear testimony in a universally understood "language." Calvin applauds the psalmist's metaphorical use of speech imagery to portray this: the heavens declare and proclaim (Ps. 19:1); they have both speech (Ps. 19:2) and voice (Ps. 19:3). Oral instruction, he notes, is more effective than visual, and thus this analogy expresses well the force of nature's witness. However, he also qualifies the psalmist's metaphorical designations in his comments on Ps. 19:4, which he translates (following the Hebrew *qawwam*, a line) as "their *writing* has gone forth into all the earth." He says that the "writing" of the heavens is a language directed toward sight, "for it is to the eyes of men that the heavens speak, not to their ears."[13] Calvin's qualification suggests the relative weakness of the natural knowledge of God that is presented to all human beings. He rejects as "allegorical" interpretations of Ps. 19:4 that apply the verse to the preaching of the gospel. Not surprisingly, the authority for this decision is Paul, who cites this passage in Rom. 10:18.[14] Paul, Calvin argues, is not referring to the spread of the gospel. Rather, Paul means only that God had always manifested his glory to the Gentiles as a kind of prelude to the fuller manifestation in the gospel. He cites Paul's statement in Acts 14:16–17 to support this.

Earlier indications of the insufficiency of the testimony to God in God's works are borne out in Calvin's treatment of God's word in his exegesis of the second part of the psalm. His opening comments on Ps. 19:7 signal the enhanced revelatory power of the word: "After having shown that the whole human race is sufficiently taught by mute creatures concerning the one God, [the psalmist] now turns toward the Jews, to whom God had been more fully known by means of his word."[15] He continues by noting that the witness to God in God's word is clearer not only because it is heard rather than seen. Rather, this witness is also more effective in light of the fallen human condition. Fallen humans are blind, and without the aid of the word, they cannot profit at all from contemplation of God's works. Instead, they are only rendered without excuse.[16] These comments on Ps. 19:7 leave no doubt as to the underlying framework of Rom. 1:18–23.

Psalm 19:7, however, does not speak of God's word but of the Torah; moreover, Calvin notes later, this praise of the law seems to conflict with Paul's severe condemnation in such passages as Romans 3 and Galatians 3. In his comments on the second half of the psalm, Calvin addresses these apparent inconsistencies. First, because the praise of the law is so lofty he concludes that "law" in this context must be understood as referring to God's covenant and promise as well as the Decalogue.[17] Law here thus implicitly includes the future gospel of Jesus Christ. This extremely broad understanding of the law as God's word of covenant and promise as well as rule of righteousness then governs Calvin's discussion of how the law restores the soul and guides God's people to salvation. In his comments on Ps. 19:8, he dwells on the law or God's word as a guiding and ordering principle for human life, noting that "God's statutes rejoice the heart" because humans, striving toward obedience, are persuaded that their lives are pleasing to God. However, Calvin cautions, this is not the ultimate ground of their assurance: "No doubt, the source from which true peace of conscience proceeds is faith, which freely reconciles us to God." He thus sets faith apart from the assurance derived from living according to God's statutes. Betraying his presuppositions, he distinguishes and gives priority to the free reconciliation of faith from and over the praiseworthy joy of observing the law.

Calvin then notes explicitly that David's eminent celebration of the law appears to contradict Paul. He attempts to resolve this difficulty by opposing the broad understanding of the law that he finds in Psalm 19 to Paul's narrower view and grounding each of these perspectives in a particular context. David, Calvin says, comprehends both the moral law and "the free promises of salvation, or rather Christ himself," but Paul, "who had to deal with perverse interpreters of the law who separated it from the grace and spirit of Christ, refers to the ministry of Moses by itself." Paul therefore treats the law without Christ and shows what it can do by itself, whereas David "speaks of the whole doctrine of the law, to which the gospel corresponds, and, therefore, under the law he includes Christ."[18]

Having demonstrated the harmony between David and Paul, Calvin continues in his comments on Ps. 19:10–11 to rely on his Pauline assumptions about salvation being apart from the law (narrowly understood) and about the law properly leading to Christ and faith (the theological use of the law) to resolve exegetical difficulties. In this discussion, Calvin appears to shift to a narrower understanding of the law as the rule of righteousness, and one sees a more "Lutheran" emphasis on the law's theological use. The mention in Ps. 19:11 of the reward for those who keep God's statutes means that God has graciously promised to reward the complete fulfillment of the law with eternal life. That, however, does not mean that there is anyone who can attain this reward. Still, he argues, believers can apply the statement about reward to themselves, since forgiveness of sins through imputation is included in the covenant of free adoption; this means that God graciously "accepts [*gratum habet*] for perfect righteousness their holy desires and earnest endeavors to obey."[19] Verse 12 represents David's confession and a prayer for this forgiveness. Calvin argues that his cry "Who can understand his errors?" destroys any confidence in works righteousness. Here Calvin claims that the conditional promises of the law lead to the realization that perfect righteousness cannot be obtained and thus drive to the refuge of God's mercy. David, he argues, is not discussing minor offenses but those larger faults that Satan obscures, an abyss of sins. Verses 13–14 consist of prayers for strength to resist temptation and to struggle against the remains of sin.

Though Calvin only mentions faith once in his exegesis of Psalm 19, even this seemingly insignificant reference illustrates that his Pauline "lenses" are firmly in place. The psalm's praise for the heavens and the law implies for him a comparison between the revelatory power of God's works and God's word. Hence he relies on Paul's judgment about this issue in Rom. 1:18–23 to relate the two parts of the psalm to one another. However, he must expand the definition of Torah in Ps. 19:7 in order to make the comparison effective, and then harmonize this praise for the law with Paul's condemnation of it later in Romans. In the context of this comparison of word and works and the related questions of knowledge of God and human salvation, Calvin treats faith as saving faith, as that which freely reconciles to God. He does not talk about faith except in the context of the word, that is, in the second part of the psalm. Despite the lofty praise for God's works in the first part, these are not the object of faith. The sight of them only points out the blindness for which humans themselves are to blame.

Calvin's Exegesis of Psalm 29: God's Voice in Nature

Psalm 29 presents a different picture of nature and nature's "speech" than that expressed in the first part of Psalm 19. Here is not a harmonious, orderly picture of the heavens but rather a powerful and even threatening voice unleashing the waters of potential chaos and natural violence. Verse 9b marks an abrupt switch from the declaration of God's thundering power to a glorification of God in God's heavenly palace. With a strategy similar to that of his interpretation of Psalm 19, Calvin uses this shift in reference to underscore the priority of the word of redemption for salvation. This time, however, this word enjoys priority not only over the manifestation of God's glory in nature but also over the divine word that underlies God's works in the natural order.

Calvin notes both in his introductory comments to the psalm and in his comments on the first verse that Psalm 29 is primarily directed toward the proud and powerful in this world, who need to be humbled and compelled by force to submit to God and God's grace. In reciting various wonders of nature in Ps. 29:3–9, each of which is linked to God's voice, David seeks to drive the torpid, the rude, and the insensible to acknowledge God's existence and in some way to submit to him. For this reason, Calvin argues, David does not speak of the glorious heavenly bodies as he did in Psalm 19 but instead selects extraordinary and violent works. These "not only testify that the world was at first created by [God] and is governed by his power, but also awaken the torpid and drag them, as it were, in spite of themselves, humbly to adore him."[20] In his comments on Ps. 29:5 Calvin criticizes the secular philosophers, who attribute these happenings to secondary or mediate causes. He implies that they do this precisely to avoid being compelled to acknowledge them to be the work of the divine hand. In contrast, the deer (mentioned in the alternative translation of Ps. 19:9a, "cause the deer to calve"), here representative of all wild beasts, submit to the power and influence of God's voice. Calvin judges: "It is base ingratitude, indeed, not to perceive [*sentire*] his providence and government in the whole order of nature, but it is a detestable insensibility that at least his unusual and extraordinary works, which compel even wild beasts to obedience, will not teach them."[21]

The shift in the middle of Ps. 29:9 to the topic of God's temple leads Calvin to contrast the voice of God that manifests itself in nature with God's voice in the church, namely, the gospel. Again, access to God via the avenue of nature is cut off: "the prophet declares that [God's] glory is celebrated only in the church because God not only speaks clearly there, but also there gently allures the faithful to himself."[22] Rather than sweetly inviting them, God's terrible voice in the thunderings of nature drives humans away. Calvin admits that David's words might be taken as a complaint that only in the church is God praised; these words would thereby function as an indictment of the rest of the world. However, he concludes that David's chief purpose in this verse is to exhort all humans to praise God and to teach them that only the word proclaimed in the church enables true knowledge and praise of God:

> In order truly to know and praise God, we need another voice than that which is heard through thunders, showers, and storms [and] in the air, in the mountains, and in the forests; for if he does not teach us clearly and kindly allure us to himself [by] giving us a taste of his fatherly love, we will continue dumb. It is the doctrine of salvation alone, therefore, which cheers our hearts and opens our mouths to sing his praises, by clearly revealing to us his grace and the whole of his will. . . . It is therefore in his word alone that there shines forth the truth that may lead us to piety.[23]

Humans are initially moved to true and pious knowledge of God neither by the works of God's providence, magnificent or terrifying, nor by the word or wisdom of which they are expressions. However, having learned from God's fatherly voice in the church, human beings do begin to view God's power in a different light. In Ps. 29:11, "Jehovah will give strength to his people," Calvin finds that David describes God "in a very different manner than he did before," namely, "not as one who overwhelms with fear and dread those to whom he speaks, but as one who upholds, cherishes, and strengthens them."[24] The godly are thus to be persuaded that God's power will be exerted on their behalf, to defend and protect them.

Whereas in his exegesis of Psalm 19 Calvin worked with a distinction between God's works and God's word, in his comments on Psalm 29 he specifies a distinction within God's word itself: the word proclaimed in creation and the word proclaimed in the church. Here, too, the priority of the word of redemption is maintained: it is the doctrine of salvation alone that opens the door to true knowledge and praise of God. Although Calvin does not explicitly treat the topic of faith in his comments, his understanding of faith as specifically resting on God's word of mercy clearly underlies his exegesis. This restriction echoes the distinction within special revelation that Calvin expressed in the 1539 *Institutes* and defended against Pighius's challenges in the 1550 *Institutes*. Though the godly embrace all aspects of God's word, faith relies especially on the promise of mercy in Jesus Christ. Yet as a result of harkening to God's fatherly voice, believers begin to view God's power no longer as menacing but rather as comforting.

Calvin's Exegesis of Psalm 33: The Providential Word

Whereas the primary audience of Psalm 29, according to Calvin, was the reprobate, the intended audience of Psalm 33 is the godly. This enables him to explore from another perspective the word by which God governs first of all the natural order and then human affairs, a perspective that he had only suggested at the end of his comments on Psalm 29. In his exegesis of Psalm 33 one finds him clearly expressing the idea of a word as the ordering principle underlying God's works in creation and the events of history. While this "providential word" (God's counsel) is not hidden to believers, who find it in the glass of scripture and contemplate its effects especially in the church, it is at the same time invisible to carnal sense. The providential word and the effects that issue from it threaten the reprobate but are an indispensable comfort to the godly.

Psalm 33 begins with a call to praise God with instruments and voice, because, as 33:4 says, "the word of Jehovah is right and all his works are in faithfulness." Discussing this last verse, Calvin notes that this relates to God's general providence over the whole world. He then states an important distinction:

> Some would have "word" and "work" to be synonymous, but I make a distinction, so that word means God's counsel or ordinance, while work signifies the effect or execution of [his counsel]. . . . Moreover, it ought to be observed that "word" is to be understood not of doctrine but of the method of governing the world.[25]

The word in this instance is the divine Logos that governs nature and history. Calvin's comments on the subsequent verses not only treat the familiar theme of the manifestation of God's glory in God's works but also discuss the character of the word of which they are an expression.

The major developments in Calvin's discussion of the word as God's method of governing the world are found in his comments on Ps. 33:6, 33:9, and 33:11. After relating the themes of God's love for righteousness and God's goodness to God's governance of creation in his comments on Ps. 33:5, Calvin treats God's word governing creation in the comments on Ps. 33:6, "By the word of Jehovah the heavens were established." Here he identifies the word as God's "eternal word, his only begotten Son."[26] He also rejects using the second half of the verse, "And all the host of them by the spirit of his mouth," to prove the deity of the Spirit. Instead, Calvin refers this to the efficacy of God's word, to the work of creation that is the word's effect. He thus underscores the word, God's Logos, as the creative and sustaining principle in the natural order and stresses the dynamic, effective power of this providential word.

For Calvin, God's providential word is especially linked to God's power, as we saw in his exegesis of Psalm 29. One finds this connection again here in his insistence on the efficacy of God's word, which alone is sufficient to create and maintain the world. Calvin argues, moreover, that the power of this word, calling forth and sustaining creation, is worthy of human adoration. He understands Ps. 33:8–9 ("Let all the earth fear Jehovah, let all the inhabitants of the world tremble") as a call for humans to fear God, that is, to submit to God's power, which is made especially evident in creating and supporting the world through the word.[27] The power of God's word alone created the world: without effort, without time, without external aids. The power of the word alone upholds and sustains the world in its existence. Thus Calvin does not view here, as he did in Psalm 29, the threatening aspect of the power in God's providential word, but instead marvels at it and says that it should be adored.

In his comments on Ps. 33:11, "The counsel of Jehovah will stand forever," Calvin takes this reverence for God's power one step farther: he calls believers not only to adore but to have faith in its greatness.[28] He thus relates the providential word to faith. Moreover, he discusses how believers apprehend this word, or, in his words, are awakened to faith in God's power. The psalmist, he claims, commends a counsel not hidden in heaven, to be honored and revered from afar. Rather, this is a revealed counsel, testifying to the steadfastness of God's love for righteousness and truth, to God's care for the righteous and good, to God's succor of the oppressed. Calvin urges his readers to "learn to look at God's counsel in the glass of his word," to be satisfied that God will perform what he has promised and that this promise is steadfast.[29] When events suggest the perversion of this counsel—this promise of guidance and protection—believers must exercise their faith in recalling this declaration of God's steadfastness. In other words, believers gain from the revealed word (in this case, scripture), and not directly from nature, an initial knowledge of God's providential word or counsel. Relying on this "counsel" (i.e., God's eternal Logos) they are persuaded of God's guidance and care.

Not only do the godly apprehend God's counsel and persuade themselves of God's providential promise, they also obtain a different perspective on the manifestations of providence. Calvin treats the visible effects of God's counsel or power especially in his comments on Ps. 33:7, 33:10, and 33: 12–13. The gathering of all the waters mentioned in Ps. 33:7 stands, according to Calvin, for all of God's works in governing the world, but it is also itself a particularly remarkable instance of the divine providence. Calvin holds to an ancient cosmological scheme that views the element of water as lighter than the earth. Therefore, the fact that the waters remain in the oceans and do not break out to overwhelm the entire earth represents for him a profound proof that God "has enclosed the waters in invisible barriers and keeps them shut up to this day."[30] Calvin finds that the psalmist returns to this topic, "that daily events are certain proofs of the providence of God," in Ps. 33:10, which declares that God scatters human counsels. Though this presents God as an adversary to human beings, Calvin finds that this is a comfort to the godly, since it declares that God's protection is set against human attempts to overturn law and justice, that God effectively checks human wantonness and the confusion they seek to bring about.[31] Thus a reliance on God's providential word enables the godly to find proofs of God's providence in nature and events and to find comfort even when these manifestations seem threatening.

Calvin's comments on Ps. 33:12–13 shed additional light on his views on the relationship between faith and God's counsel on the one hand and faith and the works of providence on the other. It is important to note that in these comments Calvin signals a distinction between the manifestation of God's providence in creation in general and the evidences of this care in the maintenance of the church. This topic will be explored in more detail in my next section, which considers God's providence in the realm of history. Nonetheless, a brief consideration of his comments is in order here. Calvin is led to the topic of the church by the claim of Ps. 33:12 that the people of God are blessed. In his comments, Calvin understands the people of God to be blessed because they not only perceive God's counsel but also have evidences of it: "The prophet, therefore, in proclaiming that they are blessed whom God receives into his protection, reminds [us] that the counsel which he had just mentioned is not hidden away but is displayed in the salvation of the church and may be there beheld."[32] Calvin does not go into any further detail about the manifestation of providence in the church or about the contemplation of these evidences. Instead, he underscores that this blessedness of the godly proceeds ultimately from divine adoption; thus the foundation for both their trust in God's providence and their ability to perceive it is God's grace.[33]

In his exegesis of the rest of the psalm, Calvin stresses the necessity of relying on God's providence. It is clear that he means a reliance on the providential word itself and not on the external manifestations of it. Accounted the people of God by "God's gracious electing love," the godly can learn, from Ps. 33:13, "that human affairs are not tossed hither and thither fortuitously, but that God secretly directs everything that happens." The psalmist's words, "Jehovah looked down from heaven; he beheld the children of Adam," lead the godly to apprehend by faith God's providential word, which only they can see:

> Now he here commends God's inspection, that we on our part may learn to behold his invisible providence with the eyes of faith. There are, no doubt, evident proofs of it continually before our eyes; but the great majority of men, notwithstanding, are blind, and, in their blindness, conceive a blind fortune.[34]

Calvin expands these insights in his comments on the remaining verses, picking up themes that I will consider later in this chapter: attempts by the ungodly to deny or thwart divine providence, the problem of affliction, the need for the godly to affirm and trust in God's secret providence. Once more, in his comments on Ps. 33:18–19, Calvin underscores the difference between the godly and the ungodly: "The whole human race, no doubt, is maintained by the providence of God, but we know that he specially vouchsafes his fatherly care to none but his own children, that they may perceive [*sentiant*] that their necessities are truly regarded by him."[35] It is only the godly, who through the eyes of faith contemplate God's counsel, who benefit: they alone perceive and rest on a providential ordering that is invisible to those without faith. They alone can properly render God the praise that God deserves.

In his exegesis of Psalm 33 Calvin views the relationship between the word of God that creates and sustains the world and the word of redemption spoken to the church from a new perspective. His reflections lead him to bring a distinct dimension of faith to fuller expression. When those who have already embraced the promise of salvation through faith perceive God's providential word, this word no longer drives them away but rather leads them to a more profound knowledge of God. This is not a natural theology in the sense of a knowledge of God arrived at either by reason or even by pious contemplation of the created order.[36] In other places, as I will show, Calvin does allow for knowledge of God's providence to be deepened through contemplation of God's works. Here, however, discussing the actual object of what I call, with Bohatec, providential faith, Calvin distinguishes this object both from its effects (the created order) and from the medium in which it is most clearly expressed or mirrored (scripture; "the glass of the word"). The object of providential faith is God's eternal Son, apprehended in faith as the creative and governing principle of the created order. Such knowledge of God as creator is not a general knowledge of God that exists prior to or even apart from the special knowledge of God as redeemer in Christ.[37] Nonetheless, faith in God's providential promise can be distinguished from saving faith, for whereas saving faith, as I have shown, rests particularly on God as redeemer, providential faith looks to God as creator and sustainer of the world. Providential faith arises out of saving faith, it cannot exist apart from saving faith, and like saving faith it is "christocentric" in that its actual object is God's Son. But whereas saving faith looks explicitly to the Son as incarnate Christ, providential faith looks to the Son as Logos.[38] In Calvin's comments on this psalm the basic outline for the idea of a providential faith emerges with particular clarity. In his exegesis of other psalms one sees him unfolding this idea and reflecting especially on the relationship between the works of providence and faith in God's providential word.

Calvin's Exegesis of Psalm 46: Creation in Turmoil

Psalm 46 praises God as a refuge and a strength in times of trouble, as a certain help in the face of natural or political threat or even disaster. Like each of the psalms that I have considered thus far, it speaks of God's activity in both nature and history: Ps. 46:2–5 praises God's power over nature and 46:6–11 extols God's triumph in battle. Yet here, too, I focus on the question of God's general providence over the natural order without treading too far on territory to be covered later in this chapter. Indeed, it is easy to maintain the boundaries of this perspective, since Calvin himself views the psalm primarily as speaking about God's general providential guidance of creation. He maintains that the psalm was written to give thanks for some particular historical deliverance (he cannot specify exactly which one) but finds that it has a general application to the church at all times: "since [the prophet] teaches us how God is accustomed to act toward all his own [people]."[39] Although Calvin's comments on Psalm 46 explicate this divine activity, they treat also the way in which God's people ought to respond to God's activity. Hence they shed light on the relationship between providential faith and the kind of violence in nature that was described in Psalm 29, on the role of the manifestations of divine providence in nature for providential faith hinted at in the exegesis of Psalm 33, and the power of God as providential faith's specific object.

In contrast to his comments on Psalm 29, Calvin stresses the benefits for believers of worldly turmoil. Verses 1–5 declare God's steadfastness among violent changes: earthquakes, collapse of mountains, raging floods. The godly recognize that God is their refuge and therefore do not fear these upheavals. They do not view these with unfeeling equanimity, but, nevertheless, when "calmness and tranquillity of heart" overcome their fear, they offer proof that they honor and rely on God's power.[40] In his comments on Ps. 46:3 Calvin stresses the need for faith to be tested through such severe conflicts as those described in these verses. Faith unfolds itself amid the utmost confusion and conquers fear. The victory of faith consists in bearing these assaults in the assurance of divine protection. Even though God's help may be slow in coming, like the gentle flowing streams mentioned in Ps. 46:4, believers derive security and peace of mind from it alone. They are not shaken by the power of the world exercised against them. Violent upheavals in the world actually drive believers to God by exercising their providential faith.

Faith obtains its victory by relying on the divine protection promised in Ps. 46:1–5. Even when God's help appears slow in coming, faith conquers fear and imparts tranquillity amid trial. In addition, faith derives consolation from consideration of previous manifestations of God's providence. Calvin argues that the prophet, in Ps. 46:6, refers to some particularly noteworthy deliverance and thus confirms from experience the doctrine that he had just advanced about the divine protection. Calvin picks up this discussion in his comments on Ps. 46:8, "come, consider the works of Jehovah." There he says that earlier manifestations of divine favor play a vital role in persuading believers of the stability of God's promise to preserve them; indeed, that consideration of God's works constitutes the best means of strengthening faith. He sees this verse also as a rebuke of those who do not take God's power as seriously as they ought, attributing things to fortune, to their own industry, or to secondary causes.[41] The psalmist's words, according to Calvin, thus condemn the ungodly for their ingratitude, and, at the same time, show that even the godly "are sluggish and languid until they are awakened."[42] Even if Ps. 46:9 refers to a particular deliverance, still, Calvin argues, the psalmist intends generally to lead the faithful to expect as much help from him in the future as they had already experienced. Hence amid the trials threatening faith in God's providence, the godly strengthen their faith in God's providential word by recalling God's providential works, which they themselves have experienced.

As we saw in his exegesis of Psalm 33, Calvin speaks of faith in God's providence as faith in the greatness of God's power. Providential faith is especially concerned with God's power over all creation, with God's superintendence of all things and events. In his comments on Ps. 46:7, "Jehovah of armies is with us: the God of Jacob is our fortress," he underscores that only those who have been embraced by God's promise of fatherly love can apply to themselves what scripture proclaims about God's infinite power. For this reason, he claims, the prophet alludes to God's adoption of Israel in the second clause of the verse. Apart from this adoption, "the commendation of God's power would only inspire us with dread."[43] Faith in God's power is impossible without faith in God's love:

> That our faith may rest firmly, we must take into consideration that these two things [exist] simultaneously in God: his immeasurable power [*virtus*], by which he is able to subdue the whole world under him, and his fatherly love, which he has manifested in his word. When these two things are joined together, there is nothing that can hinder our faith from defying all [its] enemies, nor should we doubt that God will succor us, since he has promised to do it. He is sufficiently able also to fulfill [his promise], for he is the God of armies.[44]

Providential faith, though especially concerned with God's power, is not restricted to this, but rather rests also in God's merciful love. In other words, faith in God's providence presupposes saving faith, for only the person who has embraced God's promise of adoption and fatherly love—most clearly evident in Jesus Christ—rests assured in God's promise to protect and God's ability to do so. Calvin thus links God's power to God's fatherly love and mercy and relates faith to both attributes.[45]

Note here that there is really just one faith for Calvin, but that in this one faith there are "two things joined together," namely faith in God's powerful providence and faith in God's saving love.

Returning in this psalm to the theme of creation in turmoil, Calvin develops his reflections on the relation between faith and providence by arguing that in seeking relief in times of turmoil faith rests in the promise of divine protection, looking both to God's power as well as to God's mercy. Faith in God's providence is challenged particularly by affronts to God's power, as is evident in the fact that those whom Calvin criticizes for denying God's providence are faulted for diminishing God's power by attributing events to other causes. Yet while this challenge to God's power represents the significant trial for providential faith, without a conviction of God's mercy, faith will never be able to rest firm in God's power.

Calvin's exegesis of Psalm 46 shows that providential faith leads believers to new perspectives on worldly turmoil, on the manifestations of God's providence, and God's power. Apart from faith in God's providence, human beings are driven from God by the thunderings of nature, as we saw in Calvin's exegesis of Psalm 29. However, when the godly rest their faith in God's providential word, these upheavals, though still threatening, lead them to God. Moreover, without providential faith, humans cannot see the hand of God in God's works, but the godly perceive the manifestations of God's power that they themselves have experienced and use this experience to fortify their faith. Finally, because providential faith is grounded in faith in God's promise of redemption, believers no longer fear the power of God but instead rest in it.

Calvin's Exegesis of Psalm 104: The World as a Theater

In this psalm Calvin returns to the theme of nature's witness to God's glory. His comments offer an outstanding example of how faith in God's providential care is confirmed, supported, and strengthened through pious contemplation of God's works in nature. In contrast to his comments on Psalm 19, Calvin does not dwell on the negative comparison between the external witness of nature and word of redemption but rather urges contemplation of these natural images of God's glory through the eyes of faith. For those who have been led from faith in God's saving word to faith in God's providential word, there are four consequences of seeking God in God's works in nature: a restoration of nature's original function, a confidence toward the future, more attentive reflection on the providential word, and a response consisting of praise and ethical action.

In his preface to Psalm 104, Calvin says that "presenting to us in the creation of the world and the order of nature a lively image of God's wisdom, power, and goodness, [the psalm] encourages us to praise him for the manifestation he has made of himself as a father to us in this perishable life."[46] Throughout his exegesis Calvin emphasizes that the natural order represents an accommodation of the divine nature to the human capacity.[47] He stresses that there is in nature abundant material for praising God, and he offers detailed explanations of how the elements of nature catalogued by the psalmist are so many articles of divine clothing, designed to render God, who dwells in inaccessible light, visible to human beings.

Calvin contrasts this way of knowing God not with God as revealed in the word, as he did in his exegesis of Psalm 19, but with all speculative attempts to know God. Thus, for example, in his comments on Ps. 104:2, "being arrayed with light as with a garment, and spreading out the heavens as a curtain," he observes:

> If men attempt to ascend to the height of God, although they fly above the clouds, they must fail in the midst of their course. And those who seek God in his naked majesty are certainly very foolish. That we may enjoy the sight [*conspectu*] of him, he must come forth to view with his clothing; that is, we must cast our eyes upon that very beautiful fabric of the world in which he wishes to be seen by us, [and] not be erroneously curious in searching into his secret essence.[48]

Calvin adds that the description of the heavens as a curtain does not refer to God's hiding himself but rather to God's self-manifestation. This interest in presenting creation as an effective accommodation to human nature that provides humans with abundant material for praising God suggests that faith in God's providence restores failed human vision (at least in part) and enables them to benefit from God's manifestation in nature. Indeed, Calvin indicates, concluding his comments on Ps. 104:3–4, that this goal is attainable only through the eyes of faith: "And certainly we profit little in the sight of all of nature if we do not behold with the eyes of faith that spiritual glory, an image of which presents itself to us in the world."[49]

Through the eyes of faith humans profit from creation's witness and are able to praise God. In his comments on Ps. 104:5, Calvin notes another benefit for those who have faith in God's providence: they are not anxious about their life in this world. In Ps. 104:5–9 the psalmist declares God's founding and establishment of the earth and its seas, mountains, and valleys. Calvin admits that there might be natural explanations for the position of the earth but argues that even the philosophers cannot explain why the waters, being a lighter element, do not surround and envelop the earth, except that they are held in place by God's providence. These are miracles, Calvin claims, that even experience itself shows to be true; such a powerful proof indicates the inherent fragility and instability of the natural order. Calvin returns to this theme to repeatedly in his comments on Psalm 104, each time indicating that life under such conditions would be unbearable, were it not for faith in God's providence. Hence he avers that the psalmist's words do more than stir the faithful up to praise and thanksgiving: "the prophet not only urges us to give thanks to God but also strengthens [us] in [regard to] the future, that we may not live in the world in trepidation and anxiety, as would have been the case had God not testified that he has given men a dwelling-place on the earth."[50]

In the context of his reflections on the fragility of the natural order Calvin stresses the power of God's word in maintaining and guiding creation. In his comments on Ps. 104:9, "Thou hast fixed a bound over which they shall not pass, they shall not return to cover the earth," he reiterates his view that even natural philosophers are compelled to concur with his views on the restraint of the waters. This ought to be evident even to the rudest and most stupid people. Momentary disruptions of this order (e.g., earthquakes and floods), rather than refuting the view that all things are held in place by God's providence, are actually warnings that the stability of all things is to be traced to God's word. Calvin cites a recent event as evidence:

> The Baltic sea, in our own time, inundated large tracts of land, and did great damage to the Flemish people and other neighboring nations. But by this particular flood we are warned what would happen if God's restraint [of the sea] were removed. How is it that we have not been swallowed up at the same time, but because God has held in that raging element by his word? In short, although the waters naturally can cover the earth, yet this will not happen, because, just as his truth is eternal, so this order that God has established by his word will remain steadfast.[51]

Here again one finds that the manifestations of God's providence, both past and present, not only provide material for praise and strengthen confidence toward life in this realm; they also point believers back to God's providential word itself. Calvin underscores this strengthening of providential faith in his comments on Ps. 104:24, "O Jehovah! how magnificent are thy works! thou hast made all things in wisdom." Here, he argues, the prophet touches on certain particulars of God's works in order to lead believers "to reflect on the providence by which God governs the whole world and every particular part of it."[52] He notes that the mention of wisdom alone does not exclude the divine power but only shows that the world is so carefully arranged that it cannot possibly have been put together by chance. Thus faith in God's providence is increased not just in times of trial and testing but also through contemplation of all God's works.

In his comments on the last verses of the psalm (104:31–35) Calvin returns to the need to praise God, expanding this to include not just praise of the mouth but also praise rendered to God in actions. Verse 31 expresses both of these dimensions: "Glory be to Jehovah forever: let Jehovah rejoice in his works." The second clause, Calvin points out, is not superfluous. The psalmist not only stirs humans up to praise, but also "desires that the order that God established from the beginning may be continued in the lawful use of his gifts." In other words, humans who, with the eyes of faith, can perceive the world as a theater of God's glory not only use the natural order as it was originally intended, derive confidence for life in this world, and reaffirm their faith in God's providential word; in addition, they are to lead lives of obedience, not misusing the gifts of this best of all fathers. Calvin warns that the very stability of creation depends on their adherence to this moral task; Ps. 104:32, "when he looks on the earth, it shall tremble, if he touch the mountains, they shall smoke" sets forth the consequences of the failure to do this. Concluding these arguments in his comments of Ps. 104:35, he warns: "Let us then take care so to weigh the providence of God, that being wholly devoted to obeying him, we may rightly and purely use the benefits which he sanctifies for our enjoying them."[53]

In his exegesis of Psalm 104 Calvin depicts the activity of providential faith toward the created order. Eyes of faith behold the image of God's glory presented in the world; trusting in the word of providence that they find there revealed, the faithful have no anxiety in the face of nature's instability and are free to praise and serve their creator. Though nature is fragile, providential faith recognizes that God's power is sufficient to maintain it and glimpses God's wise benevolence in this fragility itself.

In his exegesis of these five psalms Calvin creates space for but also closely circumscribes a notion of faith in God's providence. His exegesis of Psalms 19 and 29 prepares for his more explicit discussions of providential faith in Psalms 33, 46, and 104 by underscoring the priority of God's word of redemption for faith. Psalm 19 leads him to oppose the revelatory power of the promise of redemption to the failed testimony of God's works; faith, whether in its providential or saving dimension, cannot rely on external manifestations. Psalm 29 brings him to a contrast between the promise of salvation and the voice in nature, which, apart from this promise, can only drive human beings away from God. And although Calvin speaks highly of the providential word in his comments on Psalm 33, he nevertheless grounds this in the word of redemption. In other words, Calvin's comments insist on the absolute priority of saving faith over providential faith. However, it is also true that, in his exegesis of these psalms, he is far more interested in explicating the latter. His comments, especially on Psalms 33, 46, and 104, reveal that he recognizes a faith in God's providence that is grounded in faith in God's redemption. Like saving faith, providential faith relies ultimately on the promise or word and not on the manifestations of God's power or goodness. Similarly, providential faith, like saving faith, is christocentric insofar as the word that structures and stabilizes creation on which it relies is the Logos, the second person of the Trinity. But herein lies the crucial difference: providential faith looks particularly to the word that comes to expression in God's activity as creator and sustainer of all that is. This word is especially linked to God's power, and therefore providential faith appears to be concerned especially with challenges to God's power. Out of the knowledge of God's fatherly love and mercy, which is, for Calvin, initially (and perpetually) attained through saving faith in Jesus Christ, grows a faith in God's powerful providential word. It is in this way that faith "penetrates more deeply," perceiving God's hand in God's works in nature and signaling the restoration of nature to its original purpose.

Faith and History

In this section I turn to the other realm of the divine activity embraced by providential faith: the arena of human affairs, or history. In treating the relationship between faith and God's providence over history, Calvin observes the boundaries and underscores the characteristics of providential faith expressed in his discussion of faith and creation, insisting especially that the providential *word* is always the object of faith and that external manifestations of providence confirm faith in this promise. Treating these matters in his exegesis of Psalms 8, 23, and 48, he also underscores the redemptive context of providential faith by raising the providence manifest in the protection of the chosen people to special prominence. But, for Calvin, the witness of history, even that of the church's history, is more problematic than that of nature. On the one hand, he finds that God's guidance of events is a more suitable accommodation to human capacity—both to its finitude as well as its sinfulness. On the other hand, the flux of history obscures God's providential counsel to a greater extent; even the faithful have difficulty maintaining faith in the face of the confusion of history. The tension underlies Calvin's interpretation of Psalms 8, 23, and 48 and emerges especially in his comments on Psalms 9 and 73. In response to it, one finds Calvin repeatedly urging faith in God's secret, hidden counsel. Moreover, he develops further the notion of faith as an eye that not only penetrates to this secret counsel—not comprehending but reverently adoring it—but also turns back on the events of history and ascribes to them new meaning.[54]

Calvin's Exegesis of Psalm 8: The Looking-Glass of History

In his exegesis of Psalm 8 Calvin distinguishes between the natural order and the realm of human affairs as objects of divine providence and indicates the superiority of the manifestation of providence in history over that in nature. He then discusses in greater detail the character of God's providence toward the human race and where its manifestations are most clearly seen. Like his interpretation of Psalm 19, his exegesis of Psalm 8 appeals to the disruptive effects of the Fall to account for present hiddenness of God's providential care, this time, however, in history. Yet Calvin also insists on the integrity of history, both in his adherence to the "historical" meaning of the psalm and his emphasis on present, historical existence.[55] He thus upholds the ultimate visibility of God's care in the course of human affairs.

Psalm 8 opens with an exclamation expressing the wonderful nature of God's name throughout the earth and God's glory above the heavens; Ps. 8:3 speaks of the heavens as the works of God's fingers. Calvin refers this first statement to God's creation and care of the natural order but insists that this is not the main theme:

> David, it is true, sets before his eyes the wonderful power and glory of God in the creation and government of the whole world, but, only touching slightly on this subject, he applies himself to the consideration of [God's] infinite goodness toward us. For surely there is in the whole order of nature the most abundant matter for praising God. Since, however, we are more affected by our own experience, David, with great propriety, expressly commends the special favor toward the human race, for this is the brightest mirror in which we can behold his glory.[56]

The proof of God's providence toward humankind is taken up in Ps. 8:2, "out of the mouths of babes and sucklings you have founded your strength because of the adversaries, that you might put to flight the enemy and the avenger." Calvin argues that babies and nursing infants, though speechless, attest to God's liberality toward the human race: God provides nourishment for them before they are born and fits their tongues for nursing. In citing their example, David ridicules those who deny God's providence; he opposes and overcomes their violence via the mouths of children. Though the phrase "because of the adversaries" suggests that this manifestation of God's goodness is particularly designed to confound the wicked, Calvin notes that God's providence "shines forth principally for the sake of the faithful, because they alone have eyes to see it."[57] This is a view that, as I showed in the last section, he frequently asserts in his commentary on the Psalms.[58] God's providence over human affairs, just as God's providence over the natural order, is visible to those illumined by faith. The despisers of God, here presented as those who oppose the proofs of God's providence, are given over to their confusion itself as punishment.[59]

Calvin finds God's goodness toward human beings underscored in the psalmist's implicit comparison of the work of the heavens and God's attention to humans in Ps. 8:3–4: "God's wonderful goodness is seen more clearly in that such a great creator, whose majesty shines forth in the heavens, desires to adorn this miserable and worthless animal with the highest glory and to enrich [it] with innumerable treasures."[60] This special honoring of humans is confirmed by the two examples mentioned in Ps. 8:5–8; namely, that humans are "a little lower than God" and that they have dominion over God's other works. Calvin expounds the first as a reference to the endowments of human nature as created after the image of God, which are clear signs of heavenly wisdom: the ability to distinguish good and evil, the seed of religion, community with one another, a regard for what is respectable, decency, and governance by law. In his comments on Ps. 8:6, he argues that the dominion that God has granted to humans shows the greatness of God's love and is a singular honor. The evidence of this goodness, like that in the first case, is clear, and can be seen in the concrete but not exhaustive examples of human dominion given in Ps. 8:7–8.[61]

Calvin's commitment to both the literal sense and the theme of providence emerges clearly in his exegesis of Ps. 8:5 and 8:6; both verses are quoted in the New Testament in reference to Christ and Christ's kingdom (Heb. 2:7 and 1 Cor. 15:27). In his comments on Ps. 8:5 Calvin maintains that the prophet speaks of *human* excellence, but that this is legitimately applied to Christ in Heb. 2:7 insofar as Christ is both the first born (*primogenitus*) of all creatures and the restorer (*instaurator*) of the human race. David, Calvin remarks, describes human nature before the Fall. In the Fall this testimony to God's liberality was obscured, though not extinguished. Since these blessings are restored to humans through their participation in Christ, whatever excellence humans possess can be attributed to Christ and, in this way, the verse can be applied to Christ. He acknowledges nonetheless that the author of Hebrews used the verse to make a different point from that intended by David. Citing similar examples of such accommodation in Paul, Calvin legitimates Paul's use while at the same time protecting his more "historical" reading of the verse.[62]

Calvin also introduces the effects of the Fall to harmonize his interpretation of Ps. 8:6 in terms of human dominion with Paul's use of this verse in 1 Cor. 15:27 to describe Christ's dominion over all things. First he remarks that the whole order of the world is arranged to promote human happiness. Then he briefly refers his readers to his comments on the previous verse to see how the passage can be applied to Christ. Finally he addresses the question of how evident this subjection of all things is. Human dominion, like human nature, was damaged in the Fall, and is recovered fully only in Christ.[63] Calvin claims that from the fact that this state has not yet been fully actualized, Paul concludes in 1 Corinthians 15 that it will not be accomplished until death has been completely abolished. Paul's reasoning, Calvin argues, is itself based on the premise that the order of the world tends toward the promotion of human happiness.

Calvin's reconciliation of his interpretation of Ps. 8:5–6 with the New Testament application of these passages to Christ reveals not only his theological interest in promoting the doctrine of providence and but also his concern to specify its visibility in history. Calvin defends the primary meaning of the psalm as a testimony to divine providence in human affairs. In order to maintain this interpretation, he introduces the notion of a fallen creation and of providence obscured, applying the texts to unfallen human nature, on the one hand, and to human nature restored in Christ on the other. His comments thus maintain the clarity of God's providence toward human beings as "the brightest mirror in which we can behold his glory" and, at the same time, severely qualify this witness, as in his comments on Ps. 8:5: "In such corruption the liberality that David proclaims here ceased, at least in that it does not appear in its pure splendor. Although it was not altogether extinguished, nevertheless, how small a portion can be discerned among miserable ruins?"[64] Concluding his comments on the psalm, he seeks to reconcile these views. After asserting, as we saw earlier in the comments on Ps. 8:7–8, that God's providence toward humans is sufficiently evident in the ways that creation submits to them, Calvin observes that the faithful alone are led from this evidence to wonder at God's kindly grace.[65] Reflecting on God's providence in this realm, they ought be led to higher contemplation of heavenly treasures. Thus temporal blessings related by David become for the faithful a means for contemplation of the spiritual benefits offered in Christ.[66]

Though Calvin does not treat the topic of faith per se in his comments on Psalm 8, his exegesis nonetheless helps to clarify the notion of providential faith. In the realm of human affairs, divine providence has a more personal character than in nature in general. This special providential care of humans is especially evident in the integrity of original human nature and the dominion that the first humans possessed. Despite the overthrow of this order in the Fall, the vestiges of these temporal benefits are sufficient to lead those who have faith to wonder at God's grace and to rise to contemplation of the spiritual treasures that they have in Christ. The realm of history, like that of nature, both reveals and conceals God's ordering wisdom; faith opens godly eyes at least in part to this wisdom in its manifestations. It is significant that Calvin emphasizes the importance of the present life and the manifestations of providence in it. He insists that David is referring to human dominion in this life and that the faithful are to cast their eyes on these evidences of divine providence. It is through their reflection on the evidences of God's liberality toward them that they are led to a consideration of the spiritual benefits offered in Christ.

Calvin's Exegesis of Psalm 23:
The Ladder of Present Prosperity

In his comments on Psalm 23 Calvin explores the topic of present benefits as ladders for the faithful in greater detail. As in his exegesis of Psalm 8, he assumes that an awareness of God's providence toward humankind underlies the psalmist's praise. In this case, however, it is not God's liberality toward the human race in general that David celebrates but rather God's goodness toward himself in particular. Calvin attributes the composition of the psalm to the time when David enjoyed the pleasures and prosperity of kingship. David, according to Calvin, offers thanks to God for this situation and expresses his confidence that he will continue in such happiness through God's providence.[67] In his comments, Calvin explores and circumscribes the role of temporal benefits in building faith in God's providence.

Calvin opens his comments on the psalm by warning immediately against the intoxicating and blinding dangers of prosperity: "Although God, by his benefits, gently invites us to himself, as if by a taste of his fatherly sweetness, in [a state of] peace and joy we are prone to nothing more than forgetfulness of God sneaking up on us." Yet rather than being blinded by his present good fortune, David testifies that he is mindful of God and that he uses these temporal benefits as ladders for drawing closer to him. David uses the image of the shepherd to commend God's providence and acknowledges that despite all his power and riches he is but a sheep. His example, according to Calvin, teaches that God's providence, not temporal blessings, is the foundation of happiness, and that a conviction of the sufficiency of this providence is necessary in order to honor God properly.[68]

Having cautioned his readers not to forget that God's providence is the source of all good things, Calvin continues the focus on God's providential guidance of the faithful in this life in his comments on Ps. 23:2–5. He takes the references to grassy pastures and peaceful waters in Ps. 23:2 to be metaphorical statements about God's abundant providing of food, drink, and shelter. Though the restoring of the soul in Ps. 23:3 might imply justification (he refers his readers to his comments on Ps. 19:7), Calvin does not dwell on this topic but returns immediately to the theme of providence. He explicitly rejects referring the "paths of righteousness" to the direction of the Holy Spirit, since, he argues, this does not fit with the psalmist's metaphor. Instead it means easy and straight paths. In other words, Calvin understands this phrase to indicate God's protection of the faithful and not the Holy Spirit's regenerative activity.[69] That all these benefits are bestowed "for his name's sake" means that they are entirely gratuitous, deriving from God's goodness and not from David's merit.

David's declaration in Ps. 23:4 that he will fear no evil even in the valley of the shadow of death leads Calvin to discuss the need for faith in God's providence to be tried and the character of its victory over affliction. David's statement indicates for Calvin that he would lean on God's providence in any adversity.[70] David does not promise himself continued prosperity but rather acknowledges the inevitable adversities that will come. He does not rest in "carnal security" of his present prosperity but in "the repose of faith," which rests in God's protection alone. Calvin stresses that David, considering these future afflictions, truly experiences fear:

> Yet David did not mean to say that he was devoid of all fear, but only that he would surmount it so as to go without fear wherever his shepherd would lead. This appears more clearly from the context. First he says "I will fear no evil," but in immediately adding the reason he openly confesses that he seeks a remedy for his fear in looking at the staff of the shepherd. Why would he need consolation, unless fear was distressing him? Therefore we ought to remember that when David

saw in his mind those adversities that could take place, he only conquered his temptation by resting on the protection of God.[71]

In order to stress that faith in God's providence is subject to trial, Calvin assumes that David not only will be but is now afflicted by fear. Moreover, he distinguishes faith in God's care from a carnal security that rests on the present state of prosperity. He notes at the end of his comments on Ps. 23:4 that those to whom God has revealed himself as shepherd in Christ have a much clearer revelation of this than the fathers under the law. He also implies that they thus have greater obligations to render honor to God's protecting care by fixing their eyes on it and overcoming fear.[72]

In his comments on Ps. 23:6, which expresses the psalmist's confidence that God's goodness and mercy will continue throughout his life, Calvin raises the matter of the true ground of David's trust. Having already shown that David did not allow himself to be blinded by his riches but used them temperately and gave thanks to God for them, Calvin now stresses that David does not base his faith in God's continued good favor on the possession of the blessings themselves but rather on God's promise. He continues:

> For when he said to himself earlier that in the darkness of death his eyes would be intent on contemplating God's providence, he attested sufficiently that he did not depend on external things, nor did he measure the grace of God according to the judgment of his own flesh. But even where all earthly assistance failed, his faith remained confined to the word of God. Although experience led him to hope well, nevertheless he principally embraced the promise, by which God confirms his own for the future.[73]

Calvin thus circumscribes the relationship between temporal blessings and faith in God's providential word: to contemplate God's providence is to rest not on externals but on God's promise of providential care. The manifestations of God's goodness in history, like those in nature, provide occasion for wonder, thanksgiving, and praise; they even, as Calvin remarks at the end of his comments, strengthen hope in eternal life.[74] But they have this effect only for the faithful who find the ground of their faith in the word. In other words, the ladder of present prosperity is only stable when it rests on the firm floor of God's providential promise.

Calvin's Exegesis of Psalm 48: The Church as Mirror

Like Psalm 23, Psalm 48 leads Calvin to discuss God's special providential care of the godly as opposed to God's providence over human affairs in general. In this case, however, Calvin takes a broader view, focusing not on the individual example of David but rather on God's protection of the chosen people at large. In his comments Calvin develops views that he mentioned briefly in his exegesis of Ps. 29:9b and Ps. 33:12–13 and 18–19: first, that a proper apprehension of God's providential activity is restricted to the faithful, and, second, that this activity is most clearly evident to them in God's providence manifested in God's protecting and preserving of the church. As in his comments on Psalms 8 and 23, Calvin stresses the important role of the present experience of God's favor in strengthening faith. However, he underscores at the end of his comments that the assurance of God's protection of the church, too, though aided by the actual experiences of deliverance and the signs of God's promise in the temple and the steadfastness of the holy city, derives ultimately from a distinct knowledge of God's steadfastness apprehended by faith in the promise.

The first three verses of Psalm 48 extol the glory and beauty of Zion and observe that God is known as a defense or mighty help in its palaces. For Calvin this marks a distinction between the church and the rest of the world. God not only bestows a special blessing on the chosen people in setting them apart from the rest of humanity but also shows his face more visibly in the protection of the church than in the regulation of human affairs in general:

> Therefore, although his wisdom, goodness, and justice so shine forth [*refulgeant*] in the general governance of the world that no part is void of his praise, but rather material for praising him is found everywhere, the prophet, nevertheless, celebrates here the glory of God in protecting the church. He says that he is great and worthy of praise in the holy city—why not also in the whole world? Certainly, as I said, there is no corner so secluded that his wisdom, justice, goodness, and remaining attributes do not penetrate. But since [God] desires that they be chiefly beheld in his church, not without reason does [the prophet] set before our eyes this mirror, in which God more clearly exhibits and represents his face to [our] view.[75]

In his comments on these verses, Calvin specifies particular aspects of this testimony. For example, the beauty of Jerusalem is not only a natural but also a spiritual beauty that derives from its being the seat of the temple and the home of the ark of the covenant. Similarly, the phrase "joy of the whole earth" refers not to its produce or climate but to it as the place from which salvation issues. That God is in the palaces teaches that the safety of the city depended on God's power and not on the stability or magnificence of its buildings. In discussing this last verse Calvin reminds his readers about the dangers of prosperity. Even God's special favor exhibited in the care of the church can be blinding when these blessings obscure the knowledge of the power and grace of God.[76]

After these opening comments Calvin turns from a view of the church as a manifestation of God's glory to the theme of sacred history as a prominent illustration of God's providential care. He finds that Ps. 48:4–7 relates a special instance in which God delivered the Israelites. He locates this event during the reigns of Ahaz, Hezekiah, or Asa. As a result of this deliverance, Calvin claims, the Jews "experienced by clear evidence that God was the protector of the holy city, when he opposed himself to the invincible power of [their] enemies."[77] He underscores the compelling nature of this experience in his comments on Ps. 48: 8, "As we have heard, so have we seen in the city of Jehovah of hosts [*exercituum*], in the city of our God." This passage, he argues, can be understood in one of two equally suitable senses. First, it can mean that this actual experience confirms for the faithful what they had previously only heard about concerning God's steadfastness. Second, it can mean that the bare promises on which the faithful had relied finally were fulfilled, and God's grace and salvation were clearly manifested:

Therefore this would mean that the faithful not only had a testimony of God's goodness and power in histories but [also] felt from experience and application and even saw with [their] eyes [*perspicere oculis*] what they had first known from hearing and the report of the fathers. And, moreover, that God always remains like himself, repeatedly confirming the age-old instances of his grace with constant proofs. The other sense is a little more subtle but nonetheless quite fitting; namely, that God made manifest in the event itself what he had promised his people, as if the faithful said that what they had previously only heard was exhibited to their eyes, because where only the naked promises of God appear, the grace and salvation of God are hidden in hope, but in the execution they are made conspicuous.[78]

Here Calvin suggests again the view that we saw in his comments on Ps. 46:8; namely, that without actual manifestations of God's providential activity faith in the promises is exceedingly difficult.[79] Yet in that case it was recollection of God's previous deliverance, related by the psalmist, that "proved the best means of strengthening faith." In Psalm 48, however, the faithful declare that they see God's hand in the present. Moreover, Calvin's comments imply that this is a real, sensible seeing. It is noteworthy that throughout his comments he generalizes his observations about the historical city, Jerusalem, and the particular deliverance for his sixteenth-century audience.[80] He thus directs his readers' attention to the unfolding of sacred history in their own midst, applying the lessons of Psalm 48 to their own situation.

While leaving room in the exercise of faith for the ocular evidence and experience of God's present providence, Calvin explicitly restricts this apprehension to those who have already embraced the promise of adoption. He continues his comments on Ps. 48:8 by observing that "mention is made of the city of God because he has promised the same salvation not to all indiscriminately, but only to his elect and particular people." In the verse he also finds the view that the promise of adoption underlies the confession of God's providential protection: "The name Jehovah is used to express the power of God, but the faithful add immediately that he is their God in order to indicate [their] adoption, that they might dare to hope in him and familiarly take refuge in him."[81] Yet even though Calvin finds God's redemptive activity presupposed in the church's recognition of the divine hand, it is not faith's apprehension of divine election and adoption but rather faith's trust in God's providential activity that he underscores in his comments on the remaining verses. In other words, even speaking now of the God's activity toward the church, he is interested in faith's apprehension of God's providential activity, not of God's redemptive activity. In his comments on Ps. 48:9 and 48:14 Calvin discusses faith's role in the trials that the faithful faced while waiting for the divine deliverance. Verse 9, "O God, we have waited for your mercy in the midst of your temple," leads him to underscore faith's calming effect: faith overcomes external confusion and the judgment of carnal sense and waits patiently for God's help. In the absence of the manifestation of God's hand, faith looks to the visible signs of God's promise. Calvin notes that those under the old dispensation had a pledge of God's presence, and in this a promise of deliverance, in the temple; Christians, however, have an even clearer pledge of

God's presence through Christ.[82] Yet even these symbols, along with the holy city and the church, are outward things that, like the manifestation of deliverance that the Jews experienced, cannot be the ultimate object of faith. In his comments on the last verse of the psalm, "for this is our God forever and ever," Calvin says this explicitly:

> In this it is clear that the prophet did not speak of the palaces of Jerusalem so that the eyes of the godly would continue fixed on them, but so that they would raise themselves up to the beholding of God's glory. For wherever they turned, God wanted engraved marks of his grace to be discerned, indeed, that he be recognized as if present [in them]. From this we conclude that we ought to consider whatever dignity or excellence shines forth in the church as having no other purpose than that God might present [himself] to us and be celebrated in his gifts.[83]

By means of these signs, faith thus fixes the godly in a firm knowledge of God's character and purpose and holds them in calm expectation of God's help throughout the present life. Calvin observes that the word "this" in Ps. 48:14 ("that this is God") is not superfluous, since it distinguishes the true God from idols. Unbelievers have nothing firm or certain on which to stand, but since it is faith's nature to set before the godly a distinct knowledge of God, the godly do not waver. Rather, they declare here their knowledge of God's constancy in preserving the church and thus encourage and strengthen themselves for walking in the continued course of faith.[84]

In his exegesis of Psalm 48 Calvin reiterates but also develops themes that emerged in the interpretations of psalms considered earlier in this chapter: various arenas of providential activity, the role of externals and experience in building faith, faith as a certain knowledge of God's continuing care. His comments reveal a certain hierarchy of clarity among the various realms in which divine providence manifests itself. Though, as I have shown, eyes healed by faith perceive God's providence in the theater of the world and the looking-glass of history, the reality of the church most clearly reflects God's providential care. The church, Calvin remarks elsewhere, is the orchestra, or most conspicuous part, of the theater of the world.[85] He also indicates, as he had in his comments on Psalm 23, that this witness is even brighter in the church after the appearance of Christ in the flesh. Yet despite this clarity of manifestation, the external signs of God's presence in and care of the church and the actual experience of these by the faithful in the present still represent additions, however remarkable, to faith in the naked promises. In the absence of the actual experience of God's providence, faith is supported by the signs of God's presence in the church; it does not, however, remain fixed on the signs but looks through them to find its stability and certainty in God alone. Here it is worth underscoring that Calvin's restriction of the role of seeing and externals in faith reflects his general Pauline assumption that faith comes through hearing and is distinct from sight. Nevertheless, in discussions such as the one considered here, faith looks to the providential promise rather than to the gospel of salvation. Both are the word of God, and Calvin presupposes that those who grasp God's providential counsel do so only because they have already embraced the word of redemption. Still, the greater attention paid to creation and providence themes and the explicit linking of faith to God's providential activity represent a significant development in the notion of faith—underscoring that faith, for Calvin, has to do not only with future, hidden, or spiritual matters but equally with the realities of the whole of the present life.

The consideration of the relationship between faith and providence in Calvin's exegesis of Psalms 8, 23, and 48 has not only shown where faith most clearly perceives God's providence; namely, in God's care for and protection of the faithful or the church. In addition, it has shed light on what eyes healed by faith can see of God's providence in the realm of history. The faithful can glimpse God's care for the human race in general in the vestiges of human excellence and human dominion; moreover, they can perceive God's special care for the godly in temporal blessings, in past and present deliverances, and in the established signs of God's presence: Jerusalem, the sanctuary, the ceremonies and sacraments of worship. Yet faith in God's providence does not ultimately rely on these external evidences of God's ordering of history, since ultimately, for Calvin, history's witness is problematic: the Fall has diminished the clarity of human excellence and dominion, temporal prosperity now draws humans away from God, even the excellence of the church itself can obscure if human beings rest their eyes on the signs and neglect the reality to which they point. As I have just shown, Calvin finds troubling undercurrents even in such psalms as these, which praise the excellence of God's benefits in exceedingly positive tones and express confidence in God's continued favor.

Calvin confronts the theme of the hiddenness of God's providence and the problem of perception most directly in his exegesis of psalms in which the psalmist cries out to God for deliverance from a present persecution, or where the psalmist relates the depths of his despair and his subsequent rescue by God. As I have shown, in his comments on Ps. 46:3 and Ps. 23:4 Calvin insists that faith in God's providence is subject to necessary trials. Faith, relying on God's providential word, unfolds itself amid apparent disorder and conquers fear. Though, as we have seen in Calvin's exegesis of Psalm 46, faith in God's providence can be tried by turmoil in nature, it is more frequently the case in his commentary that providential faith is challenged by apparent disorder in the realm of history. Though numerous psalms lead Calvin to focus on this challenge, Psalms 9 and 73 raise the problem of the confusion of history to special prominence. His attempt to specify faith's response to this problem and its activity in the face of it in his exegesis of these two psalms reveals most clearly his concept his concept of the special trial and particular vision of providential faith.

Calvin's Exegesis of Psalm 9: The Eye of Faith

Psalm 9 praises God and tells of God's marvelous works (Ps. 9:1) in routing the psalmist's enemies and executing righteous judgment; the psalm then proclaims the perpetuity of God's judging activity and God's succor of the poor and afflicted. The psalmist repeats these themes in the latter part of the psalm (Ps. 9:13–20), in which he asks for God's mercy and predicts the downfall of the heathen, God's future judgment, and the vindication of the poor. Calvin attributes the psalm to David and dates its composition to a time in which David faces affliction from his enemies. He argues that David first recalls and celebrates God's past mercies and deliverances in order to stir himself up to pray for divine help in Ps. 9:13–20. In explaining these recollections and prayers, Calvin invokes again the idea of the perception or eye of faith to indicate how David and his readers are able both to perceive the hand of God in certain events and to rise above the confusion of the present to apprehend God's hidden providential order. In addition, Calvin offers various arguments for the necessity of affliction, finding in adversity itself evidence of divine providence.

According to Calvin, David opens the psalm by praising God and then declares that he will meditate on all the marvelous deliverances that God has accomplished on his behalf. David concentrates particularly on the miraculous manifestations of the divine power, since these more than God's ordinary works are especially suited to awaken our dead senses. In his comments, Calvin traces David's shift in perspective, from seeing the events simply in themselves to grasping, through faith, God's hand: "In the first part of the verse he narrates historically how [his] enemies were struck down or compelled to flee. Afterward he adds from the perception of faith that this did not take place by human means or by chance, but because God stood against them on the battle-front." David lifted "the eyes of his mind" to perceive that the true cause of his victory was God's hidden assistance.[86] In other words, faith functioned as an eye through which David perceived God's hidden providence *in* the events of history. Calvin urges his readers to follow David's example and not to limit their perception when they see their enemies fall.[87]

Calvin reiterates this view in his comments on Ps. 9:15–16, stressing there that the divine hand is particularly evident in situations when the wicked are caught in their own traps, a phenomenon that he elsewhere designates God's retributive providence.[88] Having prayed in Ps. 9:13–14 for God's assistance in this present trial, David now looks on his current afflictors with an attitude of confidence and triumphs over them. His statement about God's judgment in Ps. 9:16, which Calvin designates as brief and obscure, teaches nonetheless that the manifestation of such retributive judgment against the wicked is an especially evident display of God's power. As in his comments on Ps. 48:8, Calvin urges his readers to "open their eyes" to any such manifestations in their own experience, in order that their faith might be confirmed.[89] Thus perceiving God's judgments in past and present history through the eye of faith further increases faith in God's providence.

The shift to the perception of faith involves, in addition to this new perspective on events in the world, a glimpse into heaven. In Ps. 9:4–8 the psalmist proclaims that God sits on the seat of judgment, from which God vindicates the psalmist's cause and rebukes the nations, the wicked, and the enemy. Calvin refers God's activity as judge to God's ordering of history: from the throne of judgment, God executes his secret providence. He notes that there are various ways of explaining David's remarks about the desolations effected by the ungodly in Ps. 9:6. He inclines toward an ironic interpretation of David's words, which opposes the dreadful power of the enemy to God's abrupt termination of it. God's apparently sudden exercise of judgment catches the enemy by surprise. This same abruptness, however, is a comfort to the godly, who realize that it is when things are most confused that God, who always sits as a judge in heaven, will stretch forth his hand:

> God appeared at just the right time, when things were really so greatly confused. Therefore, whenever nothing but destruction presents itself to us [*nobis occurrit*], let us remember to cast [*coniicere*] [our] eyes quickly to the heavenly throne, from which God looks out for human affairs. We ought to repel all bouts of temptation with this shield: that God nevertheless sits as judge in heaven, [when] in the world it appears that we are reduced to extreme desperation. Indeed, when he hides [himself], not immediately remedying our evils, we ought to apprehend by the perception of faith his secret providence.[90]

Thus, looking to heaven, faith perceives God exercising his office as judge, even when events seem to belie his activity. More precisely, faith takes hold of God's "secret" providential ordering not yet manifest in God's works; that is, faith grasps the providential word.

Continuing these reflections in his comments on Ps. 9:8, "and he shall judge the world in righteousness," Calvin argues that David's earlier statements had testified that God's power is ever-active and not idle. In this verse, he says, David expands this view, showing that God does not confine his power to heaven but rather manifests it in helping humans. Calvin refutes the idea, which he attributes to Epicurus, that God is devoted to ease and pleasures. Even when God does not immediately succor those who are unjustly oppressed, God does not cast off his care of them.[91] In other words, when faith apprehends God's secret providence, it sees neither an idle God nor a God indulging himself in his own pleasures. Rather, it perceives God's ever-active though hidden power, ordering events and ready to comfort the godly.[92]

Waiting for God to restore order to the confusion in the world, the perception of faith not only looks to past deliverances and beholds God sitting on the judgment throne but also extends itself into the future. From the new perspective attained in the midst of his prayer, David declares, in Ps. 9:17, the impending downfall of the wicked. Calvin observes:

> Here, then, is described [that] sudden and unexpected change, by which God, when he pleases, restores to order things confused. Therefore, whenever the ungodly soar on high, devoid of all fear, let us observe attentively with the eyes of faith that a grave is prepared for them, and be certainly persuaded that the hand of God, although hidden, is very near, which can turn their course, by which they aim at heaven, back toward hell in a moment.[93]

Thus even in the present prevailing of the ungodly, the godly, through the eye of faith, have a glimpse of the manifestation of providence to come.

Throughout his development of the theme of the perception or eye of faith in his exegesis of Psalm 9, Calvin turns repeatedly to the problem of affliction. Affliction clouds the eye of faith, since it appears to contradict God's providential promise to the faithful. Yet Calvin also suggests various benefits of affliction. For example, I have already shown how Calvin finds the disorder of David's present affliction, viewed through the eye of faith, to point to God's active regulation of affairs and God's impending judgment. Indeed, God's apparent delay in putting an end to unjust affliction is a part of providence; Calvin notes in his comments on Ps. 9:8 that God postpones aid in order to exercise the patience of his people.[94] In keeping with this view, Calvin reads Ps. 9:9, which describes God as a refuge to the poor and a protection in trouble, as saying that God intentionally delays his aid until the most appropriate time. In so doing, God is not desisting from his providential duties; rather, by exercising the godly in this way, God "lights up a lamp so that his judgments appear more clearly."[95] Another benefit is described in Calvin's comments on Ps. 9:12, which says that God has not forgotten the cry of the afflicted: affliction keeps the godly from becoming overly attached to the present life.[96] Verse 18 similarly declares that the poor will not be forgotten, leading Calvin to remark that the reason why God sometimes seems to forget them for a time is to awaken them to prayer.[97] Finally, in his comments on Ps. 9:20, in which the psalmist beseeches God to strike the nations with fear, Calvin applies this request to the godly as well as the ungodly. God, he observes, subdues even his own people by fear. However, God does this mildly, while he deals more harshly with the reprobate. The godly are humbled by fear and made aware of their own weakness. The ungodly, however, do not profit from this chastisement but are only left in shame and confusion.[98]

Calvin's Pauline notion that true knowledge of God is hidden from fallen human senses forms the backdrop for his reflections. Yet this does not mean that a perception of God through the things that are made is no longer possible. Earlier I showed Calvin stressing, in his exegesis of Psalm 33, that God's providential counsel is not hidden (*absconditum*) in heaven to be viewed from afar but is revealed in the present, earthly realm: in the glass of the word and in the salvation of the church. Even here God's providence is invisible except to the eye of faith. In his exegesis of Psalm 9, Calvin explores in more detail how faith overcomes the blinding effects of external circumstances, especially affliction, to grasp God's secret providence, hidden from the eye of sense. However, in contrast to his exegesis of Psalms 33 and 48, Calvin does not dwell on the word or promise contained in scripture as the medium of revelation. Instead he focuses, as he does elsewhere in his comments on Psalm 48, on the visibility of God's providence in God's works in history. Perhaps this focus on the revelation of providence in history can be explained in part by Calvin's overriding concern in his exegesis of Psalm 9 to make sense of suffering and affliction. Rather than urging his readers to close their eyes to external circumstances and seek refuge in God's promise of providence, Calvin instead implores them here to open their eyes and find in their afflictions themselves evidence for God's providence. Reposing in the vision of God on the throne of judgment, exercising his providential counsel, faith apprehends God's secret counsel, that is, God's powerful and active providential word that structures and guides all events. Faith in this providential word then turns its eyes to external circumstances and views them in a different light. Faith offers a new perspective that makes sense of the events of history past and present and provides a glimpse into the events of the future. The eye of faith not only sees God's hand in the often sudden exercise of judgment but also realizes God's providence in the very midst of confusion and affliction, perceiving these now as divine works.

Calvin's Exegesis of Psalm 73: The View from the Watchtower

Like the book of Job, Psalm 73 raises for many interpreters the question of God's justice. While opening with a declaration of God's goodness, the psalmist quickly calls this into question by pointing to the prosperity of the wicked and to the vanity of his own integrity. Confessing, however, his own inability to understand this inequity, he asserts that he will perceive the answer to the dilemma in God's sanctuary (Ps. 73: 16–17). He thus overcomes his doubts and resolves the problem of God's apparent injustice by asserting the future judgment of the wicked and that he, in contrast, will continue forever in God's presence. For Calvin, Psalm 73, like Psalm 9, raises the problem of perception of divine providence in a time of affliction. However, Psalm 73 offers him a more dramatic portrayal of the psalmist's affliction, specifies (in Ps. 73:3) more precisely the exact nature of the psalmist's trial, and presents a more detailed account of the psalmist's shift to the new perspective on his situation in Ps. 73:17–18. In his comments, Calvin is less interested in specifying the various aspects of faith's perception of history and the various benefits of affliction. Instead, he is more concerned to contrast the false and dangerous view of events through merely carnal eyes, which he finds detailed in Ps. 73:3–9, with the perception of faith, which the psalmist ultimately obtains in Ps. 73:17–18. Psalm 73 thus presents him with a less broad but more intense account of faith's activity in affliction. In explicating this, Calvin depicts both the depths to which faith in God's providence may fall as well as the height to which it may rise in overcoming doubt.

Like earlier exegetes, Calvin finds that the mention in Ps. 73:3 of the prosperity of the wicked sets forth the central problem of the psalm, and, moreover, he links this problem to question of God's providence.[99] His comments on Ps. 73: 1–9 explore the problem in detail. In an unusually long preface to these comments, he comes immediately to the issue of faith in God's providence, noting providential faith's inherent weakness as well as the external challenges confronting it:

> We all confess that the world is ruled by divine providence, but if this were truly fixed in our hearts, the constancy of our faith would be far greater in overcoming adversity. Now when the smallest opportunity whatever shakes this knowledge from us, it is evident that we have not yet been earnestly and truly persuaded [of it]. Besides, Satan, with innumerable artifices, spreads darkness over us, and in the confused things in the world there is so great a mist that it is difficult to maintain that God takes care of [things on] earth.[100]

Their vision clouded, godly and ungodly alike imagine that chance is the arbiter of all affairs. The psalmist (who Calvin would like to believe is David) finds himself precisely in such a fog, and he therefore opens the psalm "abruptly" with a declaration designed to dispel the mist of his false imaginations. With a cry as emphatic "as if he had escaped from hell," he denounces the "judgment of his flesh," which had led him to doubt God's providence, and he declares, in essence, that despite appearances, God extends his providence especially to God's own. Calvin finds that the psalmist then explicates the details of his temptation: he envies the prosperous condition of the wicked, who enjoy good health without constant reminders of their mortality (Ps. 73:4), often appear to be free from common human afflictions (73:5), vaunt their pride and violence as if these were pieces of fine jewelry (73:6), and are led by their ever-increasing prosperity (73:7) to antinomianism (73:8) and blasphemy (73:9). In cataloging these advantages and comforts, Calvin reiterates the point he made in his comments on Ps. 9:8; namely, that God purposely spares his judgment of the ungodly and heaps these benefits on them "for the purpose of trying our faith."[101] But David does not yet realize this. Though his cry in Ps. 73:2, "my feet had well-nigh slipped," warns that all are in danger of falling unless they are retained by the power of God, nevertheless, the prosperity of the wicked pierces David to the heart.[102]

Scattered throughout Calvin's comments are references to classical literature designed to strengthen his case that judgment of events through the eyes of the flesh leads universally to a denial of divine providence.[103] In contrast to these representatives of the natural human reaction to the confusion of history, David is, in the course of the psalm, able to restrain carnal sense by taking up the perception of faith. In his comments on Ps. 73:10–17, Calvin traces the psalmist's subsequent responses to the confusion confronting him and uncovers a shift from the judgment of sense to the eye of faith. He first underscores the abysmal depths to which the psalmist and, by extension, the godly, are driven. He understands Ps. 73:10 both as a rejection of all religion by hypocrites in the church and, equally legitimately he says, as referring to the elect's departure from the path of true religion. In keeping with this latter interpretation, the question of Ps. 73:11, "How does God know?" emerges from the mouths of the faithful themselves. However, Calvin warns, they do not fall completely into blasphemy. Rather, this cry of desperation is a prayer:

> The godly, however, disburden themselves into the bosom of God before these depraved and detestable thoughts can penetrate their minds. They ask nothing but to acquiesce in his secret judgments, the reason for which escapes them. The meaning of this passage is that not only the ungodly, when they see the turbulence of things in the world, ascribe a blind government to fortune, but also the faithful themselves are led to doubt God's providence. And they are wonderfully restrained by God's hand, lest they be plunged directly into this abyss.[104]

Thus the first stage is a prayer, itself made possible only through God's protective hand.[105] David then recalls the prosperity of the ungodly and recounts the apparent vanity of his own integrity in Ps. 73:12–15. Calvin finds this problematic, since David appears to seek a reward for his innocence. Yet in Ps. 73:15–17 the psalmist's perspective changes. Calvin argues that in 73:15, which refers to God's children and concludes "I have transgressed," David perceives the sinfulness of his thoughts and bridles himself. In 73:16, "although I applied my mind to know this, it was a trouble in my sight," he admits the incomprehensibility of providence: "The intent of the words is that although he turned his mind this way and that, yet by [his] reasoning he could not comprehend how God, amid such great disorders, governs the world." It is thus necessary, Calvin notes, that whoever would be certain about God's judgments rise to a "higher level" than natural reasoning.[106]

The psalmist finally attains this higher level in Ps. 73:17, "until I entered into the sanctuaries of God, and understood their end." Calvin rejects understanding the sanctuaries merely as heavenly mansions. While it is true, he argues, that no one can judge God's providence correctly without ascending to heaven, it is simpler and more natural to understand "sanctuaries" as "heavenly teaching." In other words, it is from the word that human beings gain knowledge of God's providence: "David skillfully puts 'entering into the sanctuaries' for coming to God's school, as if he said, 'Until God be my schoolmaster, and I learn from his word what my mind otherwise could not contain, I fall short in considering the government of the world.' "[107] Especially in light of the mention of God's school, an image that he uses in the *Institutes*, Calvin appears to mean in this instance the word in scripture. He argues that this external teaching, however, is not enough; it must be accompanied by the work of the Spirit. Thus, David's language embraces both the word and the secret illumination of the Spirit. This secret illumination refers to faith, as is implied a little later, when Calvin argues that two steps are necessary in order to understand the end of the wicked and God's present work in their prosperity, that is, to profit from the contemplation of God's works: "We must first ask him to open our eyes (since those who want to have from themselves penetrating vision are nothing but fools) and then we must give authority to his word."[108] Thus implicit in the psalmist's cry is a prayer for a new, divinely given perspective grounded in God's promise of care, that is, for restored faith in God's providential word.

His faith in God's providence restored, the psalmist enjoys, in Ps. 73:18, a view of God's future restitution of order similar to that described in Ps. 9:17. Here Calvin invokes a favorite image, that of the watchtower (*specula*), to express the new perspective of faith.[109] From the vantage point of the watchtower David obtains view of things previously hidden: he sees that the wicked will fall and that they prosper now only to exercise the faith of believers. In his comments on Psalm 73:18, "surely thou has set them in slippery places; thou shalt cast them down in destruction," Calvin argues that, since David's earlier conflicts have drawn him closer to God, he now speaks with a composed mind, saying, "I now see, Lord, how you proceed; for, although the ungodly continue to stand for a while, yet they are perched on slippery places, that before long they may fall in destruction."[110] David sees that, though both the ungodly and the godly are subject to uncertainties in the present, it is only the ungodly who are on slippery places. The godly may stumble, but they are grounded in the power of God, and the hand of the Lord supports and sustains them.[111] Thus the view from the watchtower confirms and strengthens the knowledge of God's counsel (God's providential word) obtained in the sanctuaries of scripture:

> For we are not to imagine a wheel of fortune, which mixes all things in its turning, but we must hold to a counsel of God, which the prophet here mentions, and which he says is revealed to all the godly in the sanctuary; namely, that [all things] are driven by the secret providence of God.[112]

Providential faith, as I have shown repeatedly, for Calvin rests properly in the word but also illuminates God's works and is in turn made stronger through this vision. In his comments on the remaining verses of Psalm 73, Calvin reminds his readers that through faith they can see God's judgments in daily affairs.[113]

The prominence of the theme of confusion and disorder in history, raised particularly in Calvin's exegesis of Psalms 9 and 73, signals the inherent fragility of the historical order. For Calvin, history, like nature, has no intrinsic integrity. Both realms derive their stability only from God's word. And in both cases, Calvin views this inherent instability as a profound proof of God's underlying sustaining care: natural disasters and historical turmoil do not undermine but rather attest to divine providence. Nonetheless, history's witness appears more obscure, even to eyes of faith. God's glory is so manifest in the structure of the cosmos that even natural philosophers note it and the rude and simple marvel at it, though, of course, they cannot properly comprehend it without eyes of faith. But even the faithful, like David, are prone to slip when they see the confusion of history and in times of prosperity are ever in danger of delusion. Yet Calvin also presents the witnesses to providence in nature, in human affairs in general, and in the church as increasing orders of clarity. Humans are more affected by what they personally experience, and, as we saw in his exegesis of Psalm 8, the experience of history is more personal. Thus the church, as he tells his readers in his comments on Psalm 48, is the brightest mirror of God's providence. The church is the orchestra of the theater because in the church the word of salvation is spoken. Apart from this word, there can be no saving faith; without saving faith, fallen humans cannot have true knowledge of God's providence and, therefore, can have no providential faith. Moreover, providence manifests the glory of God, which is, for Calvin, most clearly evident in God's care for the elect, the crowning point of the new creation.

Calvin's exegesis of Psalms 8, 23, 48, 9, and 73 underscores that the manifestations of providence in history, as in nature, though considered with the eyes of faith, are never its proper object. Nonetheless, he maintains that eyes of faith can and do perceive God's present and ongoing care for all humans but especially for the elect. In prosperous times, eyes healed by faith perceive in the Father's bounty the manifestation of his gracious providential word. In times of trial, they trust in God's promise of protection and recognize God's sustaining and correcting hand even in their afflictions. Providential faith thus corrects their blindness and illumines the darkened mirror of history, returning it, like nature, to its original purpose as a testimony to God's goodness, power, and glory.

Conclusion

> It is true, indeed, as Paul says (2 Cor. 5:7), that as long as we wander in the world, we walk by faith and not by sight. But as we nevertheless discern God's image not only in the mirror of the gospel but in all the daily evidences of his grace, let each of us awaken from our stupor so that spiritual felicity might satisfy us until God shows himself for us to enjoy him face to face.[114]

A concern for saving faith is not completely absent in Calvin's commentary on the Psalms. It arises, for example, in his treatment of Psalm 32, the psalm cited by Paul in Romans 4. Here and elsewhere Calvin enters into discussions of the merit of works, free remission of sins, faith as the instrument of justification, and the certainty of salvation.[115] Nevertheless these issues, which clearly dominate the discussions of faith that I have considered in the *Institutes* and the New Testament commentaries, are not the focus of Calvin's depictions of faith in the Psalms. Instead, pursuing ideas that he put forth in his comments on 2 Thess. 1:5–10 and Phil. 4:4–7, Calvin here expands the view of faith that dominates in those discussions and develops the idea of a providential faith, faith in God's activity as creator and sustainer of nature and history. While this is a faith directed toward God's activity apart from redemption, providential faith nonetheless presupposes saving faith. It is not another faith but rather an extension of faith in Jesus Christ; in other words, there is one faith for Calvin, but this faith, like the knowledge of God, is twofold. For this reason providential faith exists within the same (largely Pauline) boundaries that determine Calvin's idea of faith in the New Testament commentaries. For instance, in the distinction between God's providential word and God's providential work, one senses Calvin's Pauline assumption that faith arises out of hearing and that it rests on the word and not on external manifestations of power, such as miracles. God's providential works are not the object of faith but are still contemplated by the eye of faith, supporting and sustaining providential faith in the same way that the miracles in the Gospel of John prepare for and confirm faith in God's redemptive work.

Providential faith, like saving faith, relies on the word. However, the word that is the ultimate object of providential faith is God's Logos ordering creation and history, revealed especially in scripture but also, for redeemed eyes, in God's works in nature and history. As Calvin stresses repeatedly, human beings cannot apprehend this word until they have first grasped, through faith, God's promise of mercy in Jesus Christ. As the oft-cited passage from Calvin's "Argumentum" to the Genesis commentary (1554) confirms, the apprehension of God through the creative word and in the *opera dei* is not in opposition to christological knowledge but is itself a knowledge of God through Christ.[116] Indeed, as the quotation at the head of this section suggests, God's children in a sense defraud themselves if they seek the divine image *only* in the gospel—if they limit faith to soteriological matters and "Christ" to the word's redeeming activity. Hearing the word of fatherly mercy in redemption they ought to progress to faith in God's powerful creative and providential word, because this faith provides them with new eyes that can perceive the daily evidences of God's grace. True and complete "spiritual felicity" consists not only in reconciliation with God through faith in the gospel but also in a renewed relationship to God's good creation. In establishing this link through the idea of providential faith, Calvin underscores the value of the present life: faith does not simply direct believers toward their future inheritance but fixes their eyes on God's good gifts and their own task in the present.[117] Providential faith completes the vision of God *in* this world and offers a fuller proleptic taste of the face-to-face vision to come.

5

Calvin's Twofold Notion of Faith

In an essay written thirty years after his groundbreaking study of 1952 (and subsequently incorporated into the expanded 1994 edition), Dowey explores anew the "foundational place" of knowledge and, in particular, the twofold knowledge of God, in Calvin's theological thought. He stresses again the importance of faith, arguing that faith is "the threshold of all Calvin's thought, because of the revelatory or cognitive priority of the soteriological."[1] Faith rather than scripture provides the entrance to knowledge of God; faith and not objective biblical authority resolves the problem of knowledge. Calvin's thought is therefore dominated by a soteriological center, but within his soteriology itself is "an inherent dialectic by which it is related to and is set within non-soteriological elements upon which it depends for its meaning."[2] As in his earlier book, Dowey speaks of faith with respect to the soteriological center and links scripture to the nonsoteriological material, arguing that, for Calvin, "scripture is always used in support of knowledge of the Creator, and faith in support of knowledge of the Redeemer."[3] Dowey does not deny that scripture also provides knowledge of God's redemptive work or that faith in Jesus Christ is the prerequisite for grasping the knowledge of God's creative activity expressed in scripture.[4] Nonetheless, Dowey's discussion, especially in its location as the new chapter 6 in the third edition of his book, suggests scripture and faith as two "supports" for knowledge of God that are separated on the basis of the *duplex cognitio Domini*.[5] Consistent with his intent to demonstrate that the problem of knowledge is not exhausted with the treatment of the authority of scripture in book 1, Dowey argues for a connection between the authority of scripture and faith that originates in the 1539 *Institutes* and represents Calvin's consistent view from that point on.

Yet certain aspects of Dowey's argument suggest a correlation between faith and scripture that is misleading. In 1559, the twofold character of Calvin's thought (that is, the impact of the twofold knowledge of God on his whole theology) is manifest not in the relationship between the doctrines of scripture's authority and of faith but rather in the relationship between *piety* and faith. The discussion of scripture, as I will show, needs to be related instead to Calvin's broader understanding of the word, and in particular to his twofold understanding of the divine Logos as both ordering creation and providence and manifest as the word made flesh, Jesus Christ. Indeed, Dowey says as much when discussing the concept of accommodation.[6] Nevertheless, Dowey also correlates scripture and faith in speaking of the relationship between "Scripture and the internal witness of the Spirit, on the one hand, and Christ and the illumination of the Spirit, on the other." He proposes to relate these through a dialectical "double presupposition." According to this principle, the former (scripture and the Spirit's internal witness to the authority of scripture) provides knowledge of God's creative activity that is the logical or conceptual presupposition of the knowledge provided by the witness of Christ and the illumination of the Spirit (i.e., faith) to God's redemptive activity. Concurrently, this latter knowledge is the epistemological presupposition of the former. While acknowledging the valid qualifications of his view advanced by E. David Willis, Krusche, Charles Partee, and Heiko A. Oberman, Dowey nonetheless underscores the importance of not losing the proper dialectic (against Krusche), especially through the use of the "extra" formula (against Oberman and, to a lesser degree, Willis).[7] Yet in the end, Dowey does not satisfactorily resolve the issue of the relationship between faith and scripture, as is evident in the two elements of his presupposition: God the creator and sustainer known in scripture and God the redeemer grasped in the knowledge of faith. Only those who have faith have knowledge of God the creator. As Dowey argues concerning knowledge of God's providence, "they know it through the 'spectacles' of Scripture. . . . and they know it, not directly, but through faith that their Redeemer is the God of creation-providence."[8] However, this connection between faith and knowledge of God the creator is indirect: "the knowledge of faith, properly speaking, is not God as seen in his general creative activity, but as seen in the special work of redemption in Christ."[9]

Clearly Dowey has warrant for restricting faith proper to God's redemptive activity in Christ. Not only Calvin's final placement of the discussion of faith within the context of the knowledge of God the redeemer but also his repeated distinctions within the realm of special revelation seem to demand such a limitation. However, in light of my findings in chapter 4, one must ask whether this restrictive view of faith can accurately reflect the fullness of Calvin's doctrine of faith. Consideration of his treatment of the theme "faith" in the final edition of the *Institutes* (1559) suggests that it is not. Calvin locates his main discussion of faith in the context of soteriology for polemical as well as practical reasons. While it is true that the description of saving faith in book 3 represents the primary element of faith for Calvin, the reflections in book 3 do not fully exhaust his understanding of the nature and role of faith any more than the reflections on Christ in book 2 represent all that he has to say about Christology. Rather, in 1559 he assumes a twofold notion of faith, which is not two faiths or faith in two Gods or Christs but rather one faith inevitably comprising two elements; or, alternatively, one act of believing in a twofold motion.[10] One can discern both elements when one recognizes that the correlate of the discussion of faith is not Calvin's treatment of the authority of scripture but instead the notion of piety.

Tracing the relationship between piety and faith reveals that both God's creative/ providential activity and God's redemptive activity are known through faith. Moreover, while God in God's general creative activity is not strictly speaking the object of *saving* faith, such activity *is* properly the object of a providential faith that, together with saving faith, constitutes piety.[11] Hence I agree with Dowey that faith, for Calvin, in its proper sense is knowledge of God's redemptive activity. However, it is also appropriate, proper, and, indeed, necessary to understand the knowledge of faith as including a knowledge of God in God's general creative activity as well.

The twofold notion of faith has its roots in the *duplex cognitio Domini*. Whether or not one holds, with Julius Köstlin, Dowey, and B. A. Gerrish, that this twofold knowledge constitutes the basic structure of this final edition, one can still acknowledge the significance of this feature. Evident in several specific references to a division in the material, the distinction must be taken into account in the investigation into Calvin's view of faith in the 1559 *Institutes*. Clearly the consideration of his views on faith needs to attend especially to the location and shape of the specific discussion of faith, now in book 3, as part of knowledge of God the redeemer. However, the investigation must also turn to book 1 in order to determine whether the notion of providential faith has left any noticeable imprint on the discussion of knowledge of God the creator. Indeed, the discussion of faith in book 3 itself appears to legitimate such a move, insofar as one particular addition, to be discussed hereafter, to the section on faith in book 3 actually points back to the discussion in book 1. This indication from faith to creation and providence complements the pointers in the discussions of God's creative and providential activity to the discussion of faith that emerged in the 1539 *Institutes*. Hence my investigation into the final shape of Calvin's understanding of faith turns first to his treatment of saving faith in book 3, chapters 1–2, and then to the discussion of piety, creation, and providence in book 1.

Faith and Knowledge of God the Redeemer

Attention to Calvin's discussion of faith in book 3 reveals, first of all, a new immediate context, in which faith is treated as the principal work of the Holy Spirit rather than in a preface to the discussion of the Creed. Schützeichel points out that the link between faith and the work of the Spirit stems from the explanation of the article professing belief in the Holy Spirit in the 1536 *Institutes*.[12] In 1539 Calvin included in his treatment of faith itself several paragraphs arguing, largely on the basis of Paul and John, for the need for the Spirit's inner illumination and sealing of the word.[13] Now, however, Calvin actually treats faith as part of the doctrine of the Holy Spirit, which, while not exhausted in book 3, nevertheless finds its center there. In chapter 1, three heavily revised and expanded sections on the work of the Spirit pick up the strands of earlier discussions of the Spirit's nature and activity and shift the focus to the Spirit's inner work effecting communion with Christ.[14] A fourth section, mostly new in 1559, introduces the discussion of the Spirit's principal work, faith, through which the Spirit unites people to Christ and they receive Christ's benefits. To support his assertions here of the supernatural and exclusive role of the Spirit, Calvin relies chiefly on citations from the Johannine writings and from Paul. Pauline passages and Augustine's use of John 6:44–45 also form the basis for a reiteration of these views in an expansion and a new section, added to the arguments for the Spirit's illumination, that appears later within the discussion of faith itself.[15]

Important in the 1559 edition in addition to the location of faith within the context of the soteriological work of the Spirit are the renewed emphases at several points on Christ as the object of faith and on mystical union with or engrafting into Christ as faith's principal benefit. In *Institutes* 3.1.3, Calvin cites four texts from Paul to support union with Christ. Shortly thereafter he elaborates on the theme of Christ as the true object of faith (3.2.1–2). An earlier version of this particular discussion appeared at the very beginning of the chapter following the discussion of faith in the editions of 1539 to 1554.[16] This reworked and expanded discussion renders the christocentric element not only more prominent but also more explicit. Representative of this is the rewording of a phrase specifying the one means of redressing the calamity of sin: in all earlier editions Calvin said "namely, the Lord's mercy"; in 1559 he substitutes "the appearance of Christ the redeemer."[17] In *Institutes* 3.2.6 he expands and clarifies his view that Christ as the object of faith is Christ as revealed in the word of the gospel. Addressing potential counterexamples of Naaman the Syrian (2 Kings 5:1–14; Luke 4:27), Cornelius (Acts 10), and the Ethiopian eunuch (Acts 8) in *Institutes* 3.2.32, he argues that each of these persons exhibits an obscure but true knowledge of Christ and therefore upholds rather than refutes faith's christocentric character. Finally, in *Institutes* 3.2.35, pointing to the human inability to initiate faith, Calvin sums up his views by stating that Christ, by the Spirit, not only illumines humans into faith but also engrafts them into his body.

The seeds for these ideas, of course, lie in earlier editions of the *Institutes*, especially in an addition in 1543 where Calvin argues that, because of the union that they have with Christ, believers are certain of their salvation.[18] Nonetheless, as Emile Doumergue notes, new declarations of union with Christ were added in 1559.[19] Dowey in particular explores this aspect of Calvin's discussion in book 3 and elsewhere, seeking to show that the noetic aspect of faith is not separate from a total activity of the Spirit extending to intellect, will, body, and soul. Moreover, Dowey argues, Calvin's stress on a mystical union with Christ shows that faith is concerned not simply with future salvation but also with the present life.[20] In other words, through faith in Christ the Spirit works not only justification and eternal life but also sanctification and regeneration in this life. The former gifts come through the knowledge that is faith, the latter through the obedience that is the effect of faith. A further implication of Calvin's doctrine of mystical union is the particular understanding of faith's certainty or assurance, which, as I will show, achieves further precision in this edition.

Alongside these reiterations of faith's Christocentrism, Calvin adds new discussions in which he appears more willing to accept a broader range of phenomena under the understanding of faith. Discussing the biblical examples of Naaman, Cornelius, and the Ethiopian eunuch, Calvin concedes that they have an obscure but nevertheless true knowledge of Christ.[21] This admission confirms a notion of the "implicitness" of true faith that Calvin had developed earlier in book 3.[22] His discussion merits closer examination, since it serves simultaneously to underscore and expand faith's focus on Christ.

After opening his discussion in chapter 2 by stressing faith's explicit recognition of Christ the redeemer as its proper object, Calvin turns immediately to dispute a view of implicit faith that he attributes to Rome.[23] These polemical considerations actually stem from 1539, but before 1559 they were located later in the discussion of faith.[24] In the final edition, however, Calvin moves this section forward, introducing it with a sentence that had originally led into a critique of the scholastic distinction between formed and unformed faith. He now delays his treatment of *fides informis et formata* until *Institutes* 3.2.8. Before taking up this matter, he adds two new paragraphs elaborating his statements from 1539, in which he admitted that the imperfection of faith's knowledge is such that "most things are now implicit for us." He aims to contrast this allowable type of implicitness with the ignorance that he judges characterizes the Roman idea of implicit faith as superficial reverence for the church. His subsequent remarks point to one significant difference: true faith, though imperfect and therefore implicit, is nonetheless directed toward Christ. He cites Paul (Phil. 3:15 and Rom. 12:3) to suggest that faith is not yet perfect; he also says that experience teaches this. He then details the experience of the disciples when confronted with the resurrection to show that even imperfect faith looks to Christ:

> Not that they then began to believe, but because the seed of hidden faith—which had been dead, as it were, in their hearts—at that time burst through with renewed vigor! For there was in them a true but implicit faith because they had reverently embraced Christ as their sole teacher. Then, taught by him, they were convinced that he was the author of their salvation. And finally, they believed he came from heaven that, through the Father's grace, he might gather his disciples thither.[25]

These observations clearly recall Calvin's treatment of the resurrection story in his commentary on John 20:3. The disciples had embraced Christ not only as teacher but as author of *their* salvation. However, this faith remained "hidden" and was renewed through the experience of the resurrection, which convinced them of the truth of what Christ had taught them. Thomas, of course, represents an extreme case of the hiddenness of faith.

Calvin continues by mentioning two further instances from the Fourth Gospel (the court official with the dying son and the Samaritans, both in John 4) to illustrate a kind of pious affection or reverent attention that is a preparation for full faith. This is the faith of miracles, or particular faith, that *is* the beginning of faith—a teachableness that, Calvin argues, is "far different from sheer ignorance in which those sluggishly rest who are content with the sort of 'implicit faith' the papists invent."[26] Here Calvin openly admits what he appeared only cautiously to concede in the commentary; namely, that this initial teachableness or pious disposition constitutes a beginning of faith. Still, he notes, those who have been rendered teachable are called believers "not in an exact sense [*non quidem proprie*], indeed, but insofar as God in his kindness deigns to grace that pious affection with such great honor."[27] In 1559 he thus concedes an implicitness to all faith, insofar as it is mixed with unbelief. He also allows also for an implicit faith that is a preparation for faith proper.

Despite these concessions, Calvin still maintains that, strictly speaking, faith is restricted to Christ as revealed in the gospel. The restriction is important but not absolute; Calvin invokes it to indicate the primacy of such faith for salvation (the topic currently under discussion), not to assert that this is all that faith is. He stresses this limitation in *Institutes* 3.2.6, the section immediately following his important recognition of an implicit faith. Furthermore, his distinction within special revelation and his definition of faith appear in *Institutes* 3.2.7; these considerations are now supported by several references to the Psalms, which he invokes to prove that it is particularly God's goodness and mercy that are the object of faith. Calvin seeks to allow for a degree of implicitness without detracting from faith's proper object and without diminishing the ground for faith's certainty. This confirms Dowey's judgment that, properly speaking, faith is a knowledge of God's redemptive activity. However, the discussion indicates also that some other applications of the word "faith" are not illegitimate but only not primary.

Further expansions to Calvin's notion of faith appear following the treatment of unformed and formed faith in *Institutes* 3.2.8–10, which represents a compilation of two discussions separated in earlier editions: the polemic against the scholastic distinction between *fides informis* and *fides formata* that appeared toward the end of his earlier discussions of faith and the views he gave, at the beginning of these previous presentations, on a temporary kind of faith. In contrast to the issue just outlined, his expansions pertaining to the formed and unformed distinction are not at first as easily harmonized or integrated with his assumptions about faith's certainty. Yet ultimately this discussion marks a development in his understanding of the certainty of faith and especially of the relationship between believers' experience of assurance and doubt. To see this, one needs to consider his reordering and placement of his earlier comments on the distinctions in faith and then his expansions on the theme of faith among the ungodly.

In *Institutes* 3.2.8–10, Calvin lumps together various types of knowledge of God that he says can exist among the ungodly under the designation of so-called unformed faith.[28] His difficulty with the scholastic distinction (as he interprets it) appears to be twofold. On the one hand, he thinks that the idea of an unformed faith that is not saving and a faith formed by love that is saving reduces faith to mere assent. This suggests to him that it is not faith but rather the pious disposition that is ultimately saving. I suspect that, in the end, this is the reason for his rejection of unformed faith. True faith, Calvin contends throughout *Institutes* 3.2.8–9, never exists without the necessary pious disposition. Indeed, as I have just shown, a reverent and pious attitude characterizes even the kind of implicit faith that Calvin accepts. On the other hand, the scholastic distinction appears to suggest to him that unformed faith is a kind of preparation for formed faith. His discussion of temporary faith in *Institutes* 3.2.9–10 seems designed to exclude this possibility.

Now locating his discussion of temporary faith within his treatment of unformed faith, Calvin extends the notion of unformed faith to include a temporary faith exemplified in Simon Magus (Acts 8:13, 18) and illustrated in the parable of the sower (Luke 8:5–15, Mark 4:13, Matt. 13:20). This is, he admits, a certain sort of faith; these people are not just pretending to believe but really do believe. As noted by David Foxgrover, they exemplify for Calvin a kind of lesser hypocrisy, falling between the extremes of true faith and mere pretense.[29] They apprehend God's word or are at least conquered by its majesty but fall away when the gospel fails to take living root in their hearts. The distinction between temporary and true faith is therefore the degree to which the word takes hold in the heart:

> Whatever sort of assent that is, it does not at all penetrate to the heart itself, there to remain fixed. Although it seems sometimes to put down roots, they are not living roots. The human heart has so many crannies where vanity hides, so many holes where falsehood lurks, is so decked out with deceiving hypocrisy, that it often dupes itself.[30]

Calvin does not use the expression, but it might be true to his intent to say that temporary faith is an assent that arises out of the word but is not fully formed by it. This indicates the difference between Calvin's understanding of what constitutes the formative element in faith (the word, sealed by the Spirit) and the Roman view, where the assent of faith is formed by the infused gift of *caritas*. Apparently this encounter with the word is so powerful that those who believe for a time manage to convince not only others but also themselves that they have true faith.

Another difference can be seen in the fact that the Roman teaching suggests a sequential (but not necessary) progression from unformed to formed faith. Calvin's discussion of temporary faith in *Institutes* 3.2.9–10, however, seeks to drive a wedge between true faith and temporary faith. This contrasts sharply with the potential continuity that he earlier admitted between an implicit faith and full faith. It is noteworthy that he does not speak of temporary faith as a preparation for true faith but instead views it as a kind of tragic delusion that leads away from God. Ultimately this temporary faith is inferior to demons' faith.[31] Even Calvin's statements on this shadow, image, or phantom of faith prior to 1559 refer to a delusion of the human mind that, while arising from a confrontation with the gospel and a sense of its power, nonetheless derives no stability from firm adherence to the word. In these earlier editions the discussion of the word as the object of faith followed immediately, both strengthening the contrast between true faith and this temporary apprehension of the word and diminishing the force of the latter's challenge to faith's certainty.

Ultimately, however, Calvin's stance on the *fides informis et formata*, especially in 1559, is confusing. He denies that unformed faith can be called faith. A faith lacking a pious disposition does not even qualify as a kind of preparation for full faith as just outlined. Yet Calvin also holds that there is a temporary faith and that those who believe for a time are not just pretending but really do believe. What, ultimately, accounts for the difference between a true but implicit faith and temporary faith? Both arise out of the word, but one leads to true knowledge while the other leads to delusion—one to piety, the other to idolatry. This raises, among other things, the questions of the efficacy of the word of redemption and the relationship between the Spirit and the word. How is it possible for the word to give rise to temporary faith, when in Calvin's view the word is never separated from the Spirit? His subsequent discussion provides some insight as to how this happens.

The additions in *Institutes* 3.2.11–12 seek to specify more precisely the distinction between the temporary faith that may be found among the reprobate and the true faith of the elect. To the reworked refutation of unformed and temporary faith Calvin appends nearly verbatim three of his responses to Laelius Socinus in 1555 concerning the matters of faith among the reprobate and the assurance of faith.[32] Aware of the difficulties that the concept of temporary faith raises for the certainty of the elect, Calvin offers various ways of distinguishing true faith from the nearly identical feeling that the reprobate sometimes possess. It is important to note that he is here concerned not with those who are just pretending faith but rather with those who themselves think that they are believers. There are three facets to Calvin's argument, which he repeats throughout these sections. First, he attributes both dispositions (true faith and transitory faith) to the work of the Spirit. Second, he catalogues numerous degrees of difference between them. Finally, he insists that the idea that their faith might not be genuine ought to inspire believers to self-examination. His first point seeks to explain how the reprobate appear to have faith, a phenomenon that is not only biblically but also empirically verified. Referring to Heb. 6:4–6 and the synoptic accounts of the parable of the sower, Calvin asserts that the Lord himself offers a taste of his goodness and creates faith for a time in order to render the reprobate more inexcusable. Drawing on his exegesis of the passage from Hebrews, Calvin attributes this transitory faith to the lower working of the Spirit. The reprobate are justly said to believe that God is merciful toward them, they receive the gift of reconciliation, and they seem to have the same beginning of faith as believers.

While this apparently solves the problem of how the reprobate can have faith, it raises the more pressing question of how their faith is different from that of the elect. Calvin acknowledges this objection and, referring to Gal. 4:6, responds by stressing that true faith exhibits greater confidence and springs from an incorruptible seed. He goes on to indicate other differences, all of which reflect his earlier suggestion that the distinction lies in the degree to which the word takes root in the heart: the reprobate have only a confused awareness of grace and of the gift of reconciliation; they are illumined by a light that may fade away; the seed in their hearts is not kept incorruptible. The elect, in contrast, have the Spirit as their guarantee (Eph. 1:14); the elect alone have the Spirit of adoption. Both the elect and the reprobate have an awareness of divine love, but only the elect have been adopted into this love and made members of Christ. Therefore the reprobate, who lack the Spirit of adoption and communion with Christ, possess not true confidence but only a delusion of the flesh.

True faith is based on a firm foundation while temporary faith is not. Yet experience teaches that believers do not always enjoy greater confidence or an uninterrupted sense of the divine goodness. In light of this reality, how can people be sure that they have the true testimony to adoption rather than the lower working of the Spirit? More pointedly, how is one to explain the fact that believers do not enjoy unbroken confidence in divine grace? The distinction, for Calvin, lies in the fact that the elect have from the Spirit's testimony and through their union with Christ the ability to persevere in affliction. Calvin notes that both the elect and the reprobate have an awareness of God's love but that the elect also simultaneously perceive God's wrath. This experience forces them to affirm their trust in the Spirit's testimony. Affliction leads the elect to pray that God's wrath be averted, to flee to God for refuge, and to examine their hearts. Through this process of repentance their faith advances. Those, however, who possess what Calvin designates a common or transitory faith "deceive themselves with a false opinion" when confronted with God's wrath. They become sluggish in their faith and ultimately fall away completely.

The assurance of faith thus seems intimately tied to the experience of doubt and affliction. Faith that is tested is faith that is true. True confidence manifests itself in the struggle with doubt, whereas the reprobate only persist in their deluded overconfidence. As Willis points out, faith's assurance is not subverted but confirmed by trial: "In short, part of the God-given assurance of faith is the continual testing and movement to repentance God saves for the elect by which they are assured that God has not abandoned them to the false security and fleshly confidence to which they would otherwise incline."[33] True faith is dynamic, ever moving from the apprehension of God's wondrous and righteous anger to seize the promise of mercy, on which faith ultimately rests.[34] Ironically, perhaps, it is precisely faith's response to the word of God *apart* from the gospel that shows faith to be true and living.

Calvin concludes his considerations of the various phenomena claiming the title of faith with a new section (3.2.13) openly acknowledging that scripture's own use of the term "faith" is ambiguous.[35] Of particular interest is the attention that Calvin gives to Paul's diverse uses of the word "faith." After cataloguing several of these references, Calvin reiterates his interest in discussing faith from one particular perspective:

> But now we ask, of what sort is that faith which distinguishes the children of God from the unbelievers, by which we call upon God as Father, by which we cross over from death into life, and by which Christ, eternal salvation and life, dwells in us? I believe that I have briefly and clearly explained the force and nature of that faith.[36]

Reflecting back on his earlier considerations and on the variety in the Bible, Calvin restricts faith in his present discussion to saving faith but acknowledges other possibilities. It is noteworthy, moreover, that the faith that saves is in part implicit and proves its certainty precisely in the experience of trial. In the 1559 *Institutes* Calvin thus maintains the 1536 distinction between true faith and false pretenders to faith. However, he also presents a much more nuanced understanding of true faith by delineating more precisely faith's imperfect character and the nature of faith's certainty.

A final set of additions to the 1559 discussion of faith furthers Calvin's ongoing attempt to specify faith's certainty in the face of doubt and adversity as well its relationship to God's power. As I have shown, in earlier editions Calvin backs up his quest for certainty by appealing to Pauline proof texts. In the 1559 additions, however, he appeals not so much to Paul as to Old Testament texts, and especially to the Psalms. With recourse to the Old Testament, Calvin underscores the idea he put forth in *Institutes* 3.2.12; namely, that faith that is tested is faith that is true. Doubt and affliction take on a more positive function in the life of the believer. Earlier Calvin primarily stressed the inevitability of doubt given the imperfection of faith. Now, especially with the help of the Psalms, he emphasizes the seemingly marvelous necessity of the experience of doubt, temptation, and weakness. Though this theme appeared in the 1539 *Institutes* and in Calvin's treatment of Abraham in the 1540 Romans commentary, his additions in 1559 raise it to greater prominence.[37]

In 1559 Calvin introduces the theme of the inevitable temptation of faith at an earlier point in the discussion of faith's certainty. The first instance of this appears in *Institutes* 3.2.15. Calvin interpolates an acknowledgement of weakness and unbelief in order to stress the word as the ground of certainty. He cites texts from Psalms and Proverbs to commend the word.[38] These scriptural statements about the purity of God's word serve to rebuke the unbelief that is deeply embedded in human hearts and to uproot perverse doubts. Two minor additions found in *Institutes* 3.2.21 confirm this same point.

Adding to his 1539 discussion of the inevitability of temptation in *Institutes* 3.2.17, Calvin stresses the marvelous irony that affliction and doubt actually reveal faith's assurance. He introduces David as the prime example of this struggle. David, Calvin argues, exhibits an unquiet mind throughout his life. He points explicitly to the fact that David's trial arises when he encounters God's hiddenness: "For God has forsaken him, and has turned his hand, which was once his help, to his destruction [*ad perdendum*]."[39] Nonetheless, David's faith reveals itself amid this feeling of forsakenness:

> And yet—and this is something marvelous—amidst all these assaults faith sustains the hearts of the godly and truly in its effect resembles a palm tree: for it strives against every burden and raises itself upward. So David, even when he might have seemed overwhelmed, in rebuking himself did not cease to rise up to God. He who, struggling with his own weakness, presses toward faith [*ad fidem . . . contendit*] in his moments of anxiety is already in large part victorious.[40]

A statement in Is. 7:2 concerning the unstable heart of Ahaz (king of Judah) provides Calvin with a contrast to David. This verse compares the heart of the king to the trees of the forest that are shaken by the wind. Ahaz has heard the promise but trembles nonetheless. The faith of believers, in contrast, is more like a palm tree, rising up in the face of the storm: "believers, whom the weight of temptation bends down and almost crushes, constantly rise up, although not without difficulty and trouble." A short addition to the discussion of how believers are engrafted into Christ from 1543 (*Institutes* 3.2.24) repeats this idea. Even the fact that believers are united with Christ does not prevent them from violent temptations. True faith, however, continues in its search for God.[41] Calvin returns to David's example in an addition toward the end of his discussion of faith. Here Calvin specifies the true nature of believers' peace of mind, which consists not in the unbroken or even frequent experience of tranquillity but rather in the ability to rise up in the face of temptations.[42]

Calvin also stresses faith's role in turning adversities themselves into blessings. In 1539 he already indicated this in his discussion of the expectation of eternal life as the chief assurance of faith. There he intimated that (on the basis of Eph. 2:14) all things prosper for those reconciled to God. Still, he noted, this is a certainty of things promised in the word; namely, that God will never fail, that eternal life is beyond doubt, and that earthly miseries and calamities cannot prevent God's benevolence from being the elect's true happiness. In his 1559 expansion of this discussion, he points more explicitly to the idea that these miseries and calamities themselves occasion a greater sense of God's goodness:

> In short, if all things flow unto us according to our wish, but we are uncertain of God's love or hatred, our happiness will be accursed and therefore miserable. But if in fatherly fashion God's countenance beams upon us, even our miseries will be blessed. For they will be turned into aids to salvation.[43]

These comments, supported by subsequent references to Rom. 8:35, Ps. 23:4, and Ps. 33:12, suggest again the positive function of affliction and doubt.

The benefits of adversity was a prominent theme in Calvin's commentary on the Psalms. Though his ideas about this did not originate with his commentary, the Psalms texts provided him with an opportunity to reflect on this theme and a vocabulary for expressing it. As I have shown, Calvin draws on the Psalms repeatedly to support his ideas about faith's relationship to doubt and temptation. One other theme especially evident in the Psalms has left its mark on Calvin's revisions of the section on faith: the relationship between faith and God's power. Following his response to criticisms of his idea of the distinction in special revelation, he adds an entire section reinforcing his view that the word is the object of faith proper. To support this, he cites or refers to Ps. 9:10, Ps. 119:40–42, and 119: 94. In this discussion he says, however, that God's power is *also* an object for faith.[44] Drawing first on the example of Abraham in Romans 4 and then on Paul's own confession of God's might in 2 Tim. 1:12, Calvin subsequently makes extended reference to other Old Testament examples (Second Isaiah, David, Sarah, Isaac, and Rebecca) to stress the benefits faith derives from contemplation of God's works in the order of nature and toward individuals. He points to the ever-present danger of the tendency to doubt God's power and to detract from God's might. The essence of his position is expressed in his statement that "unless the power [*virtus*] of God, by which he can do all things, confronts [*occurat*] our eyes, our ears will barely receive the word or will not esteem it at its true value."[45] He makes two important points concerning this observation. First, by "power" he refers to God's "effectual might"; that is, what God actually does, not what God by virtue of absolute freedom would be capable of doing. Moreover, piety especially looks to those manifestations of God's power that show God to be a benevolent father. Calvin also carefully reminds his readers that there is no faithful apprehension of God's works without the word and that the word is faith's ultimate source of support. The word is God's secret bridle that constrains human weakness. He thus admits the importance of God's works and, indeed, ocular perception of them, but he places these strictly within the context of the verbal testimony of God's grace.[46]

These developments in the discussion of faith in the 1559 *Institutes* reflect exegetical insights that I have traced in Calvin's commentaries, primarily those on the New Testament. While the Pauline epistles continue to be an important source for Calvin's discussion, in 1559 he incorporates other biblical viewpoints to a much greater degree. Most obvious are the influence of his work on the Gospel of John in his discussion of the implicitness of true faith and the arguments advanced in his comments on Heb. 6:4 for a faith among the reprobate, attributed here to the lower working of the Spirit. As noted earlier, the latter section has its immediate origins in a nonexegetical context. Nevertheless, one cannot overlook the exegetical underpinnings of that earlier treatise, nor should one underestimate the significance of this non-Pauline addition that so apparently challenges or even transforms the certainty of Calvin's Pauline faith. As in earlier editions of the *Institutes*, Paul's influence is especially manifest in the discussions that reinforce the notion of faith's certainty, for example, in the descriptions of faith as the work of the Spirit and of faith's mystical union with Christ. These passages build on Calvin's specifications of the Spirit's illuminating and sealing activity in passages such as 1 Cor. 2:12, Eph. 1:13, and Eph. 3:12. The renewed notions of faith's Christocentrism and the theme of participation in Christ derive their chief support from Paul and from the Johannine writings. Finally, Old Testament examples, drawn especially from the Psalms, uphold the word of mercy or grace as the particular object of faith. Calvin also relies on the Psalms to support his views of the relationship between faith and adversity. The Psalms provide the vocabulary for the dynamic character of true faith and the image of faith as a palm tree ever rising up and reaching toward God's mercy. These images confirm the idea of assurance that Calvin sets forth in his response to Socinus. Faith's certainty is not an unbroken peaceful repose; this is more likely to mark hypocritical overconfidence! Rather, the assurance of faith manifests itself in the experience of forsakenness, doubt, and the hiddenness of God. Finally, Calvin uses the Psalms and other Old Testament examples as well as Paul to suggest a positive relationship between faith and God's works apart from redemption.[47] This last instance points back to the greatly expanded discussion of the knowledge of God the creator in book 1, especially in Calvin's statement there that a vision of God's works is beneficial only when viewed in the context of piety, since piety "always accommodates God's power to use and need and especially sets before itself the works of God by which he has testified that he is a father."[48]

Faith and Knowledge of God the Creator

I have shown that Calvin incorporates themes linked in his Psalms commentary to the idea of faith's relationship to God's providence into his discussion of saving faith in chapters 1 and 2 of book 3: he develops and explicates more fully the connections between faith and God's word apart from the gospel, between doubt and certainty in faith, and between faith's apprehension of God's mercy and of God's power. He also suggests faith's contemplation of God's works (especially those that reveal God's fatherly benevolence) in the order of nature and toward individuals. Yet these matters, such as God's creative word, the hiddenness of God,

God's power and majesty, and God's works in nature and history, receive their fullest explication in book 1. To what extent does Calvin's discussion here exhibit development of the idea of faith in God's activity as creator and sustainer? As noted earlier, already in 1539 Calvin links faith to contemplation of God's works in nature, to a consideration of divine omnipotence in the context of God's benevolence, and to the expanded theme of God's glory. Hence my concern in this section will be to explore ways that Calvin strengthens these connections and develops more explicit ways of speaking of faith in God's providence. On the one hand, structural and substantive changes evidence Calvin's continued efforts to broaden the soteriological focus that shaped the earliest edition of the *Institutes*. As noted by Schreiner, these efforts to include "creation themes" were in large part driven by polemical concerns but reflect in addition Calvin's exegetical development of these themes during the 1550s in his Old Testament commentaries and sermons.[49] On the other hand, his reorganization and deepening of these themes also points to a deliberate extension of the notion of faith to apprehend both God's redemptive activity in Jesus Christ and, on the basis of this, God's fatherly benevolence manifested in creation and history. To an extent unparalleled in earlier editions of the *Institutes*, Calvin invites his readers to view natural and historical occurrences from the perspective of faith. Though he cautions repeatedly against resting faith on God's works, he nonetheless argues that when faith properly relies on God's word and views God's works through the spectacles of scripture, believers are led to a fuller awareness of God's will *erga nos*. This deepened sense of God's fatherly benevolence and power is essential for the development of true piety. Saving faith and providential faith together constitute this attitude of reverence and love of God derived from the knowledge of God's benefits as both redeemer and creator.

Clear indication of the radical redactive measures that Calvin undertook in preparing the final Latin edition of his *Institutes* appears already in book 1, "Knowledge of God the Creator." The theme of knowledge of God of course opened every edition of the *Institutes* and was treated in detail in the first chapter ever since the Latin edition of 1539. As noted in my first chapter, the focus of this discussion was not so much what humans ought to know about God as rather how humans attain proper knowledge of God. In 1559, however, Calvin treats both topics, drawing on elements from five discrete chapters of the previous edition. He begins with a reworked version of his earlier chapter 1 and continues with discussions of the impropriety of figurative representations of the divine (from the exposition of the Decalogue), the Trinity (which had previously preceded the discussion of the Apostles' Creed), creation (from the exposition of the first article of the Creed), human nature as created (from the earlier chapter 2), and providence (drawn from the exposition of the first article of the Creed and from the discussion of providence that had followed the treatment of predestination).[50] This composite discussion now leads the reader from the means of knowledge of God the creator to the content of that knowledge. Beginning with the failure of the internal and external witness to lead fallen humans to proper knowledge of God and the discussion of scripture as a more effective testimony, Calvin proceeds to the scriptural teaching about God the creator. Here he details not only the content of what can be known of God's creative and providential activity from scripture. He also presents this teaching derived from the word as a guide and norm for apprehending God's hand—at least in part—in the natural and historical realm. Or, as Calvin expresses it metaphorically in an image drawn from his 1554 commentary on Genesis, scripture functions as "spectacles" for fallen, blinded humanity.

Essential to understanding how Calvin draws on the earlier material to construct book 1 is a grasp of the twofold knowledge of God, now explicitly articulated.[51] Repeatedly throughout his discussion Calvin stresses that his subject is God's creative activity apart from God's redemptive activity in Jesus Christ. Therefore in his discussion of human nature he draws only from those parts of the former chapter 2 where he had treated the original perfection of human nature. The discussion of the Fall and the corruption of human nature now appears at the beginning of book 2, as a prelude to Calvin's exposition of redemption in Christ. Similarly, he now separates the discussion of providence from that of predestination. The result is, as Dowey puts it, "an appropriate grouping of elements that had formerly been inappropriately interspersed among purely soteriological material."[52] As I have shown, the distinction between God's creative and redemptive activity was manifest already in the editions from 1539 on. Nonetheless, Calvin's explicit designation of the twofold knowledge in the 1559 edition and his simultaneous consolidation and expansion of the material constituting the knowledge of God the creator reflect a deepened sense of a distinction in divine revelation and, correspondingly, within the means of apprehending that revelation: namely, faith.

Some care must be taken to specify exactly what this distinction entails. First, the distinction is not between God *in se* and God revealed in an accommodated way to humans. The *duplex cognitio Domini* refers instead to a distinction within the latter, *within* revelation. However, as Dowey notes, the twofold character of the knowledge of God is not synonymous with the distinction between general revelation (creation) and special revelation (scripture). Rather, scripture is a source for both types of knowledge and a guide for discovering God's entire activity in the world.[53] Nor does the twofold knowledge correspond to the division between the Old and New Testaments. I would also point out that it does not conform to the distinction *within* special revelation between the knowledge of God's mercy proclaimed in the gospel and God's word of wrath. Rather, for Calvin knowledge of God's creative activity is, as I will show, primarily awareness of God's fatherly benevolence in creating, governing, and sustaining.

As Willis points out, the knowledge of God as redeemer and creator is not two knowledges but rather "one knowledge of God inevitably comprised of two elements, available to the community of the faithful."[54] Hence the twofold knowledge reflects a distinction in the divine revelation as apprehended by human beings through faith and with the aid of scripture. It is therefore primarily a distinction in fallen humanity's apprehension of the divine activity, though it is not, as earlier treatments of this topic have suggested, a distinction in the *way* or *means by which* humanity apprehends God's activity, for example, through faith or through the authority of scripture. Rather, the distinction lies in where one looks to perceive the divine hand; it is a distinction in the locus of revelation (the particular acts of God that are recognized as revealing God's benevolence) that is viewed through the spectacles of scripture with the eyes of faith.

The need for this distinction (in both revelation and knowledge) arises as a result of human sin, as Calvin understands it. Sin disrupts the created ability of human beings to attain to proper knowledge of God through the revelation in the order of nature.[55] Through faith and the lenses of scripture, fallen human beings regain this original possibility, at least in part. Now, however, they grasp and appropriate the divine activity in a certain epistemological order: first God's saving activity in Jesus Christ and then God's providential activity in creation. By turning this theological principle into a methodological tool Calvin is able to communicate to his readers both the comprehensiveness of scriptural testimony to God and the priority of certain parts of scripture's witness (the gospel) over the rest of its message.

It would be a mistake to suppose that Calvin's distinction between God's creative and redemptive activity means that book 1 is completely isolated from all trace of soteriological concern and from every soteriological element. True, Calvin describes the content of the knowledge of God the creator as nothing but "the primal and simple knowledge to which the very order of nature would have led us if Adam had remained upright."[56] This natural knowledge, mediated through the ordered structure of creation, would obviously not have contained any elements of God's redemptive activity, since if Adam had remained upright there would have been no need for redemption. However, Calvin writes for fallen human beings not to urge them to seek God in nature apart from scripture but rather to explain how they can obtain this knowledge of God that Adam lost through the Fall. Hence though Calvin seeks to isolate his description of the content of the knowledge of God the creator from reference to God's activity as redeemer, his accounts of the means to that knowledge necessarily presuppose this very activity.

The fact that Calvin presupposes but has decided not to treat the knowledge of God the redeemer until later creates certain expositional problems. For this reason, he must include the whole series of comments that alerts the reader to that future discussion. It is significant that two of these appear at the beginning of his discussion of scripture. Technically, scripture itself is an accommodation to human fallenness and belongs to God's redemptive activity. Therefore Calvin cautions in explicit detail that he is for the present forgoing the scriptural witness to Christ the mediator and speaking only of scripture's testimony to God as creator. Nonetheless, he feels the need to digress from this testimony itself in order first to establish scriptural authority. The fact that this discussion appears at all in book 1 is itself an indication that the fallen human condition and God's saving work in Christ are presupposed even if cautiously bracketed throughout. Yet, as Dowey argues, it is a mistake to assume that this discussion completely resolves the problem of knowledge of God. I would add, however, that the objective authority of scripture is but a step toward the final answer to the problem of knowledge of God as creator as well as redeemer. Although readers learn here the content of God's creative work, they must wait for book 3 and the discussion of faith to learn the means by which they fully know God, even as creator.

Calvin's methodological pointers indicate the theological and epistemological priority of the knowledge of God the redeemer. In this regard they fulfill the same role as the sentence that ended chapter 1 of the editions of 1539–1554, pointing ahead to the coming discussion of the knowledge of faith to indicate that the problem of knowledge has not yet been resolved.[57] Despite this similarity, book 1 of the 1559 *Institutes* achieves something beyond that negative evaluation of the testimony to God in nature that issued from chapter 1 in the earlier editions. Though the general structure and discussion up through the end of the treatment of scripture in chapter 10 of book 1 follows the order of 1539, the focus of this argument shifts when the important concluding sentence, pointing the reader to the discussion of faith later in the *Institutes*, is dropped and chapters 11–18 are added.[58] Calvin has not abandoned the view that God is more clearly revealed in the face of Christ. However, he is no longer postponing, as he did in earlier editions, his discussion of the knowledge of God's creative and providential activity through faith. In those earlier editions this material followed the discussion of faith and so was already subsumed under faith in Christ. Yet, as Calvin makes absolutely clear in discussing scripture in *Institutes* 1.6.2, in 1559 he is following the order of scripture and of nature, not the order of knowing for fallen humans or the actual order of faith. Hence, the rest of the discussion of the knowledge of God the creator is no longer put off until later. All that pertains to this topic has been relocated to follow the discussion and defense of scripture, the word. Faith in God's creative and providential activity is presupposed throughout this discussion, the primary purpose of which is no longer merely to point to the knowledge of faith to come. Rather, in its explication of the content of the knowledge of God the creator, book 1 seeks to describe what believers learn about God's creative activity from scripture *and* from creation and history when these are viewed through the lenses of scripture with eyes of faith.[59] Calvin's subsequent acknowledgement in *Institutes* (1559) 2.6.1 that this knowledge is useless unless faith follows, setting forth God as father in Christ, does not diminish the positive value of this knowledge for those who already have grasped God's fatherly mercy though faith in Christ. The kind of knowledge that Calvin presents in *Institutes* (1559) 1.10–18 is not only useless without saving faith; without faith in Christ, this knowledge is impossible.

Calvin's explicit adoption of the *duplex cognitio Domini* as a methodological principle in his 1559 *Institutes* leads him to separate material dealing with faith in God's creative activity from the primarily soteriologically focused discussions that followed upon his discussion of faith in the earlier editions of the *Institutes*. Yet inasmuch as faith is the means by which humanity from Adam on apprehends divine revelation, faith is not absent from the discussion in book 1. On the one hand, Calvin's frequent indications of the discussion of God's redemptive activity to come point ahead to faith for the ultimate resolution of the problem of how human beings know God. On the other hand, a faith in God's creative and providential activity that is an outgrowth of saving faith in Jesus Christ already manifests itself in book 1. Hence I turn from my consideration of the structure of book 1 to its content, where one finds traces of providential faith in the discussions of piety, the word, creation, and providence.

The concept of piety takes on central significance to Calvin's exposition in 1559. The first indication of this is found in his reordering of some of the material at the beginning of the former chapter 1: he moves some brief comments about pious knowledge of God forward and consolidates and reorganizes his statements on the seed of religion leading to idolatry. Chapter 2 of book 1 now introduces the subject of the knowledge of God proper, declaring that there is no true knowledge of God apart from piety. Calvin defines piety as "that reverence joined with love of God that the knowledge of his benefits induces."[60] Since he explicitly says that he is treating only knowledge of God the creator, this pious awareness of God's benevolence directs itself toward God's providence:

> Moreover, although our mind cannot apprehend God without rendering some honor to him, it will not suffice simply to hold that there is One whom all ought to honor and adore, unless we are also persuaded that he is the fountain of every good, and that we must seek nothing elsewhere than in him. This I take to mean that not only does he sustain this universe (as he once founded it) by his boundless might, regulate it by his wisdom, preserve it by his goodness, and especially rule humankind by his righteousness and judgment, bear with it in his mercy, watch over it by his protection; but also that no drop will be found either of wisdom and light, or of righteousness or power or rectitude, or of genuine truth, which does not flow from him, and of which he is not the cause. Thus we may learn to await and seek all these things from him, and thankfully to ascribe them, once received, to him.[61]

Had Adam remained upright, he would have been led to this knowledge of God's benevolence by the very fabric of the universe. His natural piety would have issued in right religion and worship. I think that it is fair to judge that providential faith as set forth in Calvin's commentary on the Psalms in some respects represents a restoration of this pious recognition of God's providential goodness. The first important difference for redeemed humanity, of course, is that faith in God's providence is not read directly off of nature or history but is rather mediated through the providential promises in scripture.

In order to isolate Calvin's understanding of the second important difference between the natural piety of Adam and subsequent believers' faith in God's providence, one needs to follow his development of the theme of piety further. As I have already shown, the idea of piety emerges in *Institutes* 3.2.31 to denote the proper way of viewing God's power; namely, from the perspective of the divine benevolence. Yet how do human beings arrive at the awareness of God's goodness in the first place? Moreover, is the restoration of piety merely the reinstitution of the awareness of God as the fountain of all goodness mediated not (as for the first human pair) through the Logos ordering the world but through God's providential promises in scripture? In chapter 6 of book 2, Calvin takes up these questions as he begins his discussion of the knowledge of God the redeemer. Here he reiterates his argument that God's fatherly favor can no longer be inferred from mere contemplation of the universe.[62] Instead, faith in Christ the mediator is necessary. Though a recognition of God's benevolent fatherhood is the first step in the return to piety, this first step is not taken on the basis of evidence for the divine benevolence in the natural testimony to God's providential goodness. Rather, Christ has functioned as mediator of all true knowledge of God since the beginning of the world and has been for fallen humanity the source for saving knowledge:

> Only let the readers agree on this point: let the first step toward piety be to recognize that God is our Father to watch over us, govern and nourish us, until he gather us unto the eternal inheritance of his kingdom. Hence, what we have recently said becomes clear, that apart from Christ the saving knowledge of God does not stand. From the beginning of the world he had consequently been set before all the elect that they should look unto him and put their trust in him.[63]

Faith, which Calvin has defined since 1539 as "firm and certain knowledge of the divine benevolence toward us, based on the truth of the free promise in Christ," provides the opening to restored piety. Hence, insofar as faith recognizes God's fatherhood and evokes love and reverence for God, faith is, as Gerrish has said, the functional equivalent of piety.[64] Postlapsarian faith provides the knowledge of God's fatherly goodwill that unfallen Adam would have arrived at through the mediation in Christ in the order of nature. However, not only is the means of mediation different here, but the content of Christian piety is broader and its focus is differently placed. Gerrish argues that "although the goodness of God is still the actual object of devotion, it is now his pardoning, reconciling goodness."[65] Christian piety represents a deepening of the original prelapsarian piety of Adam and Eve. It includes both the sense of the divine powers active in regulating the universe and the epistemologically prior awareness of God's fatherly grace in Jesus Christ. Piety in the 1559 *Institutes* embraces the whole of the *duplex cognitio Domini*. To the extent that faith is the functional equivalent of piety, faith also is twofold.

The question of the mediation of pious knowledge of God occupies Calvin's discussion following the initial description of piety in book 1, chapter 2. This is a fundamentally different matter from the notion of piety itself, which, as I have just shown, has its correlate in the idea of faith developed under the knowledge of God the redeemer. Here the issue is the *source* of knowledge of God's fatherly goodness for fallen human beings: is this in God's works or in God's word (i.e., scripture)? As I showed in earlier chapters, the question of the relationship of works and word as testimonies to God's will presented itself with respect to knowledge of both God's saving and providential activity, especially in Calvin's commentaries on the Gospel of John and the Psalms. In book 1, of course, he is concerned only with the revelation of God's activity as creator. Chapters 3–5 lead the reader through the failed testimony of the internal (seed of religion) and external (nature) witness to the divine benevolence. Minor rearrangements aside, these reproduce in essence the argument from earlier editions and arrive at the same conclusion: humans are without excuse for their failure to know God properly from nature. Several expansions to the discussion merit brief mention, since they reflect Calvin's incorporation of themes that he developed in his commentary on the Psalms into his discussion. In *Institutes* 1.4.2 he relies primarily on Psalms texts to argue that those who turn from God do not deny God's existence but rather reject God's providence.[66] He draws on Psalms 104 and 11 in chapter 5 of book 1 to underscore the beauty of God's revelation in nature.[67] In the same chapter he adds a new section extending this revelation to human beings themselves, repeating elements of his exegesis of Psalm 8 to illustrate human existence as a testimony to divine goodness.[68]

As in earlier editions, this line of argumentation shuts out nature as a solely effective means of mediation of proper knowledge of God for fallen humanity. Concurrently, this discussion rejects fallen natural human faculties of reason and perception as a means of apprehending nature's revelation. As in every edition since 1539, Calvin draws on Heb. 11:3 near the end of his comments to argue that faith is necessary in order to perceive the invisible divinity manifest in these natural spectacles.[69] However, rather than pursuing the question of the means of *apprehension* further at this point, Calvin instead continues his reflections on the means of *disclosure*. He turns now to the revelation accommodated not to human finitude but to human sinfulness: scripture. The instrumentality of scripture is now wonderfully expressed in Calvin's famous image of scripture as spectacles, which is new in 1559.[70]

I have already mentioned the discussion of scripture that begins in book 1, chapter 6, in order to point out the two important references that Calvin makes to the order of the discussion according to the *duplex cognitio Domini*. Scripture's attestation to the divine goodness is, unlike the revelation in nature, twofold. Adam, Noah, Abraham, and all the other patriarchs also apprehended God in a twofold fashion from God's word.[71] But Calvin brackets here that "part of doctrine that has always separated believers from unbelieving folk, for it was founded in Christ."[72] His main goal is to present scripture as God's special accommodation of revelation to human fallenness and to oppose the clarity and efficacy of this as God's word to the general revelation in God's works. "Therefore, however fitting it may be for man seriously to turn his eyes to contemplate God's works, since he has been placed in this most glorious theater to be a spectator of them, it is fitting that he prick up his ears to the word, the better to profit."[73] This opposition between the effectiveness of the divine works and the effectiveness of the word goes all the way back to the edition of 1539 and was supported in part by reference to Psalm 19. In 1543 Calvin added a reference to John 4:22 to argue that at the time of Jesus only the Jews had access to proper knowledge of God since they alone had the word. References to the Psalms added in 1559 underscore the exclusive priority of the word in establishing proper knowledge of God. In the first instance Calvin observes that David often represents God as regnant. By this David refers not to God's power manifest in the governance of all things but rather to the doctrine by which God declares his sovereignty.[74] In other words, David indicates not God's providential works but God's providential word or the "doctrine" declaring God to be providential. In the next section, Calvin continues this opposition by quoting from Psalm 19. He then draws on his exegesis of Psalm 29 to illustrate how God's awesome voice in nature cannot be heard by unbelievers. Only those in God's "sanctuary" have God's word and can sing God's praises. Calvin confirms this insight by paraphrasing Ps. 93:5.[75]

Hence Calvin continues to direct fallen human beings away from the threatening and condemning voice of nature to the words of scripture as the proper source for their knowledge of God as creator. However, before I turn to the content of this knowledge, as Calvin sets it forth following his excursus on biblical authority in chapters 7–9, it is necessary to explore one further dimension of his understanding of the word. Here I am concerned not with the revelatory power of God's works versus that of God's word in scripture. Rather, it is necessary to consider briefly the nature of scripture's twofold testimony and the relationship of that to God's sustaining word in creation and God's reconciling word manifest in the flesh, Jesus Christ. Up to this point, I have sought to avoid what Dowey criticizes as the collapsing of faith and objective biblical authority by distinguishing between the means of apprehending divine revelation (faith) and the means of disclosing divine revelation (scripture). However, one is still in danger of such a collapse if the instrumental nature of the Bible is overlooked. If scripture is simply identified as the oracles of God, then one cannot avoid reducing faith to intellectual assent to biblical testimony. And to the extent that faith becomes mere assent to doctrine, the problem of knowledge of God is primarily resolved once the locus of doctrine is identified in book 1. However, all that we know about Calvin's views of faith from its very beginnings speaks against such a one-sided reduction. Though it is beyond doubt that he held to the view that the Bible expressed God's very words, he also held just as firmly to the witness character of scripture and to its instrumental nature. Scripture functions as *spectacles* to gather up and focus the confused knowledge of God in human minds. As this knowledge is twofold, scripture enables humans to perceive God's word manifest in the incarnate Christ and also in creation.

Corresponding to scripture's twofold testimony to God as redeemer and creator is the twofold activity of the eternal word, the second person of the Trinity: sustaining and redeeming. It is the eternal Son who from the beginning of time has been and continues to be the true mediator of knowledge of God and who is, in the end, the ultimate *object* of faith. Had he remained upright, Adam would have grown, through the exercise of his created faculties, into true knowledge of God and eternal life through contemplation of the Logos structuring and sustaining the fabric of the world. Calvin echoes this judgment, new in 1559, in several other additions found in his discussion of knowledge of God the redeemer. In his discussion of the incarnation in book 2 he observes: "Even if man had remained free from all stain, his condition would have been too lowly for him to reach God without a mediator."[76] Also in book 2, Calvin engages Osiander's position that the incarnation would have been necessary even if the Fall had not occurred. Here he argues against Osiander that if Adam had not fallen Adam would have participated in God's image only through the Son. Moreover, Adam would have, with the angels, been ordered under Christ's headship even though Christ did not appear in the flesh.[77]

Willis, the author of the most detailed investigation into these issues, concludes that Calvin uses the term "mediator" in a double sense. The primary sense is mediation as reconciliation; the mediator is *Deus manifestatus in carne*, the God-man who effects redemption. However, Calvin also extends the term to the eternal Son who, even prior to the incarnation, was the only channel between God and fallen and even unfallen humanity.[78] Willis finds the most significant development of this view in Calvin's responses to Francesco Stancaro in 1560. Here Calvin explicitly employs the name "mediator" to describe Christ's headship before the

Fall in a way that extends the notion of mediation beyond its traditional use as expiation:

> Thus we understand first that the name of Mediator applies to Christ not only because he took on flesh or because he took on the office of reconciling the human race with God. But already from the beginning of creation he was truly Mediator because he was always the Head of the Church and held primacy even over the angels and was the first-born of all creatures (Eph. 1:2; Col. 1:15ff; Col. 2:10). Whence we conclude that he began to perform the office of Mediator not only after the fall of Adam but insofar as he is the Eternal Son of God, angels as well as men were joined to God in order that they might remain upright.[79]

In this passage Calvin also explicitly extends the title "Christ" to the eternal Son as the orderer and sustainer of creation from the beginning. Usually, however, this, like the term "mediator," refers to the incarnate Son. Yet in this extended sense "Christ" and "mediator" both refer appropriately to that sustaining activity of the second person of the Trinity that *begins* with the creation of the world.

Although explicit designation of the double mediation appears first in this 1560 text, the seeds for this idea emerge already in the 1559 *Institutes*. According to this principle, Christ since the Fall exercises a twofold mediation, one as the head of angels, the other as the expiator of sin. This does not suggests two Christs any more than the twofold knowledge of God implies two Gods. The same person who ordered the unfallen creation continues to order and sustain creation after the Fall while simultaneously carrying out the proper office of reconciling mediation. In its capacity as spectacles, scripture enables fallen human beings to participate in both of these activities, as I will show when I turn to Calvin's explication of the doctrines of creation and providence. However, in closing, one final observation from the 1559 *Institutes* serves to underscore the instrumentality and temporary nature of scripture, faith, *and* Christ's double mediation. Reiterating his view that the office of reconciling mediator extends to both natures, Calvin announces that on the last day Christ will give up the mediatorial function altogether:

> Until he comes forth as judge of the world Christ will therefore reign, joining us to the Father as the measure of our weakness permits. But when as partakers in heavenly glory we shall see God as he is, Christ, having then discharged the office of Mediator, will cease to be the ambassador of his Father and will be satisfied with that glory which he enjoyed *before the creation of the world.*[80]

In the eschaton, faith will no longer look through the spectacles of scripture to gaze upon Christ the mediator and thereby apprehend God's fatherly favor. Instead, Christ as *Deus manifestatus in carne* will no more be a mediator, the spectacles will be cast aside, and faith will pass over into sight.[81] But until that day, faith must apprehend Christ as Christ is presented in scripture: as clothed in the gospel and then also as the firstborn of all creatures *and* head of the angels.

Following Calvin's cautionary advice at the beginning of book 1, chapter 10, in this last section I will be concerned to grasp only creation and providence and not "overstep the limits" and look for Christ as reconciling mediator.[82] Hence the investigation will focus on the actual character of providential faith in book 1. Moreover, I will restrict my view to the themes of creation and providence alone and leave aside Calvin's discussion of images, the Trinity, and human nature as created. Though this material belongs to the knowledge of God the creator, with the exception of the last mentioned, it does not deal directly with the divine activity itself. The discussion of images develops further the notion of piety by contrasting pious knowledge or worship of God with idolatrous formation of physical and mental images. Chapter 13 seeks to establish the trinitarian *nature* of the creator God; again, the primary purpose is to distinguish the nature of the God to whom scripture bears witness from idols. Finally, Calvin's treatment of human nature, which he expands greatly in 1559, deals not strictly with the knowledge of God but with the corresponding theme of knowledge of self. Moreover, human nature as an object of divine providence has already been the subject of detailed study.[83] In contrast, chapters 14 and 16–18 of book 1 deal directly with God's activity as creator and sustainer, with faith's apprehension of these works, and with God's providential purpose underlying them.

Calvin's discussion of the creation of the world in book 1, chapter 14, is in large part verbatim from his earlier discussions of the phrase "creator of heaven and earth" in the Creed. He expanded this treatment of this topic in 1543 to include a detailed angelology.[84] Moreover, he underscored there the role of nature as a glorious theater and explicitly designated this as an evidence for faith.[85] In 1559 Calvin prepares a new introduction to the topic of creation. These two introductory sections (1.14.1–2) link the earlier discussion to the developing opposition between knowledge of the true God and the false imaginings of those who lack God's word. Moreover, they establish proper worship as the goal of this knowledge of creation. One can see this dual purpose in the following comments on the scriptural account of creation:

> This knowledge is especially useful not only to resist the monstrous fables that formerly were in vogue in Egypt and in other regions of the earth, but also that, once the beginning of the universe is known, God's eternity may shine forth more clearly, and we may be more rapt in wonder at it.[86]

Calvin goes on to liken Moses' history of creation to a mirror in which images of God's wisdom, power, and righteousness glow. He then repeats his analogy of scripture as spectacles to stress the need for the word to provide guidance for fallen minds.[87]

Although Calvin directs his readers to the word proclaiming God's creation in six days and especially the placement of humankind in a lavishly prepared universe, he does not intend to leave their attention focused on the printed page. The very fact that God created in six days rather than in an instant suggests to Calvin that human beings ought to contemplate God's work, which is preeminently manifested in the creation of human nature.[88] Reiterating fallen humanity's weakness, Calvin suggests that the obedience of faith prepares humans to use created order for its proper purpose:

> For even though our eyes, in whatever direction they may turn, are compelled to gaze upon God's works, yet we see how changeable is our attention, and how

swiftly are dissipated any godly thoughts that may touch us. Here also, until human reason is subjected to the obedience of faith and learns to cultivate that quiet to which the sanctification of the seventh day invites us, it grumbles, as if such proceedings were foreign to God's power. But we ought in the very order of things diligently to contemplate God's fatherly love toward humankind, in that he did not create Adam until he had lavished upon the universe all matter of good things.[89]

After cataloguing various ways that the creation account depicts God as a responsible and loving parent, Calvin briefly reminds his readers that God is recognized as creator not in his bare essence but also in his eternal wisdom and Spirit. Hence Moses' narrative testifies to God's triune nature.

Following his treatment of the invisible works of God (angels and demons), Calvin returns to the theme of God's visible works in chapter 14, sections 20–22.[90] Like the discussion of angels and demons, this discussion is largely from 1543. Here Calvin briefly summarizes what can be known about creation from the biblical accounts and from the interpretations given by such men as Basil and Ambrose. Turning then to the question of how the faithful ought to view God's works themselves, Calvin points his readers to his earlier discussion of the goal of nature's witness to God.[91] From this it appears that, for the faithful, the negative and condemning effect of nature's witness apart from faith is undone. Calvin then presents the essence of his teaching on faith's apprehension of God's works:

> Therefore, to be brief, let all readers know that they have with true faith apprehended what it is for God to be creator of heaven and earth, if they first of all follow the universal rule, not to pass over in ungrateful thoughtlessness or forgetfulness those conspicuous powers that God shows forth in his creatures, and then learn so to apply it to themselves that their very hearts are touched.[92]

Believers are to apprehend God's conspicuous powers in God's works in the created realm. Apart from the word, creation only condemns and threatens. But when those who have faith in Jesus Christ view creation through the spectacles of scripture, they recover the knowledge of divine revelation that original humanity should have been able to grasp unaided. Through this apprehension believers are led to reflect first on the greatness and then on the goodness of the artificer. That this latter activity is more appropriate to faith becomes explicit in Calvin's opening to the subsequent section:

> There remains the second part of the rule, more closely related to faith. It is to recognize that God has destined all things for our good and salvation but at the same time to feel his power and grace in ourselves and in the great benefits he has conferred upon us, and so bestir ourselves to trust, invoke, praise, and love him.[93]

Hence chapter 14 leads its readers from the testimony to God's creative activity in scripture to a recognition of the works of creation as divine works—indeed, as manifestations of the divine benevolence. In 1559 Calvin places his discussion from 1539/1543 within the immediate context of the idea of scripture as lenses to guide and regulate knowledge of God's creative activity and the obedience of faith as the proper disposition for viewing these manifestations. He ushers his readers into the theater of God's glory and invites them to exercise their providential faith.

The discussion of providence proper receives more editorial attention in 1559 than the discussion of creation. This is largely due to the fact, as Schreiner has shown, that Calvin viewed providence as a doctrine under attack. He defended his views on God's providence against contemporary opponents who, he believed, undermined the particularity of divine care, imprisoned God within the chain of secondary causes, or rendered God idle and ineffectual.[94] Especially from the 1539 *Institutes* on, Calvin held (primarily on the basis of Heb. 11:3) that a correct understanding of divine providence was attained only through faith. In 1559 several of the expansions to his argument for providence provide important insight into the character of the faith by which he thinks providence is known and apprehended. Contrary to T. H. L. Parker's judgment that these chapters offer "only an extended version and detailed defense of" the discussion in *Institutes* 1.5.7–8, the discussion accomplishes a quite different purpose.[95] Whereas the earlier arguments for the witness to God's providence were designed to lead into arguments for the necessity for the revelation in scripture, the present discussion functions positively to turn believer's eyes, aided by scripture, back to the theater of providence.

Book 1, chapter 16, defends at length the view that God's sustaining hand is extended to every particular event and circumstance. If this were not the case, Calvin argues, God's fatherly favor would not be manifest.[96] Therefore Calvin rejects ideas about providence that attribute events to fortune and chance, attribute to God only a "blind and ambiguous motion," or equate Calvin's teaching with the Stoic doctrine of fate. Throughout his discussion Calvin opposes these views to scripture's teaching about the particularity and scope of divine providence, supporting his points especially with Old Testament texts. However, he recognizes that the course of events often appears to contradict this view. Hence he comes at the end of chapter 16 to discuss the hiddenness of God's providence.

Calvin begins his treatment of the inscrutability of the divine plan in *Institutes* 1.16.9 with a distinction he had made in 1539 between how things appear to believers and the view of providence that they hold in their hearts:

> Therefore I shall put it this way: however all things may be ordained by God's plan, according to a sure dispensation, for us they are fortuitous. Not that we think that fortune rules the world and men, tumbling all things at random up and down, for it is fitting that this folly be absent from the Christian's breast! But since the order, reason, end, and necessity of those things that happen for the most part lie hidden in God's purpose, and are not apprehended by human opinion, those things, which it is certain take place by God's will, are in a sense fortuitous. For they bear on the face of them no other appearance, whether they are considered in their own nature or weighed according to our knowledge and judgment.[97]

Here the conviction of providence is simply opposed to human opinion or ordinary knowledge and judgment. In 1539 Calvin gives no further clue as to how the reasons for these events lie hidden only "for the most part" or how they might be apprehended if not by human (i.e., carnal) opinion, knowledge, or judgment.

While not denying the ultimate unknowability of God's ends and reasons, in 1559 Calvin pushes the idea that these things lie hidden only in part. He observes: "In this sense the term 'fate' is often repeated in Ecclesiastes, because *at first glance* [*primo intuitu*] men do not penetrate to the first cause, which lies deeply hidden."[98] He goes on to stress the persistence of an awareness of God's providence even among the reprobate; for example, the Philistines' diviners say that they will attribute the Philistines' misfortune in 1 Samuel 6 to God and not to chance if the cows pulling the ark of the covenant go off in a certain direction. Calvin ascribes this dim awareness itself to God's government: "Meanwhile, we see them constrained from daring to think simply fortuitous what had happened unfavorably to them."[99] He finds later in the book of Samuel an especially clear instance of God controlling events by the bridle of his providence. In stating how one comes to acknowledge this, Calvin lifts up faith over ordinary ways of knowing:

> At the very moment of time in which David was trapped in the wilderness of Maon, the Philistines invaded the land, and Saul was compelled to depart [1 Sam. 23:26–27]. If God, intending to provide for his servant's safety, cast this hindrance in Saul's way, surely although the Philistines took up arms suddenly and above all human opinion, yet we will not say that this took place by chance; but what for us seems a contingency, faith recognizes to have been a secret impulse of God.[100]

While not penetrating to the hidden reasons for God's providence, in 1559 faith nonetheless enables believers to see God's hand in the sacred history related in scripture.

In chapter 17 of book 1 Calvin continues his reflections on the hiddenness of God's providence as he takes on the question of the practical application of this doctrine. The first two sections and part of the third section are new in 1559. These now prepare for Calvin's reflections on human responsibility and prudent care of life and his exhortations to meditate on divine providence that derive from the 1539 edition.

Just as the doctrine of creation serves as a guide for viewing nature, the scriptural teaching about God's providence also functions as a guide for viewing the actual manifestations of providence in the present. This is evident throughout chapter 17 but is especially clear in Calvin's statement at the beginning concerning the end for which scripture teaches that all things happen by divine ordination. Here he makes three observations. First, divine providence applies both to future and past events. Second, providence is the determinative principle of all things, working in some cases through intermediate means, sometimes without an intermediary, and at other times contrary to every intermediary. Third, the end of providence is that God may reveal his concern for the entire human race but especially for the church.[101] These principles, derived from scripture, are to be considered when reflecting on events taking place. In particular, they guide the elect from the confusion of history to pious recognition, reverence, and adoration of God's providential care. They build up faith in God's providential word: the promise of fatherly goodness manifest in this very confusion itself.

After stating his three scriptural principles, Calvin turns immediately to the problem of the confusion of history. He notes that the course of providence indeed manifests God's fatherly goodness (as well as God's judgment) but that "quiet and composed minds ready to learn" are necessary in order to grasp the reasons for events. Unfortunately, the carnal human perspective clouds this view of God's providence completely and makes it difficult for human minds to remain properly disposed to learn:

> Now this, also, ought to be added, that although either fatherly favor and benef-icence or severity of judgment often shine forth in the whole course of providence, nevertheless sometimes the causes of events are hidden. So the thought creeps in that human affairs turn and whirl at the blind urge of fortune; or the flesh incites us to contradiction, as if God were making sport of men by throwing them about like balls. It is indeed true that if we had quiet and composed minds ready to learn, the final outcome would show that God always has the best reason for his plan: either to instruct his own people in patience, or to correct their wicked affections and tame their lust, or to subjugate them to self-denial, or to arouse them from sluggishness; again, to bring low the proud, to shatter the cunning of the impious and to overthrow their devices. Yet however hidden and fugitive from our point of view the causes may be, we must hold that they are surely laid up with him, and hence we must exclaim with David: "Great, O God, are the won-drous deeds that thou hast done, and thy thoughts toward us cannot be reckoned; if I try to speak, they would be more than can be told" [Ps. 40:5].[102]

There is a struggle between carnal understanding's denial of providence and the quiet and composed mind's willingness to learn the hidden reasons for it. Or, as Calvin characterizes this in his commentary on the Psalms, the struggle is between the eye of the flesh and the eye of faith. What appears to carnal human under-standing and the physical sense of sight to be the confusion of things in the world has a deeper reason that only faith can comprehend.

In this struggle to apprehend God's providence, faith's victory appears, for the present, to be rather slight. Writing on the blind man healed in John 9, Calvin argues that human sense perception cries out against Christ's statement that the man's blindness is due not to sin but to show God's glory. Only "pure eyes" would be able to overcome the complaint of the flesh against God's apparent injustice and perceive instead God's glory manifested in the spectacle of the healing.[103] But the disturbance of worldly things is so great that minds do not remain completely composed and the eyes of faith are clouded with mist. Hence believers must infer God's providence despite appearances:

> When dense clouds darken the sky, and a violent tempest arises, because a gloomy mist is cast over our eyes, thunder strikes our ears and all our senses are benumbed with fright, everything seems to us to be confused and mixed up; but all the while a constant quiet and serenity ever remain in heaven. So we must conclude that, while the disturbances in the world deprive us of judgment, God out of the pure light of his justice and wisdom tempers and directs these very movements in the best-conceived order to a right end.[104]

Calvin urges the faithful to turn from the physical evidence clouding their senses and rest their trust in judgments that, because of their weakness, remain hidden and inscrutable.

In *Institutes* 1.17.2 Calvin continues his discussion of the secret nature of the divine plan and takes up objections that the incomprehensibility of providence conflicts with the revelation of God's will in the law. Against this claim, which is supported by Deut. 30:11–14, Calvin advances the declaration in Ps. 36:6 that God's judgments are a deep abyss. In reconciling these two statements, he distinguishes between the written testimony to God's will (scripture) and God's hidden method and reasons for governing the universe. Concerning the former there is no "abyss," since God reveals the law and the gospel and "illumines the minds of his own with the spirit of discernment." In other words, through faith believers grasp the mysteries contained in the law and gospel; moreover, scripture functions as a guide, a lamp, "and the school of sure and clear truth." In contrast to the clear revelation of scripture, God's method of governing the universe is obscure and rightly called an abyss, which though hidden ought to be adored.[105] This does not mean that God's will is manifold but means only that it appears that way to finite humans. Calvin does not suggest that God's hidden method of governance would contradict what is revealed of the divine will in law and gospel.[106] He only wants to stress that even those who have faith and walk by the light of the word do not perceive all the reasons for every event. For this reason he ends his comments in this section by distinguishing his view from the nominalistic *potentia absoluta*, which he believes separates God's justice from God's power. From providence, in contrast, "flows nothing but right, although the reasons have been hidden from us."[107]

Although scripture testifies that God governs the world by secret means (as Calvin demonstrates in his reference in this section to Deut. 29:29), in the second half of 1.17.2 Calvin is directing his readers' attention beyond the scriptural testimony to look upon providence itself: "For we see how [Moses] bids us not only direct our study to meditation upon the law, but reverently to look up to God's secret providence."[108] He cites three passages from Job and one from Augustine to underscore the need to search out God's wisdom in the secrets of nature and to be brought thereby to profound reverence for God's hidden governance.[109] Though he does not make specific reference to the Psalms, his language here as well as his earlier description of the quiet and composed mind, pure eyes, and the goal of reverent piety all echo his opening comments on Psalm 36: "For we know what a rare virtue it is, when impiety is raging without restraint and pours darkness upon us, to look up with the eyes of faith to God's providence, which, by disposing our minds to patience, holds us constantly in piety."[110] Though the reasons for providence are concealed by the confusion of history, believers are still to use the word as their guide and seek out evidences of God's righteousness, goodness, power, and wisdom in the course of events. Meditating on the manifestations of God's providence, they may not always (or even often) arrive at the reasons underlying the things that take place. Yet by the exercise of providential faith they will learn to reverence God as creator and sustainer and find their piety deepened.

These opening reflections on the confusion of history and the inscrutability of the divine plan provide a new entrance into Calvin's discussion of meditating on providence and providence as a doctrine of comfort from 1539. His discussion now illustrates how the godly mind employs the three principles outlined at the beginning of the chapter to live a life in faithful recognition of God's providence. Aware that God's providence extends both to past and future, the believer exercises due prudence and care and seeks to do nothing against God's will as revealed in God's word.[111] Recognizing the varied uses of intermediaries, the believer gives proper attention to secondary causes and recognizes God's special care, particularly in times of prosperity but also in times of adversity.[112] Finally, the godly mind knows the end toward which God's providence aims and therefore enjoys immeasurable felicity, freedom from anxiety, and comfort from the conviction that all things tend toward God's fatherly care.[113] Throughout this discussion Calvin employs numerous scriptural examples of these activities, but his goal is not to restrict his readers to scriptural evidence but to lead them to apply these principles in their own lives.

The final Latin edition of the *Institutes* clearly retains Calvin's Pauline principle that faith comes from hearing. Even providential faith is, as in the commentary on the Psalms, based on God's word in scripture. However, scripture is not the ultimate *object* of providential faith, any more than of saving faith. Rather, scripture functions as an indispensable guide for looking up to and contemplating God's providence manifest in God's works in nature and history. Though the ambivalent attitude toward sense perception that characterized Calvin's earliest articulations of the nature of faith continues to manifest itself in this his most mature formulation, here providential faith does not close but rather opens the eyes of the godly mind to God's fatherly benevolence manifest in the world: in nature and in history. True, the reasons for most occurrences remain hidden not only to physical eyes and carnal understanding but also to the inner eyes of faith. Nonetheless, these inner eyes, guided by the word, continue their quest to catch a glimpse of God's hand. The reverence for God to which this exercise gives rise is essential for the establishment of piety, from which true religion and worship of God are born.

Faith is the restoration of the pious affection with which humans in the state of integrity responded to the testimony of God in the order of creation.[114] For fallen human beings, saving faith in Jesus Christ is the essential first step in this restoration. However, in the movement from saving faith in Jesus Christ to original or even deepened piety, providential faith is the crucial second step. Providential faith is the sense of the powers of God that Calvin says near the beginning of book 1 is a fit teacher of piety.[115] His comments on Ps. 78:22 affirm this notion. Here he argues not only that faith is the root of true piety but also that faith is "to lean upon his fatherly providence." Indeed, in these very comments one can perhaps catch a hint of the necessary second step:

> "To trust in the salvation of God" is to lean upon his fatherly providence, and to regard him as sufficient for the supply of all our wants. From this we learn not only how hateful unbelief is to God, but also what is the true nature of faith and what fruits are born from it. Whence is it that men quietly submit themselves to him, but because they are persuaded that their salvation is singularly precious to him and are fully assured that whatever is needful will be given [to them] and thus that they permit themselves to be governed by his will? Faith, then, is the root of true piety.[116]

The persuasion that one's salvation is precious to God is the persuasion of saving faith. The assurance that God will provide whatever is needful belongs to saving faith as well. However, with respect to things of this world, this assurance is perhaps most appropriately the conviction of a faith in God's providential and protecting care that is mentioned here. Only when these two steps have been taken will believers turn to God in pious reverence and love, willingly submitting to God's will. As described at the end of my chapter 4, true and complete spiritual felicity consists not only in reconciliation with God through faith in the gospel but also in a renewed relationship to God's good creation. The road to piety encompasses both.

A Theology of Nature and Divine Hiddenness

By way of conclusion I turn now to two larger questions implied by Calvin's twofold notion of faith: first, whether the notion of a faith in God's activity apart from redemption implies a natural theology, and, second, how the idea of a twofold notion of faith affects Calvin's characteristic emphasis on the knowledge, certainty, and perception of faith.

The twofold character of faith does not imply a natural theology, if this is taken to mean the ability to receive the revelation efficaciously in creation unaided by scripture or apart from faith in Christ. Although it means dredging up again the debate between Emil Brunner and Karl Barth on this issue, I must clarify how God's activity apart from redemption is known by faith.[117] As my chapter 4 makes clear, providential faith is not a knowledge of God derived directly from nature or through natural human capacity. Rather, providential faith as faith in God's activity as creator and sustainer necessarily exists alongside the knowledge of God's redemptive promise manifest in Jesus Christ; it is, moreover, in its own way "christocentric" (in the larger sense noted by Willis). Yet providential faith's relationship to saving faith needs to be considered in light of Brunner's use of the word *Ergänzung* to express the relation of the knowledge of God from God's works to that given in God's word for the Bible-believing Christian.[118] The issue at stake is the understanding of the sufficiency of the scriptural witness, *sola scriptura*. Peter Barth criticizes Brunner's use of this term and argues that it implies the possibility of setting aside the spectacles of scripture, leading inevitably to a vision without the guidance of scripture.[119] For his part Brunner maintains that through scripture another source for knowledge of God is indeed opened up.[120] Moreover, he claims that Peter Barth contradicts himself when he later quotes Calvin's "Argumentum" to Genesis. As Dowey points out, for all the heat of the debate, it appears that Brunner and Peter Barth nonetheless agree "that for Calvin only the Christian can see the true God in creation, and then only by the aid of the 'spectacles' of Scripture, not as if his 'sight' had been perfectly restored."[121]

This study of Calvin's Psalms commentary and his *Institutes* (especially the 1559 edition) has made abundantly clear that Calvin views scripture as a temporary and instrumental but necessary and for the present indispensable means through which faith gains divine knowledge. Until the last day, scripture cannot be done away with or surpassed. In calling his readers to a knowledge of and faith in divine providence, Calvin inevitably invites them to the glass of God's word in scripture. That he also urges them to grasp the providential word by which God governs all things and which is manifest in the divine works occurring in their midst does not mean that he does away with scripture. He never suggests that believers apprehend or even glimpse God's hand without looking through the spectacles of scripture. So far, then, I am in agreement with Dowey's conclusion regarding this debate.

My findings confirm and even help to clarify the relationship between the witness to God in God's word in scripture and that in God's works by showing that scripture is always, for Calvin, the primary witness to God's creative and redemptive work. My findings also point to a further deficiency in the portrayal of Calvin's theology advanced by both sides in the debate.[122] While both sides acknowledge that scripture's testimony to the divine activity is twofold, both ignore the fact that *Christ's mediation is also duplex*. For example, Karl Barth opposes "creation" and "Christ" as two sources of knowledge of God without acknowledging that the knowledge of God as creator, even for humans in the state of integrity, is itself a knowledge centered on Christ, although not on the incarnate Christ.[123] Earlier studies of the Barth-Brunner debate have either missed or not paid sufficient attention to the fact that, in discussing faith's relationship to God's activity apart from redemption, Calvin not only differentiates between two forms of revelation (i.e., God's works and God's word as scripture) but also distinguishes both from the word as the eternal Son creating, governing, and ordering creation.[124] For Calvin, *all* knowledge of God comes through the mediation of Christ. Even in the very order of nature that would have led humans in the state of integrity to pious knowledge of God it is the *ordo*, namely, the Logos, the eternal Son, that bridges the gap between God and human beings.[125]

The failure to understand the knowledge of God the creator as a christocentric knowledge in the broader sense reflects a one-sided emphasis on Christ's redemptive activity to the neglect of Christ's sustaining activity as head of the angels and all creation. "Christocentric" comes to mean "redemptorcentric." Certainly the distinction between God's work as creator and as redeemer is crucial for fallen human beings who need to arrive at knowledge of God in a certain epistemological order; however, maintaining this distinction does not mean opposing one element of knowledge of God to the other. Such one-sidedness yields a skewed understanding of the whole of Calvin's thought, particularly with respect to the doctrines of creation, Christology, and faith. As Willis remarks, "Calvin's delight in creation as a source of confirming knowledge of God is missed too easily in a theology which sets Christological knowledge in virtual opposition to the knowledge of God from creation."[126] Similarly, Calvin's reverence for divine providence is obscured when faith is restricted to Christ's redemptive work alone. When the work of Christ apprehended by faith is reduced to the saving work of *Deus manifestatus in carne*, then it is obvious that debate will arise over how this other aspect of the divine activity is known, whether humans can obtain such knowledge "naturally," and whether it is in some sense an addition or complement to the revelation in Christ. However, Calvin held a twofold mediation of Christ and presented faith as apprehending both aspects of this mediation. Hence for fallen human beings, the witness to God in nature fulfills a dual function that is similar to the first and third uses of the law. Apart from faith, the word, and the Spirit, the natural order condemns and threatens. But when viewed through the spectacles of scripture by eyes healed by faith, nature and history are returned (at least in part) to their original revelatory function. Contemplating this order to the extent that it can, faith penetrates more deeply to arrive at true piety.

A word of caution is in order, however, both to guard against making Calvin's understanding of word and works more systematic than it can be reasonably claimed to be and also to underscore an important, if often overlooked, piece of evidence for the view of faith as new perception of heavenly and earthly realities. Providential faith is a knowledge of God through God's creative and providential works, as illuminated by the word of scripture and as revealing Christ the eternal Son. Saving faith is a knowledge of God's redemptive works, as illuminated by the word of scripture and as revealing Christ incarnate. What is often missed is the role of God's works, and in particular the visible evidences of the sacraments, in saving faith. As Thomas Torrance has detailed, Calvin held that in paradise certain "ancient sacraments," such as the tree of life and the tree of the knowledge of good and evil, exhibited Christ the word in a special way that is analogous to the presentation of Christ the redeemer in the Christian sacraments.[127] A simple opposition between the revelatory efficacy of God's word versus God's works (implied in the debate over Brunner's use of *Ergänzung*), or alternatively a view that links the word to knowledge of God the redeemer and works especially to knowledge to God the creator, does nothing to clarify Calvin's doctrines of knowledge of God and faith. Instead, one must take into account the complex ways in which the word as Christ, the word as scripture, visible works in general, and sacramental signs in particular work together to mediate, through the special agency of the Spirit, both aspects of the twofold knowledge of God.

The twofold notion of faith raises further issues, and it is helpful to return to the heuristic trinity of knowledge, certainty, and perception that guided my investigation earlier. The last two in particular raise critical questions that are in themselves worthy of much more detailed attention than I can provide at this point. My goal for the present is primarily to suggest possibilities for further research.

An investigation devoted solely to analysis of Calvin's evolving understanding of the certainty of faith would be an exceptionally worthwhile undertaking.[128] This study has traced Calvin's exegetical underpinnings of this notion to the Pauline epistles and, less directly, to the idea of faith as knowledge that he derives from the Johannine writings. I have also shown that in the final edition of the *Institutes* Calvin appears to integrate his concern with certainty with his interest to uphold the reality of doubt in an interesting way. Further attention to these discussions might be able to determine whether this final presentation of faith in 1559 reinforces or undermines Calvin's insistence on the certainty of faith. Clearly his willingness to acknowledge an implicitness to faith, to speak of the lower working of the Spirit in effecting faith among the reprobate, and to extend faith to God's activity apart from redemption all signal difficulties for his quest for certainty.[129] Moreover, the renewed emphasis on union with Christ also affects Calvin's views on the certainty of faith. A more detailed investigation into these matters would also need to attend more closely to Calvin's doctrine of predestination. As noted earlier, the relationship between predestination and faith has been treated and ultimately criticized by Schützeichel and Victor Shepherd. One might build on these earlier investigations by considering the scriptural underpinnings of Calvin's views on certainty, their development over time, and their relationship to a twofold notion of faith.

Finally, Calvin's final views on the perception of faith, especially as this relates to the perception of God's providence in nature and history, both retain the profound ambivalence of and exhibit greater complexity than his discussions in the 1530s. Do these statements about faith's perception of providence, both of the secret counsel of God's providential word and the limited glimpse of its manifestation in God's works in the present realm, mitigate or reinforce the notion of divine hiddenness, as this is expressed by Gerrish?

> But even for the redeemed, whose vision has been restored, the divine purpose in the world order cannot simply be read off from the face of nature and history. Calvin's doctrine of providence, so far from being inferred from the visible tokens of God's presence, is in fact developed despite God's hiddenness. We do not invariably *see* that God's hand is at work; we *believe* it on the basis of the Word. However things may be disposed in the design of God, to us, Calvin, admits, they are fortuitous.[130]

Does the eye of faith actually *see*, or is at the end of the day only the case that it *trusts* in a hidden reality? From Calvin's repeated recourse to Psalm 104 it appears that in the realm of nature the elect do indeed see something of God's providential ordering. In the realm of history, however, the eye of faith emerged with particularly clear vision only in the most dire of circumstances. Faith's glimpse from the watchtower into the future appears to be a rare instance of such an apprehension. In this respect, it is noteworthy that Calvin underscores his argument in the 1559 *Institutes* that things ordained by God's plan appear fortuitous even to the redeemed. Nevertheless, one must also consider Calvin's addition to this discussion in 1559, where he says that "what for us seems a contingency, faith *recognizes* [*agnoscet*] to have been a secret impulse from God."[131]

On the basis of my consideration of Calvin's commentaries and the *Institutes* I can hazard a provisional judgment. The apprehension of faith in this realm appears to be more than a blind trust in things hidden. True, believers with their restored vision do not simply read the reasons for providence off of nature and history but view these always in the mirror of the word. Moreover, they are not ultimately concerned with the purpose for which God does this or that but rather to perceive only that it is God who regulates all events. Though not yet able to understand the reasons for God's providential ordering of events, believers nevertheless recognize the divine hand and are led to wonder and reverence. Perhaps the strongest evidence for this argument is the simple fact that Calvin repeatedly resorts to visual terminology and images to characterize the nature and activity of providential faith. Although the notion of providential faith emerges most clearly in Calvin's commentary on the Psalms, more work needs to be done to fill in the outlines that I have traced here. Only then will it be possible to answer definitively the question of faith's perception. Such an investigation would need to attend especially to Calvin's commentaries on Genesis, Isaiah, and Jeremiah as well as to

Calvin's sermons on Job, 1 and 2 Samuel, and Genesis.[132] Moreover, any serious attempt to trace the relationship between faith and divine hiddenness would have to turn again to the knowledge of God the redeemer and take up the question of the eternal decree.[133]

In establishing the exegetical underpinnings of Calvin's understanding of faith and demonstrating the existence of a twofold notion of faith in Calvin's theology, this study hopes, finally, to suggest a *via media* in the debate over the ultimate principle of organization in the 1559 *Institutes*: Is this the Apostles' Creed, or the twofold knowledge of God? Proponents of the first position often hold that Calvin has expanded the Creed, previously prefaced by the discussion of faith, and organized all the material around these articles of faith. Advocates of the latter view hold that Calvin's increasing preoccupation with knowledge, especially knowledge of God, provides the structural basis for the final *Institutes*. Regardless of the view one takes, the twofold notion of faith is implied in both cases. This, in turn, suggests an alternative way of viewing the structure of this edition. In following the order of the Creed or the twofold knowledge of God, the doctrine of faith, like the doctrine of God (incorporating the doctrine of the word and the doctrine of the Spirit), extends over the entire work.[134] Calvin's discussions of these key doctrines are clearly concentrated in specific *loci*. Yet he did not let his doctrinally ordered presentation overwhelm an obvious sense of the inner coherence of Christian belief and his sensitivity to the variety of the scriptural witness to these topics.

Notes

Abbreviations

CCL   *Corpus Christianorum: Series Latina*. Turnhout: Brepols, 1953–.

CO   John Calvin, *Ioannis Calvini opera quae supersunt omnia*. Ed. Wilhelm Baum, Edward Cunitz, and Edward Reuss. 59 vols. Vols. 29–87 of the *Corpus Reformatorum*. Brunswick: C. A. Schwetschke and Son (M. Bruhn), 1863–1900.

Comm. Gal. et. al.   John Calvin. *Commentarii in Pauli Epistolas ad Galatas, ad Ephesios, ad Philippenses, ad Colossenses*. Ed. Helmut Feld. Vol. 16 of *Ioannis Calvini Opera Omnia: Series 2: Opera Exegetica Veteris et Novi Testamenti*. Geneva: Librairie Droz, 1992.

Comm. Heb.   John Calvin. *Commentarius in Epistolam ad Hebraeos*. Ed. T. H. L. Parker. Vol. 19 of *Ioannis Calvini Opera Omnia: Series 2: Opera Exegetica Veteris et Novi Testamenti*. Geneva: Librairie Droz, 1996.

Comm. Rom.   *Iohannis Calvini: Commentarius in Epistolam Pauli ad Romanos*. Ed. T. H. L. Parker. Studies in the History of Christian Thought 22. Leiden: E. J. Brill, 1981.

Comm. Sec. Cor.   John Calvin. *Commentarii in secundam Pauli Epistolam ad Corinthios*. Ed. Helmut Feld. Vol. 15 of *Ioannis Calvini Opera Omnia: Series 2: Opera Exegetica Veteris et Novi Testamenti*. Geneva: Librairie Droz, 1994.

Commentaires   *Les Commentaires à l'Ancien et au Nouveau Testament*. Publication sous les auspices de la Société calviniste de France. Geneva: Labor et Fides, 1960–.

In Johannem   John Calvin. *In Evangelium Secundum Johannem Commentarius Pars Prior*. Ed. Helmut Feld. Vol. 11/1 of *Ioannis Calvini Opera Omnia: Series 2: Opera Exegetica Veteris et Novi Testamenti*. Geneva: Librairie Droz, 1997.

Institutes (1536)   John Calvin. *Institutes of the Christian Religion: 1536 Edition*. Translated and annotated by Ford Lewis Battles. 1975; rev. ed., Grand Rapids: Eerdmans, 1986.

Institutes (1559)	John Calvin. *Calvin: Institutes of the Christian Religion*. Ed. John T. McNeill and trans. Ford Lewis Battles. 2 vols. Library of Christian Classics, vols. 20–21. Philadelphia: Westminster Press, 1960. Cited according to book, chapter, and section.
LW	*Luther's Works*. American Edition. Ed. Jaroslav Pelikan and Helmut T. Lehmann. 55 vols. St. Louis: Concordia Publishing House and Philadelphia: Fortress Press, 1955–1986.
OS	John Calvin. *Ioannis Calvini opera selecta*. Ed. Peter Barth, Wilhelm Niesel, and Dora Scheuner. 5 vols. Munich: Chr. Kaiser, 1926–1952.
PL	*Patrologiae Cursus Completus, Series Latina*. Ed. J.-P. Migne. Paris, 1841–1864.
Romans	John Calvin. *The Epistles of Paul the Apostle to the Romans and to the Thessalonians*. Trans. Ross Mackenzie. Grand Rapids: Eerdmans, 1961.
WA	Martin Luther. *D. Martin Luthers Werke: Kritische Gesamtausgabe*. Weimar, 1883–1957.

Introduction

1. *Catecheses* V.ix, in *Cyrilli Hierosolymarum archiepiscopi opera quae supersunt omnia*, ed. W. C. Reischl and J. Rupp (Munich, 1848; rpt. Hildesheim: Georg Olms Verlagsbuchhandlung, 1967), 1:149; in English, "Lenten Lectures," in vol. 1 of *The Works of St. Cyril of Jerusalem*, trans. Leo P. McCauley and Anthony A. Stephenson, vol. 61 of *The Fathers of the Church* (Washington: Catholic University of America Press, 1969), pp. 145–46.

2. In addition to the monographs cited in the next two notes, several "dissertations" from the late nineteenth and early twentieth centuries (average length is thirty pages), short journal articles, books, and unpublished scholarly dissertations treat Calvin's understanding of faith (sometimes in conjunction with other topics). The journal articles tend to restrict their view to the *Institutes*; see, for example, [?] Frerichs, "Der Glaube nach Calvins Unterricht in der christlichen Religion," *Reformierte Kirchenzeitung* 69 (1919): 19–22, 26–27; James M. Bulman, "The Place of Knowledge in Calvin's View of Faith," *Review and Expositor* 50 (1953): 323–29; George Gordh, "Calvin's Conception of Faith," *Review and Expositor* 50 (1953): 207–15. The following do not add anything to the monographs' conclusions about Calvin's understanding of faith; moreover, they also vary greatly in the accuracy of their portrayals of Calvin's views on this topic: P. E. Massot, *La notion de la foi d'après l'Institution chrétienne de Calvin* (Montauban, 1871); Benjamin Blondiaux, *De la notion de la foi d'après l'Institution chrétienne de Calvin* (Montauban, 1874); Alfred Boegner, *Quid Joannes Calvinus in libro tertio Institutionis christianae religionis de fide senserit exponitur et aestimatur* (Argentorati, 1876); Henry Booth Hazen, "Calvin's Doctrine of Faith" (B.D. thesis, University of Chicago, 1903); Johannes Fritz, *Der Glaubensbegriff bei Calvin und den Modernisten*, Freiburger Theologische Studien 11 (Freiburg: Herdersche Verlagshandlung, 1913); W. A. Hauck, *Christusglaube und Gottesoffenbarung nach Calvin* (Gütersloh: Bertelsmann, 1939); J. M. Jones, "The Problem of Faith and Reason in the Thought of John Calvin" (diss., Duke University, 1942); Paul Sebestyen, "The Object of Faith in the Theology of Calvin" (diss., University of Chicago, 1963); Joel R. Beeke, *Assurance of Faith: Calvin, English Puritanism, and the Dutch Second Reformation*, American University Studies, series 7, Theology and Religion 89 (New York: Peter Lang, 1991), pp. 47–77.

3. Simon Pieter Dee, *Het geloofsbegrip van Calvijn* (Kampen: J. H. Kok, 1918). A review and summary of Dee's book by A. G. Honig appears as "Het Geloofsbegrip van Calvijn," *Gereformeerd Theologisch Tijdschrift* 21 (1920): 132–46; 178–86; Walter E. Stuermann, *A Critical Study of Calvin's Concept of Faith* (Ann Arbor: Edwards Brothers, 1952); Edward A.

Dowey, *The Knowledge of God in Calvin's Theology* (1952; expanded ed. Grand Rapids: Eerdmans, 1994); Heribert Schützeichel, *Die Glaubenstheologie Calvins*, Beiträge zur Oekumenischen Theologie 9, ed. Heinrich Fries (Munich: Max Hueber, 1972).

4. Victor A. Shepherd, *The Nature and Function of Faith in the Theology of John Calvin*, NABPR Dissertation Series, no. 2 (Macon, Ga.: Mercer University Press, 1983).

5. Here the worst offenders are Shepherd, *The Nature and Function of Faith*, and Peter Brunner, *Vom Glauben bei Calvin: Dargestellt auf Grund der Institutio, des Catechismus Genevensis und unter Heranziehung exegetischer und homiletischer Schriften* (Tübingen: J. C. B. Mohr [Paul Siebeck], 1925). B. A. Gerrish points to one significant flaw in Shepherd's censure (*Grace and Gratitude: The Eucharistic Theology of John Calvin* [Minneapolis: Fortress Press, 1993], p. 62, note 47).

6. This is the case, for example, in Dee, *Het geloofsbegrip*; Stuermann, *Calvin's Concept of Faith*; Dowey, *Knowledge of God in Calvin's Theology*; W. A. Hauck, *Christusglaube und Gottesoffenbarung*; Frerichs, "Der Glaube nach Calvins Unterricht in der christlichen Religion"; see also Schützeichel, *Glaubenstheologie*, pp. 61 and 65–66.

7. For example, Schützeichel, *Glaubenstheologie*; Richard A. Muller, "*Fides* and *Cognitio* in Relation to the Problem of Intellect and Will in the Theology of John Calvin," *Calvin Theological Journal* 25/2 (November 1990): 207–24; William J. Bouwsma, *John Calvin: A Sixteenth-Century Portrait* (New York: Oxford University Press, 1988).

8. The most important recent literature includes: Richard C. Gamble, "Calvin as Theologian and Exegete: Is There Anything New?" *Calvin Theological Journal* 23 (1988): 178–94; Alexandre Ganoczy and Stefan Scheld, *Die Hermeneutik Calvins: Geistesgeschichtliche Voraussetzungen und Grundzüge*, Veröffentlichungen des Instituts für Europäische Geschichte 114 (Wiesbaden: Steiner, 1983); Alexandre Ganoczy, "Calvin als paulinischer Theologe," in *Calvinus Theologus*, ed. W. H. Neuser (Neukirchen: Neukirchener, 1976), pp. 39–69; Benoit Girardin, *Rhétorique et Théologique: Calvin, Le Commentaire de l'Épître aux Romains* (Paris: Éditions Beauchesne, 1979); Elsie Anne McKee, "Calvin's Exegesis of Romans 12: 8—Social, Accidental, or Theological?" *Calvin Theological Journal* 23 (1988): 6–18; Richard A. Muller, "The Hermeneutic of Promise and Fulfillment in Calvin's Exegesis of the Old Testament Prophecies of the Kingdom," in *The Bible in the Sixteenth Century*, ed. David Steinmetz (Durham, N.C.: Duke University Press, 1990), pp. 68–82; T. H. L. Parker, "Calvin the Exegete: Change and Development," in *Calvin Ecclesiae Doctor*, ed. W. H. Neuser (Kampen: J. H. Kok, 1981), pp. 33–46; *Calvin's New Testament Commentaries* (Grand Rapids: Eerdmans, 1971); *Calvin's Old Testament Commentaries* (Edinburgh: T. and T. Clark, 1986); David L. Puckett, *John Calvin's Exegesis of the Old Testament*, Columbia Series in Reformed Theology (Louisville: Westminster/John Knox Press, 1995); Susan E. Schreiner, "Exegesis and Double Justice in Calvin's Sermons on Job," *Church History* 58/3 (September 1989): 322–38; "'Through a Mirror Dimly': Calvin's Sermons on Job," *Calvin Theological Journal* 21 (November 1986): 175–93; *Where Shall Wisdom Be Found? Calvin's Exegesis of Job from Medieval and Modern Perspectives* (Chicago: University of Chicago Press, 1994); David C. Steinmetz: "Calvin and Abraham: The Interpretations of Romans 4 in the Sixteenth Century," *Church History* 57 (1988): 443–55; "Calvin and the Patristic Exegesis of Paul," in *The Bible in the Sixteenth Century*, pp. 100–18; *Calvin in Context* (New York: Oxford University Press, 1995); John L. Thompson, *John Calvin and the Daughters of Sarah: Women in Regular and Exceptional Roles in the Exegesis of Calvin, his Predecessors, and his Contemporaries* (Geneva: Droz, 1992); Thomas F. Torrance, *The Hermeneutics of John Calvin* (Edinburgh: Scottish Academic Press, 1988); Marten H. Woudstra, "Calvin Interprets What 'Moses Reports': Observations on Calvin's Commentary on Exodus 1–19," *Calvin Theological Journal* 21 (1986): 151–74; David F. Wright, "Calvin's Pentateuchal Criticism: Equity, Hardness of Heart, and Divine Accommodation in the Mosaic Harmony Commentary," *Calvin The-*

ological Journal 21 (1986): 33–50. Note also one early study: Louis Goumaz, *La Doctrine du Salut d'après les commentaires de Jean Calvin sur le Nouveau Testament* (Lausanne: Payot, 1917). Several of the English-language articles just listed and other important articles on Calvin's hermeneutics have been reprinted in *Calvin and Hermeneutics*, vol. 6 of *Articles on Calvin and Calvinism*, 14 vols., ed. Richard C. Gamble (Hamden, Conn.: Garland, 1992).

9. "First, as much in the fashioning of the universe as in the general teaching of scripture the Lord shows himself to be simply the creator. Then in the face of Christ he shows himself the redeemer. Of the resulting twofold knowledge of [God] we shall now discuss the first aspect; the second will be dealt with in its proper place" (*Institutes* [1559], 1.2.1; OS 3:34).

10. Josef Bohatec, "Calvins Vorsehungslehre," in *Calvinstudien: Festschrift zum 400. Geburtstag Johann Calvins* (Leipzig: Rudolph Haupt, 1909), pp. 348–93 and 434. To illustrate the character of providential faith, Bohatec draws not only on the discussions in the *Institutes* and various polemical treatises but also heavily on the commentary on the Psalms. It is noteworthy that he derives most of his information about the content of providential faith from the *Institutes* and the polemical treatises (pp. 352–86). An exception to this is his frequent citation of the Psalms commentary in his discussion of faith in God's meaningful government of the world (pp. 379–86). His primary source for the character (*Art*) of providential faith is the Psalms commentary (pp. 387–93).

11. Numerous scholars have followed Julius Köstlin, maintaining that the *duplex cognitio dei* constitutes the organizational principle of the 1559 edition ("Calvins Institutio nach Form und Inhalt, in ihrer geschichtlichen Entwicklung," *Theologische Studien und Kritiken* [1868]:6–62; 410–86). Battles notes that the explicit designation of a twofold knowledge was added in the 1559 edition, and he argues that this distinction "is basic to the structure of the completed work" (*Institutes* [1559], p. 40, note 3). Some are also inclined to see an implicit reference to the twofold knowledge as a principle of arrangement in Calvin's explicit declaration of his satisfaction with the final edition. In an addition to the preface originally composed in 1539 for the second Latin edition, Calvin writes, "each time the work has been reprinted since then [i.e., 1539], it has been enriched with some additions. Although I did not regret the labor spent, I was never satisfied until the work had been arranged in the order now set forth" (*Institutes* [1559], p. 3). Thus Calvin discusses knowledge of God the creator in book 1, which now contains all the material from chapter 1 of 1539, along with the discussion of the trinity that followed the exposition of faith in earlier editions, a new discussion of creation, and the section on providence (with some additions) from the chapter on predestination and providence. Knowledge of God the redeemer is discussed in books 2–4. See Dowey, *Knowledge of God in Calvin's Theology*; François Wendel, *Calvin: The Origins and Development of his Religious Thought*, trans. Philip Mairet (New York: Harper and Row, 1963; rpt. Durham, N.C.: Labyrinth Press, 1986), p. 121; Gerhard Ebeling, "Cognitio Dei et hominis," in *Geist und Geschichte der Reformation: Festgabe Hanns Rückert zum 65. Geburtstag*, ed. H. Liebing and K. Scholder (Berlin: Walter de Gruyter, 1966), pp. 304–5; compare Randall Zachman, *The Assurance of Faith: Conscience in the Theology of Martin Luther and John Calvin* (Minneapolis: Fortress Press, 1993), p. 93; B. A. Gerrish "Theology within the Limits of Piety Alone: Schleiermacher and Calvin's Notion of God," in *The Old Protestantism and the New: Essays on the Reformation Heritage* (Edinburgh: T. and T. Clark, 1982), pp. 199–201. Dowey defends his position and reinforces his claim that the *duplex cognitio Domini* "lies at the root of the dialectical structure of Calvin's thought" ("The Structure of Calvin's Theological Thought as Influenced by the Two-Fold Knowledge of God," in *Calvinus Ecclesiae Genevensis Custos*, ed. W. H. Neuser [Frankfurt am Main: Peter Lang, 1984], pp. 141–48, quotation is from p. 142; rpt. as "Influence of the Twofold Knowledge on Calvin's Theology," chapter 6 in the 1994 edition of

Knowledge of God in Calvin's Theology, quotation on p. 252). E. David Willis disagrees with Köstlin's ordering but also thinks that T. H. L. Parker's criticisms of Dowey are off the mark (*Calvin's Catholic Christology: The Function of the So-Called Extra Calvinisticum in Calvin's Theology*, Studies in Medieval and Reformation Thought, vol. 2 [Leiden: E. J. Brill, 1966], p. 103). See also Brian G. Armstrong, "*Duplex Cognitio Dei*, Or ? The Problem and Relation of Structure, Form, and Purpose in Calvin's Theology," in *Probing the Reformed Tradition: Historical Studies in Honor of Edward A. Dowey, Jr.*, ed. E. A. McKee and B. G. Armstrong (Louisville: Westminster/John Knox Press, 1989), pp. 135–53.

12. *Knowledge of God in Calvin's Theology*, p. 151. All references to this work are to the 1994 edition.

13. Schützeichel, *Glaubenstheologie*, p. 65.

14. *Knowledge of God in Calvin's Theology*, pp. 152–53 and 153, note 20.

15. Stuermann, *Calvin's Concept of Faith*, pp. iv, 37, and 73.

16. See Schützeichel, *Glaubenstheologie*, p. 131; compare H. Jackson Forstman, *Word and Spirit: Calvin's Doctrine of Biblical Authority* (Stanford: Stanford University Press, 1962), p. 90.

17. Dowey, *Knowledge of God in Calvin's Theology*, pp. 173–80; compare Werner Krusche, *Das Wirken des heiligen Geistes nach Calvin* (Göttingen: Vandenhoeck and Ruprecht, 1957), pp. 259–61.

18. "Now we shall possess a right definition of faith, if we say that faith is a firm and certain knowledge of the divine benevolence toward us, which, founded on the truth of the free promise in Christ, is both revealed to our minds and sealed on our hearts through the Holy Spirit" (CO 1:456; compare *Institutes* [1559], 3.2.7).

19. Dowey argues against Peter Brunner's emphasis on illumination as overcoming "the absolute distance between the finite thinking of men and the in-every-respect infinite object of faith's knowledge" (*Vom Glauben bei Calvin*, p. 131, quoted in Dowey, *Knowledge of God in Calvin's Theology*, p. 178). As Dowey sees it, the problem is much more blindness occasioned by sin than the gulf between finite and infinite. That blindness is the fundamental problem in the fallen world is, as Dowey points out, particularly evident in some of Calvin's New Testament commentaries, especially in the commentaries on the Fourth Gospel and the Pauline epistles (see pp. 178–79).

20. On this point, see Elsie Anne McKee, "Exegesis, Theology, and Development in Calvin's *Institutio*: A Methodological Suggestion," in *Probing the Reformed Tradition: Historical Studies in Honor of Edward A. Dowey, Jr.*, ed. E. A. McKee and B. G. Armstrong (Louisville: Westminster/John Knox Press, 1989), pp. 154–74.

One. From Fiducia to Cognitio

1. I am using the term "Lutheran" rather loosely to refer to the general movement whose adherents were in some way sympathetic to and identified themselves with Luther's theological reforms—in particular, with the doctrine of justification by faith alone. Calvin's relationship to Luther is a notoriously vexed and complicated question. For a discussion of what Calvin explicitly said about Luther, see B. A. Gerrish, "The Pathfinder: Calvin's Image of Martin Luther," in *The Old Protestantism and the New*, pp. 27–48; see also Wendel, *Calvin*, pp. 123, 131–35; David C. Steinmetz, *Luther in Context* (Bloomington, Ind.: Indiana University Press, 1986), pp. 85–97; Suzanne Selinger, *Calvin against Himself: An Inquiry into Intellectual History* (Hamden, Conn.: Archon Books, 1984), pp. 11–56. Further suggestions as to the influence of Luther on Calvin's early theology can be found in Köstlin, "Calvin's *Institutio*," p. 428; Wilhelm Diehl, "Calvins Auslegung des Dekalogs in der ersten Ausgabe seiner *Institutio* und Luthers Katechismen," *Theologische Studien und Kritiken* (Gotha, 1898);

August Lang, "Zwingli und Calvin," *Monographien zur Weltgeschichte*, fasc. 31 (Bielefeld, 1913), p. 106; "Die Quellen der Institutio von 1536," *Evangelische Theologie*, 3. Jahrgang (Munich: Chr. Kaiser, 1936; rpt. Amsterdam: John Benjamin N. V., 1969). On the particular character of Calvin's reformational origins, see Heiko A. Oberman, *Initia Calvini: The Matrix of Calvin's Reformation*, Mededelingen van de Afdeling Letterkunde, Nieuwe Reeks 54, no. 4 (Amsterdam: Koninklijke Nederlandse Akademie von Wetenschappen, 1991); rpt. in *Calvinus Sacrae Scripturae Professor: Calvin as Confessor of Holy Scripture*, ed. Wilhelm H. Neuser (Grand Rapids: Eerdmans, 1994), pp. 113–54.

2. Prior to the *Institutes* Calvin had published only prefaces to Olivétan's translation of the Bible into French (CO 9:787–90) and had written, but most likely not yet published, his treatise *Psychopannychia* (ed. W. Zimmerli, Quellenschriften zur Geschichte des Protestantismus 13 [Leipzig, 1932]). On the publication of the *Psychopannychia*, see Rodolphe Peter and Jean-François Gilmont, *Bibliotheca Calviniana: Les oeuvres de Jean Calvin publiées au XVIe siècle*, Travaux d'Humanisme et Renaissance 255 and 281 (Geneva: Librairie Droz, 1991, 1994), 1:115–16; and Alexandre Ganoczy, *The Young Calvin*, trans. David Foxgrover and Wade Provo (Philadephia: Westminster Press, 1987), pp. 77–78 and 99–100.

3. John Calvin, *Christianae religionis Institutio* [1536] (OS 1:11–280; CO 1:9–248). The quotation is from OS 1:92; CO 1:78; *Institutes* (1536), pp. 63, 64.

4. OS 1:44; CO 1:34; *Institutes* (1536), p. 21.

5. See also Dowey, "The Structure of Calvin's Theological Thought as Influenced by the Two-Fold Knowledge of God," p. 137; *Knowledge of God in Calvin's Theology* (1994), p. 246.

6. Ganoczy, *The Young Calvin*, p. 191.

7. Ganoczy, *The Young Calvin*, p. 190; see also pp. 191–92. Ganoczy points out that the "systematic Christ-centered approach to all issues is not original with Calvin." He traces this approach also to theologians influenced by the modern devotion (Erasmus, Lefèvre) and, of course, to Luther (p. 357, note 18). It is important to note that the substance of Luther's Christocentrism differs from the devotion to Christ influencing such figures as Erasmus and Lefèvre, who stressed the imitation of Christ. Marc Lienhard argues for three essential differences between Luther and the adherents of modern devotion: Luther is more interested in the incarnate Christ than imitating the man, Jesus; Christ, for Luther, is primarily the redeemer, not an example to be imitated; and Luther emphasizes the unity of cross and resurrection (*Luther: Witness to Jesus Christ: Stages and Themes of the Reformer's Christology*, trans. Edwin H. Robertson [Minneapolis: Augsburg, 1982], pp. 35–36).

8. Here it is necessary to disagree with Ganoczy's claim that "[n]either [Calvin nor Luther] pauses to analyze the *being* of the eternal Son of God made man, that is, to describe the hypostatic union; but they proceed directly to the exposition of his *work* of redemption" (*The Young Calvin*, p. 139). Actually, Calvin spends roughly half the space allotted to the discussion of this article defending the hypostatic union and at one point offers an analogy for conceiving it (OS 1:79; CO 1:66; *Institutes* [1536], p. 52). He also takes considerable pains to explicate the communication of properties. Yet this is all done within the context of Calvin's overarching soteriological concern.

9. In 1557 Calvin asserted that he wrote the *Institutes* in response to persecutions in France, with the hope that he might vindicate those whose religious sympathies he shared (CO 31:23). He also claimed that the first edition was meant as an instruction in the doctrine of salvation for the learned; see the "Argument du livre" for the 1541 French edition of the *Institutes*, which appears in English (mistakenly designated as the preface to the 1560 French edition) on pp. 6–8 of Battles's translation of the 1559 edition. Scholars thus generally acknowledge a twofold aim (e.g., Lang, "Die Quellen der Institutio von 1536," pp. 104–5). However, because the first four chapters of the 1536 edition follow the

pattern of Luther's catechisms, some have argued that this is a catechism turned apology. Wendel says that since Calvin subjected the apologetic sections to little revision in later editions while making "profound modifications" in the theological exposition, Calvin himself thought the theological content to be more important (*Calvin*, p. 146); Köstlin argues that the first three chapters make up three major parts designed to catechize, while the remaining chapters form appendices that take a polemical and apologetic turn, thereby transforming the clearly catechetical intent of the first three chapters ("Calvins Institutio," pp. 21–31); compare Peter and Gilmont, *Bibliotheca Calviniana*, 1:36–38. However, just because Calvin revised and expanded the theological exposition does not mean that in 1535, when he was writing the first edition, he did not conceive its primary purpose to be apologetic. Moreover, even though Calvin says that he wanted to set down the rudiments of evangelical faith for the French people "hungering and thirsting for Christ," he in fact did not simply do this but was driven by necessity to write an apology for that faith. One cannot maintain, with Köstlin, that the first three chapters are not permeated with the polemical and apologetic points of view that characterize the last three chapters (p. 26) or that these last three chapters do not especially explicate the question of justification (p. 25). Simply because the catechetical intent was an initial aim does not make it the primary one in the final product. Parker places the 1536 *Institutes* among the writings that were "occasional, called forth by some situation or another" (*Calvin's New Testament Commentaries*, p. 4). Olivier Millet also criticizes the catechism-turned-apology view held by Köstlin. Arguing, in my view correctly, for the literary unity of the 1536 edition, Millet also contends that the apologetic element does not determine the strategy and composition of the text (*Calvin et la dynamique de la parole: Étude de rhétorique réformée*, Bibliothèque Littéraire de la Renaissance, série 3, vol. 28 [Paris: Librairie Honoré Champion, 1992], pp. 585–87).

10. OS 1:21; CO 1:9; *Institutes* (1536), p. 1.

11. OS 1:37; CO 1:27; *Institutes* (1536), p. 15. For a discussion of the knowledge of God and self in the editions of 1536, 1539, and 1559, as well as a comparison of Calvin with Zwingli and Luther, see Ebeling, "Cognitio dei et hominis," pp. 271–322.

12. OS 1:39–40; CO 1:30; *Institutes* (1536), p. 17.

13. OS 1:41; CO 1:31; *Institutes* (1536), p. 18.

14. OS 1:68; CO 1:56; *Institutes* (1536), p. 42.

15. OS 1:96; CO 1:82; *Institutes* (1536), p. 68.

16. OS 1:119; CO 1:103; *Institutes* (1536), p. 88.

17. OS 1:162; CO 1:141; *Institutes* (1536), p. 124. See O. Millet's treatment of this chapter, in which he argues that it is no mere appendix (*Calvin et la dynamique*, pp. 583–84).

18. OS 1:223; CO 1:195; *Institutes* (1536), p. 176.

19. See Jean-Daniel Benoit, "The History and Development of the *Institutio*: How Calvin Worked" in *John Calvin: A Collection of Distinguished Essays*, ed. G. E. Duffield (Grand Rapids: Eerdmans, 1966), p. 103. Recall Calvin's words to the king, stating that he has here "embraced almost the sum of that very doctrine." The second edition (1539) appears to acknowledge this overstatement (though with no less modesty with respect to its own achievements) by substituting the words: "now at last truly corresponding to its title."

20. For a discussion of the shape of this concept in the 1536 edition, see Ganoczy, *The Young Calvin*, pp. 188–190. Ganoczy points out that Calvin followed scripture in conceiving of the glory of God in terms of royalty and that he "stressed two ways of celebrating the glory of God: service and praise" (p. 189).

21. OS 1:23; CO 1:11; *Institutes* (1536), p. 3.

22. OS 1:25; CO 1:14; *Institutes* (1536), p. 4.

23. OS 1:37; CO 1:27; *Institutes* (1536), p. 15.
24. OS 1:104; CO 1:89; *Institutes* (1536), p. 75.
25. OS 1:66; CO 1:54; *Institutes* (1536), p. 40.
26. OS 1:103; CO 1:88; *Institutes* (1536), p. 74.
27. OS 1:33; CO 1:23–24; *Institutes* (1536), p. 12.
28. OS 1:24–25; CO 1:13–14; *Institutes* (1536), p. 4.
29. OS 1:58; CO 1:47; *Institutes* (1536), p. 33.
30. OS 1:59; CO 1:47–48; *Institutes* (1536), p. 34.
31. For a discussion of medieval theories about faith, see Elisabeth Gössmann, "Glaube V. Mittelalter," *Theologische Realenzyclopädie* (New York: de Gruyter, 1977–), 17:308–18. On a broader note, Olga Weijers has explored the various shifts in meaning of words expressing the notions of "faith" and "belief" in the medieval period in "Some Notes on 'Fides' and Related Words in Medieval Latin," *Archivum Latinitatis Medii Aevi* 40 (1977): 77–102. She notes that in the Middle Ages the word *fides* came to be associated primarily with Christian faith, leading to a decline from the number of other meanings the word once represented. Thus, for example, "*fides*, being the technical term for Christian faith, tended to lose its aptitude for performing a second particular function, viz. that of the feudal fidelity or oath, which was taken over by *fidelitas*" (p. 94). Along with this crowding out of other applications there is a shift in emphasis from one of the classical meanings of the word to the other. In antiquity, *fides* meant primarily "guarantee" or "reliability," but in medieval texts this meaning is nearly eclipsed by the meaning "trust" or "faith," in the sense of believing or giving credence to something. At the same time, *fides* came to be distinguished from *fiducia* and *confidentia* "by the fact that the concept of 'Christian doctrine' (viz. the contents of Christian Faith, the collection of articles that are and should be believed) is expressed by *fides* but never by *fiducia* or *confidentia*. This means that *fides* can have an objective application, whereas *fiducia* and *confidentia* only allow a subjective one" (p. 97). In some ways, Luther's frequent identification of *fides* and *fiducia* marks a further narrowing of the meaning of *fides* through a new shift in stress from the objective to the subjective application of the word. See also Susan E. Schreiner, "Faith," in *The Oxford Encyclopedia of the Reformation*, ed. Hans Hillerbrand et al. (New York: Oxford University Press, 1996), 2:89–93.
32. OS 1:69; CO 1:57; *Institutes* (1536), p. 43. P. Brunner's insistence that Calvin concentrates almost exclusively on the *fides quae creditur* and shows little interest in the *fides qua creditur* is curious (see *Vom Glauben bei Calvin*, pp. 113–15). Even in the 1536 *Institutes*, in which the instructional element is perhaps most pronounced, Calvin discusses faith in the section devoted to that topic from the perspective of the act of believing.
33. John B. Payne notes a similar lack of precision with respect to the distinction between the *fides quae* and the *fides qua* in Erasmus; see "Erasmus: Interpreter of Romans," in *Sixteenth Century Essays and Studies*, ed. Carl S. Meyer (St. Louis: Foundation for Reformation Research, 1971), p. 21. Walther von Loewenich discusses the relationship between *fides qua* and *fides quae* in Luther, arguing that for Luther the two are never to be separated (*Wahrheit und Bekenntnis im Glauben Luthers dargestellt im Anschluß an Luthers Großen Katechismus*, Institut für Europäische Geschichte Mainz Vorträge 57 [Wiesbaden: Steiner, 1972]). Against certain existentialist interpretations of Luther, von Loewenich underscores the importance of the *fides quae*, insisting that "the *fides qua creditur* is based on the *fides quae creditur*" (p. 22). Compare this to P. Brunner's similar claim for Calvin (*Vom Glauben bei Calvin*, p. 115).
34. P. Brunner, *Vom Glauben bei Calvin*, pp. 139–40, note 3; compare Wendel, *Calvin*, p. 240. Brunner locates the distinction in Luther's "Eine kurze Form der zehn Gebote, eine kurze Form des Glaubens, eine kurze Form des Vaterunsers" (1520), which appeared in Latin translation as "Enchiridion piarum precationum" (WA 7:215). On Melanchthon, see

Ganoczy, *The Young Calvin*, pp. 147–48. For additional summary of other literature contributing to Calvin's views, see the notes to Battles's translation of the 1536 *Institutes*, pp. 252–55. For other similarities to the notions of faith in Melanchthon and Bucer, see Krusche, *Das Wirken des heiligen Geistes*, p. 257.

35. See, for example, Augustine, *Enarrationes in Psalmos* 77, sec. 8 (CCL 39:1073). Schützeichel points out that this is the only place that Augustine uses "God" as the object; elsewhere he speaks of *credere Christum, Christo, et in Christum: In Iohannis Evangelium Tractatus CXXIV*, tract. 29, sec. 6 and tract. 53, sec. 10 (CCL 36:287, lines 33–41, and 36: 456); *Enarrationes in Psalmos* 130, sec. 1 (CCL 40:1898); *Sermones ad populum*, sermon 144, chap. 2, sec. 2 (PL 38:788). See also Thomas Aquinas, *Summa Theologiae*, part 2–2, quest. 2, art. 2, and the additional references given by Schützeichel, *Glaubenstheologie*, p. 76, note 19. Christof Gestrich notes the importance of Augustine's views on faith in his interpretation of John 6 and 7 for the understanding of faith in the sixteenth century and for Zwingli in particular: "Nach Augustin besteht also der seligmachende, mit Christus vereinigende Glaube aus dem Zusammenwirken der drei theologischen Tugenden: Glaube, Hoffnung und Liebe." The recovery of this idea by Luther and Zwingli marks, according to Gestrich, a distinctive feature against scholastic theology (*Zwingli als Theologe: Glaube und Geist beim Zürcher Reformator*, Studien zur Dogmengeschichte und systematischen Theologie 20 [Zürich: Zwingli, 1967], pp. 149–51).

36. Heiko A. Oberman, *The Harvest of Medieval Theology: Gabriel Biel and Late Medieval Nominalism* (1963; rpt. Durham, N.C.: The Labyrinth Press, 1983), p. 465. This concept is apparently more difficult to define than the others; David Steinmetz defines it as "a loving confidence in God" (*Luther in Context*, p. 34). Mark D. Jordan, speaking specifically (and deliberately with caution) with respect to Thomas, calls it "believing for the sake of attaining God as one's last end, as the goal of one's willing" (In Thomas Aquinas, *On Faith: Summa Theologiae, Part 2–2, Questions 1–16 of St. Thomas Aquinas* [Notre Dame: University of Notre Dame Press, 1990], pp. 69–70, note 14).

37. OS 1:68–69; CO 1:56; *Institutes* (1536), p. 42. Compare the similar statements in Philip Melanchthon's *Loci communes* (1521) (*Loci communes theologici* [1521], in *Philippi Melanchthonis Opera quae supersunt omnia*, ed. C. G. Bretschneider and H. E. Bindsell, 28 vols., in *Corpus Reformatorum*, vols. 1–28 [Brunswick: C. A. Schwetschke and Son (M. Bruhn), 1854; rpt. 1963], 21:161, lines 15–20; English translation in *Philip Melanchthan and Martin Bucer [Selections]*, *Melanchthon and Bucer*, ed. Wilhelm Pauck, Library of Christian Classics, vol. 19 [Philadelphia: Westminster Press, 1969], pp. 91–92). Wendel says that Calvin may have known the 1521 edition of the *Loci* and certainly knew the 1535 edition, because he wrote a preface to the French translation of that edition in 1546 (*Calvin*, pp. 134–35), in fact, the translation was likely made from a later edition of the *Loci*, probably the Basel edition of 1545. Reinhard Schwarz points to Luther's designation of two kinds of faith, a *fides acquisita* and a *fides infusa*, in his marginal comments on Peter Lombard's *Sentences* (1509/1510). The latter is never separated from justifying grace, whereas the former has nothing to do with it. Schwarz argues that this distinction of two kinds of faith represents a break with the entire medieval tradition, insofar as Luther collapses unformed and acquired faith and unites infused faith with love (*Fides, Spes und Caritas beim jungen Luther. Unter besonderer Berücksichtigung der mittelalterlichen Tradition*, Arbeiten zur Kirchengeschichte 34 [Berlin: de Gruyter, 1962], p. 42; compare Martin Luther, WA 9: 90.24–34). In exploring the origin of the *fides historica* in Zwingli, Gestrich notes that this term appears with any frequency in Luther's works only after 1531; he points out also that Luther, in distinction to Zwingli's use of the term, uses it primarily to cover the scholastic *fides acquisita* and *fides informis*. Gestrich concludes that Zwingli most likely derives his understanding of *fides historica* from Melanchthon, and he quotes the 1521 version of the passage just cited (*Zwingli als Theologe*, pp. 29–31, note 36).

38. OS 1:69; CO 1:56; *Institutes* (1536), p. 42.

39. According to Augustine, demons believe both that Christ is and that what Christ says is true. "Nam ipsum esse Christum et daemones crediderunt, nec tamen in Christum daemones crediderunt. Ille enim credit in Christum, qui et sperat in Christum et diliget Christum. Nam si fidem habet sine spe ac sine dilectione, Christum esse credit, non in Christum credit" (*Serm. ad pop.*, serm. 144, chap. 2, sec. 2 [PL 38:788]). "Nam et daemones credebant ei, et non credebant in eum" (*In Iohannis Evangelium*, tract. 29, sec. 6 [CCL 36: 287]).

40. In contrast to Calvin, at least at this point, Bucer acknowledges that scripture uses both phrases *credere Deo* and *credere in Deum* to indicate both temporary belief and genuine faith; see *Metaphrases et enarrationes perpetuae epistolarum D. Pauli Apostoli . . . Tomus primus. continens metaphrasim et enarrationem in Epistolam ad Romanos* (Strasbourg, 1536; 2d ed. Basel, 1562); English translation of the discussion of faith from 1562 in *Common Places of Martin Bucer*, trans. and ed. D. F. Wright, Courtenay Library of Reformation Classics 4 [Appleford, England: The Sutton Courtenay Press, 1972], pp. 172–200).

41. OS 1:93–94; CO 1:79; *Institutes* (1536), p. 65.

42. OS 1:94; CO 1:80; *Institutes* (1536), p. 66.

43. Schwarz, *Fides, Spes und Caritas*, p. 48, note 110. For a list of medieval literature pertaining to *fides informis*, *fides acquisita*, and *fides daemonum*, see Schützeichel, *Glaubenstheologie*, p. 83, note 20. For a discussion of these terms in Biel, Bonaventure, and d'Ailly, see Schwarz, *Fides, Spes und Caritas*, pp. 43–48. For an assessment and a critique of Calvin's understanding of the *fides informis*, see Schützeichel, *Glaubenstheologie*, pp. 85–88.

44. OS 1:95; CO 1:80; *Institutes* (1536), p. 66.

45. For lists of literature relating to the use of 1 Cor. 13:2 to support distinctions in faith, see Schützeichel, *Glaubenstheologie*, pp. 86–87, and Battles's notes to p. 66 in the 1536 *Institutes* (notes are on p. 267; see especially notes to "power").

46. "This Paul teaches in his definition, calling it a 'substance of things hoped for, and the proof of things not seen.' By substance or hypostasis (as the Greek has it) he understands a support on which we lean and recline. It is as if he said: faith is a certain and sure possession of those things that God has promised us." Calvin goes on to stress that in order to possess such lofty things, we must exceed our own nature, press our vision, and surpass ourselves. These things are possessed in hope and are secure even though not seen. He continues "while he calls it an indication and proof (in Greek *elenchus* [*sic*], demonstration) of things not appearing, he is speaking as if to say that the evidence of things not appearing is the vision of things which are not seen, the perception of things obscure, the presence of things absent, the proof of things hidden." He then concludes concerning this second kind of faith, "This sort of faith is far different from the first one. Whoever has this kind of faith cannot but be accepted by God; on the contrary, without it, it cannot happen that anyone will ever please him" (OS 1:69–70; CO 1:57; *Institutes* [1536], p. 43).

47. See Kenneth Hagen, *Hebrews Commenting from Erasmus to Bèze: 1516–1598*, Beiträge zur Geschichte der Biblischen Exegese 23 (Tübingen: J. C. B. Mohr [Paul Siebeck], 1981), p. 8, note 15.

48. On Luther's use of this term, see Schwarz, *Fides, Spes und Caritas*, pp. 311–13, and Helmut Feld, *Martin Luthers und Wendelin Steinbachs Vorlesungen über den Hebräerbrief: Eine Studie zur Geschichte der Neutestamentlichen Exegese und Theologie*, Veröffentlichungen des Instituts für Europäische Geschichte 62 (Wiesbaden: Steiner, 1971), pp. 181–82.

49. That Heb. 11:1 represented a definition of faith was held by some, but not all, earlier exegetes; on this point and the others raised see Schwarz, *Fides, Spes und Caritas*, pp. 58–61 and 63–64 (especially notes 148, 151, and 152).

50. Schwarz argues that Luther's first Psalms lectures (1513–1515) mark an important

stage in the development of this view; see his section entitled "Der Glaube as Zeichen und Besitz der Zukunft," in *Fides, Spes und Caritas*, pp. 154–72.

51. OS 1:69; CO 1:57; *Institutes* (1536), p. 43.

52. OS 1:88; CO 1:74; *Institutes* (1536), p. 60.

53. OS 1:91; CO 1:77; *Institutes* (1536), p. 63.

54. "But if finally even after long waiting our senses cannot learn the benefit received from prayer, or perceive any fruit from it, still our faith will make us sure of what cannot be perceived by sense, that we have obtained what was expedient" (OS 1:117; CO 1:101; *Institutes* [1536], p. 86).

55. "Adeoque haec fidei natura est, aures arrigere, oculos claudere, hoc est, promissioni attendere, cogitationem avertere ab omni hominis dignitate vel merito" (OS 1:60; CO 1: 48; *Institutes* [1536], p. 34). Schwarz discusses the view of faith as light and vision in Luther's first Psalm lectures and notes a similar ambiguity toward physical sense perception (*Fides, Spes und Caritas*, pp. 140–53, especially pp. 142–43, 149–50). Of course, the issue of perception in both Luther and Calvin is linked to the theme of illumination, which has a particularly rich history in the tradition and finds one of its foremost representatives in Augustine, as noted by Schwarz on p. 140, note 192.

56. William J. Bouwsma, *John Calvin*, p. 158. See also E. David Willis's observation that "Calvin emphasizes the priority of hearing over seeing as a means of receiving revelation" (*Calvin's Catholic Christology*, p. 118); compare P. Brunner, *Vom Glauben bei Calvin*, pp. 109–10.

57. OS 1:119; CO 1:103; *Institutes* (1536), p. 88. See also OS 1:121–22; CO 1:105; *Institutes* (1536), p. 90.

58. Underlying Calvin's rejection of Zwingli's spiritualizing of the sacraments are a less dualistic anthropology and a different understanding of faith. Ganoczy notes that in the 1536 *Institutes* Calvin quotes a passage directly from Zwingli's *Commentary on True and False Religion* (1525) that expresses the view that faith cannot be increased by the sacraments and then goes on to reject this position (*The Young Calvin*, pp. 152–53). On Zwingli, see Gestrich, *Zwingli als Theologe*, pp. 25–27, 42–54.

59. Calvin describes this in the chapter on the sacraments; see OS 1:121; CO 1:104; *Institutes* (1536), p. 89.

60. OS 1:84; CO 1:71; *Institutes* (1536), p. 57.

61. "And, as he [God] once established, so now he sustains, nourishes, activates, [and] preserves by his goodness and power, apart from which all things would immediately collapse and fall into nothingness. But when we call him almighty and creator of all things, we must ponder such omnipotence whereby he works all things in all and such providence whereby he regulates all things—not of the sort those Sophists fancy: empty, insensate, idle. By faith are we to be persuaded that whatever happens to us, happy or sad, prosperous or adverse, whether it pertains to the body or to the soul, comes to us from him (sin only excepted, which is to be imputed to our own wickedness); also by his protection we are kept safe, defended, and preserved from any unfriendly force causing us harm" (OS 1:76; CO 1:63; *Institutes* [1536], p. 49). For a short summary of the treatment of providence in the 1536 edition, see J. Bohatec, "Calvins Vorsehungslehre," p. 342.

62. Recall that Calvin explicitly says that he has shown faith to be "trust in the one God and Christ [*in unum Deum ac Christum fiduciam*]" (OS 1:93–94; CO 1:79; *Institutes* [1536], p. 65; compare OS 1:37, 42, 69, 75; CO 1:27, 32, 56, 63; *Institutes* [1536], pp. 15, 19, 42–43, 49). P. Brunner observes, "Besonders häufig in der ersten Ausgabe der Institutio hat Calvin den Glauben als Vertrauen bestimmt" (*Vom Glauben bei Calvin*, p. 139).

63. "But this cannot have its seat in a devious, perverted and false heart, nor can it be begun or sustained except by God's grace alone" (OS 1:70; CO 1:57; *Institutes* [1536],

p. 43). Schwarz finds the linking of faith and the word in Luther's first lectures on the Psalms (1513–1515) to be much closer than in his earlier comments on the *Sentences* and views this as a starting point for new theological thinking (*Fides, Spes und Caritas*, pp. 157 and 221–23).

64. "This is what God requires of us by the First Commandment of his law. Having first said that he is the one Lord our God, he adds that we are not to have other gods before him. This obviously means that in no one else but him are our hope and trust to rest, for they are owed to him alone. He also hints that, if our hope and trust look to another, we have another god" (OS 1:70; CO 1:57; *Institutes* [1536], p. 44). Compare to Luther in "The Freedom of a Christian" (*LW* 31:352–53) and "The Large Catechism" ("Großer Katechismus," in *Die Bekenntinisschriften der evangelisch-lutherischen Kirche* [Göttingen: Vandenhoeck und Ruprecht, 1986], p. 560; in English, "Large Catechism," in *The Book of Concord: The Confessions of the Evangelical Lutheran Church*, trans. and ed. Theodore G. Tappert [Philadelphia: Fortress Press, 1959] p. 365). Compare also Schwarz, *Fides, Spes und Caritas*, p. 257–59.

65. For more detailed discussions, see Ganoczy, *The Young Calvin*, pp. 91–131; Wendel, *Calvin*, pp. 46–68. On Calvin in Geneva, see Richard Hörcsik, "John Calvin in Geneva, 1536–38—Some Questions about Calvin's First Stay in Geneva," in *Calvinus Sacrae Scripturae Professor: Calvin as Confessor of Holy Scripture*, ed. William H. Neuser (Grand Rapids: Eerdmans, 1994), pp. 155–65.

66. Ganoczy thinks it is likely that Calvin knew Oswald Myconius, Simon Grynaeus, and Wolfgang Capito; he may also have met Heinrich Bullinger, Guillaume Farel, Pierre Viret, Pierre Caroli, Elie Courrand, Claude de Feray, and Pierre Toussaint (*The Young Calvin*, pp. 92–93).

67. CO 5:245; OS 1:295. The two epistles, written in Italy in 1536 and published together the following year, are entitled "De fugiendis impiorum illicitis sacris, et puritate Christianae religionis observanda" and "De Christiani hominis officio in sacerdotiis Papalis ecclesiae vel administrandis, vel abiiciendis" and were published as "Epistolae duae de rebus hoc saeculo cognitu apprime necessariis" (CO 5:233–312; OS 1:287–362). It is generally thought that the former letter was addressed to Nicolas Duchemin, at this time an ecclesiastical official in France, and the latter to Gerard Roussel, recently ordained bishop (see Ganoczy, *The Young Calvin*, p. 112). For details about the writing and publication of the letters, see Wendel, *Calvin*, p. 47, and OS 1:285.

68. In the 1536 *Institutes*, Calvin speaks about the mass in extremely harsh terms, presenting it as a satanic corruption, as blasphemy and sacrilege. Still, at one point he implies that it is possible to receive its benefits and that to partake with the proper frame of mind is not idolatrous (OS 1:143–44; CO 1:124; *Institutes* [1536], p. 108). In "On Fleeing the Illicit Rites of the Wicked ("De fugiendis," n. 67), Calvin intensifies his criticism of the adoration of the sacrament such that it becomes to his mind equally if not more problematic and detrimental to true piety than the idea of mass as sacrifice. The theme of idolatry is not a prominent one in chapter 4 of the 1536 *Institutes*, appearing only at one point (OS 1:144; CO 1:125; *Institutes* [1536], pp. 108–9). However, it is the major concern of this epistle.

69. Parker gives five reasons for supposing that the subject of the lectures, given between 1536 and 1538, was Paul's epistle to the Romans. See *Comm. Rom.*, p. ix.

70. CO 5:276; OS 1:327. And, further, "The things that I put before you are not things that I quietly pondered with myself in my privacy but those to which God's invincible martyrs always submitted themselves amid crosses, flames, and ravenous beasts" (CO 5:278; OS 1:328).

71. "Instruction et confession de foy dont on use en l'Eglise de Geneve" (1537), CO

22:5–96. For views on the authorship of the confession from 1536 (CO 9:693–700), which was combined with Calvin's catechism (instruction), see CO 22:9–18 and Peter and Gilmont, *Bibliotheca Calviniana* 1:44–46.

72. On Caroli's challenge to Calvin's views on the Trinity, see Ganoczy, *The Young Calvin*, pp. 114–17. In September 1537 Calvin participated in a colloquy at Bern, along with Capito, Bucer, Myconius, Grynaeus, Farel, and Viret. This colloquy yielded a common confession of faith concerning the eucharist that expressed Calvin's view of how the eucharistic gift is received. While denying with Zwingli the local presence of Christ's glorified body, the *Confessio fidei de Eucharistia* (OS 1:435–36; CO 9:711–12) affirmed against the Zwinglian view a real and substantial eating and a real presence in the Supper. It also said that the Spirit is the bond of participation in the eucharist.

73. See Ganoczy, *The Young Calvin*, pp. 119–125.

74. *Iacobi Sadoleti romani cardinalis epistola ad senatum populumque Genevensem* and *Ioannis Calvini responsio*, OS 1:437–88; CO 5:365–416; in English, *John Calvin and Jacopo Sadoleto: A Reformation Debate*, ed. John C. Olin (1966; rpt. Grand Rapids: Baker Book House, 1976).

75. Wendel, *Calvin*, p. 61; Parker, *Calvin's New Testament Commentaries*, p. 10; Anette Zillenbiller, *Die Einheit der katholischen Kirche. Calvins Cyprianrezeption in seinen ekklesiologische Schriften*, Veröffentlichungen des Instituts für Europäische Geschichte (Mainz: Philipp von Zabern, 1993), pp. 35–43; Cornelius Augustijn, "Calvin in Strasbourg," in *Calvinus Sacrae Scripturae Professor: Calvin as Confessor of Holy Scripture*, ed. Wilhelm H. Neuser (Grand Rapids: Eerdmans, 1994), pp. 166–77.

76. See the discussion of these matters in Ganoczy, *The Young Calvin*, pp. 131 and 287–307. The last quote is from p. 297. While I agree with Ganoczy that the documents from 1539 show a new, more confident attitude in the legitimacy of Calvin's own calling (p. 292), I find that the prophetic tone of the two letters from 1537 already indicates a movement in this direction. In these, Calvin writes with a much greater sense of his own authority than he does in the 1536 *Institutes* and, to some extent, *does* commit himself to public action, if not yet as a pastor, at least as a prophet. Yet this awareness is not at all complete until, as Ganoczy so persuasively demonstrates, Calvin experiences the victories and defeats in Geneva and profoundly questions the origin of his call.

77. On the successive editions of the *Institutes*, see CO 1:xxx–xliv; Köstlin, "Calvin's Institutio"; Wendel, *Calvin*, pp. 111–122 and 144–49; Schützeichel, *Glaubenstheologie*, pp. 62–67; Wulfert de Greef, *The Writings of John Calvin: An Introductory Guide*, trans. Lyle D. Bierma (Grand Rapids: Baker Books, 1993), pp. 195–202; and the introduction to the English translation of the 1559 edition, 1:xxix–xlii.

78. In the 1536 edition: "Summa fere sacrae doctrinae duabus his partis constat: Cognitione Dei ac nostri" (OS 1:37; CO 1:28). In the 1539 edition: "Tota fere sapientiae nostrae summa, quae vera demum ac solida sapientia censeri debeat, duabus partibus constat: cognitione Dei, et nostri" (CO 1:279). Regarding this change, Bouwsma makes the following interesting observation: "This rather absolute wording suggested that he held, in 1536, a traditional conception of theology as *God's* truth rather than ours. But the second edition, three years later, made an interesting change, as though something had troubled him about the earlier wording. Now, for 'sacred doctrine,' he substituted 'our wisdom . . . ,' that is, the best sort of knowledge we limited creatures can manage." Bouwsma suggests that Calvin understood theology to be a "remarkably human enterprise" that states truths not in absolute terms and adds that Calvin may not have realized this "immediately or fully" (*John Calvin*, p. 160). See also Ebeling, "Cognitio Dei et hominis," pp. 289–90.

79. Augustine, *Epistola* CXLIII, PL 33:586.

80. See Wendel, *Calvin*, pp. 144–49.

81. CO 1:255.

82. Wendel, *Calvin*, pp. 147–49.

83. In the dedication to his Romans commentary, dated October 18, 1539, Calvin recalls a friendly discussion that he and Simon Grynaeus had three years earlier about the best way to interpret scripture. See *Comm. Rom.*, p. 1.

84. Aside from the rare instances where Calvin identifies his source or the easily detectable influence of certain biblical texts (such as Romans) or patristic writings (such as those by Augustine or Chrysostom), it is difficult, if not impossible in most cases, to isolate the particular biblical texts or patristic writings that shaped Calvin's expression of these views in 1539.

85. Peter Barth, "Fünfundzwanzig Jahre Calvinforschung," *Theologische Rundschau*, Neue Folge 6 (1934): 164. This statement echoes earlier ones by Köstlin ("Calvin's Institutio," p. 39) and Benjamin Warfield (*Calvin and Calvinism* [New York: Oxford University Press, 1931], p. 30). See also Wendel, *Calvin*, p. 115. Schützeichel says that the 1539 edition formed the theological foundation for all later editions (*Glaubenstheologie*, p. 62). H. Strohl discusses the effect of Calvin's statements in 1539 on providence and predestination on his later presentation of these topics ("La Pensée de Calvin sur la Providence divine au temps où il était réfugié à Strasbourg," *Revue d'Histoire et de Philosophie Religieuses* 22 [1942]: 154–69).

86. On the role of knowledge in Calvin's theology, especially as this pertains to knowledge of God, see Dowey, *Knowledge of God in Calvin's Theology*, especially chaps. 1–2; Bouwsma, *John Calvin*, chaps. 6 and 9; and T. H. L. Parker, *Calvin's Doctrine of the Knowledge of God* (1952; rev. ed., Grand Rapids: Eerdmans, 1959). Parker notes specifically that the concept of knowledge is not a major theme in 1536 (pp. 1–2).

87. In treating each of these topics in turn, Calvin follows the pattern that he adopted in the catechisms of 1537 (French) and 1538 (Latin), where, as noted by Jacques Pannier, the ideas developed here are often formulated in identical words. Pannier also points out that Guillaume Farel's *Sommaire* (1524) began with an opening chapter entitled "de Dieu" and a second chapter "de l'homme" (Jean Calvin, *Institution de la religion chrestienne* [Geneva, 1541], ed. J. Pannier [Paris: Societe les belles lettres, 1936; rpt. 1961], 1:307, note *a* to page 39). For further discussion of Farel's influence on Calvin, see Charles Partee, "Farel's Influence on Calvin: A Prolusion," (1983; rpt. in Gamble, *Articles*, 1:73–85). For a discussion and evaluation of the literature tracing the distinction between knowledge of God and self to Zwingli (P. Wernle, A. Lang, F. Blanke), Clement of Alexandria (the editors of the OS), and Guillaume Budé (J. Bohatec), see Ebeling, "Cognitio Dei et hominis," pp. 281–82.

88. Bouwsma notes that a general crisis about knowledge dominated the intellectual climate of the fourteenth to seventeenth centuries. He argues that Calvin's concern with the problem of knowledge needs to be understood in this context (*John Calvin*, p. 150 and all of chap. 9). On this point see also Charles Trinkaus, "Renaissance Problems in Calvin's Theology," in *Studies in the Renaissance*, vol. 1, ed. W. Peery (New York: Renaissance Society of America, 1954), pp. 59–80. Finally, Ganoczy points out that Calvin's discussion of what ought to be known, what can be known, and how it is known also shows the influence of his reading of Romans 1 ("Calvin als paulinischer Theologe," p. 60).

89. The discussion appears in CO 1:279–82.

90. See Bouwsma, *John Calvin*, p. 100; compare the quotations from Calvin given on pp. 99 and 103.

91. For example, "Just so, an eye to which nothing is shown but black objects judges something dirty white or even rather darkly mottled to be whiteness itself. Indeed, we can discern still more clearly from the bodily senses how much we are deluded in estimating

the powers of the soul. For if in broad daylight we either look down upon the ground or survey whatever meets our view round about, we seem to ourselves endowed with the strongest and keenest sight; yet when we look up to the sun and gaze straight at it, that power of sight that was particularly strong on earth is at once blunted and confused by a great brilliance, and thus we are compelled to admit that our keenness in looking upon things earthly is sheer dullness when it comes to the sun" (CO 1:280–81). For the editions of 1539–1554 I have relied on the English translations of the corresponding passages in the 1559 edition by Battles but have occasionally altered the quotations without notation.

92. Dowey, *Knowledge of God in Calvin's Theology*, p. 26; see the full discussion of this topic on pp. 24–31. Compare also the similar arguments advanced by Krusche (*Das Wirken des heiligen Geistes*, pp. 50–51) and Muller, "*Fides* and *Cognitio*," p. 219.

93. CO 1:285. Ganoczy argues that even though Calvin first offers a definition of piety and explicitly links it to knowledge of God in 1539, the idea underlies the presentation in the 1536 *Institutes*, especially in the Dedicatory Epistle (*The Young Calvin*, pp. 194–209).

94. "And here again we ought to observe that we are called to a knowledge of God: not that knowledge that is content with empty speculation but that which will be sound and fruitful if we duly perceive it" (CO 1:288–89; compare *Institutes* [1559], 1.5.9, which adds two phrases: "non quae inani speculatione *contenta in cerebro tantum volitet*, . . . si *rite* percipiatur a nobis, *radicemque agat in corde*" [1559 additions in italics]).

95. On this point, see Ebeling, "Cognitio Dei et hominis," pp. 285–86, 290–96.

96. "Yet there is, as the eminent pagan says, no nation so barbarous, so people so savage, that they have not a deep-seated conviction that there is a God" (CO 1:282). The reference is to Cicero, *On the Nature of the Gods*, 1.16.43; compare the references to other classical literature in OS 3:38, note 1.

97. CO 1:284–85.

98. CO 1:286.

99. CO 1:290–91.

100. For a discussion of Calvin's meaning of "inexcusable," see Parker, *Calvin's Doctrine of the Knowledge of God*, pp. 121–23.

101. CO 1:292–93.

102. CO 1:293–303; see Krusche, *Das Wirken des heiligen Geistes*, pp. 202–18.

103. CO 1:303; compare *Institutes* (1559), 1.10.1.

104. CO 1:304.

105. "The reason why the author of the letter to the Hebrews elegantly calls the universe the appearance of things invisible is that this skillful ordering of the universe is for us a sort of mirror in which we can contemplate God, who is otherwise invisible" (CO 1:286; compare *Institutes* [1559], 1.5.1).

106. "[S]ed ad illam perspiciendam non esse nobis oculos, nisi interiore Dei revelatione per fidem illuminentur" (CO 1:291; compare *Institutes* [1559], 1.5.14). See Stuermann, *Calvin's Concept of Faith*, p. 6.

107. CO 1:496. The double consolation is, first, that faith knows that there is sufficient ability to do good in him, whose arms extend to rule, manage, and dispense all things, in whose possession are heaven and earth, at whose nod all creatures respond to promote the salvation of the godly, and second, faith sees that there is enough assurance of his protection, to whose will are subject all the harmful things that, whatever their source, we fear, whose authority bridles Satan, with all his machinations, and whatever else is opposed to our salvation. The discussion of providence in chapter 8 begins with the statement that providence supports faith (see CO 1:889).

108. "For even though the minds of the impious too are compelled by merely looking upon this earth to rise up to the creator, faith has its own peculiar way of contemplating

God as creator of heaven and earth. For this reason the apostle says that 'by faith we understand that the universe was created by the word of God.' [For without faith] we do not properly perceive what it is to call God the creator of everything, however we may seem both to comprehend with the mind and confess with the tongue. Carnal knowledge, once confronted with the power of God in the creation, remains there, and when it goes farther, at most weighs and considers only the wisdom and power of the author in accomplishing such a work. . . . It contemplates, moreover, some general preserving and governing activity, from which the force of motion derives. But faith ought to penetrate more deeply. Having found him creator of all, it ought to recognize him as everlasting governor and preserver, not only in that he drives the celestial frame as well as its several parts by a universal motion, but also in that he sustains, nourishes, and cares for everything he has made by a certain particular prerogative, even to the least sparrow" (CO 1:511; compare *Institutes*, [1559], 1.16.1; in 1550 Calvin changed "praerogativa" to "providentia").

109. CO 1:889.

110. CO 1:890.

111. CO 1:893.

112. CO 1:889.

113. "We are all created in order that we may know the majesty of our creator, that having known it, we may esteem it above all and honor it with all awe, love, and reverence" (CO 22:33).

114. A most explicit example of the priority of the concept is found in Calvin's response to Sadoleto. Calvin criticizes Sadoleto for concentrating so much on salvation and eternal life in his letter urging the Genevans to return to the Roman communion. Calvin argues that sounder theology would set zeal to illustrate the glory of God as a more appropriate motivating factor (OS 1:463–64; CO 5:391–92; *A Reformation Debate*, p. 58).

115. See H. Strohl, "La Pensée de Calvin sur la Providence divine au temps oú il était réfugié à Strasbourg." Bohatec also finds that the treatment of the theme of providence in the exposition of the first article of the Creed is "wesentlich erweitert" in the editions subsequent to 1536 ("Calvins Vorsehungslehre," p. 342).

116. *Praefationes Bibliis Gallicis Petri Roberti Olivetani*, CO 9:791–822. An English translation is found in *Calvin: Commentaries*, ed. and trans. Joseph Haroutunian, Library of Christian Classics, vol 23 (Philadelphia: Westminster Press, 1958), pp. 58–72.

117. Wendel, *Calvin*, p. 114.

118. See Luther's exposition of the first article of the Creed in the Larger Catechism (1529). See also Zwingli's *De vera et falsa religione commentarius* (in *Corpus Reformatorum* 90:645–54; in English as *Commentary on True and False Religion*, ed. Samuel Macauley Jackson and Clarence Nevin Heller [1929; rpt. Durham, N.C.: Labyrinth Press, 1981], pp. 64–65) and his sermon at Marburg, *De Providentia Dei* (in *Werke. Erste vollständige Ausgabe*, ed. M. Schuler and J. Schulthess [Zurich, 1828–1848], 4:79–144; in English in *Zwingli: On Providence and Other Essays* [1922; rpt. Durham, N.C.: Labyrinth Press, 1983], pp. 128–234), which Wendel says Calvin perhaps knew (*Calvin*, p. 177, note 84). Bohatec argues that Calvin's arguments in the 1539 *Institutes* for a providence known by faith and not by reason, a discussion that eventually opens the treatment of providence in the 1559 edition, derives from Melanchthon, even though Melanchthon ultimately assessed the role of reason in apprehending providence more positively ("Calvins Vorsehungslehre," pp. 342 and 350–51; see CO 1:511; compare *Institutes* [1559], 1.16.1 and, for Melanchthon, *Loci* [1535] [in *Corpus Reformatorum* 21:271]). Susan Schreiner finds parallels between Calvin and Melanchthon also in Calvin's later sermons on Job (1554–1555) (*The Theater of His Glory: Nature and the Natural Order in the Thought of John Calvin*, Studies in Historical Theology 3 [Durham, N.C.: Labyrinth Press, 1991], p. 132, note 167).

119. On this point, see Dowey, *Knowledge of God in Calvin's Theology*, pp. 46–49; Parker, *Calvin's Doctrine of the Knowledge of God*, p. 2.

120. Battles, *Institutes* (1536), p. xlix.

121. CO 1:454.

122. CO 1:456.

123. CO 1:457.

124. In actuality, Calvin has little scriptural basis in Paul for the claim that faith is knowledge. As chapters 2 and 3 will demonstrate, the Johannine writings provide him with more direct support for this idea. The fact that Calvin nonetheless appeals to Paul to legitimate his definition indicates the significance of Pauline authority for Calvin's theology.

125. CO 1:457; compare 1:473: "sed explicitum requirit divinae bonitatis agnitionem." On the centrality of the concept of recognition for Calvin's understanding of faith, see B. A. Gerrish, *Grace and Gratitude*, pp. 66–67, 75.

126. CO 1:457.

127. CO 1:455.

128. CO 1:459. See also his reference to the eyes of our mind (CO 1:458), as well as his statements that believers "contemplate the glory of God with such efficacy through the gospel that they are transformed into God's image" (CO 1:460), that faith's light is never snuffed out (CO 1:461), and that the single goal of faith is "the mercy of God, to which it ought, so to speak, to look with both eyes" (CO 1:686).

129. Yet another example, in which Calvin uses two different senses, sight and taste, to characterize faith's activity: "Not that anyone has ever seen the Father but him who was sent by God. Therefore, as we cannot come to Christ unless we be drawn by the Spirit of God, so when we are drawn we are lifted up in mind and heart above our understanding. For the soul, illumined by him, takes on a new keenness, as it were, to contemplate the heavenly mysteries, whose splendor had previously blinded it. And man's understanding, thus beamed by the light of the Holy Spirit, then at last truly begins to taste those things that belong to the kingdom of God, having formerly been quite foolish and dull in tasting them" (CO 1:469).

130. In addition to the 1536 *Institutes*, Calvin's 1537 catechism expressed the idea of faith as confidence (CO 22:47; *Instruction in Faith* [1537], trans. Paul J. Fuhrmann [1949; rpt. Louisville: Westminster/John Knox, 1992], pp. 39–40). Note also the perceptual language that Calvin employs here.

131. CO 1:458; compare *Institutes* (1559), 3.2.15.

132. In this regard it is interesting to note Calvin's reformulation of his statement in 1536 identifying faith as *fiducia*. He has deleted the reference to love as faith's companion, since he has moved the discussion of 1 Cor. 13:2 to an earlier point. More important, however, is the fact that he also leaves out the statement "which we previously showed to be trust in the one God and Christ": "Yet wherever this living faith is, it must have along with it the hope of eternal salvation as its inseparable companion" (CO 1:684; compare *Institutes* [1559], 3.2.42).

133. "From this it is also clear that faith is much higher than human understanding. And it will not be enough for the mind to be illumined by the Spirit of God unless the heart is also strengthened and supported by his power. In this matter the Schoolmen go completely astray, who in considering faith identify it with a bare and simple assent arising out of knowledge and leave out confidence and assurance of the heart. In both ways, therefore, faith is a singular gift of God, both in that the human mind is purged so as to be able to taste the truth of God and in one's heart is established therein. This is indeed considered most paradoxical: when it is said that no one, unless faith be granted to him, can believe in Christ. But this is partly because men do not consider either how secret and

lofty the heavenly wisdom is, or how very dull men are to perceive the mysteries of God; partly because they do not have regard to that firm and steadfast constancy of heart that is the chief part of faith" (CO 1:468; compare *Institutes* [1559], 3.2.33).

134. CO 1:458.

135. See Stuermann, *Calvin's Concept of Faith*, p. 80.

136. Dowey, *Knowledge of God in Calvin's Theology*, p. 185.

137. Though he arrives at this same conclusion, Stuermann's resolution of the relationship between *fides* and *fiducia* is puzzling insofar as he sees *fiducia* as a movement of the will (heart) to be quite distinct from both the certainty that is sealed by the Spirit on the heart (pp. 106–7) and from the *certitudo* of the knowledge of faith (p. 88). He thus concludes that *fiducia* is completely an effect of faith and in no way an integral part of it (p. 108). Dee and Krusche hold, in contrast, that *fiducia* is an integral part of faith; see Dee, *Het geloofsbegrip*, pp. 36–42, and Krusche, *Das Wirken des heiligen Geistes*, p. 264; compare Muller, "*Fides* and *Cognitio*."

138. It should be noted that Calvin, in discussing the need for the Spirit to seal the truth of the divine promise on the human heart, asserts that this is all the more necessary since "the heart's distrust [*diffidentia*] is greater than the mind's blindness" (CO 1:468; compare *Institutes* [1559], 3.2.36). This, however, is a statement against a purely intellectualistic notion of faith—precisely the notion of faith that Calvin wishes to do away with through his expansion of the meaning of the concept of knowledge.

139. For an excellent discussion of the interrelationship of the intellect and the will in Calvin's view of faith see Muller, "*Fides* and *Cognitio*." Muller cleans up the muddy terminology of intellectualism and voluntarism, places Calvin's views within their medieval context, and shows that Calvin "balances the functions of intellect and will in his conception of faith rather than argue either a purely intellectualist or a purely voluntarist definition" (p. 220). To demonstrate that Calvin's view of faith was not intellectualistic was, as discussed in the introduction, one of the main goals of Stuermann's *Calvin's Concept of Faith* and Dowey's *Knowledge of God in Calvin's Theology*; compare the earlier endeavors to demonstrate this by Dee (*Het geloofsbegrip*) and P. Brunner (*Vom Glauben bei Calvin*). For support for this position see also Krusche, *Das Wirken des heiligen Geistes*, pp. 261–64; Gerrish, *Grace and Gratitude*, pp. 62–86; and Forstman, *Word and Spirit*, pp. 100–105. In spite of these arguments, Bouwsma maintains the view that Calvin tended toward a more intellectualistic view of faith: "Such sentiments point to a tendency in Calvin to understand faith less as trust in God's promises than as intellectual assent to a body of propositions" (*John Calvin*, p. 99).

140. Olivier Millet, "*Docere/Movere*: Les catégories rhétoriques et leurs sources humanistes dans la doctrine calvinienne de la foi," in *Calvinus Sincerioris Religionis Vindex: Calvin as Protector of the Purer Religion*, ed. Wilhelm H. Neuser and Brian G. Armstrong, Sixteenth Century Essays and Studies, vol. 36 (Kirksville, Mo.: Sixteenth Century Journal, 1997), pp. 35–51.

141. Krusche explores this same question and concludes: "Würde der Glaube als *fiducia* definiert (also als Willensakt), so käme die *cognitio* außerhalb des Glaubens zu stehen, während umgekehrt die Definition des Glaubens als *cognitio* das Vertrauenselement einschließt" (*Das Wirken des heiligen Geistes*, p. 264); compare Stuermann, *Calvin's Concept of Faith*, pp. 103–8, especially the citations to P. Brunner and Wernle on p. 106. Gestrich explores the reasons why Zwingli speaks of faith in primarily noetic rather than fiducial terms yet without excluding the fiducial character of faith. He argues that Zwingli combines faith with knowledge to distinguish it from opinion and to underscore faith's certainty (*Zwingli als Theologe*, pp. 61–65). As I will show especially in chapter 3, Calvin, too, uses noetic terms for these reasons. This affinity does not necessarily imply, of course, that by faith as knowledge Calvin and Zwingli meant the same thing.

142. CO 1:461.

143. Stuermann discusses four possible explanations for these apparently antithetical conclusions (*Calvin's Concept of Faith*, pp. 240–43).

144. CO 1:470. For an extremely detailed discussion of Calvin's understanding of scholastic theology's moral conjecture, see Schützeichel, *Glaubenstheologie*, pp. 101–12.

145. See Gerrish, *Grace and Gratitude*, p. 69: "although the goodness of God is still the actual object of devotion, it is now his pardoning, reconciling goodness."

146. CO 1:466.

147. See Dowey, *Knowledge of God in Calvin's Theology*, pp. 155–63. Dowey has called this Calvin's "bold distinction within the realm of special revelation" (p. 159). According to Dowey, Calvin never fully reconciled the idea of faith's acceptance of the entire scripture with faith's exclusive reliance on Christ. For a discussion of the relationship between the authority of scripture and Calvin's christocentric view of faith, see pp. 160–63, and B. A. Gerrish, "The Word of God and the Words of Scripture: Luther and Calvin on Biblical Authority" in *The Old Protestantism and the New*, pp. 58–68. Other discussions of the relationship between faith and the word are found in Stuermann, *Calvin's Concept of Faith*, pp. 143–48, and Shepherd, *The Nature and Function of Faith*, pp. 5–28.

148. Dowey, *Knowledge of God in Calvin's Theology*, p. 157.

149. CO 1:466–67.

150. CO 1:891, 496.

151. Throughout the chapter, Paul remains the most frequently cited biblical source; in the course of his exposition, Calvin draws on Ephesians, Colossians, 1 and 2 Corinthians, 1 Timothy, Romans, and the Hebrews 11:1 reference from 1536. Significantly, in describing faith he also refers to the Gospel and first epistle of John. There are, in addition, scattered references and allusions to the Old Testament: to Genesis, the Psalms, Proverbs, Job, Ecclesiastes, Malachi, and Joel.

152. For details on the various editions of the *Institutes*, see Wendel, *Calvin*, pp. 115–22, and Joh. Wilhelm Marmelstein, *Étude comparatives des textes latins et français de l'Institution de la religion chrétienne* (Groningen: J. B. Wolters, 1923).

153. Schützeichel, *Glaubenstheologie*, p. 135. See also Susan E. Schreiner, " 'The Spiritual Man Judges All Things': Calvin and the Exegetical Debates about Certainty in the Reformation," in *Biblical Interpretation in the Era of the Reformation: Essays Presented to David C. Steinmetz in Honor of his Sixtieth Birthday*, ed. Richard A. Muller and John L. Thompson (Grand Rapids: Eerdmanns, 1996), pp. 189–215.

154. Schützeichel, *Glaubenstheologie*, pp. 101–13.

155. Schützeichel, *Glaubenstheologie*, pp. 107–8.

156. Schützeichel, *Glaubenstheologie*, p. 108.

157. Schützeichel concludes that much of what Calvin has to say about the certainty of faith is to be found in scholastic discussions of hope and the certainty of hope. Medieval theologians held these to be of a different order: the certainty of faith was a certainty of the intellect, whereas the certainty of hope was an affective certainty (pp. 112–13; see also p. 137). For Calvin, the certainty of faith appears to be more of an affective certainty: Faith "requires a full and fixed certainty, of the sort that should be concerning things experienced and proved" (CO 1:457). This reflects Calvin's expansion of the concept of the knowledge of faith to include both the intellect and the will as well as his insistence that the heart's distrust is greater than the mind's blindness.

158. Schützeichel, *Glaubenstheologie*, p. 109; for references to Bonaventure, Thomas, and Biel see note 54.

159. Schützeichel, *Glaubenstheologie*, pp. 154–55.

160. *Acta Synodi Trindentinae cum Antidoto* (CO 7:365–506); in English in John Calvin, *Tracts and Treatises*, trans. Henry Beveridge (Grand Rapids: Eerdmans, 1958), 3:17–

188. See also Theodore W. Casteel, "Calvin and Trent: Calvin's Reaction to the Council of Trent in the Context of his Conciliar Thought," *Harvard Theological Review* 63 (1970): 91–117.

161. Eph. 3:11–12: "This was in accordance with the eternal purpose that he has carried out in Christ Jesus our Lord, in whom we have access to God in boldness and confidence through faith in him."

162. CO 1:457–58.

163. CO 1:461.

164. CO 1:462.

165. On Calvin's polemic against these "half-papists," see Manfred K. Bahmann, "Calvin's Controversy with Certain 'Half-Papists,'" *Hartford Quarterly* 5 (1965): 27–41; rpt. in Gamble, *Articles* 5:337–51. Bahmann argues that the half-papists are Protestants who, in Calvin's view, divorce justification from sanctification. He notes that Calvin's criticisms parallel in some respects his later polemics against Andreas Osiander. On the basis of what he himself admits is "a thin thread of evidence," Bahmann links the two discussions and conjectures that the "half-papists" are Nuremberg evangelicals.

166. CO 1:462–64.

167. D. Willis-Watkins, "The Unio Mystica and the Assurance of Faith according to Calvin," in *Calvin: Erbe und Auftrag: Festschrift für Wilhelm Heinrich Neuser zum 65. Geburtstag,* ed. Willem van't Spijker (Kampen: Kok, 1991), p. 83.

168. Peter and Gilmont, *Bibliotheca Calviniana,* 1:186; compare the changes "non magni momenti" noted by the editors of the OS, 3: xxiii–xxiv.

169. The phrase added in 1545 is in small capitals; the phrases in italics are from 1550: "[I]deo nostram definitionem inde petimus [SUMPSIMUS], quae tamen ab illa Apostoli VEL DEFINITIONE VEL DESCRIPTIONE POTIUS, *quam suae disputationi accommodat,* minime aliena est: ubi docet esse rerum sperandarum subsistentiam, indicem non apparentium. Nam per hypostasin (quo vocabulo utitur) quasi fulcrum intelligit, cui pia mens innitatur et incumbat. Acsi diceret fidem ipsam certam quandam esse ac securam possessionem eorum quae nobis a Deo promissa sunt; *nisi quis hypostasin pro fiducia accipere malit; quod non displicet: quanquam illud quod receptius est amplector*" (CO 1:474; compare OS 4:51; I have relied on the notes from the OS; the CO attributes the entire phrase "vel definitione . . . disputationi accommodat" to the 1545 edition). Note that the sentence interpreting hypostasis as *fulcrum* and *possessio* is nearly verbatim from the 1536 edition (see note 54 earlier).

170. This point is somewhat obscured in the English translation. In 1539 Calvin attributes the "definition" to the "apostle" instead of to Paul and then lifts his discussion from 1536 practically verbatim. However, whereas he had in 1536 maintained Paul as the subject throughout he must, in 1539, explicitly introduce Paul's name when he comes to a genuinely Pauline verse (Rom. 8:24) that he claims makes the same point as Heb. 11:1. This can be seen in the fact that in 1536 Paul is the subject of the verbs ("Paulus . . . docet, . . . ut significaret. . . . Addidit . . . ut ipse alibi scribit, spes que videtur"), but in 1539 the apostle is the subject up until the reference to the Romans passage ("quae tamen ab illa Apostoli [definitione] minime aliena est, ubi docet . . . quo vocabulo utitur . . . ut significat . . . addidit . . . siquidem evidentia, ut Paulus scribit, spes non est."). After this, Calvin turns back to the Hebrews passage and the word *elenchos,* and the subject of the remaining verbs (*loquitur, diceret*) is again the unspecified apostle (CO 1:57, 474).

171. Albert Pighius, *Controversiarum praecipuarum in comitiis Ratisponensibus tractarum, et quibus nunc potissimum exagitatur Christi fides et religio, diligens et luculenta explicatio* (Cologne, 1542), chap. 2, folios 94r–96r (reference is to the microfilm in the Joseph Regenstein Library, University of Chicago. The OS, Battles (*Institutes* [1559]), and Schützeichel (*Glaubenstheologie*) all give the citation as roughly folios 58a–60a; this reference did not corre-

spond to the edition I consulted). In the same year Pighius published another work, *De liberio hominis arbitrio et divina gratia libri decem* (Cologne, 1542), which criticized ideas expressed by Calvin in the 1539 *Institutes*. Books 1–6 dealt with the freedom of the will. Books 7–10 argued against Calvin's view of predestination. The following year Calvin responded to books 1–6 in his tract *Defensio sanae et orthodoxae doctrinae de servitute et liberatione humani arbitrii adversus calumnias Alberti Pighii Campensis* (CO 6:225–404); in English, *The Bondage and Liberation of the Will: A Defence of the Orthodox Doctrine of Human Choice against Pighius*, ed. A. N. S. Lane, trans. G. Davies, Texts and Studies in Reformation and Post-Reformation Thought 2 (Grand Rapids: Baker Books, 1996). This work defended the evangelicals' understanding of the bondage of the will. In 1552 Calvin published a response to Pighius and others' criticisms of his views on predestination, *De aeterna Dei predestinatione qua in salutem alios ex hominibus elegit alios suo exitio reliquit: item de providentia qua res humanas gubernat, Consensus pastorum Genevensis ecclesiae* (CO 8:249–366); in English, *Concerning the Eternal Predestination of God*, trans. J. K. S. Reid (Cambridge: James Clarke, 1961; rpt. Louisville: Westminster/John Knox Press, 1997). On this polemical exchange, see L. F. Schulze, *Calvin's Reply to Pighius* (Potchefstroom, Republic of South Africa: Pro Rege—Press, 1971).

172. CO 1:467; appears as 3.2.30 in the 1559 *Institutes*. Dee wrongly attributes this addition to the 1543 *Institutes* (*Het geloofsbegrip*, p. 74).

Two. The Just Shall Live by Faith

1. All references, unless otherwise specified, are to the first published edition of each commentary; in the case of 1 and 2 Thessalonians, references are to the 1551 edition appearing in the collected Pauline epistles, since no copies of the 1550 first editions survive. For the commentaries other than Romans, Calvin made very few changes in subsequent editions; on this point, see Peter and Gilmont, *Bibliotheca Calviniana*, 1:418. Most of the modifications for the 1551 edition are especially minor; in preparing the commentaries for the 1556 edition Calvin did little rewriting but occasionally expanded his comments on individual verses, again with the exception of Romans, where the additions are more substantial. The editors of the *Calvini Opera* indicate many, but not all, of these additions by printing them in italics. However, in addition to ignoring some changes to the 1556 edition altogether and neglecting to give earlier readings, they also do not signal modifications made for the 1551 edition. See the more recent editions of the Romans commentary (cited in chapter 1), of the commentaries on Galatians, Ephesians, Philippians, and Colossians, of the commentary on 2 Corinthians, of the commentary on Hebrews, and of the first half of the commentary on John cited in the bibliography and the list of abbreviations. For a discussion of the literary history of Calvin's commentaries on the New Testament, see Parker, *Calvin's New Testament Commentaries*, pp. 1–25; further details are provided in Peter and Gilmont, *Bibliotheca Calviniana*.

2. Calvin published a short commentary on Jude in French in 1542; however, both Parker and Louis Goumaz argue that this is an "occasional piece" or intermediate work that does not fit the pattern of the Romans commentary, the subsequent commentaries on the Pauline epistles, or the Latin commentary on Jude from 1551 (Parker, *Calvin's New Testament Commentaries*, p. 10; Louis Goumaz, *La Doctrine du Salut d'après les commentaires de Jean Calvin sur le Nouveau Testament* [Lausanne: Payot, 1917] p. 50). Calvin's views on the authorship of Hebrews will be treated in chapter 3.

3. See, for example, Girardin, *Rhétorique et Théologique*; Ganoczy, "Calvin als paulinischer Theologe"; Ganoczy and Scheld, *Die Hermeneutik Calvins*, especially p. 47; David C. Steinmetz, "Calvin and Abraham"; "Calvin and the Patristic Exegesis of Paul"; and "Calvin

and the Natural Knowledge of God," in *Via Augustini: Augustine in the Later Middle Ages, Renaissance, and Reformation*, ed. Heiko A. Oberman and Frank A. James, III, Studies in Medieval and Reformation Thought, vol. 49 (Leiden: E. J. Brill, 1991), pp. 142–56.

4. Recent work in the history of exegesis has underscored the importance of recognizing that exegetical decisions are not made in isolation from the antecedent tradition and contemporary discussions. This is especially true for Calvin. Observations on the use of Paul and Paul's understanding of faith among Calvin's exegetical predecessors and contemporaries will appear in the notes, since their purpose is not to establish the sources of particular arguments or views. To attempt that extremely difficult task would take me far afield of the present topic. Instead, these comparisons will illustrate some traditional and contemporary understandings of the view of faith arising out of the Pauline epistles and will serve to show where Calvin acknowledges or ignores, adopts or rejects them. For this chapter, the following works have been consulted: Origen, *Commentarii in Epistulam ad Romanos*, in vol. 14 of *Patrologiae Cursus Completus, Series Graeca*, ed. J.-P. Migne (Paris, 1857–1912; rpt., Turnhout: Brepols; hereafter abbreviated *PG*), cols. 839–1291; *Commentarii in Epistulam ad Romanos/Römerbriefkommentar*, 2 vols., translated with an introduction by Theresia Heither (New York: Herder, 1991–1992); *Der Römerbriefkommentar des Origenes. Kritische Ausgabe der Übersetzung Rufuns, Buch 1–3*, ed. Caroline P. H. Bammel, Vetus Latina. Aus der Geschichte der lateinischen Bibel, vol. 16 (Freiburg: Herder, 1990); John Chrysostom, *Homiliae XXXII in Epistolam Ad Romanos*, in *PG* 60:13–384; *Homiliae XLIV in Epistolam Primam Ad Corinthios*, in *PG* 61:9–380; *Homiliae XXX in Epistolam Secundam Ad Corinthios*, in *PG* 61: 381–610; *Homilies on the Acts of the Apostles and the Epistle to the Romans*, A Select Library of the Nicene and Post-Nicean Fathers of the Christian Church, series 1, vol. 11 (rpt. Grand Rapids: Eerdmans, 1969), pp. 335–566; *Homilies on First and Second Corinthians*, A Select Library of the Nicene and Post-Nicean Fathers of the Christian Church, series 1, vol. 12 (rpt. Grand Rapids: Eerdmans, 1969); Augustine, *De Spiritu et littera*, PL 44:199–246 (in English as *The Spirit and the Letter* in *Augustine: Later Works*, Library of Christian Classics, vol. 7 [Philadelphia: Westminster Press, 1955], pp. 182–250); Augustine, *Epistolae ad Romanos inchoata Exposito*, in *PL* 35:2087–2104; *Expositio quarumdam propositionum ex Epistola ad Romanos*, in *PL* 35:2063–2086; *Expositio quarumdam propositionum ex Epistola ad Romanos* and *Epistolae ad Romanos inchoata Expositio* in *Augustine on Romans*, text and trans. Paula Fredriksen Landes (Chico, Calif.: Scholars Press, 1982); Martin Luther, *Der Brief an die Römer* (1515/1516), WA 56:3–528 and LW 25; Philip Melanchthon, *Commentarii in Epistolam Pauli ad Romanos* (Wittenberg, 1532), citations from *Römerbrief-Kommentar 1532*, ed. Rolf Schäfer, in *Melanchthons Werke in Auswahl*, vol. 5 [Gütersloh: Gerd Mohn, 1965]). An English translation of Melanchthon's edition of 1540 has been published as *Commentary on Romans*, trans. Fred Kramer (St. Louis: Concordia, 1992). Further details on Calvin's sources can be found in the introduction to the Feld edition of the Commentary on Galatians, Ephesians, Philippians, and Colossians (*Comm. Gal. et al.*, pp. xxi–xxvi).

5. Parker, *Calvin's New Testament Commentaries*, p. vii. On the importance of commentaries on Romans in the sixteenth century, see his *Commentaries on the Epistle to the Romans 1532–1542* (Edinburgh: T. and T. Clark, 1986).

6. Steinmetz, "Calvin and Abraham," p. 444; see his notes 5 and 6 for a detailed listing of sixteenth-century and antecedent literature.

7. For discussions of various aspects of this multifaceted interest in Paul, see Ganoczy and Scheld, *Die Hermeneutik Calvins*, pp. 22–48; John B. Payne, "Erasmus: Interpreter of Romans," pp. 1–35; "Erasmus and Lefèvre d'Étaples as Interpreters of Paul," *Archiv für Reformationsgeschichte* 65 (1974): 54–83; "Interpretations of Paul in the Reformation," *Encounter* 36 (Summer 1975): 196–211; Helmut Feld, "Die Wiedergeburt des Paulinismus im Europäischen Humanismus," *Catholica: Vierteljahresschrift für Oekumenische Theologie* 36

(Münster: Aschendorff, 1982): 294–327; David Steinmetz, *Luther and Staupitz: An Essay in the Intellectual Origins of the Protestant Reformation* (Durham, N.C.: Duke University Press, 1980), pp. 96–125.

8. See Ganoczy and Scheld, *Die Hermeneutik Calvins*, pp. 23, 24, 32, and 44–45.

9. For a list of patristic and medieval Latin literature on Romans, see Werner Affeldt, *Die weltliche Gewalt in der Paulus-Exegese: Röm. 13,1–7 in den Römerbriefkommentaren der lateinischen Kirche bis zum Ende des 13. Jahrhunderts* (Göttingen: Vandenhoeck und Ruprecht, 1969), appendix 1, pp. 256–85. Maurice F. Wiles offers a lucid study of the interpretation of Paul among major patristic exegetes (*The Divine Apostle: The Interpretation of St. Paul's Epistles in the Early Church* [Cambridge: Cambridge University Press, 1967]). See also Karl Hermann Schelkle, *Paulus, Lehrer der Väter: Die Altkirchliche Auslegung von Römer 1–11* (Düsseldorf: Patmos, 1956); Alexander Souter, *The Earliest Latin Commentaries on the Epistles of St. Paul* (Oxford: Clarendon Press, 1927); and Karl Froehlich, "Which Paul? Observations on the Image of the Apostle in the History of Biblical Exegesis," in *New Perspectives on Historical Theology: Essays in Memory of John Meyendorff*, ed. Bradley Nassif (Grand Rapids: Eerdmans, 1996), pp. 279–99. For the sixteenth century, see Susi Hausammann, *Römerbrief-auslegung zwischen Humanismus und Reformation: Eine Studie zu Heinrich Bullingers Römer-briefvorlesung von 1525*, Studien zur Dogmengeschichte und Systematischen Theologie, vol. 27 (Zurich: Zwingli, 1970); compare Fritz Büsser, "Bullinger as Calvin's Model in Biblical Exposition: An Examination of Calvin's Preface to the Epistle to the Romans," in *In Honor of John Calvin, 1509–64*, ed. E. J. Furcha (Montreal: Faculty of Religious Studies, McGill University, 1987), pp. 64–95; rpt. in Gamble, *Articles*, 6:434–65; Joel Edward Kok, "The Influence of Martin Bucer on John Calvin's Interpretation of Romans: A Comparative Case Study" (Ph.D. diss., Duke University, 1993). Also interesting to note are the interpretations implied by the translation of Paul's Greek into Latin (e.g., in the Vulgate, by Valla, Faber, Erasmus) and, eventually, German (Luther). Some of these nuances in translation are conveyed by Parker (*Commentaries on Romans*); for close study of Romans 3 in particular, see Heinz Bluhm, *Luther: Translator of Paul: Studies in Romans and Galatians* (New York: Peter Lang, 1984), pp. 9–223.

10. Steinmetz, "Calvin and Abraham," p. 446.

11. *Comm. Rom.*, p. 5, lines 9–11; *Romans*, p. 5. Unless otherwise designated, citations are to the 1540 edition. Most translations are from the English translation of the 1556 edition (*Romans*). Where no reference is given to this edition, the translations are my own. On the special status of Romans in Western biblical exegesis, see Karl Froehlich, "Which Paul?" pp. 291–95.

12. In summarizing scriptural discussions here and elsewhere, I have relied on modern commentaries and discussions not in order to determine whether Calvin's interpretation is "correct" but only to provide a foundation for trying to understand what Calvin understood Paul or the other biblical authors to be saying. For discussions of Paul's theology in general and his understanding of faith in particular, see John Ziesler, *Pauline Christianity*, rev. ed. (New York: Oxford University Press, 1990); Gerhard Friedrich, "Glaube und Verkündigung bei Paulus" in *Glaube im Neuen Testament: Studien zu Ehren von Hermann Binder*, ed. Ferdinand Hahn and Hans Klein (Neukirchen: Neukirchner, 1982). On Romans in particular see Ulrich Wilckens, *Der Brief an die Römer*, 3 parts, vol. 6 of *Evangelisch-Katholischer Kommentar zum Neuen Testament* (Zürich: Benzinger; Neukirchen-Vluyn: Neukirchener, 1978–), especially 6/1:199–202. Modern debates over justification by faith in Paul are summarized in Payne, "Interpretations of Paul in the Reformation," pp. 207–11.

13. Ziesler, *Pauline Christianity*, p. 89.

14. In Paul, *pistis* can refer both to a body of beliefs, i.e., to what later theology designates a *fides quae creditur* (e.g., Gal. 1:23 and 6:10; compare also Rom. 12:6), and to

the quality of faithfulness (e.g., Rom. 3:3). Or, as in this instance, it can designate the human response to divine grace proclaimed in the gospel, a *fides qua creditur*. Infrequently, Paul speaks of this act of belief as an intellectual assent to a proposition (Rom. 6:8 and 10: 9, 1 Thess. 4:14; compare James 2:19). However, according to the general Pauline usage, faith means a believing acceptance of the kerygma about Jesus Christ that not only assents to but also embraces this message in a way that is determinative for one's existence (cf. G. Barth, *pistis, pisteuo* in *Exegetisches Wörterbuch zum Neuen Testament*, ed. H. Balz and G. Schneider, 2d. ed. [Stuttgart: W. Kohlhammer, 1992], 3: 226; Otfried Hofius, "Wort Gottes und Glaube bei Paulus: Wilfrid Werbeck zum 60. Geburtstag" in *Paulusstudien*, Wissenschaftliche Untersuchungen zum Neuen Testament 51 [Tübingen: J. C. B. Mohr (Paul Siebeck), 1989], pp. 155–57; Karl Kertelge, *"Rechtfertigung" bei Paulus: Studien zur Struktur und zum Bedeutungsgehalt des paulinischen Rechtfertigungsbegriffs* [Münster: Aschendorff, 1967], pp. 172–75). However, this response is "not an action to be performed with effort, indeed it is almost a non-thing" (Ziesler, *Pauline Christianity*, p. 84).

15. It is noteworthy that Calvin also recognizes Paul's concern for Jewish-Gentile relations among the followers of Christ and the difficulties that Christianity's Jewish heritage raised regarding the salvation of the Gentiles. But, as his comments on Rom. 3:28 and 3: 29 attest, this issue is clearly secondary for him. Concerning Rom. 3:28, "We reckon therefore that a man is justified by faith without the works of the Law," Calvin writes: "Paul states his main proposition as being now incontrovertible"; he designates Rom. 3:29, "Or is God the God of the Jews only? Is he not also the God of the Gentiles? Yes, of the Gentiles also," as the second proposition (*Comm. Rom.*, p. 77, lines 65–66; *Romans*, pp. 79–80).

16. *Comm. Rom.*, p. 68, line 51; *Romans*, p. 70. Schelkle notes that for the patristic exegetical tradition the understanding of "works" in Rom. 3:27–28 sheds light on the understanding of "righteousness" in Rom. 3:21, since many interpreters understood Rom. 3: 28 to exclude all boasting about a righteousness based on works (*Paulus, Lehrer der Väter*, p. 111). Yet while the patristic tradition might have understood Rom. 3:27–28 to be excluding works in general from justification, neither Origen nor Chrysostom applied Rom. 3:21 to works in general. Origen argues that the first time law appears in this verse it refers to the natural law, and the second time it refers to the Mosaic law (compare Schelkle, *Paulus, Lehrer der Väter*, p. 114). Chrysostom applies the law in Rom. 3:21 to the entire Old Testament (compare Chrysostom's comments on Rom. 3:19). In *The Spirit and the Letter*, Augustine understands the law in Rom. 3:20 as the moral law, which does not itself bestow righteousness but which acts as a tutor conducting to grace. When he turns to explain the law of works and the law of faith of Rom. 3:28, he understands the law of works as the moral law enjoined with threatenings. The law of faith, Augustine explains, has its precepts also; however, this law teaches that these precepts can be fulfilled only by grace (pp. 202–12). Melanchthon (1532) understands "without the law" to apply to the whole law, both ceremonial and moral (*Römerbrief-Kommentar*, p. 103, lines 14–18). He opposes the law, which, though it contains the promises, attaches to these a condition, to the gospel, which promises unconditionally (*Römerbrief-Kommentar*, p. 104, lines 23–37). Bullinger, according to Parker, understands "without the law" to be put for work or merit (*Commentaries on Romans*, p. 33; compare Hausammann, *Römerbriefauslegung*, p. 269).

17. Calvin returns to this issue in the first edition several times; see especially his comments on Rom. 4:6 (*Comm. Rom.*, p. 83). Parker points out the abbreviated and somewhat confusing argument advanced in Calvin's 1540 comments on Rom. 3:20. Calvin says that some interpreters understand the phrase "works of the law" to refer to the whole law while others restrict it to the ceremonies. He then identifies Chrysostom, Origen, and Jerome with the former position. Confusion arises when he claims that they adopted this

interpretation because of the addition of the word "law" in order to "prevent the passage from being understood of all works" (*Comm. Rom.*, p. 66, lines 85–86, *Romans*, p. 69; see Parker, *Commentaries on Romans*, pp. 193–95). Yet after criticizing them, he goes on to refute those who restrict the meaning to the ceremonial law by arguing that Paul does mean the whole law in this verse. The problem is compounded by the fact that the position that Calvin attributes to Origen and Chrysostom is not to be found in their commentaries on Rom. 3:20. This distinction does appear, however, in the commentary of Pseudo-Jerome (Pelagius). It seems to me that Calvin agrees with the position that Paul refers to the whole law but that he rejects the reason for this interpretation that he attributes to Origen, Chrysostom, and Jerome. According to Calvin, Paul speaks of the works of the law in order "to remove more explicitly the power of justification from all works" (*Comm. Rom.*, p. 66, line 89; *Romans*, p. 69). For a discussion of the introduction of this distinction between ceremonial and moral law by patristic interpreters, see Wiles, *The Divine Apostle*, pp. 66–94 and 133–34. Schelkle notes that Theodoret and Pelagius understood Rom. 3:19 to be referring to the ceremonial law, and that Augustine explicitly rejects such an interpretation in *Spirit and the Letter* (8,14); see Schelkle, *Paulus, Lehrer der Väter*, pp. 105–6; compare Augustine, *Spirit and the Letter*, p. 204. Among Calvin's contemporaries, Bucer (1536), Marino Grimani (1542), and Philibert Haresche (1536) adopted the view that "works of the law" referred to the ceremonies (Parker, *Commentaries on Romans*, pp. 143–44, 163–64, and 180–81). According to Parker, Bucer, who claimed that this interpretation was held by all except Augustine, understood Paul to be using the works of the ceremonial law as synecdoche, so that the point is that (in Parker's words) "no works of the law, whether moral or ceremonial, could justify" (Parker, *Commentaries on Romans*, p. 181).

18. *Comm. Rom.*, p. 76, lines 9–13. Melanchthon also links merit and boasting in his comments on 3:27–28, actually identifying *gloriatio* (boasting) with *meritum de condigno* (*Römerbrief-Kommentar*, p. 115, lines 2–3).

19. In referring to James 2:24 in the context of this discussion, Calvin is following in the footsteps of earlier exegetes, including Pelagius and Cyril of Alexandria (see Schelkle, *Paulus, Lehrer der Väter*, p. 113). Luther refers to James 2:26 in his comments on Rom. 3: 20. Here he reconciles the two statements by making a distinction between works of the law (works done outside of faith and grace for the purpose of obtaining righteousness) and a living faith that produces its own works (WA 56:248–50). Melanchthon treats the apparent inconsistency between James 2:24 and Paul in his "Argumentum." According to Melanchthon, James is talking about works after faith; works of righteousness are necessary, but they will not please God unless the person has already been accepted by trust in mercy (*Römerbrief-Kommentar*, p. 49, line 9–p. 50, line 29).

20. "Conciliatio potissimum est in animadversione duplicis paralogismi. Quia iustificatio apud Iacobum, non pro imputatione, sed pro declaratione ac testificatione iustitiae posita est, fidei autem vocabulum abusive: per concessionem usurpatum est" (*Comm. Rom.*, p. 77, notes to lines 50–59). At this point, Calvin breaks off the discussion and refers his readers to the *Institutes*. See *Institutes* (1539) (CO 1:787–88); the same discussion appears in *Institutes* (1559), 3.17.11–12.

21. For a discussion of Calvin's understanding of a broad and a narrow sense of the law and their relationship to the gospel in light of the issue of the unity of scripture, see Krusche, *Das Wirken des heiligen Geistes*, pp. 190–95. Krusche argues that, for Calvin, the difference between law even in its narrow or actual (*prägnant*) sense and the gospel lies not in content but in the way this content is conveyed (not in *Lehrinhalt* but in *Lehrgehalt*, i.e., *forma docendi*). Both law in its narrow sense and the gospel express God's righteousness, but whereas the law (in its narrow sense) presents this as a demand, the gospel witnesses to it as obtained and given to us by Jesus Christ.

22. Compare also Calvin's comments on Rom. 4:15 ("For the law works wrath"): "Since the law produces nothing but vengeance, it cannot bring grace. The law would, it is true, show the way of life to those who are good and pure, but since it orders the sinful and corrupt to do what they ought without supplying them with the power to do it, it brings them guilty before God's tribunal" (*Comm. Rom.*, p. 91, lines 82–85 and notes) and on Rom. 3:20: "By itself it [the law] teaches righteousness and life, but because of human corruption it profits nothing in this way" (*Comm. Rom.*, p. 67, lines 35–40 and notes).

23. *Comm. Rom.*, p. 79, lines 13–17 and notes. Calvin uses the language of effect and cause and the image of fruit from a tree to illustrate the relationship between the imputed righteousness of faith and the actual righteousness of works attained through the process of sanctification (*Comm. Rom.*, p. 85, line 98; *Romans*, p. 87).

24. See Calvin's comments on Rom. 3:21: "It is not certain why he calls the righteousness which we obtain by faith the righteousness of God, whether it is because it alone stands in the presence of God, or because the Lord in his mercy confers it on us. As both interpretations will suit, we do not argue for one or the other" (*Comm. Rom.*, p. 68, lines 45–49; *Romans*, p. 70). In 1556 Calvin adds a sentence in his comments on the phrase in Rom. 3:22, in which he argues that the fact that "of God" is reintroduced seems to indicate that Paul makes God the author and not merely the approver of righteousness. He touches on this theme in his comments on Rom. 3:26 ("that he might himself be just") and, in 1556, revises his comments to bring out the fact that God's justice is particularly evident in communicating righteousness to those he justifies through faith in Christ (*Comm. Rom.*, p. 75, lines 91–98 and notes; *Romans*, pp. 77–78). For a discussion of patristic interpretation of the passage, see Schelkle, *Paulus, Lehrer der Väter*, pp. 108–13. Augustine, in the *Spirit and the Letter* (9,15), anticipates Luther's alleged "insight" and argues "the righteousness of God, not that by which God is righteous, but that wherewith he clothes man, when he justifies the ungodly" (PL 44:209; *Spirit and the Letter*, p. 205). Luther, in his comments on Rom. 3:26, argues that here "as above," righteousness of God "describes that by which he makes us righteous" (WA 56:262). Melanchthon, in his comments on Rom. 3:21, says that righteousness of God in this case does not mean a quality but "signifies the acceptation by which God accepts us" (*Römerbrief-Kommentar*, p. 99, lines 11–17). See also the discussion of the righteousness of God, including a summary of the history of the interpretation of this concept, in Wilckens, *Der Brief an die Römer*, part 1, pp. 223–233.

25. Expressed clearly in Calvin's comments on Rom. 4:3 and 4:6 (*Comm. Rom.*, p. 82, lines 55–58; p. 83, lines 36–39). See also under Rom. 3:22 (*Comm. Rom.*, pp. 71–72, lines 76–78; compare *Romans*, p. 74); and under Rom. 3:26 (*Comm. Rom.*, p. 75, notes to lines 89–1). Other examples are found in additions made in 1556, e.g., in the comments on Rom. 4:3: "If there were any righteousness by the law or by works, it would reside in men themselves. But men get the faith that they lack from elsewhere. Therefore it is rightly termed the imputed righteousness of faith" (*Comm. Rom.*, p. 81, lines 49–51; *Romans*, p. 83); and on Rom. 3:25: "This definition or explanation confirms again what I have frequently hinted at, viz. that men are justified not because they are such in reality, but by imputation" (*Comm. Rom.*, p. 74, lines 45–47; *Romans*, p. 76).

26. As Calvin says in discussing Rom. 3:26, "Therefore, they are justified because they are counted as just, even if they are not, for the obedience of Christ is imputed to them for righteousness (*Comm. Rom.*, p. 75, notes).

27. *Comm. Rom.*, pp. 70–71; *Romans*, p. 73.

28. See, e.g., Calvin's comments on Rom. 4:6–8 (*Comm. Rom.*, p. 85, lines 73–74; *Romans*, p. 87). He states the same idea more forcefully in 1556 in his comments on Rom. 4:3: "We conclude from this that the question is not what men are in themselves, but how God regards them, not because of purity of conscience and integrity of life are distinguished

from the free favor of God, but because, when it is asked why God loves us and recognizes us as just, it is necessary that Christ should appear [as the one] who clothes us with His own righteousness" (*Comm. Rom.*, p. 82, lines 81–85; compare *Romans*, p. 84).

29. Compare his comments on Rom. 3:24, where he adds that the final cause is the glory of the divine justice and goodness (*Comm. Rom.*, p. 72, lines 94–97; *Romans*, p. 75). For similar statements in the *Institutes* (1539), see CO 1:766 and 768. The same discussions appear in *Institutes* (1559), 3.14.17 and 21. See Stuermann, who notes the irony in Calvin's persistent use of this scheme in light of his criticism of a similar analysis advanced by the Council of Trent (*Calvin's Concept of Faith*, p. 179). It is significant that the Council designated baptism, and not faith, as the instrumental cause of justification; see chapter 7 of the Sixth Session in *Concilium Tridentinum: Diariorum, Actorum, Epistularum, Tractatuum Nova Collectio* (Freiburg: Herder, 1964), 5:793; in English, *Canons and Decrees of the Council of Trent*, text and trans. H. J. Schroeder (St. Louis: B. Herder, 1941), p. 33.

30. Late medieval theories of justification typically distinguished between justification and salvation, holding that justification was a part of a process culminating, one hopes, in salvation. For a discussion of Luther's rejection of the notion of justification as a process, see Heiko A. Oberman, " 'Iustitia Christi' and 'Iustitia Dei': Luther and the Scholastic Doctrines of Justification," in *The Dawn of the Reformation: Essays in Late Medieval and Early Reformation Thought* (1966, rpt. Edinburgh: T. and T. Clark, 1986), pp. 104–25. Joseph Wawrykow's otherwise interesting study of conceptual similarities between Thomas Aquinas and John Calvin speaks of a "salvific process" in Calvin's theology and does not stress sufficiently that Calvin also virtually identifies justification and salvation ("John Calvin and Condign Merit," *Archiv für Reformationsgeschichte* 83 (1992): 73–90). While Calvin undoubtedly understood regeneration (sanctification) as a process leading toward holiness, salvation strictly understood rested only on God's free justification of the sinner, as is evident in Calvin's comments on Romans 3–4. Though justification involves the perpetual forgiveness of sin and the imputation of Christ's righteousness, it is not, for Calvin, a process.

31. *Comm. Rom.*, p. 84, lines 47–49; *Romans*, p. 86.

32. "According to Numbers 25:6–9, Phinehas, the grandson of Aaron the priest, stopped a plague in the Israelite camp by killing an idolatrous Jew and his Midianite mistress. Psalm 106:31 celebrates the zealous action of Phinehas and announces in language echoing Genesis 15:6 that his act was counted to him for righteousness. In other words, while Abraham was justified by faith, Phinehas was justified by works. Or to state the matter even more sharply, Phinehas was justified by a double homicide. On what theological principle, then, is Genesis 15:6 and the faith of Abraham given precedence over Psalm 106:31 and the zeal of Phinehas?" ("Calvin and Abraham," pp. 447–48). Steinmetz notes that many sixteenth-century interpreters addressed this problem in their commentaries on Romans (see his note 14).

33. *Comm. Rom.*, p. 84–85, lines 63–73 and notes; *Romans*, p. 86–87; see also Steinmetz, "Calvin and Abraham," p. 451.

34. A similar image, that of the root and fruit, is at least as old as Origen's commentary on this passage; see *Commentarii in Epistulam ad Romanos*, trans. Heither, 2:176.

35. *Comm. Rom.*, p. 91, lines 72–76; *Romans*, p. 93. In his comments on Rom. 4:14, Melanchthon also advances a "definition" of faith as trust in the promise of mercy. He opposes this to historical knowledge, since faith "non tantum notitia quaedam, sed est velle et accipere id, quod offert promissio" (*Römerbrief-Kommentar*, p. 141, lines 9–10). The identification of faith as *fiducia misericordiae* or *fiducia promissae misericordiae* appears many times in Melanchthon's exegesis of this passage; see, e.g., the "Argumentum" (p. 40, lines 7–17) and the comments on Rom. 3:21 (p. 99, lines 20–21) and Rom. 4:3 (p. 126, lines

12–13; p. 127, lines 19–26; p. 130, line 15), and the "Disputatio" to Rom. 4:13–16 (p. 149, lines 30–33; p. 150, lines 1–2); compare the comments on Rom. 4:25 (p. 155, lines 18–20).

36. *Comm. Rom.*, p. 80, lines 35–38; *Romans*, p. 82. For some patristic solutions to the fragmentary character of Paul's expression in Rom. 4:2, see Schelkle, *Paulus, Lehrer der Väter*, pp. 124–25. Many earlier interpreters, e.g., Origen, Chrysostom, Augustine (in his commentary on Psalm 31), and Ambrosiaster, assumed that Abraham did have reason to boast before God but that this was not because of his works but because of his faith. Calvin, in contrast, denies that Abraham has any reason to glory at all.

37. *Comm. Rom.*, pp. 80–81, lines 44–47; *Romans*, p. 83.

38. *Comm. Rom.*, p. 76, lines 25–27; *Romans*, p. 78.

39. Compare also Calvin's comments on Rom. 4:4, where he declares that he is agreeing with Bucer's assessment of the form of the argument: "Faith is reckoned as righteousness not because we merit anything at all, but because we lay hold of the goodness of the Lord. Therefore righteousness is not our due, but is freely bestowed." In 1556 Calvin revised this sentence to stress the activity of faith but at the same time to show that it is not a human work: "Faith is reckoned as righteousness not because it [faith] brings any merit from us, but because it lays hold of the goodness of God" (*Comm. Rom.*, p. 82, lines 1–3 and notes; compare *Romans*, p. 85). Schelkle notes that some early interpreters wanted to view faith as a work. He finds Origen referring to such a view in his commentary on John and thinks that Chrysostom and Ambrosiaster tend toward this view (*Paulus, Lehrer der Väter*, p. 113). Erasmus says that Abraham was considered righteous because of his "merit of faith" (1517) or "merit of trust" (1521) and that by his faith he merited the name of the righteous man and the promise (*In epistolam Pauli Apostoli ad Romanos paraphrasis*, in English in *Paraphrases on Romans and Galatians*, ed. Robert D. Sider, translated and annotated by John B. Payne et al., vol. 42 of *Collected Works of Erasmus* [Toronto: University of Toronto Press, 1984], pp. 27 and 29–30; the notes to pp. 29 and 30 point to the fact that Erasmus follows Origen in attributing merit to faith).

40. Discussing the various polemics against Roman theology found in the commentary, Girardin notes that the position most frequently denounced by Calvin was the teaching concerning the uncertainty of salvation (*Rhétorique et Théologique*, p. 142).

41. Though Calvin rarely names his theological adversaries, it is likely that here he has in mind the general scholastic teaching on what kind of certainty one can have of being in a state of grace. This is clear from his refutation of the notion of *conjectura moralis*. As I showed in the last chapter, the Roman Catholic views on certainty and doubt (especially those advanced by the Council of Trent) continued to provide impetus for Calvin's polemics throughout the 1540s and into the 1550s.

42. This is also an exceedingly prominent concern in Melanchthon's commentary on Romans.

43. *Comm. Rom.*, p. 92, lines 18–26 and notes; compare *Romans*, p. 92. The polemic against moral conjecture is a frequent one and is often joined with criticism of uncertainty about final perseverance; see, e.g., Calvin's comments on Rom. 5:2: "This passage demolishes the two most troublesome doctrines of the sophists, first, that in which they bid Christians be satisfied with moral conjecture in discerning the grace of God toward them, and second, that in which they teach that we are all in a state of uncertainty concerning our final perseverance" (*Comm. Rom.*, p. 103, lines 57–62; *Romans*, p. 105).

44. Calvin translates these verses as follows: "Ac fide minime debilitatus, non consideravit suum ipsius corpus iam emortum, centenarius quum fere esset: nec emortuam vulvam Sarae: Nec vero in Dei promissionem per incredulitatem disquisivit: sed roboratus est fide, tribuens gloriam Dei" (*Comm. Rom.*, p. 95, lines 9–12).

45. *Comm. Rom.*, p. 96, lines 49–52 and 56–58 and notes; *Romans*, p. 98.

46. "When therefore a message is brought to the saints concerning the works of God, the greatness of which exceeds their comprehension, they break out in expressions of wonder and even astonishment, but from wonder they soon pass on to a contemplation of the power [*virtutem*] of God (*Comm. Rom.*, pp. 96–97, lines 67–70; *Romans*, p. 98).

47. Calvin's language in this passage sounds much like Luther's descriptions of *Anfechtung*. The believer is assailed by circumstances that suggest the exact opposite of what God promises: "He promises us immortality—yet we are surrounded by mortality and corruption. He declares that he accounts us just—yet we are covered with sins. He testifies that he is propitious and benevolent toward us—yet outward signs threaten his wrath" (*Comm. Rom.*, p. 97, lines 82–85 and notes; compare *Romans*, p. 99). Similarities and differences between Luther's *Anfechtung* and Calvin's understanding of tribulation are discussed by Zachman (*Assurance of Faith*, pp. 63–68 and 183–87). On Luther see also Heiko A. Oberman, *Luther: Man between God and the Devil*, trans. E. Walliser-Schwarzbart (New Haven: Yale University Press, 1989), pp. 75–79. For additional discussion of Calvin's views on the trials of faith, see Ronald S. Wallace, *Calvin's Doctrine of the Christian Life* (Grand Rapids: Eerdmans, 1959), pp. 251–70.

48. *Comm. Rom.*, p. 97, lines 88–90 and notes; compare *Romans*, p. 99. Compare the fuller explanations of this issue in Calvin's commentary on Genesis 17:17, 18:12–15 (1554) (CO 23:245, 253–56). In these passages, Calvin refers to Romans but is not as concerned with spelling out Abraham's certainty as in the Romans commentary.

49. Calvin expresses this bias in 1540 in his comments on Rom. 4:19 and 4:20. In the first case, Calvin's criticism of the sense of perception follows clearly from Paul's statements suggesting that the promise of God was contrary to all appearances. Calvin writes, "Abraham withdrew his mind from what he could see and, as it were, forgot himself in order to make room for divine truth. . . . It was a mark of greater constancy to withdraw his attention from that fact which thrust itself freely before his eyes than if he had never contemplated any such thing" (*Comm. Rom.*, p. 95, lines 21–23 and 28–30; compare *Romans*, p. 97). In his comments on Rom. 4:20, he suggests the following as the remedy against appearances that contradict God's promise: "What then are we to do? We ought to pass over ourselves and all things of ours with closed eyes, so that nothing will impede or hold us back from believing that God is true" (*Comm. Rom.*, p. 97, lines 85–87 and notes; compare *Romans*, p. 97). Calvin reaffirmed these views in 1556 when he added the following sentences to his comments on Rom. 4:18: "There is nothing more inimical to faith than to bind our minds to our eyes, so that we seek the substance of our hope from their sight. . . . If . . . faith does not ascend on heavenly wings so as to look down from afar on all feelings of the flesh, it will always stick fast in the mud of the world" (*Comm. Rom.*, p. 94, lines 90–91 and 93–95; compare *Romans*, p. 96).

50. "We tend to make the excuse that our doubts about his promises do not detract from his power since the reason is the defect that is in us. However, we do not sufficiently exalt the power [*potentiam*] of God if we do not consider it greater than our weakness. Faith, therefore, ought not to look to our weakness, misery, and defects but should attend with all eagerness to the power [*virtutem*] of God alone. For if it relied on our righteousness and dignity it would not remain fixed in consideration of God's power [*potentia*]. The proof of unbelief [*incredulitas*], which he mentioned before, is the measuring of the power [*potentiam*] of God by our own standard" (*Comm. Rom.*, p. 98, lines 8–18 and notes; compare *Romans*, pp. 99–100).

51. Calvin's understanding and evaluation of God's omnipotence and the relation of this to faith is complex. It will be considered in more detail in chapter 4. In general, Calvin is critical of the nominalistic distinction between God's absolute and ordained power (*potentia absoluta et ordinata*); he especially dislikes the term "absolute power," since he thinks

this makes God a tyrant by separating God's power from God's justice. Nonetheless, Calvin maintains the theological principle underlying the distinction between the two powers; namely, that God's will is the rule of righteousness. However, according to Oberman, he transforms the understanding of the *potentia absoluta* to refer not to what God could have done but to what God actually does, the reasons of which are hidden from us. The best discussion of Calvin's relationship to the medieval concept of the absolute power of God appears in Steinmetz, "Calvin and the Absolute Power of God," *Journal of Medieval and Renaissance Studies* 18/1 (Spring 1988): 65–79; see also Heiko A. Oberman, "The 'Extra' Dimension in the Theology of Calvin," 1970; rpt. in *The Dawn of the Reformation*, pp. 256–57; *Initia Calvini: The Matrix of Calvin's Reformation*; Richard Stauffer, *Dieu, la création et la Providence dans la prédication de Calvin*, Basler und Berner Studien zur historischen und systematische Theologie, vol. 33 (Las Vegas: Peter Lang, 1978), pp. 112–16; S. Mark Heim, "The Powers of God: Calvin and Late Medieval Thought," *Andover Newton Quarterly* 19 (1979): 156–66 (rpt. in Gamble, *Articles*, 4:3–12); Schreiner, *Theater of His Glory*, pp. 34–35.

52. *Comm. Rom.*, p. 98, lines 28–29; *Romans*, p. 100.

53. See Calvin's frequent statements opposing the law or human works and God's mercy, e.g., in his comments on Rom. 3:21 (*Comm. Rom.*, pp. 68, lines 55–57 and p. 69, lines 1–4; *Romans*, pp. 71, 72); compare his comments on Rom. 3:24 (*Comm. Rom.*, p. 72, lines 98–102 and notes; *Romans*, p. 75).

54. Calvin speaks of the general content of Abraham's faith in his comments on Rom. 4:3: "Abraham, therefore, seized the kindness of God which was offered to him in the promise, and by which he perceived that righteousness was being communicated to him" (*Comm. Rom.*, p. 81, lines 71–73; *Romans*, p. 84). Discussing Rom. 4:17, Calvin views Abraham as a type or pattern of the general calling of a Christian to new life. Since Abraham's body was as if dead; similarly, the Gentiles are barren and dead and yet are "brought into the fellowship." Likewise, Christians are called from death into new, future life in the kingdom of God (*Comm. Rom.*, pp. 93–94, lines 65–85 and notes; *Romans*, pp. 95–96).

55. Moreover, for Calvin, as we have seen in chapter 1, firm and certain knowledge of God's benevolence, that is, faith, leads ineluctably to certainty of salvation; therefore, whenever Paul treats the topics of faith and justification or salvation, Calvin finds an open door to discuss certainty. Passages elsewhere in Romans (e.g., Rom. 5:1–5, 5:9–11, 8:1–2, 8:15–18, 8:31–39) led interpreters for whom the question of psychological certainty was a highly polemical issue to view the whole of Paul's theology through this lens. In addition, recall that in the 1539 *Institutes* Calvin cites Paul (Eph. 3:12) to legitimate a distinction between *fides* and *fiducia* that enabled Calvin to lay greater emphasis on the element of certainty in faith. He underscored this, again on the authority of Paul, in the addition to this section of the *Institutes* in 1543 (CO 1:457–58).

56. *Comm. Rom.*, p. 79, lines 8–11; p. 99, lines 53–54; *Romans*, pp. 81, 101. Schelkle points out that patristic interpreters tended to understand faith in Rom. 3:31 as *fides quae* (*Paulus, Lehrer der Väter*, pp. 120–21).

57. Parker points out that Calvin's exegesis of the passage Rom. 3:19–28 in 1540 totaled about two thousand words; in revising the passage, Calvin made this section half again as long (*Commentaries on Romans*, p. 193). The revisions to chapter 4 were not quite as extensive but nonetheless amounted to almost 30 percent of the original length.

58. See *Acta Synodi Trindentinae cum Antidoto* (CO 7:365–506; in English in *Tracts and Treatises* 3:17–188); Casteel, "Calvin and Trent"; Adolf Stakemeier, *Das Konzil von Trient über die Heilsgewißheit* (Heidelberg: F. H. Kerle, 1947).

59. See Augustine, *Spirit and the Letter* (9, 15): "not that justification is without our will, but the weakness of our will is discovered by the law, so that grace may restore the

will and the restored will may fulfill the law" (PL 44: 209; *Spirit and the Letter*, p. 205). Melanchthon (1532) had already criticized the view that faith justifies because it is the beginning of renovation; he attributed the origin of this view to Augustine. Like Calvin, Melanchthon found that such a view undermined the certainty of faith (*Römerbrief-Kommentar*, p. 100, line 5–p. 101, line 25). The view that justifying faith included the gift of new life was also set forth by Sadoleto in his commentary on Romans. See Parker's summary of Sadoleto's exegesis of Rom. 3:20–28, where he cites Sadoleto's rejection of the view that justification consists of the forgiveness of sins and formulation of the view that God adorns those whom he has pardoned with righteousness and then receives them by adoption. Parker cautions, however, that it is difficult to know how literally to take Sadoleto in this section (*Commentaries on Romans*, pp. 170–71). Nonetheless, in his letter to the Genevans (1539), Sadoleto did advance a definition of "faith alone" that suggests the view that Calvin rejects here: "we hold that in this very faith love is essentially comprehended as the chief and primary cause of our salvation" (OS 1:447; CO 5:375; *A Reformation Debate*, p. 36). Calvin may also have in mind the decree on justification issued at the end of the sixth session of the Council of Trent (January 13, 1547), which declared that justification consists in the remission of sins and the sanctification and renewal of the inward man. See Calvin's "Acts of the Council of Trent, with Antidote," in which he argues, largely on the basis of Romans 4, that justification does not include the gift of regeneration (CO 7:448–51; *Tracts and Treatises* 3:115–19 and 122–25). For a summary of Calvin's views on merit and his criticism of even the "sounder schoolmen," see Gerrish, *Grace and Gratitude*, pp. 98–102. For an overview of Calvin's use of Augustine in his exegetical works, see Jan Marius J. Lange van Ravenswaay, *Augustinus totus noster: das Augustinusverständnis bei Johannes Calvin*, Forschungen zur Kirchen- und Dogmengeschichte 45 (Göttingen: Vandenhoeck und Ruprecht, 1990), pp. 113–15.

60. *Comm. Rom.*, p. 68, lines 66–68; compare *Romans*, p. 71.

61. *Comm. Rom.*, p. 72, lines 79–84; *Romans*, p. 74.

62. *Comm. Rom.*, p. 93, lines 35–39; *Romans*, p. 94.

63. Discussing Rom. 4:25 in 1540, Calvin says that Paul has not yet begun to deal with the topic of newness of life (*Comm. Rom.*, p. 101, lines 14–15; *Romans*, p. 103).

64. *Comm. Rom.*, p. 82, lines 95–96; *Romans*, p. 84. For the soteriological focus in general, see the statement that Paul's subject is eternal salvation at Rom. 4:13 (*Comm. Rom.*, p. 89, lines 24–25; *Romans*, p. 91).

65. See, e.g., Calvin's comments at Rom. 4:5 (1556): "[Paul] clearly shows that faith brings us righteousness, not because it is a meritorious virtue, but because it obtains for us the grace of God" (*Comm. Rom.*, p. 83, lines 14–16; *Romans*, p. 85).

66. See, e.g., Calvin's comments on Rom. 3:24 (1556): "Here again the fiction of those who make righteousness a quality receives its best refutation. If we are accounted righteous before God because we are redeemed at a price, we certainly borrow from some other source what we do not have" (*Comm. Rom.*, p. 72, lines 6–9; *Romans*, p. 75). Compare similar statements at 4:3 (1556) and 4:5 (1556) (*Comm. Rom.*, p. 81, lines 49–51; p. 83, lines 19–20; *Romans*, p. 83, 85).

67. See, e.g., Calvin's comments on Rom. 3:25 (added in 1556): "This definition or explanation confirms again what I have already frequently hinted at, viz. that men are justified not because they are such in reality, but by imputation" (*Comm. Rom.*, p. 74, lines 45–47; *Romans*, p. 76).

68. Discussing Rom. 4:3, where Paul quotes Gen. 15:6 (1556): "Let us simply note that those to whom righteousness is imputed are justified, since Paul uses these two expressions as synonyms. We conclude from this that the question is not what men are in themselves, but how God regards them, not because purity of conscience and integrity of

life are distinguished from the free favor of God, but because, when the reason for God's love to us and his acknowledgment of us as just is questioned, it is necessary that Christ should be seen to be the one who clothes us with his own righteousness" (*Comm. Rom.*, p. 82, lines 79–85; *Romans*, p. 84).

69. *Comm. Rom.*, p. 69, lines 75–77; *Romans*, p. 71. Later, concluding this addition to the comments on Rom. 3:21, Calvin refers again to the peace of conscience, says that it is "disturbed on the score of works," and asserts that it is a lifelong phenomenon (*Comm. Rom.*, p. 69, lines 97–98; *Romans*, p. 72).

70. *Comm. Rom.*, p. 89, lines 17–19; compare *Romans*, p. 91.

71. *Comm. Rom.*, p. 81, lines 58–71; *Romans*, pp. 83–84; compare Melanchthon, *Römerbrief-Kommentar*, p. 127, line 14-p. 128, line 9.

72. *Comm. Rom.*, p. 81, lines 65–66; *Romans*, pp. 83–84.

73. In his "Antidote" to the Council of Trent, Calvin relied heavily on Rom. 4:14 to support his arguments for the certainty of faith (CO 7:456; compare 7:448; *Tracts and Treatises* 3:126, compare 3:115).

74. 1540: "We see that the apostle calls hesitation and doubt 'incredulity,' by which faith is abolished and the promise abrogated." 1556: "We see that the apostle, estimating faith by its firm and unshakable certainty, considers hesitancy and doubt as unbelief, by which faith is abolished and the promise abrogated" (*Comm. Rom.*, p. 92, lines 22–25 and notes; compare *Romans*, p. 94)

75. *Comm. Rom.*, pp. 92–93, lines 34–40; *Romans*, p. 94.

76. *Comm. Rom.*, p. 96, lines 51–52; *Romans*, p. 98.

77. *Comm. Rom.*, p. 98, lines 18–22; compare *Romans*, p. 100.

78. CO 23:213.

79. CO 23:208.

80. For a discussion and assessment of Calvin's appreciation for different scriptural uses of the word "faith," see Schützeichel, *Glaubenstheologie*,pp. 122–24.

81. See Calvin's comments on 1 Cor. 12:9 and 13:2 (CO 49:499–500 and 509). Calvin equates this *fides particularis* with Chrysostom's *fides signorum*. Faith is taken as the first principles of religion or as sound doctrine (a *fides quae*) in Calvin's comments on Rom. 12: 6 and 1 Tim. 1:19, 3:9, 4:1, 4:6, and 6:21. Since Calvin assumed Pauline authorship of the Pastoral epistles, he also considered their more prominent usage of *fides quae* to be genuinely Pauline. On faith in the Pastoral epistles, see G. Barth, *pistis, pisteuo*, 3:230–31.

82. Compare the comments on Rom. 4:14 (*Comm. Rom.*, p. 91); Rom. 10:10: "I maintain that faith is a firm and effectual confidence and not just a bare idea" (*Comm. Rom.*, p. 229, lines 80–83; *Romans*, p. 228); 1 Cor. 2:12: "Hence we may know the nature of faith to be this, that the conscience has from the Holy Spirit a certain testimony of the divine benevolence toward it [and] relying on this it does not hesitate to invoke God as father" (CO 49:342); Phil. 3:10 and Col. 1:6 (*Comm. Gal. et al.*, pp. 356, 391).

83. See Calvin's comments on Rom. 10:14–17, where he underscores at several different points the connection between faith and the preached gospel. Calvin understands this connection to be not a necessary one but rather a result of God's special providence. Several additions that he makes in 1551 reinforce the idea, expressed in 1540 in the comments on Rom. 10:17, that "by itself preaching is profitless, but when the Lord is pleased to work, it is the instrument of his power" (*Comm. Rom.*, p. 234, lines 56–58; *Romans*, p. 233).

84. Passages important for certainty include 1 Cor. 2:10–16; Gal. 4:6; Phil. 2:13. Calvin often opposes faith and opinion and engages in polemic against moral conjecture and uncertainty about final perseverance. See, e.g., his comments on Col. 1:23 ("if you continue, grounded and settled in faith"), which he takes as an exhortation to perseverance and a

proof text for certainty: "For faith is not like opinion, which is shaken by various movements, but has a firm constancy that resists all the machinations of hell. Therefore the whole papal theology will never afford the slightest taste of true faith, [since] it considers it axiomatic that we must always be in doubt concerning the present state of grace, as well as concerning final perseverance" (*Comm. Gal. et al.*, p. 407, lines 9–16). Similar expressions are found in the comments on 1 Cor. 11:24, 2 Cor. 13:5, Col. 2:2, and Titus 1:1.

85. This observation is in tension with Stuermann's view that Paul and Calvin stand together against other Christian thinkers in their view of faith as knowledge, although Stuermann also holds that Calvin "developed" the idea beyond Paul (*Calvin's Concept of Faith*, pp. 72–73).

86. CO 1:457. In the commentary on Ephesians, Calvin's comments on this passage ("[that you] may have power to comprehend with all the saints what is the breadth and length and height and depth and to know the love of Christ, which exceeds knowledge, so that you may be filled with all the fullness of God") first argue that this knowledge of the greatness of Christ's love springs from faith. The love of Christ is the perfection of wisdom and is all that is needful to know. Calvin asserts that the fact that it is beyond knowledge does not mean that it cannot be known with certainty that the elect enjoy the grace of God. He maintains that the knowledge of faith [*scientia*] is higher than all knowledge [*cognitio*] and is certain because "it is acquired through the teaching of the Holy Spirit and not through the acuteness of our intellect" (*Comm. Gal. et al.*, p. 217, lines 6–8). Calvin also finds the link between faith and knowledge [*scientia*] in his comments on 2 Tim. 1:12 ("For I know whom I have believed"): "Therefore faith neither leans on human authority nor rests on God in such a way that it hesitates but must be joined with knowledge [*sed cum scientia coniuncta esse debet*]" (CO 52:355), and he finds faith joined with knowledge [*agnitio*] in his comments on Titus 1:1 (CO 52:404–5).

87. "Accordingly, Paul is not content with this general declaration but defines what the gospel is and what it contains. He declares that his doctrine is the true gospel, lest it be sought elsewhere. Of what profit was it to profess respect for the gospel and not know what it meant? Among the papists, where implicit faith thrives, that might be sufficient. But among Christians there is no faith where there is no knowledge [*cognitio*]" (*Comm. Gal. et al.*, p. 19, lines 1–7). Compare also Calvin's comments on Phil. 3:10 ("so that I may know [Christ]"): "He describes the strength and nature of faith: that it is the knowledge of Christ, and that not bare and confused, but such that the power of his resurrection is felt [*percipitur*]" (*Comm. Gal. et al.*, p. 356, lines 27–29); and on Col. 1:6 ("since the day you heard [the gospel], and knew the grace"): "It is with propriety that the faith of the gospel is called the knowledge of God's grace, since no one has ever tasted the gospel except one who knew himself to be reconciled to God and grasped hold of the salvation that is offered in Christ" (*Comm. Gal. et al.*, p. 391, lines 7–9; this statement stems from 1556). Ephesians 4:13 ("and of the knowledge of the son of God") provides Calvin with an opportunity to stress faith's christocentric character by underscoring that faith consists in the son of God being known [*filius Dei cognoscitur*] (*Comm. Gal. et al.*, p. 233, lines 33–34).

88. Calvin also derives the idea of blindness as the fundamental human problem directly from 2 Cor. 4:3–4, which says that the god of this world has blinded the minds of those who do not believe so that they cannot perceive the light of the gospel. For further sources of the theme of blindness, compare also Calvin's exegesis of 1 Cor. 1:21–25 and 2:8–10, Gal. 4:9, and Titus 2:13. On the unique way that Calvin interprets this theme into his exegesis of Rom. 1:18–32, see Steinmetz, "Calvin and the Natural Knowledge of God," pp. 151–54.

89. "But what does Paul wish for the Ephesians? The spirit of wisdom and the illumination of the eyes of their understanding [*cordis*]. Did they not have these? Yes, but at

the same time they needed increase [*incrementis*], so that having received a larger measure of the Spirit and being more and more enlightened, they might more clearly and deeply maintain what they already hold" (*Comm. Gal. et al.*, p. 170, lines 4–7). As noted earlier, Calvin develops in the comments on 1 Cor. 2:5–7 the notion of the gospel as a hidden wisdom distinct from the wisdom of the world; it is on this hidden wisdom that faith is founded.

90. Calvin's interpretation of Rom. 1:18–23 clearly guides his reading of 1 Cor. 1:21 ("For since, in the wisdom of God, the world did not know God through wisdom, it pleased God to save those who believe by the foolishness of preaching"). According to Calvin, this verse says that the witness to God in creation only renders human beings inexcusable and therefore saving knowledge of God must be sought in the gospel: "This is a most beautiful passage, from which is clear the extent of the blindness of the human mind, which in the midst of light discerns nothing. For it is true that this world is like a theater, in which the Lord shows to us a clear manifestation [*figura*] of his glory; nevertheless, even though we have such a spectacle placed before our eyes, we are blind, not because the revelation is obscure but because we are alienated in mind. We lack not only the will but also the ability for this matter. For even though God shows himself openly, it is only with the eye of faith that we can see him, except [for the fact] that we receive a slight taste of divinity that renders us inexcusable. Therefore when Paul denies here that God is known through his creatures, you must understand him to mean that a pure knowledge of him is not attained [*non apprehendi puram eius notitiam*]" (CO 49:326). Compare also Calvin's comments on Acts 14:17 (1554). Here he not only raises the theme of inexcusability but also stresses that faith comes from hearing the word of salvation and not from beholding heaven and earth (CO 48:327–29).

91. "Those things that he mentions as 'given by Christ' [*a Christo donata*] are the blessings [*beneficia*] that we obtain from his death and resurrection: that when we have been reconciled to God and obtained the remission of sins, we know that we are adopted to the hope of eternal life [and] that we are made new creatures by the sanctification of the spirit of regeneration, so that we might live to God [*ut vivamus Deo*]" (CO 49:342).

92. CO 49:341.

93. CO 49:341–42.

94. CO 49:342. The exegesis of Tit. 1:1 also demonstrates how faith as knowledge answers the problem defined on the basis of Romans 1. In discussing the phrase "the knowledge of truth, which is according to piety," Calvin says first that this explains the nature of faith but does not provide a full definition of it. As knowledge, faith is distinguished both from opinion and from implicit faith. "Truth" reflects the certainty of faith's object, the right and sincere knowledge of God. By limiting this knowledge to that which is according to piety, it is shown that Paul's doctrine aims at the proper worship of God (CO 52:404–405). The soteriological context of this knowledge is brought out in the comments on Titus 1:2, which Calvin translates "on account of the hope of eternal life." Here he understands salvation to be the cause or ground of the worship of God. Nonetheless he cautions his readers against valuing their salvation more than the glory of God; the hope of heavenly life is essential for piety, but it is not the ultimate goal of proper knowledge of God. The idea that the glory of God is final cause of salvation arises, as I have shown, in Calvin's comments on Rom. 3:22 and 3:24; compare his comments on Eph. 1:4, 5, 12 (*Comm. Gal. et al.*, pp. 158, 160–61 and 165).

95. "The true conviction [*persuasio*] that the faithful have of the word of God, of their own salvation, and of religion in general, does not spring from the judgment of the flesh, or from human and philosophical arguments, but from the sealing of the Spirit, which makes their consciences so certain that all doubt is removed. The foundation of faith would

be frail and unsteady if it was placed in human wisdom" (*Comm. Gal. et al.*, p. 166, line 30-p. 167, line 5).

96. *Comm. Gal. et al.*, p. 167, lines 10–12.

97. "First Paul denominates it the faith of Christ, meaning that everything that faith ought to regard is exhibited to us in Christ. Hence it follows that we should not understand as faith an empty and confused knowledge [*nudam et confusam notitiam*] of God but [rather] that [knowledge] which aims at Christ in order to seek God there. This will not be done unless the power and office [*virtus et officium*] of Christ are understood. Boldness and confidence proceed from faith, [which] brings with itself from these the latter first. There are three stages. First we believe the promises [*promissionibus credimus*] of God. Then, resting on these, we receive confidence, so that we are heartened and peaceful. Then boldness follows, which, since fear has been overcome, enables us to commit ourselves calmly and firmly to God" (*Comm. Gal. et al.*, p. 210, lines 10–20). Gerrish notes that Calvin's narrowing of *fides* here to believing the promises is counter to his usual tendency: "It is more characteristic of him to represent faith as grasping the divine will in the promises" (*Grace and Gratitude*, p. 64, note 57).

98. *Comm. Gal. et al.*, p. 210, lines 20–28.

99. Stuermann has a discussion of the relationship between *fides* and *fiducia* (*Calvin's Concept of Faith*, pp. 103–8). However, he seems to distinguish too sharply between the certainty of faith and *fiducia*, arguing at one point that it is precisely the certain character of faith that distinguishes *fides* from *fiducia* (p. 88). More true to Calvin's intent are, to my mind, Dowey's comments, showing a link between the certain character of faith and the confidence of the believer: "Although this certainty [described in the comments on Eph. 1:13] has God's veracity and the authority of the word behind it, its real nature is seen in man's personal individual appropriation of God's promise. It is not an abstract or syllogistic certainty, but personal, existential assurance" (*Knowledge of God in Calvin's Theology*, p. 181).

100. An important proof text for this is Eph. 3:17–19.

101. In 1556 Calvin made this even more explicit by adding the following to his comments on 1 Cor. 2:10: "By the 'deep things' [*profunditates*] do not understand the secret judgments, into which we are forbidden to inquire, but the entire doctrine of salvation, which would have been set forth in the scriptures in vain unless God elevated our minds to it by his Spirit" (CO 49:341).

102. CO 49:509.

103. "Nunc tenemus quid sit fides, nempe Dei ac divinae voluntatis cognitio, quam per ecclesiae ministerium consequimur: vel, si mavis, fides universalis et proprie accepta" (CO 49:515). The words *hoc loco* appearing in the CO edition were added in 1551. At first glance, Calvin's willingness to distinguish between the fuller sense of faith in 1 Cor. 13:13 and the *fides particularis* that he finds earlier in the passage might seem to legitimate precisely the distinction between unformed and formed faith that Calvin rejects. Despite the similarities (for example, both Calvin's *fides particularis* and the scholastic *fides informis* refer to faith apart from "love"), for Calvin it is not the fact that the *fides particularis* lacks love that renders it incapable of justifying. Rather, such "faith" has an incomplete conception or knowledge of Christ. This topic receives fuller treatment in Calvin's discussion of the miracle stories in the Fourth Gospel and will be discussed in chapter 3.

104. A similar discussion of the relationship of love and faith is found in Calvin's comments on 1 Tim. 1:5 (CO 52:253). First Cor. 13:13 was a major countertext among Roman Catholic polemicists who argued that faith provided the beginning or foundation of justification, which was completed by hope and love; compare Schützeichel, *Glaubenstheologie*, p. 206.

105. CO 49:514.

106. CO 49:514.

107. In his comments on 2 Cor. 3:18, Calvin seeks to reconcile the view expressed in that passage (that we behold God with unveiled face) with the obscurity of the vision asserted in 1 Cor. 13:12. He concludes that God is openly beheld only insofar as this is advantageous for our salvation and as much as our capacity allows (*Comm. Sec. Cor.*, p. 66, lines 29–31).

108. Calvin defends his translation of the Greek word *eidos* into the Latin *aspectum* rather than the more usual *species* (e.g., Erasmus). He argues that few people understood the meaning of *species* in this instance (*Comm. Sec. Cor.*, p. 91, lines 3–4).

109. *Com. Sec. Cor.*, p. 91, lines 7–9.

110. *Com. Sec. Cor.*, p. 91, lines 16–17. John Chrysostom also cross-references 1 Cor. 13:12 and 2 Cor. 5:6–7 in his homilies on these passages and, like Calvin, addresses the difficulty posed by Paul's statement that we are absent from God. However, he uses the category of knowledge to explain the images of visual perception used to describe apprehension of God. For example, in the homily in which he covers 1 Cor. 13:12, Chrysostom relies on John 6:46 to interpret seeing as "the most perfect knowledge." In the homily on 2 Cor. 5:6–7, he asks: "Are we then estranged while we are here? [Paul] in anticipation corrected such a thought, saying, 'For we walk by faith, not by sight.' Even here indeed now we know him, but not so clearly. As he says also elsewhere, 'in a glass and darkly'" (John Chrysostom, *Homilies on First and Second Corinthians*, pp. 203, 328).

111. Another example of this opposition is found in Calvin's comments on 2 Cor. 4:18 ("while we look not at those things which are seen but at those which are not seen. For those things which are seen are temporal but those which are not seen are eternal"): "This is what will make all the miseries of this world easy for us to endure: if only we transfer our thoughts to the eternity of the heavenly kingdom. . . . Moreover, the apostle's words mean that we are deceived by the view of present things, because there is nothing there that is not temporal, [and] there is therefore nothing for us to rest on except the confidence of eternal life. Observe this expression, 'looking at things which are not seen,' for the eye of faith penetrates farther than every sense of a natural human being, *and faith is therefore also called a 'vision [adspectus] of invisible things'*" (*Comm. Sec. Cor.*, p. 85, lines 24–26; the italicized phrase is an addition in 1556). See also the commentary on 1 Tim. 6:16 (CO 52: 332–33).

112. Calvin also hints at this in his exegesis of 1 Cor. 1:21. See again the comments on 1 Tim. 6:16 ("who inhabits unapproachable light"): "By faith therefore we enter into the light of God but only in part [ingredimur ergo per fidem in lucem Dei, sed ex parte]" (CO 52:332).

113. The important analogy between the sacraments' revelation of God the redeemer and nature and history's ongoing (but vain, at least for fallen humanity) testimony to God the creator has been noted by Stephen K. Moroney, who also points to the glaring absence of discussions of the sacraments in most treatments of Calvin's understanding of the knowledge of God. See "The Noetic Effects of Sin: An Exposition of Calvin's View and a Constructive Theological Proposal" (Ph.D. diss., Duke University, 1995), pp. 125–27.

114. This should not imply that the theme of God's providence over creation and history appears in complete isolation from the concern for salvation. Indeed, given the conditions of the Fall, it is precisely at the point of God's orderly guidance of the world and events that any absolute distinction between God's creative and redemptive activity breaks down: is God's maintenance of order an extension of the original creative activity, or is it, in so far as it involves the restoration of creation, more appropriately a function of the redemptive activity? Mary Potter Engel, drawing on Calvin's three levels of providence,

speaks therefore of "creative providence," "redemptive providence I," and "redemptive prov-idence II" in describing Calvin's understanding of the divine activity. See *John Calvin's Perspectival Anthropology*, American Academy of Religion Series, number 52 (Atlanta: Scholars Press, 1988), pp. 207–9; compare pp. 123–49.

115. See, for example, Calvin's comments on Rom. 8:35–39. Here Calvin acknowl-edges in the 1540 edition that afflictions torment for a variety of reasons, one of which is the fact that those suffering do not realize that these things happen through God's provi-dence. Nonetheless, in the text of 1540 and the subsequent additions, Calvin understands the danger to lie primarily in the threat to faith in adoption and God's mercy. He takes Rom. 8:38 as a proof text for the certainty of salvation; see *Comm. Rom.*, pp. 188–91; *Romans*, pp. 186–89.

116. See Calvin's comments on Eph. 6:12–16, which he claims, in his comments on Eph. 6:14, is a discussion not of justification but of a "blameless life," i.e., sanctification. Feld notes that this interpretation is not found in any of the commentaries used by Calvin (*Comm. Gal. et al.*, p. 286, lines 5–10 and note 33). Calvin characterizes the darkness in Eph. 6:12 as "unbelief and ignorance of God" and, in his comments on Eph. 6:16, explores the protective power of faith when combined with the word (*Comm. Gal. et al.*, pp. 283 and 287, lines 32–36). Compare also his comments on 1 Thess. 5:8, which describes faith and love together as a breastplate (CO 52:169–70). Calvin mentions this verse in his comments on Eph. 6:16.

117. See Calvin's comments on 2 Thess. 1:4: "And certainly there is nothing that sustains us in tribulations other than faith. This is sufficiently manifest in that we completely fall to pieces [*collabimur*] as soon as the promises of God leave us" (CO 52:188).

118. CO 52:188.

119. "[H]oc alterum sine controversia sequetur, praesentem ataxian esse demonstrati-onem iudici quod nondum apparet" (CO 52:189). The restoration of order is an important theme in Calvin's theology. In chapters 3 and 4 I will show Calvin returning again and again to this central idea. On this topic, see R. Wallace, *Calvin's Doctrine of the Christian Life*, pp. 103–92; Lucien Joseph Richard, *The Spirituality of John Calvin* (Atlanta: John Knox Press, 1974), pp. 111–16; Schreiner, *Theater of His Glory*, pp. 97–114. The studies by Wal-lace and Schreiner are particularly distinguished for their broad use of Calvin's commentaries and sermons.

120. See Calvin's comments on 2 Thess. 1:5: "God furnishes tokens of a future judg-ment when he now abstains from the office of a judge. And if things were now arranged in a tolerable way so that the judgment of God might be recognized as complete [*ut agnosci posset absolutum Dei iudicium*], this kind of moderation would detain us on earth. Therefore God, in order to excite us to hope of a future judgment, judges the world at present only to a certain extent. Of course, he supplies many proofs [*documenta*] of his judgment, but in such a way as to compel us to extend our hope farther. Truly a remarkable passage, since it teaches in what manner our minds ought to be raised up [*excitandae sint*] above all the obstacles of the world whenever we suffer any adversity—that the righteous judgment of God, which will raise us above this world, might come into our mind" (CO 52:189).

121. The following lines were added in 1556: "Finis est, ut pii quasi oculis clausis praetereant breve hoc terrestris vitae iter, semper mente ad futuram regni Christi manifes-tationem intenti. Quorsum enim pertinet mentio adventus in potentia, nisi ut spe trans-siliant ad beatam illam resurrectionem quae adhuc abscondita est?" (CO 52:192). Other passages where Calvin urges contemplation of the last day, God's righteous judgment, or the coming of Christ are found in his comments on Tit. 2:13 (where he explicitly says that one should contemplate by faith the last day and the revelation of God's majesty), 1 Thess. 1:10, 1 Tim. 6:13–14, and 2 Tim. 4:8. It is interesting to note that Calvin made additions

to his comments on each of these last three passages in 1556; in the case of 1 Thess. 1:10 and 2 Tim. 4:8 the comments either introduced or strengthened the idea that the faithful need to close their eyes to the present and look to their future deliverance. Outside of the Pauline corpus, see also Calvin's comments on 2 Pet. 2:9.

122. CO 52:193.

123. CO 52:188–89.

124. Calvin mentions the example of Dionysius the Younger also in his comments on Pss. 10:5, 73:3, and 133:1.

125. CO 52:191.

126. "*Sermon du Dernier Advenement de Nostre Seigneur Iesus Christ*" (CO 52:225–38). In this sermon Calvin directs his audience's attention to the future judgement. However, the themes he develops in this regard relate not to the problem of the confusion of history but rather to the need for faith in the gospel, to faith and certainty of salvation, and to faith's role in sanctification. He emphasizes that faith in the gospel is all that God requires and that to believe is not only to find the gospel to be true and holy but to love and revere it; it is because of their failure to believe that the wicked will be judged (cols. 227–28). He engages in polemic against the "papists," who trust in their works and merits and have no faith (cols. 228–29). Those who do not obey the gospel—which is possible only through proper faith—do not know God and are without excuse (cols. 229–30). Yet all who believe the gospel can boast without any doubt that Jesus will come as their redeemer (col. 231). Because Christ will return to be admired in his saints and glorified in them and not merely to judge the wicked, the faithful should not fear his return (cols. 233–34). Referring at only one point in the sermon to the condition of the faithful in this world, Calvin also remarks that this teaches them not to seek their glory in this world but to look to its manifestation when Christ returns to be glorified in them (cols. 234–35). Paul's statement "to those who have believed" proves that faith is the true source and origin of all holiness. Faith is the guarantee of sanctification (col. 235).

127. CO 52:192.

128. CO 52:197.

129. CO 52:205. See also the similar judgment in the comments on Col 3:6 ("on account of which things the wrath of God comes"): "Paul speaks here, however, of eternal destruction, a mirror of which appears only in the reprobate. In short, whenever God threatens he shows us the punishment in an indirect way [*oblique*], so that beholding this in the reprobate we may be deterred from sinning" (*Comm. Gal. et al.*, p. 446, lines 23–26).

130. See Calvin's comments on Phil. 3:18–21 (*Comm. Gal. et al.*, pp. 363–67).

131. *Comm. Gal. et al.*, p. 372, lines 20–24.

132. *Comm. Gal. et al.*, p. 373, lines 17–22.

133. On these proverbs, see *Comm. Gal. et al.*, p. 373, notes 32 and 33.

134. *Comm. Gal. et al.*, p. 374, lines 7–13.

135. *Comm. Gal. et al.*, p. 374, line 36–p. 375, line 2.

136. *Comm. Gal. et al.*, p. 375, lines 19–26.

137. CO 52:174.

138. CO 52:175.

139. See, for example, Calvin's concluding comments on 1 Thess. 4:14: "Therefore, let the grief of the godly be mixed with consolation, so that this may train them to patience. The hope of blessed immortality, which is the mother of patience, will effect this" (CO 52:165).

140. CO 52:174.

141. Schreiner notes that the theme of the confusion of history arises also in at least

two sermons on Pauline texts: a sermon on Eph. 1:7–10 (CO 51:283–96) and one on Eph. 3:7–9 (CO 51:457) (*Theater of His Glory*, pp. 130–31, notes 140 and 144). However, these sermons are much later than the commentaries on Paul. They were first published in 1562; according to Parker, Calvin preached on Ephesians in 1558 (*Oracles of God: An Introduction to the Preaching of John Calvin* [London: Lutterworth Press, 1947], p. 162).

Three. From Faith to Faith

1. *Comm. Heb.*, pp. 11–12 and 180–81. On Calvin's views on Pauline authorship, see Parker, *Calvin's New Testament Commentaries*, p. 73, and Hagen, *Hebrews Commenting from Erasmus to Bèze*, pp. 62–64.

2. Erich Grässer, *Der Glaube im Hebräerbrief*, Marburger Theologische Studien, vol. 2 (Marburg: N. G. Elwert, 1965), p. 13. For discussions of faith in the letter to the Hebrews, see, in addition to Grässer, G. Barth, *pistis, pisteuo*, 3:228–29.

3. Calvin discusses the relationship between faith and hope as early as the 1536 *Institutes*; however, he expands the discussion considerably in 1539 (CO 1:684–86). He specifies hope as the hope of eternal salvation and stresses its importance for refreshing and strengthening faith. He acknowledges that this close connection causes scripture sometimes to use the words "faith" and "hope" interchangeably. Indeed, in the commentary on Romans, Calvin finds an example of this in Rom. 4:18: "If we adopt this reading [i.e., "Qui praeter spem super spe credidit"] the sense will be that when there was no good reason—indeed, when all things were against [him]—he nonetheless did not cease to believe. We can also read 'above hope' [*Supra spem*], and perhaps more appropriately, as if he were saying that by his faith he had far surpassed any conception that he could have formed. In the second instance the word 'hope' means the faith given by God; the meaning is, that when he had no grounds for hope he still relied [*incubuit*] in hope [*spe*] on the Lord's promise and considered that what the Lord had promised was sufficient for hope." In 1551 Calvin added the following to the beginning of the last sentence, making the use of hope for faith even more explicit: "Paul uses the word hope twice; in the first place he means the reason for hope that can be derived from nature and carnal reason." See *Comm. Rom.*, p. 94, lines 86–100 and notes. See also Stuermann, *Calvin's Concept of Faith*, pp. 250–54; Schützeichel, *Glaubenstheologie*, pp. 189–92.

4. See Grässer, *Glaube*, pp. 102–5 and 115–17.

5. On the meaning of Heb. 4:2, see Grässer, *Glaube*, pp. 14–15.

6. See his comments on Heb. 6:11 and 6:19, where Christ as the object of faith is presupposed.

7. In his comments on this passage, Calvin paraphrases Rom. 1:16–17 and attacks so-called faith among demons and those who have not heard the word (compare James 2:19) in order to make his point that the word must be received by faith (*Comm. Heb.*, pp. 59–60). Compare Calvin's comments on Rom. 10:14–17 (*Comm. Rom.*, pp. 231–41; *Romans*, 229–33).

8. *Comm. Heb.*, pp. 64–68. Calvin applies this to the word of God in general, not just to the law, claiming that Christ "pierces" (i.e., brings to light the deepest human thoughts) "for the most part by the gospel" and that the word as a "discerner" means that "it brings the light of knowledge to the human mind." In exegeting this verse, Calvin makes frequent reference to passages from the Pauline epistles.

9. Erich Grässer, *An die Hebräer: 1. Teilband: Hebr 1–6*, vol. 17/1 of *Evangelisch-Katholischer Kommentar zum Neuen Testament*, ed. N. Brox et al. (Braunschweig: Benzinger and Neukirchen-Vluyn: Neukirchener, 1990), pp. 28–29.

10. *Comm. Heb.*, p. 87.

11. *Comm. Heb.*, p. 88.

12. Grässer (*An die Hebräer*, p. 33, note 27) reports this claim by the fourth-century bishop Filastrius of Brescia in *Diversarum haereseon liber*, 89.3 (CCL 9:256) and *Ephiph Haer*, 59.2.1 (*Die griechischen christlichen Schriftsteller der ersten drei Jahrhunderte* [Leipzig: Hinrichs, 1897–], 31:365). According to Kenneth Hagen, medieval exegetes followed four different "avenues of interpretation" in attempts to get around the Novatian interpretation of Heb. 6:4–6. The dominant interpretation was that the verses do not deny second repentance but only second baptism; repentance can be referred to baptism since the phrase "crucifying the Son of God" in Heb. 6:6 means to die with Christ in baptism. Other interpretations were that the passage denies the possibility of repentance after this life, that "impossibility" means "difficult" (a view represented only by Nicholas of Lyra), or that to "fall away" means to sin against the Holy Spirit (held by Pseudo-Hugh of St. Victor). This latter view appears in Bugenhagen's commentary on Hebrews (1524) and is also the approach taken by Calvin. Moreover, some exegetes (e.g., Luther and Bugenhagen) found an argument against Pauline authorship in the denial of a second repentance in Heb. 6:4–6. See Hagen, *Hebrews Commenting from Erasmus to Bèze*, pp. 8–12. In his comments on Heb. 6:4, Calvin explains and rejects two of the medieval possibilities: that "impossible" means "difficult" and the idea that the repentance that is denied is the catechumen's repentance preparing for initial baptism (this is linked to the dominant medieval interpretation).

13. *Comm. Heb.*, p. 90. Calvin makes similar observations in his comments on Heb. 10:26 and finds his views confirmed in Heb. 10:28 (*Comm. Heb.*, p. 168–71).

14. "But we must notice in passing the names by which he distinguishes the knowledge of the gospel [*cognitio evangelii*]. He calls it 'illumination'; hence it follows that human beings are blind until Christ, who is the light of the world, enlightens them [*illis affulgeat*]. He calls it a 'taste of the heavenly gift,' which means that the things that Christ confers on us are above nature and the world and yet they are tasted by faith. He calls it the 'partaking of the Spirit,' because it is [the Spirit] who distributes to everyone all the light and understanding he desires [*quia is est qui unicuique distribuit prout vult quidquid est lucis et intelligentiae*], [and] without [the Spirit] no one can say that Jesus is Lord [1 Cor. 12:3]; he opens for us the eyes of our minds and reveals to us the secret things of God [*patefacit Dei arcana*]. He calls it a 'taste of the good word of God,' by which he means that the will of God is revealed in it not in any sort of way [*non quovis modo*] but in such a way as to sweetly delight us. In short, by this title is pointed out the difference between the law and the gospel, for the former has nothing but severity and condemnation, but the latter is a sweet testimony of divine love toward us and fatherly indulgence. Lastly he calls it a 'taste of the powers of the world to come,' by which he means that we are admitted by faith as it were into the kingdom of heaven, so that we see in spirit [*cernamus spiritu*] that blessed immortality that is hidden from our senses. Let us know, therefore, that the gospel is not properly known other than by the illumination of the Spirit. Being thus drawn away from the world we are raised to heaven, and knowing the goodness of God we rely on his word [*agnita Dei bonitate in eius verbum recumbamus*]" (*Comm. Heb.*, p. 92).

15. *Comm. Heb.*, pp. 92–93. Calvin expresses a similar judgment in his commentary on John. See the comments on John 13:18, where Calvin acknowledges that the reprobate are sometimes endued with the gifts of the Spirit but without the gift of sanctification (CO 47:311). In the commentary on the parable of the word sown as seed on different types of soil in his Harmony of the Gospel (1555), Calvin says that those who have so-called temporary faith not only profess to be disciples for a time but also think that they have faith. However, they are not renewed by that incorruptible seed that cannot spoil (CO 45: 365). Another biblical example of temporary faith (to be discussed in chapter 5) is that of Simon Magus in Acts 8:13, 8:18–24.

16. Calvin's interpretation of this passage both picks up an idea raised in an earlier interpretation of a passage from 1 Corinthians (1546) and provides an example to confirm his later exegesis of a passage in 1 Thessalonians (1550/1551). In his comments on Heb. 6:4–6, Calvin appears to return to the notion of a special faith (*fides particularis*), which he had briefly mentioned in his comments on 1 Cor. 13:2, and to expand this idea by providing a more detailed picture of faith among the reprobate. Here as well as in 1 Cor. 13:2 the faith that can be lost is distinguished from true faith in its lack of the Spirit of sanctification. In the 1 Corinthians passage, however, it appeared that special faith could not save because it grasped Christ only as a miracle worker and not in his full significance. Here Calvin expresses this failure in different terms—not in terms of its inadequate apprehension of Christ but in terms of instability apart from the gift of repentance. Moreover, he goes beyond the earlier passage in explicitly portraying temporary faith as a divine work. It is not the idea of faith among the reprobate but rather the warning to persevere in repentance that finds its way back into Calvin's interpretation of Paul. In the comments on 1 Thess. 5:19, Calvin extends the concept of quenching the Spirit beyond the particular disdain of prophecy (compare 1 Thess. 5:20) to those who through their neglect of the task of repentance "make void the gifts of God." According to Calvin, the meaning of the phrase "quench not the Spirit" is "be enlightened by the Spirit of God. See that you do not lose that light through your ingratitude." He follows this comment with a reference to Heb. 6:4, which, he claims, shows that those who, though once enlightened, reject God's gift are struck "with a dreadful blindness" as a negative example for the elect. As he argues in the interpretation of Heb. 6:4 itself, the admonition does not detract from the efficacy of divine grace but serves to stimulate the indolent flesh to seek God's help. See CO 52:175–76.

17. Calvin's translation of Heb. 6:11: "Desideramus autem unumquemque vestrum idem ostendere studium ad certitudinem spei usque in finem" (*Comm. Heb.*, p. 97).

18. "The word 'hope' is here to be taken for faith because of [their] affinity. It appears that the apostle could do this intentionally because the topic concerned perseverance" (*Comm. Heb.*, p. 98). Grässer notes that earlier exegetes also understood this passage to be talking about faith, perhaps because of the identical construction in Heb. 10:22 (*plerophoria pisteus*) or simply because of the context. He also lists traditional translations of the phrase: *ad expletionem spei* (Theophylakt, Vulgate, Luther), *perfecta spes* (Ephraem), *ad confirmationem* (Latin Version). See Grässer, *Glaube*, pp. 26–27, notes 77 and 79. See also Schützeichel, *Glaubenstheologie*, p. 137.

19. Calvin's comments on Heb. 10:23 not only explain this but also reveal his underlying assumption that some in the community, like some in certain Pauline churches, paid too much attention to the ceremonies of the law: "Since here he is exhorting the Jews to perseverance he mentions hope rather than faith. For just as hope is born of faith, so it nourishes and sustains it [faith] to the end. Moreover, he requires confession, because faith is not true faith unless it shows itself before human beings. And he seems to touch indirectly the dissimulation of those who for the sake of their people paid too much attention to legal rituals [*legales ritus nimis religiose servabant*]. He therefore orders them not only to believe with the heart but also to demonstrate this and to profess how much they honored Christ" (*Comm. Heb.*, p. 165).

20. *Comm. Heb.*, p. 98.

21. See Grässer, *An die Hebräer*, pp. 383–86.

22. "For nowhere does a haven appear to our eyes, but wherever we direct our senses only water shows itself, indeed, waves rise up and threaten. But the anchor is cast through the waters into a dark and hidden place [*locum obscurum et abditum*] and while it rests there it keeps the ship beaten by the waves in place, lest it be overwhelmed. In the same way we ought to fix [*figenda*] our hope on the invisible God. There is a difference: the anchor

is cast downward into the sea, because the earth is at the sea's bottom. But our hope rises upward and soars aloft [*sursum attollitur et evolat*], for in the world it finds nothing on which it can stand, nor ought it cling to created things but only to God" (*Comm. Heb.*, pp. 103–4).

23. *Comm. Heb.*, p. 104.

24. *Comm. Heb.*, p. 99.

25. Calvin says that the author proves his intention "by this argument, that when God promised a countless offspring to Abraham, it seemed to be an incredible thing." Because he relied on God's word (*ab ore Dei pendet*), Abraham "was made a partaker of this blessing" (*Comm. Heb.*, p. 99).

26. *Comm. Heb.*, p. 99.

27. See Calvin's comments on Rom. 6:2 (1540): "The truth is, the grace of justification is never apprehended without regeneration. Indeed, we are justified for this purpose, so that by being regenerated we may glorify the Lord in purity of life" (*Comm. Rom.*, p. 120, lines 35–39 and notes).

28. See, for example, Thomas Aquinas, *Summa Theologiae* 2–2, q. 4, a. 1. On the nuances of Thomas's exegesis of Heb. 11:1, see C. Spicq, "L'exégèse de Hébr. XI,I par S. Thomas d'Aquin," *Revue des Sciences Philosophiques et Théologiques* 31 (1947): 229–36. Other examples of traditional views are given by Schützeichel, *Glaubenstheologie*, p. 185, notes 16 and 17. See also Feld, *Luthers und Steinbachs Vorlesungen*, pp. 174–82. Schwarz shows that not all medieval theologians took this as a definition; some understood it rather as a description (*Fides, Spes und Caritas*, pp. 64–66, especially notes 148, 150, and 151, and pp. 154 and 310–13). Gestrich briefly compares the interpretations of Heb. 11:1 offered by Luther and Zwingli (*Zwingli als Theologe*, pp. 35–38). For a detailed discussion of Calvin's translation and exegesis of Hebrews 11:1, see Schützeichel, *Glaubenstheologie*, pp. 183–87. For additional perspectives and a criticism of views seeking a definition of faith in this verse, see Grässer, *Glaube*, p. 46, note 197.

29. "Hence it is also evident that those who think that an exact definition [*iustem definitionem*] of faith is given here are greatly mistaken, for the apostle is not talking about the whole nature of faith [*tota fidei natura*] but selects the part that fits with his purpose, namely, that patience is always joined to it" (*Comm. Heb.*, p. 180). Here Calvin breaks even with Luther, who, though he does not designate Heb. 11:1 a definition, was able, with the help of Paul, to interpret the verse so as to find the view of faith as clinging to the word of God: "Igitur cum fides nihil aliud sit quam adhaesio verbi Dei, ut ad Rom. I., sequitur, quod sit possessio verbi Dei, id est aeternorum bonorum." (WA 57:3.228, lines 17–19; see Feld, *Luthers und Steinbachs Vorlesungen*, p. 182); compare Schwarz, *Fides, Spes und Caritas*, pp. 50–60. According to Grässer, "the connection that Calvin established between 10:39 and 11:1 has become *communis opinio* among exegetes" (*Glaube*, p. 45, note 190). Chapter 11:1 emphasizes the necessary transcendental referent of faith proper, without which it could easily be misunderstood to be "eine bloß innerweltlich zu begreifende Tapferkeit" (*Glaube*, p. 190).

30. *Comm. Heb.*, p. 178.

31. "Fides, inquit, est hypostatis, hoc est fultura vel possessio, in qua pedem figimus" (*Comm. Heb.*, p. 181). Luther notes that recent commentators understand *substantia* as cause or foundation (*causa, fundamentum*) but says he will leave it to others to determine whether that is the meaning of substance in this verse (WA 57:3.226). After considering some interpretations of the next part of the verse, he suggests the meaning "possession," citing Luke 8:43 and 1 John 3:17: "Therefore, since faith is nothing else than a clinging to the word of God, as is stated in Rom. 1, it follows that the possession of the word of God, that is, of everlasting goods, is at the same time also the taking away (at least so far as affection and clinging are concerned) of all present goods, as Ps. 72 [Ps. 73:28] states 'For

me it is good to cling to God.' Therefore the apostle, as a wise and faithful agent of his Lord, properly calls the Hebrews, who founded their substance on this world, back to 'a better substance, which is the gaining of the soul' (compare Heb. 10:34, 39)." Luther refers this understanding back to Jerome's commentary on Galatians (WA 57:3.228–29; LW 29: 230–31; compare Feld, *Luthers und Steinbachs Vorlesungen*, pp. 180–81, and Kenneth Hagen, *A Theology of Testament in the Young Luther: The Lectures on Hebrews*, Studies in Medieval and Reformation Thought 12 [Leiden: Brill, 1974], pp. 84–87). It is noteworthy that Calvin, as he does in the *Institutes*, uses the word *possessio*, though his meaning seems broader than Luther's. Luther distinguishes his view from Chrysostom's interpretation of *substantia* as essence, by which he means the new spiritual essence that the Christian gains in Christ (Feld, *Luthers und Steinbachs Vorlesungen*, p. 94). Chrysostom's understanding as presence of future salvation found representation in Theodoret, Oecumenius, and Theophylakt (Grässer, *Glaube*, pp. 46–47, note 199). Kenneth Hagen explores the interpretation of *substantia* among medieval exegetes (Thomas, Peter of Tarantasia, Nicholas of Lyra, Dionysius the Carthusian, Faber Stapulensis) and shows that faith was taken as the foundation, beginning, or cause of salvation that needed to be formed by works of love. Hagen shows how Luther's understanding of possession departs from this line of interpretation (*A Theology of Testament*, pp. 79–87; compare Feld, *Luthers und Steinbachs Vorlesungen*, pp. 174–76).

32. "[D]emonstratio eorum quae non videntur" (*Comm. Heb.*, p. 181). In his lectures on Hebrews, Luther rejects the view that *argumentum* means *probatio, convictio*, or *repraehensio*. The first two terms suggest to him that faith relies on the fact that someone else (the patriarchs and other saints) believed; Luther reasons that if this were the case, then Adam and Abel couldn't have believed. Reproof is an effect of true faith but not faith itself. He notes that Peter Lombard has *convictio* and that Chrysostom takes it to mean *coniunctio*, but in cautioning "unless perhaps the manuscript of one or the other has been corrupted" Luther says that *elenchos* means *argumentum, compraehensio*, and *inditium*. In the gloss he has *indicium, signum* (WA 57:3.226–28 and 62:1.17; compare Feld, *Luthers und Steinbachs Vorlesungen*, p. 181). Calvin, in contrast, likes the language of proof, evidence, and demonstration. He admits that the idea of a demonstration of things not seen is paradoxical, since "demonstration makes things appear or be seen and is commonly applied to what is subject to our senses." But this is not inconsistent with respect to faith, because "the Spirit shows [*demonstrat*] hidden things to us, the knowledge of which cannot reach our senses." Calvin says he does not disapprove of Augustine's occasional rendering of *elenchos* as *coniunctio* (Fr. "un nom qui vient du verbe convaincre"), "conviction," but that *demonstratio* is less forced (*quia minus est coactum*).

33. "Promised to us is eternal life, but [it is promised] to the dead; to us is the word of a happy resurrection, but meanwhile we are involved in corruption; we are pronounced just, and sin lives in us; we hear that we are happy, but meanwhile we are overwhelmed with infinite miseries; we are promised an abundance of all good things, but we still often hunger and thirst; God declares that he will come to us quickly, but he seems to be deaf to our cries" (*Comm. Heb.*, p. 181). Feld notes that the point of traditional exegesis of Heb. 11:1 was to demonstrate precisely that faith was not "Widersinniges," or contradictory (*Luthers und Steinbachs Vorlesungen*, p. 177).

34. *Comm. Heb.*, p. 203.

35. *Comm. Heb.*, p. 205.

36. *Comm. Heb.*, p. 182.

37. *Comm. Heb.*, pp. 184–85. Calvin repeats this point at least twice in his exegesis of this verse alone: "He confirms what I have already stated, that no works coming from us can please God until we ourselves have been received into his favor. Or, more briefly, no works are reckoned just before God except those of a just man." "Let us learn therefore

that no right work can proceed from us until we until we are justified before God." Calvin makes similar claims with respect to Noah. From Noah's example (Heb. 11: 7) "it is evident that in all ages men have neither been approved by God nor done anything worthy of praise otherwise than by faith" (p. 189). When the verse declares that Noah became the heir of that righteousness that is according to faith, Calvin writes: "Moses reports that he was just. Because that history does not report that the cause and root of his righteousness was faith, the apostle declares this from the matter itself. This is true not only because no one ever devotes himself sincerely in service to God unless, relying on God's promises of fatherly benevolence, he trusts that his life will be approved by him. [It is true] also because when estimated according to God's standard no one's life, however holy, can please God without pardon. Therefore it is necessary that righteousness rest on faith" (p. 191).

38. "The apostle does not mean that men ought to feel assured that there is some god, for he speaks only of the true God; it will not be sufficient for you to understand any god you please, but you must understand what sort of being the true God is" (*Comm. Heb.*, pp. 186–87).

39. "The second clause [of Heb. 11:6] is that we ought to be fully persuaded that God is not sought in vain. This persuasion includes the hope of salvation and eternal life. . . . But let us remember that this must be believed and not held as an opinion, for even the ungodly may sometimes entertain such a notion, but nonetheless they do not come to God because of it since they do not have a firm and stable faith. This then is the other part of the faith by which we obtain favor with God: when indeed we hold as certain that salvation is laid up for us in him" (*Comm. Heb.*, p. 187). Luther's exegesis also raises the themes of *pro nobis* and individual certainty of salvation. After criticizing a human faith, called "dead" by James and called by others both "acquired" and a faith that only believes that God will reward others but never believes this about itself—Luther calls this a faith about God (*de Deo*) and not in God (*in Deo*)—he writes, "For this reason another faith is needed, namely, the faith by which we believe that we are numbered among those for whom God exists and is a rewarder" (WA 57:3.233; LW 29:235). See also Feld, *Luthers und Steinbachs Vorlesungen*, pp. 182–83.

40. *Comm. Heb.*, p. 187. Compare Calvin's comments on Rom 3:28 (1540): "The moral law is truly confirmed and established through faith in Christ, since it was given to teach man of his iniquity and to lead him to Christ, without whom the law is not fulfilled. [The law] can do nothing except increase inordinate desires, in order to finally bring upon man greater condemnation. When, however, we come to Christ, we first find in him the exact righteousness of the law, and this also becomes ours by imputation" (*Comm. Rom.*, p. 79, lines 8–15; compare *Romans*, p. 81).

41. "If anyone desires a fuller discussion of this topic, he should begin with the point that we attempt all things and struggle in vain unless we look to God. The only true end of life is to promote his glory. This can never be done unless there is first knowledge of him. Yet this is only half of faith, and it will profit little unless confidence is added. Therefore faith is only then complete in its members for obtaining God's favor for us when we will trust that we do not seek him in vain and thus give ourselves the hope of certain salvation from him" (*Comm. Heb.*, p. 188).

42. "But by faith alone we understand [*percipimus*] that the world was created by God. Therefore it is no wonder that faith shone forth in the fathers above all other virtues. But it could be asked here, why does the apostle assert that [the very thing—namely, that the world was created by God—] acknowledged by even infidels is understood by faith [i.e., not by natural intelligence]? For the appearance of heaven and earth constrains even the ungodly to recognize some maker. And hence Paul convicts all of ingratitude because they did not, after having known God, give him the honor due to him (Rom. 1:21). And no

doubt religion would not have so prevailed among all peoples if human minds had not been impressed with the conviction that God is the creator of the world. Thus it appears that this knowledge, which the apostle ascribes to faith, exists apart from faith [*Videtur itaque extra fidem locum habere haec cognitio quam apostolus in fide includit*]" (*Comm. Heb.*, pp. 182–83).

43. "The godly do not hold a slight opinion about God being the creator of the world but have a conviction deeply impressed on their hearts and behold the true God. Furthermore, they understand the power of his word, not that power which showed itself instantaneously in the creation of the world but that which perpetually sets itself forth in its preservation. Nor do they only perceive [*concipiunt*] a sense of power but [also] of goodness, wisdom, and justice. Hence they are led to worship, love, and honor God" (*Comm. Heb.*, p. 183).

44. Compare the Vulgate's translation: *ut ex invisibilius visibilia fierent*. According to Calvin, the phrase does not express the point that things seen arise from things not seen but rather means that the things seen in the world are themselves visible manifestations of invisible things. He argues first on philological grounds, maintaining that the reading *ex non apparentibus* is not an accurate rendering of the Greek, which, in order to support such a translation (or that of the Vulgate) would have to be *ek mē phainomenōn* instead of *mē ek phainomenōn*. Moreover, he claims, this meaning cannot be supported by the context (*Comm. Heb.*, pp. 183–84). For a history of the interpretation of this passage, see Franz Josef Schierse, *Verheißung und Heilsvollendung: Zur Theologischen Grundfrage des Hebräerbriefes*, Münchner Theologische Studien, vol. 9 (Munich: Karl Zink, 1955), pp. 72–79.

45. *Comm. Heb.*, p. 184. Luther also refers fleetingly to Rom. 1:20: "In this passage the 'things which do not appear [*invisibilia*]' does not mean 'chaos' and that 'primordial matter' of nature from which they say the world was created. No, it means the same thing that is stated in Rom. 1[:20], namely, that 'the invisible things of God are clearly understood through the things that are made' " (WA 57:3.229; LW 29:231).

46. Commenting on Rom. 1:19 ("because that which is known of God") (1540) Calvin writes: "By this [Paul means] what is right or expedient for us to know of God. [He] moreover understands all that refers to the showing forth of the glory of the Lord, or, which is the same thing, whatever ought to induce and excite us to glorify God" (*Comm. Rom.*, p. 29, lines 19–22; *Romans*, pp. 30–31). Commenting on Rom. 1:20 ("For the invisible things of him since the creation of the world are clearly seen") (1540) Calvin writes: "God is invisible in himself, but since his majesty shines forth in all his works and in all his creatures, men ought to have acknowledged him in these, for they clearly demonstrate their creator [*nam artificem suum perspicue declarant*]." And on the phrase "that they may be without excuse" he states: "We must, therefore, make this distinction, that the manifestation of God by which he makes his glory known among his creatures is sufficiently clear as far as its own light is concerned. It is, however, inadequate on account of our own blindness" (*Comm. Rom.*, p. 29, lines 36–38 and p. 30, lines 48–51; *Romans*, p. 31). Recall the similar comments on 1 Cor. 1:21 (CO 49:326), cited earlier in chapter 2, note 90.

47. *Comm. Rom.*, p. 30, lines 54–55.

48. *Comm. Heb.*, p. 184.

49. "By saying 'God manifested it' he means that man was formed to be a spectator of the created world and that he was endowed with eyes for the purpose of his being led to God himself, the author of the world, by contemplating so magnificent an image" (*Comm. Rom.*, p. 29, lines 33–35; *Romans*, p. 31).

50. Compare the discussion the *Institutes* (1550), CO 1:467.

51. "To this I reply that faith indeed properly is born from the promises; it is founded on them; it rests in them. Therefore we say that Christ is the real object [*scopus*] of faith,

[for] in him the heavenly Father is propitious to us and in him all the promises of salvation are sealed and confirmed. Nonetheless there is no reason why faith should not look to God and reverently accept whatever he himself says. Or, if you prefer a briefer statement, it is a strict property of faith to hear God whenever he speaks and to embrace without doubt whatever proceeds from his sacred mouth. So faith is subject to commands and threatenings as well as to the gratuitous promises. But no one is ever moved as much as he ought or sufficiently to obey God's commands nor is stirred up enough to deprecate God's wrath unless he has taken hold of the promises of grace in order to acknowledge him as a benevolent father and the author of salvation. Therefore from the principal part [a praecipua parte] the gospel is called through synecdoche the word of faith, and the mutual relationship between the one and the other is set forth. Faith then though it rightly applies itself to the promises of God, yet looks on his threatenings so far as it is necessary for it to be taught to fear and obey God" (Comm. Heb., p. 190; compare Calvin's comments at the end of Hebrews 11:11, p. 194).

52. Comm. Heb., p. 204.

53. "And I do not tarry over the barkings of Pighius and dogs like him when they attack this restriction, as if by tearing faith to pieces they might grab up a single piece. I admit, as I have already said, that God's truth is, as they call it, the common object of faith, whether he threaten or hold out hope of grace. Therefore, the apostle attributes to faith the fact that Noah feared the world's destruction when it was not as yet visible" (CO 1:467; appears as Institutes [1559], 3.2.30).

54. CO 1:787–88; the same discussion appears in Institutes (1559), 3.17.11–12. Discussion in commentary is in CO 55:403–7.

55. Ganoczy and Scheld find in Calvin's interpretation of this passage not only that certain presuppositions (largely Pauline) influence Calvin's reading of James but also that the underlying assumptions about faith, works, and justification point to fundamental difficulties and questionable aspects of Calvin's exegesis as a whole; see Die Hermeneutik Calvins, pp. 193–201.

56. "Vulgaris Dei notitia" (CO 55:405); "frigida et nuda Dei notitia" (CO 55:403).

57. See the comments on James 2:14 (CO 55:403). Calvin also claims that the distinction between formed and unformed faith cannot be derived from James 2:22 (CO 55:406).

58. "Ergo ne in paralogismum incidamus, qui sophistas fefellit, notanda est haec amphibologia: Iustificandi verbum, Paulo esse gratuitam iustitiae imputationem apud Dei tribunal: Iacobo autem esse demonstrationem iustitiae ab effectis, idque apud homines" (CO 55:406).

59. "Non iustificatur homo sola fide, hoc est, nuda et inani cognitione Dei. Iustificatur operibus, hoc est, ex fructibus cognoscitur et approbatur eius iustitia" (CO 55:407).

60. Luther's oft-cited judgment that James is "a right strawy epistle, for it has nothing of the nature of the gospel about it" appears in Vorrede auff das newe Testament, WA Deutsche Bibel [DB] 6:10. Compare Vorrede auff die Epistel S. Jacobi und Jüde (1546 [1522]), WA DB 7:385, and Luther's remark, "Ich werde ein mal mit dem Jekel den offen hitzen" (WA Tischreden 5:382 [no. 5854]). See Gerrish, "The Word of God and the Words of Scripture," p. 54 and notes 24–25.

61. Ganoczy and Scheld argue that Calvin interprets certain assumptions into this passage from James. First, the fact that Calvin does not recognize gradations in the perfection of [justifying] faith means that he can only understand the faith that James rejects as a common knowledge of God. Second, he reads into the letter the idea of works flowing from faith as fruit from a tree, even though this is precisely what the author contradicts.

They judge that Calvin's presuppositions about justification as an event that consists in faith alone, that is considered a work of God, and that does not depend on any human influence impede a true understanding of the epistle's presentation of the relationship between faith and works (*Die Hermeneutik Calvins*, pp. 195, 197). Each of these presuppositions can be traced to Calvin's reading of Paul.

62. On 1 John, see Hans-Josef Klauck, *Der erste Johannesbrief*, vol. 23/1 of *Evangelisch-Katholischer Kommentar zum Neuen Testament*, ed. N. Brox et al. (Braunschweig: Benzinger Verlag and Neukirchen-Vluyn: Neukirchener, 1991). References to literature on the Gospel of John appear hereafter.

63. CO 55:297–98. Calvin returns to this point in his comments on 1 John 4:7: "we have said that [the epistle] is made up of the doctrine of faith and the exhortation to love. [The author] pursues these two points in such a way that he continually passes from one to the other" (CO 55:352).

64. See, for example, Calvin's comments on 1 John 1:1: "For all these things, 'what we have seen, what we have heard, what we have looked upon,' etc., serve to ratify [*ad sanciendam*] our faith in the gospel"; that is, as Calvin immediately afterward makes clear, to render the truth of the gospel more certain so that faith can subscribe to its truth as fully proved (CO 55:299).

65. Calvin finds this idea expressed, e.g., in 1 John 2:3 ("in this we know that we know him, if we keep his commandments"): "After having treated that doctrine of the gratuitous remission of sins he returns to the exhortations connected to it and dependant on it. And first he reminds [*admonet*] [us] that the knowledge [*notitia*] of God that is received [*concipitur*] from the gospel is not idle but that obedience comes forth from it" (CO 55: 310); and in 1 John 2:29 ("if you know that he is righteous"): "He again passes on to exhortations so that he mingles these continually with doctrine throughout the epistle. However, he proves by many arguments that faith is necessarily connected with a holy and pure life" (CO 55:328).

66. See, e.g., his comments on 1 John 2:1, which he understands to be a refutation of the notion that the free forgiveness of sins gives license to sin: "He is not, however, silent as to the gratuitous remission of sins; for though heaven should fall and all things be confounded, yet this part of truth ought never to be omitted. Rather, Christ's office ought to be preached clearly and distinctly" (CO 55:308). He stresses the need for continual forgiveness in his comments on the second part of the verse ("And if any man sin, we have an advocate with the Father, Jesus Christ the righteous"): "By these words he confirms what we have already said, that we are very far from perfect righteousness; indeed, that we contract new guilt daily, and that yet there is a remedy for reconciling us to God [*ad placando*], if we flee to Christ (CO 55:308). He remarks shortly thereafter that "[t]he intercession of Christ is a continual application of his death for our salvation" (CO 55:309).

67. Calvin's comments on 1 John 2:12 make the need for such a distinction clear: "Surely we ought to urge holiness of life, we ought carefully to enjoin the fear of God, we ought to goad men sharply to repentance, we ought to commend newness of life, together with its fruits, but still we ought always to take heed, lest the doctrine of faith be smothered, which teaches [*statuit*] that Christ is the only author of salvation and of all blessings. On the contrary, we ought to maintain such moderation that faith might always hold the first place [*ut primas semper fides obtineat*]. John prescribes this rule for us when, having faithfully spoken of good works, lest he should seem to give them more importance than he ought to have done, he carefully calls us back to the grace of Christ" (CO 55:316).

68. This is essentially the view ratified by the sixteenth session of the Council of Trent (January 1547). For a discussion of the view of justification as a process involving

works of love to fulfill the law as the common denominator among medieval scholastics (Biel, Scotus, and Thomas), see Oberman, " '*Iustitia Christi*' and '*Iustitia Dei*,'" pp. 116–120.

69. CO 55:334.

70. See, for example, the comments on 1 John 2:3 ("And hereby we know that we know him, if we keep his commandments"), where Calvin discusses the efficacy of true, living knowledge of God, which issues in obedience. He notes at the end of his comments on the first part of the verse that the apostle "means that obedience is so connected with knowledge [*scientia*] that the latter is nevertheless the first in order, as the cause is necessarily before its effect." But in the comments on the second part of the verse, he switches to faith: "But we are not hence to conclude that faith rests on works. For even though everyone has a testimony to his faith from his works, yet it does not follow that it is founded on them, since this evidence is added later as a sign. And so the certainty of faith rests on the grace of Christ alone, but piety and holiness of life distinguish true faith from that knowledge of God which is fictitious and dead, for the truth is, that those who are in Christ (as Paul says in Col. 3:9) have put off the old man, etc." (CO 55:311). Compare also the comments on 1 John 4:16 ("we have known and believed the love that God has toward us"): "we have known by believing" (CO 55:356).

71. See, e.g., Calvin's comments on 1 John 4:14 ("and we have seen"): "and by seeing [*adspectus*] he does not mean any sort of seeing but what belongs to faith [*fidei adiunctum*], by which they recognized the glory of God in Christ" (CO 55:356).

72. In his comments on 1 John 2:27 Calvin notes that "faith is not a naked and frigid apprehension of Christ, but a lively and real sense of his power, which produces [*generat*] confidence" (CO 55:328); compare his comments on 1 John. 5:8: "but from these words we may learn that faith does not lay hold of a bare or empty Christ but that his power is at the same time vivifying" (CO 55:366). Calvin's insistence on the exclusivity of knowledge of God in Christ is evident also in his extended criticisms on christological positions that he designates as inadequate. See especially his comments on 1 John 2:23–24 and 4:1–3 (CO 55:325–27; 345–49).

73. Calvin continues: "What the sophists say, that God foresees those who are worthy to be adopted, is plainly refuted by these words. In this way the gift would not be gratuitous. It is especially worthwhile to hold this point of doctrine among the first, for since the only cause of our salvation is adoption, and since the apostle testifies that this flows from the mere love of God alone, there is nothing left to our worthiness or to the merits of works. For why are we sons? Because God began to love us freely, when we deserved hatred rather than love" (CO 55:329).

74. CO 55:330.

75. CO 55:330.

76. CO 55:331.

77. CO 55:331.

78. "Quatenus autem renovatur in nobis Dei imago, oculos habemus ad Dei adspectum comparatos. Et nunc quidem Deus imaginem suam instaurare in nobis incipit: sed quantula ex parte? Ergo, nisi omni carnis nostrae corruptione exuti Deum facie ad faciem adspicere non poterimus" (CO 55:331).

79. CO 55:332. Calvin also refers briefly to Augustine's exegesis of this passage. He rejects Augustine's "refined questions." Calvin refers to his epistles to Paulinus and Fortunatus, to the *City of God* (book 22, chapter 29), and to "other places." Augustine was very interested in exploring the issue of the vision of God, citing 1 John 3:2 over a hundred times in his writings and dedicating an entire epistle (found in *Corpus scriptorum ecclesias-*

ticorum latinorum [Vienna, 1866–], 44:274–332) to the matter (Klauck, *Der erste Johannes-brief*, p. 184).

80. CO 1:457.

81. *Institutes* (1539), CO 1:457. Compare Calvin's observations on 1 John 3:2: "The word 'know' shows the certainty of faith in order to distinguish it from opinion. Neither simple nor universal knowledge is here intended, but that which every one ought to have for himself, so that he may feel assured that he will be sometime like Christ. Though the manifestation of our glory depends on the coming of Christ, our knowledge of this is well founded" (CO 55:331). Another passage cited by Calvin to stress the knowledge character of faith is 1 John 5:19–20. In his comments on Rom. 8:16 in 1540 he had said that no one can be called a son of God unless he acknowledges (*agnoscat*) himself as such and that this acknowledgement (*cognitio*) is called *scientia* by John to denote its certainty (*Comm. Rom.*, p. 171, lines 20–22; compare *Romans*, p. 171). In an addition in 1556, Calvin supplied 1 John 5:19–20 as the biblical reference for this statement. Calvin's exegesis of this passage in the commentary reiterates his view that the knowledge character entails confidence in divine adoption and excludes the scholastic notion of probable conjecture (CO 55:374). 1 John 5:20 shows that through Christ the elect have a "sure knowledge of the true God," that is, of the God who is really God. Calvin quotes John 17:3 ("this is eternal life, to know you, the eternal God, and Jesus Christ, whom you have sent") to confirm this. He also mentions Col. 2:9 and 2 Cor. 4:6 to underscore that Christ manifests God in the flesh and thus provides in this way, along with the illumination of his Spirit, true understanding of God (CO 55:375).

82. CO 55:315. This judgment might be extended to the interpretation of the entire exhortation to love in 1 John 2:7–11.

83. CO 55:339. Compare also Calvin's comments on 1 John 2:3, which says: "In this we know that we know him, if we keep his commandments." Calvin takes this verse as proof that knowledge of God is efficacious and that it issues in obedience and love. Works are evidence of faith, but faith depends not on works for its certainty but on the grace of Christ alone. In support of his argument he cites 2 Cor. 3:18 and Col. 3:9 to show that transformation into the image of God and piety and holiness of life flow from true knowledge of God (CO 55:308–12).

84. CO 55:340. See also Calvin's comments on 1 John 3:19: (CO 55:342), cited later in note 87; on 1 John 2:3, a passage dealing with exhortations: "but piety and holiness of life distinguish faith from a feigned and dead knowledge of God" (CO 55:311); and on 1 John 4:15: " 'Faith' and 'confession' are used indiscriminately in the same sense. For though hypocrites may falsely [*mendaciter*] boast of faith, yet the apostle here acknowledges none of those who ordinarily confess [*in ordine confitentium*] except those who believe truly and from the heart" (CO 55:356).

85. Klauck, *Der erste Johannesbrief*, pp. 219–21.

86. "If we truly love our neighbors, we have a testimony that we are born of God, who is truth, or that the truth of God dwells in us. But we must always remember that we do not have the knowledge, which the apostle mentions, from love, as though we were to seek from it the certainty of salvation. And doubtless we do not know that we are children of God in any other way than [by God] seal[ing] his free adoption on our hearts by his own Spirit and [by our] embrac[ing] by faith the sure pledge of it offered in Christ. Then love is accessory or an inferior aid, a prop to our faith not a foundation on which it rests [*Est igitur caritas accessio vel adminiculum inferius ad fidei fulturam: non fundamentum quo nititur*]" (CO 55:341–42).

87. Calvin continues, "not that assurance arises from it or depends on it, but that we

are only then really and not falsely assured of our union with God when by the efficacy of his Holy Spirit he manifests himself [*se profert*] in our love. For it is always fitting to consider what the apostle handles. Since he condemns a feigned and false [*fictam et fallacem*] profession of faith, he says that we cannot have firm assurance before God unless his Spirit produces in us the fruit of love. Nevertheless, though a good conscience cannot be separated from faith, yet no one should hence conclude that we must look to our works in order that our assurance may be certain" (CO 55:342).

88. CO 55:343.

89. "When he says 'because we keep his commandments,' he does not mean that confidence in praying is founded on our works. Rather he teaches only that true piety and the sincere worship of God cannot be separated from faith. Nor ought it appear strange that he uses a causal particle even though he does not speak of a cause, for an inseparable addition is sometimes mentioned as a cause. As one says, because the sun shines over us at midday, there is more heat. *But it does not follow that heat comes from light*" (CO 55:344; the italicized sentence is from 1556).

90. "Nam Paulus de gratuitae adoptionis certitudine loquitur, quam spiritus Dei cordibus nostris obsignat: Iohannes autem hic effectus respicit, quos profert spiritus in nobis habitans. Quemadmodum et Paulus ipse, quum dicit eos esse Dei filios, qui spiritu Dei aguntur. Nam illic quoque de mortificatione carnis, et vitae novitate disserit" (CO 55:345); compare Calvin's comments on Rom. 8:14–16 (*Comm. Rom.*, pp. 168–72; *Romans*, pp. 166–71).

91. Calvin writes, "the 'name' [as in 'we should believe in the name of his son, Jesus Christ'] refers to preaching. We ought to take note of this connection, since few understand what it is to believe in Christ [*in Christum credere*]. From this way of speaking we can easily conclude that the only right faith is that which embraces Christ as he is preached in the gospel. Hence it is also shown that there is no faith without teaching, as Paul also teaches [in] Rom. 10:14" (CO 55:345).

92. CO 55:363. Prefacing this is Calvin's exegesis of 1 John 5:3 ("this is the love of God, that we keep his commandments, and his commandments are not grievous"), which draws heavily on Romans 7 to show that the difficulty that believers experience in fulfilling the law lies not in the nature of the law itself—thus the commandments are not grievous—but in the "flesh,", i.e., the not yet regenerate part of the believer. Moreover, Calvin cautions, John speaks of the law in a broad sense, expressing both God's commands and fatherly indulgence. The commands are not burdensome because they are mitigated by the promise of pardon. In the comments on 1 John 5:4, faith is declared the victory because faith, perpetually effected by the Spirit, strengthens believers for their battle against the world and their corrupt nature. John uses "has overcome" to express that victory, though not yet finally achieved, is certain; "it depends on faith alone, and faith receives from another that by which it overcomes."

93. Whereas for the author of Hebrews, faith consisted primarily of patience and hope, for the author of 1 John, faith is characterized by love. Despite this close interrelationship, however, faith is not ultimately reduced to love in the epistle; see Klauck, *Der erste Johannesbrief*, p. 225.

94. Knowledge and belief are joined in John 6:69, 10:38, 17:3, and 17:8; cf. John 14:20; 1 John 4:16. For a treatment of these issues by patristic interpreters, see Maurice Wiles, *The Spiritual Gospel: The Interpretation of the Fourth Gospel in the Early Church* (Cambridge: Cambridge University Press, 1960).

95. See Calvin's comments on John 12:45 ("and he who sees me sees him that sent me"): "The word 'see' is here taken for 'knowledge' [*cognitio*], for he refers us to the Father in order to give true and complete tranquillity to our consciences, which would otherwise

have been constantly subject to various agitations. Therefore the stability of faith is certain and firm because it is above the world" (CO 47:302). Compare the comments on John 14: 7 ("if you had known me, you would have known my Father also; henceforth you know him and have seen him"): "The word 'see' expresses the certainty of faith" (CO 47:325).

96. See Calvin's comments on John 6:69 and 10:38 (CO 47:163, 254).

97. For a discussion of faith in the Gospel of John, see G. Barth, *pistis, pisteuo*, 3: 226–28. Barth discusses the relationship between seeing, knowledge, and faith (3: 227). See also Rudolf Schnackenburg, "Das johanneische Glauben," excursus 7 in *Das Johannesevangelium*, in *Herders Theologischer Kommentar zum Neuen Testament* (Freiburg: Herder, 1965–1984), 1:508–24. On the exegesis of John in the sixteenth century, see Timothy J. Wengert, *Philip Melanchthon's Annotationes in Johannem in Relation to Its Predecessors and Contemporaries* (Geneva: Librairie Droz, 1987) and Craig S. Farmer, *The Gospel of John in the Sixteenth Century: The Johannine Exegesis of Wolfgang Musculus* (New York: Oxford University Press, 1997).

98. In his comments on John 6:30, Calvin compares this attitude to those in the present day: "At first, because they promise themselves that Christ will flatter their vices, they eagerly take up his gospel and desire no proof of it. But when they are called to deny the flesh and bear the cross, then they begin to abrogate faith in [what] Christ [says] [*fidem Christo*] and ask questions about the source of the gospel [*quaerunt unde ortum sit evangelium*]" (*In Johannem*, p. 201).

99. *In Johannem*, p. 143. For confirmation of this reading of Calvin's exegesis of John 4, see Dowey, *Knowledge of God in Calvin's Theology*, pp. 169–70. Shepherd disagrees with Dowey's conclusion that "no general trust in Christ as a prophet is accepted as a beginning of faith. Such, however great, is entirely superseded by knowledge, however slight, of Christ as God's salvation" (p. 170). Shepherd argues that the term "loosely" is to be preferred to "improperly" to designate the Samaritans' belief. Shepherd finds that Calvin "certainly implies that under the initiative of God (q.v. *Comm.* Luke 19:1) a confession of Christ as prophet becomes, ultimately, that 'entrance to faith' wherein Christ is confessed as God's salvation" (*The Nature and Function of Faith*, p. 112). I agree there are passages in Calvin that contradict the first part of Dowey's statement; however, I fail to see how Dowey pushes Calvin into what Shepherd designates as a false dichotomy. Shepherd seems to want to impose greater continuity on the transition from these kinds of preparation for faith and faith itself than Calvin's comments really warrant. In this instance, the distinction between these two is clear. Calvin is struggling with the text, which tells him that the Samaritans believed and thereby contradicts his presuppositions about faith. He therefore says that they are improperly said to believe; this is like a beginning of faith but it is clearly something different from the full faith that follows. According to Calvin's strictest definition, no "such general trust" is worthy of the name of faith proper, even when it in fact is followed by full faith in Christ. Shepherd is correct to note that it is true that the confession of Christ as prophet may function as an entrance to faith. Calvin's willingness to admit this indicates the extremes to which this Gospel in particular pushes his theological assumptions. However, Calvin always distinguishes carefully between the preparation for/beginning of faith and faith proper in instances where the evangelist, to Calvin's mind, confuses the two (see the next note for additional examples).

100. See Calvin's comments on John 2:23, which describe the faith of the people as a "cold and shadowy faith"; an "appearance of faith" that might be changed into true faith later; a faith "directed exclusively to the world and earthly things"; a "cold [faith]; a persuasion unaccompanied by true feelings of the heart." It "depended solely on miracles and had no root in the gospel, therefore it could not be fixed or stable" (*In Johannem*, pp. 79–80). Calvin's comments on John 7:31: "The word 'believe' [*credendi*] is used improperly

here, because they depended on miracles rather than relied on doctrine, not yet convinced that Jesus was the Christ. But as they were prepared to listen to him and offered themselves as ones ready to be taught by him [*ei tanquam magistro se dociles praebebant*], such a preparation for faith [*praeperatio fidei*] is called faith" (*In Johannem*, p. 246); on John 8:30: "But the evangelist improperly calls 'faith' that which was only a sort of preparation for faith. For he says nothing more of them than that they were disposed to receive that doctrine of Christ" (*In Johannem*, p. 278); on John 11:45: "Accordingly by the word 'believe' we ought not to understand anything else to be meant than a willingness to embrace the doctrine of Christ [*docilitas ad amplexandam Christi doctrinam*]" (CO 47:270). On the matter of using the word "faith" or "believing" improperly, compare also Calvin's comments on John 6:29, where he says that Christ himself, in calling faith a work, speaks improperly [*improprie loqui*] (*In Johannem*, p. 200); on John 20:3, where Calvin, speaking of Peter on the way to the tomb, writes: "Though this feeling of piety [*sensus pietatis*] was confused and accompanied by much superstition, I nonetheless improperly attribute to it the name of 'faith,' since it was produced by the doctrine of the gospel and did not aim toward anything but Christ. From this seed [*semine*] sprang true and sincere faith, which after leaving the tomb might ascend to Christ's heavenly glory [*quae relicto sepulcro ad coelestem Christi gloriam conscenderet*]" (CO 47:428); on John 20:8, which says that the disciple accompanying Peter "saw [the abandoned linens and the empty tomb] and believed," where Calvin comments that saying that he believed is not "inconsistent with the fact that Peter and John returned home still in doubt and perplexed [*suspensi adhuc et perplexi*], for in other passages above John has used this way of speaking to describe the increase of faith [*quum fidei profectum notare vellet*]" (CO 47:429); and the similar judgment in the comments on John 20:10 (CO 47:430).

101. See Calvin's comments on John 6:15: "They learned from the word of God that the redeemer who was promised would be a king, but out of their own heads they contrive an earthly kingdom and assign to him a kingdom outside of the word of God. Therefore, whenever we mix up our opinions with the word of God, faith degenerates into frivolous conjectures" (*In Johannem*, p. 192).

102. Calvin comments on John 6:29 ("that you believe in him whom he has sent"): "We said in the third chapter what is meant by the word 'believe' [*credendi*]. We ought always to remember that in order for the power of faith to remain steadfast among us [*ut vis fidei nobis constet*] we must determine [*definiendum esse*] what Christ is, in whom we believe, and for what reason he was given to us by the Father" (*In Johannem*, p. 200); on John 6:47 ("he who believes in me has eternal life"): "I have already explained what it is to believe in Christ [*in Christum credere*]. We must not imagine a confused and empty [*inanis*] faith that deprives Christ of his power, which is the sort [of faith] among the papists, who believe [only] as much as they like about Christ [*qui de Christo credunt quantum libuerit*]" (*In Johannem*, p. 212); and John 7:38 ("he who believes in me, as the scripture says, out of his belly shall flow living water"): "He now shows the manner of coming, which is that it is proper to approach not with the feet but by faith; indeed, to come is nothing other than to believe [*credere*], if, of course, you define 'believe' correctly. As was already said, we believe in Christ [*in Christum nos credere*] when he is embraced as he puts himself forth in the gospel: filled with power, wisdom, righteousness, purity, life, and all the gifts of the Spirit" (*In Johannem*, p. 251). Compare Calvin's comments on John 6:40 ("whoever sees the Son and believes in him will have eternal life"): "Moreover, these words show that faith flows from knowledge of Christ [*ex Christi notitia*], not that it desires anything beyond the simple word of God but because, if we rely on Christ [*Christo fidamus*], we should perceive [*sentire*] what he is and what he brings to us" (*In Johannem*, p. 208); on John 9:37 (Jesus to

the man whose sight he restored, "You have both seen him [the Son of God] and it is he who speaks with you"): "By these words of Christ the blind man could not be carried higher than a very small cold and barren portion of faith. For Christ does not mention his power, or the reason why he was sent by the Father, or what he has brought to human beings. But the chief part of faith is to know that sins are expiated by the sacrifice of his death and that we are reconciled to God, that the resurrection is a triumph over vanquished death, that we are renewed by his spirit, so that being dead to the flesh and sin we may live to righteousness, that he himself is the only mediator, that his spirit is the pledge of our adoption, in short, that in him are found all elements of eternal life." Calvin thus concludes that Jesus must have said more to the man than what the evangelist relates (CO 47:232); and Calvin comments on John 16:28 ("I came out from the Father and have come into the world; again, I leave the world and go to the Father"): "We now understand in what way we ought to embrace Christ, that is to say, so that our faith reflects on the purpose and power of God, by whose hand he is offered to us. For that he came out of God is not to be received coldly, but at the same time we must understand for what reason or to what end he came out of God [*quorsum vel in quem finem exierit*], namely, that he might be wisdom, sanctification, righteousness, and redemption for us (1 Cor. 1:30)" (CO 47:372). Note that the need to know the purpose of Christ's life, death, and resurrection is contrasted to bare history in Calvin's "Argument to the Gospel of John" that prefaces the epistle (*In Johannem*, p. 8). Calvin shares the view of Luther and others that the fourth evangelist does a better job of presenting this than the other three (compare Luther, "Prefaces to the New Testament [1522]," WA DB 6:10; LW 35:361–62).

103. The comments on John 3:16 treat a variety of issues and make several related points that all coincide with the chief themes that Calvin elaborates in his exegesis of Paul: God's love for the world as a motivation for sending the Son means that works and merits have no place in justification; faith looks to Christ, especially to Christ's death; only the elect have faith in Christ; and faith "bestows life" not through the regeneration that it effects but rather through the nonimputation of sins (*In Johannem*, pp. 98–101). Calvin reiterates this last point in his comments on John 3:36 ("He who believes in the Son has eternal life"): "Moreover, though I acknowledge that it is true that we are renewed by faith so that the spirit of Christ governs us, yet I say that we ought first to consider the free remission of sins, by which we are made acceptable to God [*qua fit ut Deo accepti simus*]. I say again that all confidence of salvation is founded on and consists in this alone, because righteousness *coram Deo* cannot be imputed to us except when sins are not imputed to us" (*In Johannem*, p. 114).

104. *In Johannem*, p. 100.

105. The Gospel of John is important for the development of Calvin's thinking about this mystical union. See also Calvin's comments on John 14:20 and 17:3; compare Dowey, *Knowledge of God in Calvin's Theology*, pp. 197–204.

106. "[E]vangelio credere nihil esse aliud quam Dei oraculis subscribere" (*In Johannem*, p. 111); compare Fr. "que Croire à la Evangile n'est autre chose que consentir et souscrire à la vérité procédée de Dieu" (*Commentaires*, 2:66).

107. "He now describes the manner of bestowing life; namely, when he enlightens the elect in the knowledge of God. For he does not now speak of the enjoyment of life that we hope for but only of the manner in which men obtain life. . . . Where he has shone, we possess him by faith, and, therefore, we also enter into possession of life. And this is the reason why the knowledge of him is truly and justly called saving, or bringing salvation. Almost every one of the words has its weight; for it is not every kind of knowledge that is here described, but that knowledge that forms us anew into the image of God from faith

to faith, or rather, which is the same as faith, by which, having been ingrafted into the body of Christ, we are made partakers of divine adoption and heirs of heaven" (CO 47: 376).

108. See, e.g., Thomas Aquinas, who is concerned to speak about faith formed by love in his comments on John 3:16 and 6:29 (*Commentum in Matthaeum et Joannem Evangelistas*, vol. 10 of *Sancti Thomae Aquinatis Doctoris Angelici Ordinis Praedicatorum opera omnia* [Parma: P. Fiaccadori, 1861; reprint, New York: Musurgia Publishers, 1949], 350, 409; in English, *Commentary on the Gospel of St. John*, part 1, trans. J. A. Weisheipl with F. R. Larcher, vol. 4 of Aquinas Scripture Series [Albany, N.Y.: Magi Books, 1980], 203, 360). Compare Denis the Carthusian, *Enarratio in Evangelium secundum Joannem*, vol. 12 of *Opera omnia* (Monstrolii: S. M. De Pratis, 1901), 316, 321, 331, 419. Furthermore, both Thomas and Denis relate the faith mentioned in John 1:12 to faith formed by love. Patristic exegetes also distinguished different types or degrees of faith in their interpretations of John; see Maurice Wiles, *The Spiritual Gospel*, pp. 50, 87–91.

109. Note also the paralytic at the pool of Bethesda (John 5:13), to whom Calvin attributes a secret movement of faith.

110. Calvin's comments on John 4:53 illustrate this well. It is this verse, and not 4: 50, that Calvin sees as referring to the beginning of actual faith: "It may seem absurd that the evangelist designates this as the beginning of faith [*initium fidei*] in that man, whose faith he had already praised [in John 4:50, "the man believed the word that Jesus had spoken to him"]. Yet the word 'believe' cannot be referred, at least in this place, to the increase of faith [*ad fidei progressum*]. We must understand that this man, a Jew and educated in the doctrine of the law, had already obtained some taste of faith before he came to Christ. Then when he believed in the words of Christ [*sermoni Christi*], that was a special faith [*particularis fides*], which did not extend any farther than [to expect] the life of his son. But now he began to believe in a different manner, that is to say, because he, embracing the doctrine of Christ, openly professed that he was one of his disciples. Thus not only does he now hope that his son will be returned to him safe and sound simply through the kindness of Christ, but he recognizes [*agnoscit*] that Christ is the Son of God and enlists in [the service of] his gospel" (*In Johannem*, pp. 149–150). Recall that Calvin also spoke of a *particularis fides* (a faith that believes in miracles that can exist apart from the spirit of regeneration) in his comments on 1 Cor. 13.

111. *In Johannem*, p. 70; compare Martin Bucer, *Enarratio in Evangelion Iohannis* (1528, 1530, 1536), ed. Irena Backus, vol. 2 of *Martin Buceri Opera Latina, Martin Buceri Opera omnia*, series 2 (Leiden: E. J. Brill, 1987), p. 114; Thomas Aquinas, *Summa Theologiae*, 3a q. 43, a. 3.

112. As evident in Calvin's comments on John 2:11 (where it is said, after the miracle at Cana, "and his disciples believed in him [*in eum*]"): "If they were disciples, they must have already been imbued with some faith. But since up to this point they had not followed him with a certain and explicit faith, they began now to devote themselves to him and acknowledge him as the Messiah, such as he had already been announced to them. . . . Thus they who already believed, to the extent that they daily make progress toward the goal, begin to believe. . . . This also shows the fruit of miracles, namely, that they ought to be referred to the confirmation and progress of faith" (*In Johannem*, p. 70); and on John 11:15 (Jesus' statement that, on account of the disciples, he rejoices that he was not present at the death of Lazarus, "so that you may believe"): "He does not mean that this was the first rudimentary beginning of faith in them but that it was the confirmation of a faith already begun [*incohatae iam fidei confirmationem*], which as yet was extremely small and weak [*exiqua et debilis*]. Yet he suggests that unless the hand of God had been openly displayed, they

would not have believed [*nisi palam exserta fuisset Dei manus, ipsos non fuisse credituros*]" (CO: 47:260). Confirmation of the disciples' faith is also the purpose of the miracle of walking on the water; see Calvin's comments on John 6:16. This particular miracle illustrates, according to Calvin, the dangerous nature of the knowledge that is attained through the sign or work alone; when Jesus comes toward the boat, the disciples are terrified (John 6:19). Calvin generalizes that such simple demonstrations of divinity lead people to fall into their own imagination and form idols for themselves. This "wandering in our understanding" leads to "trembling and confused terror of heart." But when Christ speaks, a "clear and solid knowledge [*liquidam . . . solidamque notitiam*]" is obtained, which brings joy and peace (*In Johannem*, p. 194). That the disciples already possessed faith (in its proper sense) is confirmed for Calvin by Peter's confession (John 6:69), "And we have believed and known that you are the Christ, the Son of the living God"): "even if the twelve did not all at once understand everything that Christ had taught, nonetheless it is enough that according to the small measure of their faith [*pro fidei suae modulo*] they confessed him to be the author of salvation and submitted themselves to him in all things" (*In Johannem*, pp. 227–28).

113. Calvin interprets this to mean that as long as Christ dwelt in the world the grace of the Spirit was not openly manifest (*In Johannem*, p. 253). Compare also Calvin's reading of John 6:65 (*In Johannem*, pp. 225–26). However, Calvin does not mention the Spirit as the author of faith in his treatment of passages where Jesus promises to send the Spirit (John 14:16–17; 15:26) or of John 20:22, which relates the actual imparting of the Spirit. In his comments on these passages, Calvin is concerned to establish that the Spirit is sent by both the Father and the Son (CO 47:329–30), that the Spirit imparts certainty to faith (CO 47:354–55), and that the resurrected Jesus' breathing on the disciples is not inconsistent with the Pentecost account in Acts 2:3 (CO 47:438–40).

114. See, for example, Calvin's comments on John 8:32 (*In Johannem*, pp. 278–79).

115. See Calvin's comments on John 11:22 (CO 47:261). Calvin takes the fact that Mary falls at Jesus's feet (John 11:32) as a sign that she is convinced that he is the son of God, yet the fact that she voices the same wish as her sister is evidence that her faith is also too limited to Christ's bodily presence (CO 47:264). Martha evidences distrust [*diffidentia*] and a confused and weak faith once again in her objection to removing the tombstone (John 11:39): "Moreover, we may perceive in Martha how numerous are the failings of faith, even in the most excellent people. She was the first that came to meet Christ; this was not a common testimony of piety, and yet she did not desist from throwing impediments in his way" (CO 47:267).

116. "Christ justly rebukes Philip because he does not have eyes of faith [that are] pure [*puros fidei oculos non habuerit*]" (CO 47:325).

117. "Manebat igitur semen aliquod fidei in eorum cordibus, sed ad tempus suffocatum, ut nescirent se habere quod habebant" (CO 47:428).

118. It is difficult to know exactly why Calvin introduces the term *pietas* in his comments on John 20:3. Here he seems to use it synonymously with faith, and hence the seed of faith is synonymous with the sense of piety. He asserts that it is not possible that piety motivated the disciples to seek Christ. Rather, some seed of faith remained in their hearts as a concealed root—as a confused *sensus pietatis*. Calvin also mentions the seed of piety in connection with Nicodemus in John 3:2.

119. "Though this feeling of piety, which they possessed, was confused and accompanied by much superstition, I nonetheless attribute to it—though improperly—the name of faith, because it was produced by nothing but the doctrine of the gospel and aimed at nothing but Christ. From this seed appeared at length true and sincere faith, which, leaving

the sepulchre, ascended to the heavenly glory of Christ" (CO 47:428). Compare the similar view in the comments on John 16:31 (Jesus responding to the disciples' declaration that they know that he is from God, saying "Do you now believe?") (CO 47:373).

120. See Calvin's comments on John 20:28 (CO 47:443–44). On the peculiarity of Calvin's exegesis of John 20 (in light of his general assumptions about faith), see also Willis, *Calvin's Catholic Christology*, p. 115.

121. "[I]t was not by mere touching or seeing that Thomas was brought to believe that Christ is his God, but, being awakened from sleep, he recalled to remembrance the doctrine that he had nearly forgotten earlier. Faith cannot flow from a mere experience of things [*ex nudis rerum experimentis*] but must draw its origin from the word of God. Christ [in John 20:29], therefore, rebukes Thomas for rendering less honor to the word of God than he ought, and for binding faith, which is born from hearing and ought to be completely intent on the word, to the other senses" (CO 47:445).

122. CO 47:445.

123. "Quare sensus verborum est, scripta haec esse ut credamus, quatenus signis adiuvari potest fides" (CO 47:447).

124. See Calvin's comments on John 3:2, 11:45, and 20:31 (*In Johannem*, p. 84 and CO 47:270 and 446–47).

125. For example, in his comments on John 6:44, Calvin says that "a new understanding and a new perception [*nova mente et novo sensu*]" are necessary to receive the gospel (*In Johannem*, p. 210); in his comments on John 6:69 he calls faith "the eye of the understanding [*fides ipsa vere mentis oculus est*]" (*In Johannem*, p. 228); in his comments on John 8:56, 8:58, and 14:19 he speaks about "the eyes of faith [*oculis fidei*]" (*In Johannem*, pp. 295 and 296 and CO 47:330). His comments on John 16:16 discuss how Christ is seen "not with eyes, yet his presence is known [*cognoscitur*] by the experience of faith." Calvin goes on to quote 2 Cor. 5:6–7 and concludes by stating: "Thus the grace of the Spirit is a mirror for us in which Christ wishes to be seen" (CO 47:365).

126. *In Johannem*, p. 279.

127. Grässer, *Glaube*, p. 149, note 12. Grässer notes that Paul deals with the preservation and increase of faith, pointing to Rom. 11:20, 1 Thess. 3:10, 2 Cor. 10:15, Rom. 4:21, Rom. 14:1–5, and 1 Thess. 1:5, but judges correctly that this is not Paul's central theme.

128. Grässer, *Glaube*, p. 149.

129. Grässer, *Glaube*, p. 149, note 13.

Four. Providential Faith

1. CO 1:511; compare "In summa, quum inferiores causae, tanquam vela, Deum e conspectu nostro subducere ut plurimum soleant: fidei oculo altius penetrandum est, ut Deum manum in his organis operantem cernat" (*De aeterna Dei praedestinatione* [1552] [CO 8:352]).

2. "Contre la secte phantastique et furieuse des Libertins qui se nomment spirituelz" (1545) (CO 7: 149–248); "Advertissement contre l'astrologie qu'on apelle judiciaire et autres curiosités qui régnent aujourd'huy au monde" (1549) (CO 7:514–42; English translation "A Warning against Judiciary Astrology and other Prevalent Curiosities, by John Calvin," translated with an introduction by Mary Potter, *Calvin Theological Journal* 18 [1983]: 157–89); *De aeterna Dei praedestinatione* (1552) (CO 8:249–366); *Calumniae nebulonis cuiusdam quibus odio et invidia gravare conatus est doctrinam de occulta Dei providentia, et ad easdem responsio* (1558) (CO 9:273–318). In addition to these works, the section concerning predestination and providence in the 1550 *Institutes* was published as a separate treatise in Geneva in 1550.

3. A comparison of Calvin's ideas about providence with those of his contemporaries and predecessors is beyond the scope of this study; however, parallels and divergences have been indicated or investigated in previous discussions. The best treatment of the issue of Calvin's opponents and his perception of them is given by Schreiner, *Theater of His Glory*, pp. 16–22; compare also pp. 8–15 and 115–19. Schreiner makes the important point that attempts to identify these opponents precisely is "like entering a labyrinth." While she offers "informed suggestions" as to identity whenever possible, she shows that Calvin perceived his opponents, whoever they were, as guilty of similar errors that led him to think that they either imprisoned God in creation or sought to remove God from creation. See also Bohatec, "Calvins Vorsehungslehre," pp. 342–43; later in the same article Bohatec suggests broad comparisons with Luther and Zwingli and considers in detail the distinction between Calvin's doctrine of providence and the Stoic understanding of fate (pp. 391–93 and 415–27). Charles Partee locates the distinction between Calvin and classical philosophy in Calvin's greater concern with the particularity of divine providence (*Calvin and Classical Philosophy*, Studies in the History of Christian Thought 14 [Leiden: E. J. Brill, 1977], pp. 126–45). Mary Potter Engel discusses Calvin's understanding of providence and its relationship to human freedom (*John Calvin's Perspectival Anthropology*); compare Charles Trinkaus, "Renaissance Problems in Calvin's Theology."

4. *Theater of His Glory*, pp. 4–5.

5. See, for example, Henri Chaix, *Le Psautier Hugenot: sa Formation et son Histoire dans l'Église Réformée* (Geneva: Imprimerie Romet, 1907), chaps. 1–4; Dowey, *Knowledge of God in Calvin's Theology*, pp. 194–95; the introduction to J. Calvin, *Der Psalter auf der Kanzel Calvins*, edited with an introduction by E. Mülhaupt (Neukirchen: Neukirchener, 1959), pp. 8–24; R. Martin-Achard, "Calvin et les Psaumes" (1960; rpt. in *Approche des Psaumes*, Cahiers Theologique 60 [Neuchatel: Éditions Delachaux et Niestlé, 1969]), p. 9; Richard A. Hasler, "The Influence of David and the Psalms upon John Calvin's Life and Thought," *Hartford Quarterly* 5 (1965), rpt. in Gamble, *Articles*, 1:87–99; Rodolphe Peter, "Calvin and Louis Budé's Translation of the Psalms" in *John Calvin: A Collection of Distinguished Essays*, ed. G. E. Duffield (Grand Rapids: Eerdmans, 1986) pp. 193–95; Parker, *Calvin's Old Testament Commentaries*, pp. 29–32; *Le Psautier de Genève: Images Commentées et Essai de Bibliographie* (Geneva: Bibliothèque publique et universitaire, 1986), chaps. 1–2; Heribert Schützeichel, "Ein Grundkurs des Glaubens: Calvins Auslegung des 51. Psalms," *Catholica: Vierteljahresschrift für Oekumenische Theologie* 44 (Münster: Aschendorff, 1990), p. 203; Barbara Pitkin, "Imitation of David: David as a Paradigm for Faith in Calvin's Exegesis of the Psalms," *Sixteenth Century Journal* 24/4 (1993): 843–63; James A. De Jong, " 'An Anatomy of All Parts of the Soul': Insights into Calvin's Spirituality from His Psalms Commentary," in *Calvinus Sacrae Scripturae Professor: Calvin as Confessor of Holy Scripture*, ed. Wilhelm H. Neuser (Grand Rapids: Eerdmans, 1994), pp. 1–14.

6. Bohatec, "Calvins Vorsehungslehre," p. 343; Schreiner, *Theater of His Glory*, pp. 4–5 and 7. See also Stauffer, *Dieu, la création et la Providence*.

7. In his discussion of providential faith Bohatec establishes the notion by tracing Calvin's arguments that providence is known by faith and not by reason. He then focuses on the content of providential faith, i.e., what faith knows *about* providence. Here he summarizes Calvin's various defenses of special providence, raises the questions of human freedom and whether God is the author of sin, and, in the last section of this discussion, entitled "Glaube an Gottes zweckvolle Weltregierung," treats the twofold goal of providence: human salvation and the glory of God. After this Bohatec discusses the character of providential faith ("Die Art des Vorsehungsglaubens") and demonstrates its fundamentally Christian underpinnings. It is significant that the bulk of the textual evidence for his arguments for the importance of the glory of God and the Christian character of faith in

providence is derived from the commentary on the Psalms ("Calvins Vorsehungslehre," pp. 348–93, especially 379–93).

8. See, for example, Calvin's comments on Ps. 40:5 (CO 31: 409–10, verse 6). Citations to the Psalms will follow standard modern numeration for both psalm number and verse. In cases such as the present one where the verse number in the CO differs from modern enumeration, this number will be given parenthetically following the column number.

9. See *Institutes* (1539) (CO 1: 287–88). In the 1545 treatise against the Libertines, Calvin distinguishes three aspects of the divine government: a universal operation that governs the order of nature, God's defense of his own and the punishment of the wicked, and his guidance of the faithful by the Spirit (CO 7:186–90). In *De aeterna Praedestinatione Dei* Calvin distinguishes four "grades": the general governance of the world and then the care of its particular parts, the particular management of human affairs, and the special protection of the church. Here Calvin stresses that providence is recognized by the perception of faith (*agnoscitur fidei sensu*) (CO 8:347–49). For a summary of these discussions and of Calvin's view of special providence, see Partee, *Calvin and Classical Philosophy*, pp. 126–33. Étienne de Peyer distinguishes three levels (general providence, particular providence, and special providence) and links the last two to common grace and saving grace, respectively ("Calvin's Doctrine of Divine Providence," *Evangelical Quarterly* 10 [1938]: 30–44). Krusche links the levels to the threefold distinction of a *providentia universalis, specialis,* and *specialissima* and identifies the last of these with predestination (*Das Wirken des heiligen Geistes nach Calvin,* pp. 13–32); compare Bohatec, "Calvins Vorsehungslehre," p. 353; Wendel, *Calvin,* pp. 179–80.

10. See the following literature: Hans-Joachim Kraus, *Psalmen, Erster Teilband: Psalmen 1–59, Zweiter Teilband: Psalmen 60–150,* vols. 25/1 and 25/2 of *Biblischer Kommentar Altes Testament* (1961; 5th ed., Neukirchen: Neukirchener, 1978), 1:298, 306–7; Artur Weiser, *Die Psalmen,* 2 vols., *Erster Teil: Psalm 1–60, Zweiter Teil: Psalm 61–150,* vols. 14 and 15 of *Das Alte Testament Deutsch* (Göttingen: Vandenhoeck und Ruprecht, 1950), 14:124. On the history of the interpretation of the Psalms, see H. J. auf der Maur, *Das Psalmenverständnis des Ambrosius von Mailand* (Leiden: E. J. Brill, 1977), which contains a summary of other studies on the interpretation of the Psalms in early Christianity (pp. 4–10); R. Gerald Hobbs, "An Introduction to the *Psalms* Commentary of Martin Bucer" (diss., University of Strasbourg, 1971); Hans Hermann Holfelder, *Tentatio et Consolatio: Studien zu Bugenhagens "Interpretatio in Librum Psalmorum,"* Arbeiten zur Kirchengeschichte 45 (Berlin: de Gruyter, 1974); Gerhard Hammer and Karl-Heinz zur Mühlen, eds., *Lutheriana: Zum 500. Geburtstag Martin Luthers,* vol. 5 of *Archiv zur Weimarer Ausgabe der Werke Martin Luthers* [hereafter AWA] (Cologne: Böhlau, 1984); William L. Holladay, *The Psalms through Three Thousand Years: Prayerbook of a Cloud of Witnesses* (Minneapolis: Fortress Press, 1993).

11. CO 31:194.

12. See, e.g., Calvin's comments on Ps. 19:1: "It cannot be but that the beholding of the heavens lift us up to him who is their creator, and that the wonderful arrangement, which appears in them, [their] excellence and splendor, furnish a brilliant testimony to his providence. Scripture, indeed, sets forth the time and manner of creation, but the heavens themselves, although God should be silent, proclaim that they have been fashioned by his hands. And this of itself abundantly suffices to bear testimony to his glory" (CO 31:195). Compare Calvin's comments on Ps. 93:1, which argue that a look at the world ought to sufficiently attest to divine providence (CO 32:16–17).

13. CO 31:197.

14. Translations and interpretations of Ps. 19:4 often seek to reconcile the Masoretic text's *qawwam* (a line) with Paul's citation of the Septuagint's *ho phthongos* (speech, voice)

in Romans 10:18; see, e.g., Luther, *Operationes in Psalmos* (1519–1521) WA 5:547–48; R. Gerald Hobbs notes that Zwingli follows the Septuagint in his *Enchiridion Psalmorum* (1532 [CR 100: 467–836]) and translates *ho phthongos* as *oratio eorum;* however, in the 1525 German Psalter he follows the Hebrew and renders the phrase as *ir mess.* Hobbs cites the former as an instance of Zwingli's general preference for the Septuagint. He finds that Zwingli's position on the relative merits of the Septuagint and the Masoretic text in some ways runs counter to the current of the sixteenth-century exegetes who gave priority to the Hebrew ("Zwingli and the Study of the Old Testament," in *Huldrych Zwingli, 1484–1531: A Legacy of Radical Reform,* ed. E. J. Furcha [Montreal: McGill University Press, 1985], pp. 160–61 and 167–68).

15. CO 31:199. For the hints about this point in the first half of his exegesis, see Calvin's comments on Ps. 19:2: "If we were as attentive as we ought to be, even one day would bear sufficient testimony to us of the glory of God. . . . [T]here is now left to men no pretext for ignorance, for since the days and nights perform so well the office of teachers, we may acquire sufficient knowledge under their tuition" (CO 31:195, 196); on Ps. 19:3: "but the heavens have a common language to teach all men without distinction, nor is there anything but carelessness to hinder even those who are most strange to each other from profiting, as it were, at the mouth of the same teacher" (CO 31:196); and on Ps. 19: 4: "Therefore [David] was pleased by means of common expression to reprove the whole world of ingratitude, if, in beholding the sun, they do not make progress in piety" (CO 31: 198).

16. CO 31:199.

17. See Calvin's comments on Ps. 19:7: "Farther, under the term law, he not only means the rule of living righteously or the ten commandments, but he also comprehends the whole covenant by which God had distinguished that people from the rest of the world, and the whole doctrine of Moses, the parts of which he afterwards enumerates under the terms testimonies, statutes, and other [names]. These utterances, by which he commends the law, would not agree with the ten commandments alone unless there were, at the same time, joined [to them] a free adoption and the promises which depend on it; and, in short, the whole body of doctrine of which true religion and piety consists" (CO 31:199). Compare Calvin's comments on Ps. 19:10: "From this we may again deduce that David's words are not to be understood simply of the commandments and of the dead letter, but that, at the same time, the promises by which the grace of God is offered to us are comprehended" (CO 31:203).

18. CO 31:201.

19. CO 31:204.

20. CO 31:287.

21. CO 31:290.

22. CO 31:290.

23. CO 31:290.

24. CO 31:291.

25. "Verbum et opus quidam volunt esse synonyma: sed ego ita distinguo, ut verbum tantundem valeat ac consilium Dei, vel mandatum: opus vero sit eius effectus et exsequutio. . . . Interea notandum est, verbum non accipi pro doctrina, sed pro mundi gubernandi ratione" (CO 31:325).

26. "[V]ere tamen et certo hinc colligitur, mundum per aeternum Dei sermonem, qui Filius est unigenitus, fabricatum esse." Calvin makes implicit reference to John 1: "The scriptures often teach in other places that the world was created by that eternal word, who, being the only begotten Son of God, appeared afterward in the flesh" (CO 31:327). On Calvin's views of the second person of the Trinity as the ordering principle of creation,

and for a discussion of the christological implications of these views, see Willis, *Calvin's Catholic Christology*, and Peter Wyatt, *Jesus Christ and Creation In the Theology of John Calvin*, Princeton Theological Monograph Series 42 (Allison Park, Penn.: Pickwick Publications, 1996); compare E. Emmen, *De Christologie van Calvijn* (Amsterdam: H. J. Paris, 1935); Oberman, "The 'Extra' Dimension in the Theology of Calvin"; Krusche, *Das Wirken des heiligen Geistes*, pp. 24–25.

27. "For to fear and revere Jehovah is simply to submit [*suscipere*] to [God's] mighty power" (CO 31:328).

28. "The prophet thus extols the immense power of God in order to build up our faith in its greatness [*ut in eius altitudine fidem nostram aedificet*]" (CO 31:329).

29. "In the first place, then, let us learn to look at God's counsel in the glass of his word [*Dei consilium inspicere in verbi speculo*], and when we have determined that he has promised nothing but what he has determined to perform, let the steadfastness of which the prophet speaks immediately present itself to us" (CO 31:329).

30. CO 31:328; compare Calvin's comments on Ps. 24:2 (CO 31:244). For a discussion of Calvin's cosmological views and traditional theories about the waters, see Schreiner, *Theater of His Glory*, pp. 22–28.

31. CO 31:329.

32. "[S]ed vigere et spectari in ecclesiae salute" (CO 31:330).

33. On adoption as the basis for providential faith, see Bohatec, "Calvin's Vorsehungs-slehre," p. 388.

34. "Porro, Dei intuitum ideo commendat, ut nos vicissim fidei oculis invisibilem eius providentiam adspicere discamus. Etsi enim ob oculos nobis assidue versantur clara eius documenta, maior tamen pars hominum caecutit, et pro sua caecitate fortunam caecam fabricat" (CO 31:331).

35. CO 31:333.

36. On the matter of Calvin's view of natural theology and faith's role in apprehending God the creator, see Krusche, *Das Wirken des heiligen Geistes nach Calvin*, pp. 76–79, especially "das sola fide gilt nicht nur in der Rechtfertigungslehre, sondern in derselben Exklusivität auch für die Erkenntnis Gottes des Schöpfers."

37. See Krusche's explication of Calvin's position and his criticisms of the interpretations of H. Heppe and van der Linde (*Das Wirken des heiligen Geistes nach Calvin*, pp. 79–84).

38. See Willis, *Calvin's Catholic Christology*, pp. 109–31; compare Erwin Mülhaupt's introduction to Calvin, *Der Psalter auf der Kanzel Calvins*, pp. 23–24.

39. CO 31:460, verse 2.

40. See, e.g., Calvin's comments on Ps. 46:2 (CO 31:460–61).

41. "The evidences [*documenta*] of God's grace, which he has shown in preserving us, ought to be kept continually before our eyes that they might establish the faith[fulness] of the promises in our hearts. By this exhortation we have tacitly rebuked the indifference of those who do not make so great account of the power of God as they ought; or rather, the whole world is charged with ingratitude, because there is scarcely one in a hundred who acknowledges that he has sufficient protection in God, so that they are all blind to the works of God, or rather wilfully shut their eyes [to that] which would prove the best means of strengthening their faith" (CO 31:464, verse 9).

42. CO 31:465, verse 9.

43. CO 31:464, verse 8. Underlying such judgments as this is Calvin's concern to avoid separating the divine power from the divine justice. As noted in chapter 2, Calvin rejects the medieval distinction between the *potentia absoluta* and the *potentia ordinata* be-

cause he thinks that the former term attributes to God a totally arbitrary and tyrannical power. See Steinmetz, "Calvin and the Absolute Power of God."

44. CO 31:464, verse 8; compare Calvin's comments on Ps. 62:11 (CO 31:592, verse 12).

45. As noted in chapter 2, Calvin relates faith to God's power in his consideration of Abraham in Rom. 4:21. There, however, doubts concerning God's power arise when the sinner considers his or her own unrighteousness, weakness, misery, and defects. In other words, it is specifically God's power to *save* that is there called into question. In the Psalms, questions arise not so much concerning God's power to save but rather regarding God's power to regulate, order, and judge all that is and happens.

46. CO 32:84.

47. See Calvin's comments on Ps. 104:3: "That we may not imagine that there is anything in him derived, as if he was enhanced by the creation of the world, we must remember that he clothes himself [with the created order] for our sake [*eum nostra causa vestem induere*]" (CO 32:85).

48. CO 32:85, verse 1.

49. "Et certe male proficimus in spectaculo totius naturae, nisi fidei oculis speculamur spiritualem illam gloriam, cuius imago in mundo nobis apparet" (CO 32:86).

50. CO 32:86–87.

51. CO 32:88.

52. CO 32:93.

53. CO 32:97.

54. On Calvin's views of history, see Heinrich Berger, *Calvins Geschichtsauffassung,* Studien zur Dogmengeschichte und systematischen Theologie 6 (Zurich: Zwingli, 1955); Josef Bohatec, "Gott und die Geschichte nach Calvin," *Philosophia Reformata* 1 (1936): 129–61; *Budé und Calvin: Studien zur Gedankenwelt des französischen Frühhumanismus* (Graz: Böhlau, 1950); Trinkaus, "Renaissance Problems in Calvin's Theology"; E. Harris Harbison, "Calvin's Sense of History," in *Christianity and History* (Princeton: Princeton University Press, 1964); Gerrish, " 'To The Unknown God': Luther and Calvin on the Hiddenness of God," in *The Old Protestantism and the New*, pp. 141–45; Schreiner, *Theater of His Glory*, pp. 111–14; Pitkin, "Imitation of David," pp. 860–63.

55. Calvin's great appreciation for the literal, grammatical, or "plain" sense of the text is part of a general trend beginning in the Middle Ages and becoming especially influential in the sixteenth century. However, Calvin's particular view of the historical and exemplary nature of the Psalms is rather different than, for example, Luther's and leads to some surprising exegetical twists, particularly with respect to some elements that were traditionally read christologically. It is likely that Calvin's interest was influenced by Bucer, who also insisted on a more strictly historical reading of the Psalms. On the literal sense in the Middle Ages, see Henri de Lubac, *Exégèse médiévale: les quatres sens de l'écriture,* 4 vols. (Paris: Aubier, 1959–1964); James Samuel Preus, *From Shadow to Promise: Old Testament Interpretation from Augustine to the Young Luther* (Cambridge, Mass.: Harvard University Press, 1969); Beryl Smalley, *The Study of the Bible in the Middle Ages,* 2d ed. (Oxford: Basil Blackwell, 1952). A detailed discussion of Calvin's relationship to the preceding tradition can be found in Ganoczy and Scheld, *Die Hermeneutik Calvins;* see also Muller, "The Hermeneutic of Promise and Fulfillment." For the Psalms in particular, see E. A. Gosselin, *The King's Progress to Jerusalem: Some Interpretations of David during the Reformation Period and Their Patristic and Medieval Background* (Malibu, Calif.: Undena Publications, 1976); and Pitkin, "Imitation of David." A rather different (and to my mind problematic) assessment of Calvin's christological reading of the Psalms is ventured by W. McKane, who claims that

Calvin's "Messianic interpretation of the Psalms is extensive, extending to Psalms which are not expressly attributed" ("Calvin as an Old Testament Commentator," *Nederduitse Gereformeerde Teologiese Tydscrif* 25 [1984]: 258; rpt. in Gamble, *Articles*, 6:250–56); compare S. H. Russell, "Calvin and the Messianic Interpretation of the Psalms," rpt. in Gamble, *Articles*, 6:261–72. Clearly more work needs to be done on Calvin's christological and historical interpretation of the Old Testament; a beginning appears in Puckett, *John Calvin's Exegesis of the Old Testament*. On Bucer, see R. Gerald Hobbs, "How Firm a Foundation: Martin Bucer's Historical Exegesis of the Psalms," *Church History* 53 (1984): 477–91. Hobbs has also explored the sixteenth century's emergent interest in relating the Hebrew origins of the Psalms with apostolic or traditional christological interpretations; see "Bucer on Psalm 22," in *Histoire de l'Exégèse au XVI siècle*, Études de philologie et d'Histoire 34, ed. O. Fatio and P. Fraenkel [Geneva: Droz, 1978], pp. 144–63) and "Hebraica veritas *and* Traditio Apostolica: Saint Paul and the Interpretation of the Psalms in the Sixteenth Century," in Steinmetz, *The Bible in the Sixteenth Century*, pp. 83–99. Bucer's commentary on the Psalms (*Sacrorum Psalmorum libri quinque* [Strasbourg]) was published pseudonymously in 1529, with a second edition in 1532. Calvin mentions Bucer's commentary and that of Wolfgang Musculus (*In sacrosanctum Davidis Psalterium commentarii* [Basel, 1551]) with approval in the preface to his own commentary (CO 31:13, 14).

56. CO 31:88. See Calvin's similar observations on Ps. 8:3 (CO 31:91, verse 4); compare Kraus, *Psalmen*, 1:206.

57. "Fateor quidem lucere Dei providentiam praesertim fidelium causa, quia soli oculati sunt ad eam spectandam" (CO 31:89, verse 3). Compare Luther (commenting on Ps. 8:5 in his *Operationes in Psalmos* [1519–1521]): "Opera dei sunt haec incomprehensibilia, nisi per fidem" (AWA 2/2:481, lines 22–28).

58. Compare also, for example, Calvin's comments on Ps. 9:10: "Sed quia plurimi ad Dei iudicia caecutiunt, profectum hunc David ad solos fideles restringit, et certe ubi nulla est pietas, nullus est operum Dei sensus" (CO 31:101, verse 11).

59. "But it is asked, how does God put to flight his enemies, whose impious slanders do not cease to strike out with violence against all proofs of divine providence? I answer, they are not put to flight by being compelled to humility, but because they along with their blasphemies and canine barkings are left over to their vile confusion" (CO 31:90, verse 3).

60. CO 31:91.

61. Calvin comments that the prophet does not cover every instance of human dominion but sets forth only that part of it "which is sufficiently evident even to rude and stupid people." He continues, "There is no one of so dull or slow a mind who, if he opens his eyes, will not see that it is by the wonderful providence of God that horses and cows yield their service to men, and that sheep produce wool to clothe them, and that all sorts of animals supply them with food from their own flesh. And the more that the evidence of this dominion is apparent, as often as we eat food or enjoy the remaining comforts, the more ought we to be touched by a sense of the divine grace" (CO 31:94–95, verse 8).

62. Calvin notes that the author of Hebrews uses this verse to indicate that Christ's humiliation would be of short duration. In so doing, the author is not interpreting Ps. 8:5 but rather accommodating the text to a different purpose: "Therefore, when the apostle alluded to the terms humiliation and honor, he was not considering what David meant; he applied the former to the death of Christ and the latter to the resurrection" (CO 31:93, verse 6). Calvin points out that Paul similarly accommodates scripture to his own purpose in Rom. 10:6 and Eph. 4:8.

63. On the fallen aspects of creation, see Schreiner, *Theater of His Glory*, pp. 28–30.

64. CO 31:93, verse 6.

65. "And although by the defection of man that condition has been almost entirely ruined, there remain nonetheless certain remnants of that divine liberality that suffice to fill us with admiration. But in this wretched overthrow that legitimate order of nature no longer shines forth; the faithful, however, whom God gathers to himself under Christ, their head, possess in part the remnants of the good things of which they were deprived in Adam, to such an extent that they have enough material for marveling at how kindly they are treated by him" (CO 31:95, verses 8–10).

66. CO 31:95.

67. Calvin says this in the argument to Psalm 23: "and he not only acknowledges that [this] tranquillity now to act free from all inconveniences and troubles is [due to] the goodness of God, but trusts that by his providence he will continue happy until the end" (CO 31:237).

68. CO 31:238–39.

69. "Furthermore, he posits ways of righteousness for easy and even [ways]. As he still persists in his metaphor, it would be absurd to understand this of the direction of the Holy Spirit. Just as he stated above, that he will procure in abundance and kindly from God whatever things pertain to the preservation of life, so he now adds that he is protected from all trouble. The point is, God in no way lets the faithful down, since he both sustains, invigorates, and vivifies them by his power and averts all evils, so that they might walk at ease on even paths" (CO 31:239).

70. "[S]e recumbere in Dei providentiam" (CO 31:240).

71. CO 31:240.

72. CO 31:240.

73. CO 31:242. On the hermeneutical priority of the word or promise, compare the comments on Ps. 18:30, Ps. 27:8–9, and Ps. 116:7. On an extreme form of experimental or experiential knowledge among the wicked, with similarities to the faith among the reprobate described in the comments on Hebrews 6:4–6, see Calvin's comments on Ps. 83:18.

74. "It is therefore certain that David was lifted up by the help of present blessings to the hope of eternal life" (CO 31:242–43).

75. CO 31:472–73.

76. "Indeed, since this depravity is inborn in us, so that earthly wealth, dazzling our eyes, leads us to forget God, we ought to meditate with all our attention on this doctrine, lest whatever seems in us to be worthy of value obscure the knowledge of the power and grace of God. Rather the glory of God ought always to shine forth in all the gifts with which we are adorned, so that we reckon that we are happy nowhere else but in him" (CO 31:474).

77. CO 31:475.

78. CO 31:476.

79. Other passages in which Calvin indicates the benefit of the manifestations of God's providence added to God's word are in his comments on Pss. 40:4, 41:11, 43:3, 58:11, 80:11, and 119:52.

80. See Calvin's observations at the end of verses 2, 6, 8, and 9.

81. CO 31:477.

82. CO 31:478.

83. CO 31:480.

84. "For although the unbelievers boldly usurp the name of God and prate about religion, if one inquires more closely, he finds that nothing certain or firm underlies this, for indeed, those who are not founded in true faith must necessarily sink along with their figments into oblivion. It is, thus, the nature of faith to put before us a distinct knowledge

of God, in which we do not waver. . . . Moreover, in order to encourage and strengthen themselves for walking in the continued course of faith, the faithful declare that God will be perpetually steadfast in preserving the church" (CO 31:480).

85. See Calvin's comments on Ps. 135:13–14: "Et certe sicuti totus mundus theatrum est divinae bonitatis, sapientiae, iustitiae, virtutis: pars tamen illustrior, instar orchestrae, est ecclesia" (CO 32:361, verse 13). For other statements about the church as the principle arena for perceiving divine providence, see Calvin's comments on Ps. 68:7, Ps. 76:2, and Ps. 113:7.

86. CO 31:97, verse 4.

87. "Therefore wherever we see our enemies fall, we must take care not to limit our perception to this sight, just as profane men are blind while seeing. But let this doctrine present itself to us, that when they are turned back, they are overthrown by the face of the Lord" (CO 31:98, verse 4).

88. See, for example, Calvin's comments on Ps. 7:15, Ps. 18:42, and Ps. 35:8.

89. "Whenever God ensnares the ungodly in their own wickedness, it is open and manifest to all that God is fulfilling the office of a judge. In short, David declares that, whenever God turns back against them whatsoever kinds of evil-doing they devise, his judgment is too evident for it to be ascribed either to nature or chance. If God should clearly stretch forth the power of his hand, let us, too, learn to open [our] eyes so that these judgments, which he exercises against the enemies of the church, might confirm our faith" (CO 31:105, verse 17).

90. CO 31:99, verses 7–8. Compare Calvin's comments on Ps. 92:5–9 (CO 32:11–14, verses 6–10).

91. CO 31:100, verse 9.

92. For other instances in which Calvin asserts or implies that faith apprehends God's secret or invisible providence, see his comments on Ps. 13:1 (CO 31:132, verse 2); on Ps. 13:5 (CO 31:134, verse 6); on the title of Psalm 36 (CO 31:358, verse 2); on Ps. 36:5 (CO 31:361, verse 6); and on Ps. 40:3 (CO 31:407, verse 4). In his comments on Ps. 40:5, Calvin discusses the incomprehensibility of providence, and he argues that believers need to close their eyes in order to trust entirely in it. This, however, is not a contradiction of his view in Ps. 9:3, but rather a means of emphasizing that God's providence in God's works cannot be seen with physical eyes apart from faith or the illumination of the Spirit. Calvin maintains that believers are to meditate upon God's works *and* discern in them God's hand (CO 31:409, verse 6).

93. CO 31:106, verse 18.

94. CO 31:100, verse 9.

95. CO 31:100, verse 10.

96. CO 31:103, verse 13.

97. CO 31:106, verse 19.

98. CO 31:107–8, verse 21. Wallace discusses the Christian's simultaneous experience of affliction and God's restoring grace. Citing passages from Calvin's commentary on the Psalms, he notes that even though Christians already enjoy tokens of God's restoration of creation in this life, for various reasons affliction is still necessary. Nonetheless, amid affliction God still furnishes believers with actual experimental (experiential) evidence of his grace (*Calvin's Doctrine of the Christian Life*, pp. 133–35).

99. Augustine does not dwell on the question of providence; however, he mentions the temptation to doubt it and to think all is ruled by chance in his comments on Ps. 73:16 (Vulgate, Psalm 72). For other examples, see also the comments of Gerhoh of Reichersberg (1093–1169) on the opening verse, where he not only implies the challenge to providence but also dwells in detail on the problem of perception (PL 194:337–38); the comments of

Nicholas of Lyra (ca. 1270–1340) on the first two verses of this psalm in his *Postilla Litteralis* (in *Biblia cum glosa ordinaria, Nicolai de Lyra postilla, moralitatibus eiusdem, Pauli Burgensis additionibus, Matthiae Thoring (= Doering) replicis* [Basel, 1506–1508], p. 188r col. b, sec. D); and the more succinct characterization of the theme of this psalm of Denis the Carthusian (1402–1471) (*Super librum Psalmorum* in *Doctoris Estatici D. Dionysii Carthusiani Opera Omnia*, 42 vols. in 44, ed. Monks of the Carthusian Order [Monstroli: S. M. De Pratis, 1896–1913, 1935], 6:212).

100. CO 31:673.

101. CO 31:676.

102. CO 31:675–676.

103. Calvin relates incidents from the lives or legends of the Stoic philosopher Brutus (in his prefatory comments), the tyrant king Dionysius of Sicily (in his comments on Ps. 73:3), and the king Demetrius (in his comments on Ps. 73:7). He also cites from Ovid and another unnamed Latin poet (at Ps. 73:11); see CO 31:674, 675–76, 677–78, and 679. Reference to the figure of Dionysius of Sicily (ca. 400 B.C.E.) and his judgment that, since nothing impeded his plundering of the temple at Syracuse, the gods favor the wicked appears elsewhere; see Calvin's comments on Pss. 10:5 and 133:1, as well as the comments on 2 Thess. 1:5 (discussed in chapter 2), where Calvin also cites the line from Ovid. Dionysius is mentioned by Cicero in *De natura deorum*, trans. H. Rackham, ed. E. H. Warmington, Loeb Classical Library (Cambridge, Mass.: Harvard University Press, 1967), 3.34.83; compare Calvin's commentary on Seneca's *De clementia* (1532), book I, chapter xii (*Calvin's Commentary on Seneca's de Clementia*, translated with introduction and notes by Ford Lewis Battles and André Malan Hugo [Leiden: E. J. Brill, 1969], p. 205). In the comments on Ps. 73 Calvin mentions two other classical figures to make points unrelated to providence: Julius Caesar in comments on Ps. 73:4, Plautus in the comments on Ps. 73:21 (CO 31:676, 685).

104. CO 31:680.

105. For similar instances, see, for example, Calvin's comments on Ps. 10:1 (CO 31: 108), Ps. 10:12 (CO 31:115), Ps. 11:4 (CO 31:123–24), and Ps. 13:1 (CO 31:132; verse 2). For a discussion of Calvin's exegesis of these passages, see Pitkin, "Imitation of David."

106. CO 31:682.

107. CO 31:682. Calvin attributes the view referring the sanctuaries to celestial mansions to the "Hebrews"; other traditional interpretations include viewing them as sacred scripture (Nicholas of Lyra) or Christ.

108. CO 31:683.

109. The image of the watchtower often appears in Calvin's discussion of texts that predict the downfall of the wicked through God's judgment on them. See, for example, Calvin's comments on Pss. 37:37, 83:5, and 94:13 (CO 31:385, 775 [verse 6], 32:25); compare the comments on Ps. 87:3 (CO 31:801). Some passages, without specifically mentioning the watchtower, represent the godly beholding the future judgment of the wicked; see the comments on Pss. 1:4 ("fidei oculis contemplari quod alioqui incredibile videre posset"), 9:17, and 36:12 (CO 31:40, 105, and 364–65 [verse 13]).

110. CO 31:683; compare Calvin's comments on Ps. 58:8 (CO 31:562). That this view is available to all the godly is a point that Calvin makes elsewhere in his comments on the psalms; see, e.g., his comments on Ps. 55:23 (CO 31:545).

111. CO 31:683.

112. CO 31:683.

113. See the comments on Ps. 73:19: "Yet at the same time he warns that God is daily working in such a way that, if we were not lacking eyes, we would have proper occasion for wonder. Rather, if from the eminence of faith we would look out on the judgments of

God, nothing new or difficult to be believed would come to pass [*Imo se fide eminus pros-piceremus iudicia Dei, nihil novum vel difficile creditu contingeret*]" (CO 31:684); compare his comments on Ps. 73:20: "This [awakening] occurs not only when God restores a tolerable order to turbulent things but when by dispelling the darkness he also clears up our minds" (CO 31:684–85).

114. CO 31:168.

115. Aside from the extended treatment of these themes in the exegesis of Psalms 32 and 130, the soteriological perspective emerges only sporadically in the commentary. See, for example, Calvin's comments on Pss. 5:12, 6:1, 7:8, 17:5, 37:39, 38:22, 39:8, 40:11, 44:25, 50:16, 51:9–10, 61:11, 79:9, 85:2, 103:3, 106:31, and 143:2. See also Calvin's introduction to the commentary.

116. CO 23:10–11; compare Willis, *Calvin's Catholic Christology*, 126–27.

117. See Bohatec's discussion of the value of the present life, which contains numerous references to Calvin's Psalms commentary ("Calvins Vorsehungslehre," pp. 427–35).

Five. Calvin's Twofold Notion of Faith

1. Dowey, *Knowledge of God in Calvin's Theology*, p. 255.

2. Dowey, *Knowledge of God in Calvin's Theology*, p. 247. Dowey goes on the explain his use of the word "dialectic": "By dialectic we mean here the interrelationships of elements of thought belonging to the same universe of discourse that can neither be stated in a continuous logical sequence, nor be systematically related to one another in a rationally consequent system—and yet, cannot be separated from one another or asserted as independently true propositions, without losing their proper meaning."

3. Dowey, *Knowledge of God in Calvin's Theology*, p. 255. Dowey faults Köstlin and Wendel for assimilating "the entire problem of the knowledge of the Redeemer to the question of Scripture." It is true that neither Köstlin nor Wendel explicitly treats the cognitive character of faith in light of the issue of knowledge of God raised in book 1 of the *Institutes*.

4. See Dowey, *Knowledge of God in Calvin's Theology*, pp. 87–88, 144–46, 221–22, and 238–42; compare Willis, *Calvin's Catholic Christology*, p. 103. Dowey is struggling with an issue raised earlier by Benjamin Warfield: the confusion that arises when Calvin separates the discussion of the authority of scripture from the discussion of faith. See Warfield, *Calvin and Calvinism*, pp. 70–72.

5. See especially Dowey, *Knowledge of God in Calvin's Theology*, pp. 253–55; compare pp. 150–51.

6. Dowey, *Knowledge of God in Calvin's Theology*, p. 250; compare pp. 9–17, 157.

7. Dowey, *Knowledge of God in Calvin's Theology*, pp. 256–57; see also Willis, *Calvin's Catholic Christology*, pp. 120–22 and 130–31; Krusche, *Das Wirken des heiligen Geistes*, pp. 127–28; Partee, *Calvin and Classical Philosophy*, p. 45, note 11; Oberman, "The 'Extra' Dimension in the Theology of Calvin."

8. Dowey, *Knowledge of God in Calvin's Theology*, pp. 239–40.

9. Dowey, *Knowledge of God in Calvin's Theology*, p. 256; compare p. 239.

10. I am adopting terminology employed by Willis to describe the knowledge of God; see Willis, *Calvin's Catholic Christology*, p. 128; compare pp. 124 and 131.

11. The notion of piety emerges in Calvin's thought from his earliest writings but becomes especially prominent in the 1559 *Institutes*. Richard has traced the semantic history of the term *pietas* and the relationship of this term to *devotio* (*The Spirituality of John Calvin*, pp. 78–96). He notes that *pietas* took the place of *devotio* (which had become especially

popular among the advocates of the so-called *Devotio Moderna*) in the early Renaissance (e.g., in the writings of Erasmus and Juan de Valdes). The substitution of "piety" for "devotion" indicates the fundamental difference between the spiritualities of modern devotion, which tended to be anti-intellectual, and those of the Renaissance. "Although the Renaissance authors shared the objections of the *Devotio Moderna* against the *eruditio* of the scholastics, they in no way opposed learning. True piety was a *sancta eruditio*" (p. 92). Interestingly, *pietas* was closely linked to or even identified with the idea of wisdom (*sapientia*). Wisdom in this case refers to divine wisdom, caused by divine illumination and grasped only by divine illumination. John Colet expresses this in his exposition of Corinthians: "This faith is a kind of light infused into the soul of man from the divine sun, by which the heavenly virtues are known to be revealed without uncertainty or doubt; and it far excels the light of reason as certainty does uncertainty. The wisdom of the intellect is faith . . . the illumination and infused light, by which the soul may see perfect truths, is faith" (quoted in Richard, p. 91). Richard goes on to note that for Colet "*sapientia* was achieved not by an intellectual analysis of ideas, but by the passive reception of understanding given by God to those who are morally good" (p. 92). Though Calvin clearly would reject "moral goodness" as a condition for the passive reception of divine wisdom, he, too, understands piety to entail a certain knowledge of the divine obtained in a special way *and* involving a moral dimension. On Calvin's concept of piety, see Gerrish, "Theology within the Limits of Piety Alone."

12. Schützeichel, *Glaubenstheologie*, p. 63, note 15. For other discussions of the changes to the section on faith in 1559 see Schützeichel, *Glaubenstheologie*, pp. 63–68; Dowey, *Knowledge of God in Calvin's Theology*, pp. 151–53. Somewhat surprisingly, Köstlin does not consider the special topic of faith in his consideration of the development of the successive editions of the *Institutes* ("Calvin's Institutio").

13. Found in *Institutes* (1559), 3.2.33, 34, 36.

14. The Spirit's activity spans the entire breadth of the 1559 *Institutes*, as is clear in Krusche's study of Calvin's pneumatology (*Das Wirken des heiligen Geistes*).

15. *Institutes* (1559), 3.2.33, 35. Calvin quotes, paraphrases, or alludes to 2 Tim 1:14, Gal 3:2, 2 Cor. 4:13, 2 Thess. 1:11, 1 Cor. 2:4–5, and Eph. 1:13 and 4:30.

16. Compare CO 1:477–78.

17. *Institutes* (1559), 3.2.1.

18. CO 1:462–64; appears in *Institutes* (1559), 3.2.24. On Calvin's idea of mystical union with Christ, see Wilhelm Kolfhaus, *Christusgemeinschaft bei Johannes Calvin*, Beiträge zur Geschichte und Lehre der Reformierten Kirche 3 (Neukirchen: Buchhandlung des Erziehungsvereins, 1939); Otto Gründler, "John Calvin: Ingrafting into Christ," in *The Spirituality of Western Christendom*, ed. E. Rozanne Elder (Kalamazoo: Cistercian Publications, 1976), pp. 169–87; Dowey, *Knowledge of God in Calvin's Theology*, pp. 197–204; Krusche, *Das Wirken des heiligen Geistes*, pp. 265–72; Willis-Watkins, "The Unio Mystica and the Assurance of Faith according to Calvin."

19. Emile Doumergue, *Jean Calvin, les hommes et les choses de son temps* (Lausanne: Georges Bridel, 1899–1917; Neuilly, 1926–1927), 4:241; see also Dowey, *Knowledge of God in Calvin's Theology*, pp. 152–53. Paul Jacobs notes that Calvin develops the statements about mystical union with Christ in the polemic with Osiander (*Prädestination und Verantwortlichkeit bei Calvin* [Kassel: Oncken, 1937], p. 128); compare Dowey, *Knowledge of God in Calvin's Theology*, p. 198; Wilhelm Niesel, *Die Theologie Calvins* (Munich: Kaiser, 1938), pp. 121–27 and 133–34; Wendel, *Calvin*, pp. 235–42.

20. Dowey, *Knowledge of God in Calvin's Theology*, pp. 200–204; see also Stuermann, *Calvin's Concept of Faith*, pp. 190–93, 196, and 220–25. Stuermann criticizes Peter Brunner for failing to see the connection between the mystical union and repentance in the present;

compare Brunner, *Vom Glauben bei Calvin*, pp. 85–86. While agreeing that through faith the Spirit both justifies and sanctifies, Shepherd argues against Stuermann that faith *is* union with Christ (*The Nature and Function of Faith*, p. 230). However, as noted earlier, Gerrish has shown that union was clearly an effect of faith for Calvin (*Grace and Gratitude*, p. 62, note 47).

21. See also Schützeichel, *Glaubenstheologie*, p. 165.

22. *Institutes* (1559), 3.2.4–5. See Dee, *Het geloofsbegrip*, pp. 89–93.

23. *Institutes* (1559), 3.2.2–3.

24. CO 1:472–74.

25. *Institutes* (1559), 3.2.4.

26. *Institutes* (1559), 3.2.5.

27. *Institutes* (1559), 3.2.5.

28. Schützeichel criticizes this unnuanced presentation of the *fides informis* (*Glaubenstheologie*, pp. 85–87).

29. David Foxgrover, " 'Temporary Faith' and the Certainty of Salvation," *Calvin Theological Journal* 15 [1980]: 227; compare Zachman, *The Assurance of Faith*, p. 182; Krusche, *Das Wirken des heiligen Geistes*, pp. 249–50.

30. *Institutes* (1559), 3.2.10. The passage is originally from 1539.

31. It is noteworthy that Calvin concludes his treatment of Simon in Acts 8 by suggesting, against the patristic exegetical tradition, that Simon eventually repented of his error. Peter's condemnation of Simon appears to have awakened in him what he previously lacked, despite having perceived the truth of the gospel from Philip's preaching: namely, denial of himself. His latent ambition leads him to reveal his hypocrisy before Peter (Acts 8:18). In response (Acts 8:20–23), Peter both strikes Simon with a sense of divine judgment and raises him up to hope in God's pardon. It is this, apparently, and not his earlier temporary faith, that leads him to yield fully to God, and provides the basis for Calvin's conjecture (CO 48:184–87).

32. *Institutes* (1559), 3.2.11–12. Calvin's response to Laelius Socinus, *Calvini ad Laelii Socini quaestiones Responsio Nonis Iun. 1555*, is found in CO 10/1:160–65. On this exchange of ideas, see David Willis, "The Influence of Laelius Socinus on Calvin's Doctrines of the Merits of Christ and the Assurance of Faith," in *Italian Reformation Studies in Honor of Laelius Socinus*, ed. John A. Tedeschi (Florence: Felice le Monnier, 1965) 4:233–41; rpt. in Gamble, *Articles*, 5:59–67; see also Krusche, *Das Wirken des heiligen Geistes*, pp. 248–55. Willis notes that Laelius's questions are no longer extant but suggests possible formulations. From his hypothetical proposals, it appears that one issue underlying the matter of the assurance of faith and faith among the reprobate is the reliability and immutability of the divine will (pp. 238–39). Schützeichel observes that Calvin's debates over predestination in the 1550s lie behind the discussion of faith among the reprobate (*Glaubenstheologie*, p. 67). Krusche also provides an excellent discussion of the relationships among the idea of faith among the reprobate, the certainty of the elect, and Calvin's doctrine of predestination. (*Das Wirken des heiligen Geistes*, pp. 243–51).

33. Willis, "The Influence of Laelius Socinus," p. 240.

34. See Gerrish, "To the Unknown God," pp. 147–49. Both Willis and Krusche note the contrast between Calvin's view here and the later notion of a *syllogismus practicus* (the view that one's outward conduct or peace and prosperity lead one to conclude that one is elect). Though Calvin does suggest at times that the elect can discern signs of their election in their sanctification, he insists that their assurance of election (and of their faith) rests solely in the testimony of the Spirit and in their communion with Christ. Here, however, he intimates that not the experience of peace and prosperity but rather that of doubt and affliction is a more compelling mark of election (see Willis, "The Influence of Laelius

Socinus," pp. 239–40; Krusche, *Das Wirken des heiligen Geistes*, pp. 244–48). For a discussion of how tensions in Calvin's understanding of these matters might have led to the development of the practical syllogism, see Susi Hausammann, " 'Leben aus Glauben' in Reformation, Reformorthodoxie und Pietismus," *Theologische Zeitschrift* 27 (1971): 263–89.

35. On the discussion in *Institutes* (1559), 3.2.13, see Stuermann, *Calvin's Concept of Faith*, pp. 81–84.

36. *Institutes* (1559), 3.2.13.

37. See *Institutes* (1559), 3.2.21–23; note that in section 23 Calvin focuses on the experience of God's majesty rather than the experience of hiddenness in particular.

38. Psalms 12:6, 18:30; Prov. 30:5. Calvin also mentions that Psalm 119 is devoted to commendation of God's word.

39. *Institutes* (1559), 3.2.17. In this section, Calvin cites or refers to Ps. 42:5, 11; Ps. 31:22; Ps. 77:7, 9, 10; Ps. 116:7; Ps. 27:14; and Ps. 119:43.

40. *Institutes* (1559), 3.2.17.

41. *Institutes* (1559), 3.2.24.

42. *Institutes* (1559), 3.2.37. In this section, Calvin cites or refers to Ps. 46:2–3, Ps. 35, Ps. 37:7; Is. 30:15; Heb. 10:36.

43. *Institutes* (1559), 3.2.28.

44. "Yet in the meantime we do not exclude God's power in respect to which [*cuius intuitu*] unless faith sustains itself it can never render to God the honor due to him" (*Institutes* [1559], 3.2.31).

45. *Institutes* (1559), 3.2.31 (OS 3:41).

46. Calvin's initial discussion of the word as the object of faith in *Institutes* (1559) 3.2.6–7 is also the first place that he makes the distinction within special revelation. In 1559 he underscores the fact that it is God's word of mercy that is the particular object of faith by proof-texting from the Psalms, where frequent reference is made to God's mercy and truth.

47. Recall that the idea of God's power as an object for faith appeared already in Calvin's exegesis of Rom. 4:21 in 1540. Calvin underscored and expanded this idea in his revisions to the commentary in 1556.

48. "[Q]uia pietas, ut alibi visum fuit, Dei potentiam semper ad usum et opus accommodat: praesertim opera Dei sibi proponit quibus se patrem esse testatus est" (*Institutes* [1559], 3.2.31 [OS 3:41]). The French edition of 1560 renders *pietas* as *foy*.

49. Schreiner, *Theater of His Glory*, p. 5.

50. See also Köstlin, "Calvin's Institutio," pp. 52–53.

51. The distinction between the knowledge of God as creator and the knowledge of God as redeemer is evident in the specific references that Calvin makes in *Institutes* (1559) 1.2.1, 1.6.1, 1.6.2, 1.10.1, 1.13.9 (compare also 1.13.11), 1.13.23, 1.13.24, and 2.6.1. Some interpreters (Battles, Dowey) also find this distinction expressed in 1.14.20 and 1.14.21 (these passages derive from 1543). For a detailed discussion of several of these passages, see Dowey, *Knowledge of God in Calvin's Theology*, pp. 41–49.

52. Dowey, *Knowledge of God in Calvin's Theology*, p. 46.

53. "Yet I repeat once more: besides the specific doctrine of faith and repentance that sets forth Christ as Mediator, scripture adorns with unmistakable marks and tokens the one true God, in that he has created and governs the universe, in order that he may not be mixed up with the throng of false Gods" (*Institutes* [1559], 1.6.2). This clearly says that scripture is the source of information about God's reconciliation in Christ *and* God's governance of the world. Yet interpreters have obscured this on the basis of Calvin's statement in *Institutes* (1559) 1.2.1: "Quia ergo Dominus primum simpliciter creator tam in muni opificio, quam in generali Scripturae doctrina, deinde in Christi facie redemptor apparet:

hinc duplex emergit eius cognitio." Dowey faults Karl Barth and Wilhelm Niesel for implying that Calvin held that the twofold knowledge refers to knowledge from creation and
in Christ. But Dowey's own formulation, though derived directly from this statement in
1.2.1, is also misleading insofar as it appears to imply that scripture is somehow only a
source for knowledge of God's creative activity: "The knowledge of God the Creator has
two sources: creation and the 'general doctrine' of Scripture; and the knowledge of the
Redeemer has one source, Christ" (*Knowledge of God in Calvin's Theology*, p. 43; for references to Barth and Niesel, see note 7). Clearly Dowey does not wish to imply this, since
he continues his discussion by arguing that both biblical Testaments contain both "orders
of the knowledge of God."

54. Willis, *Calvin's Catholic Christology*, p. 128.

55. See Dowey, *Knowledge of God in Calvin's Theology*, pp. 252–53, and Ebeling, "Cognitio Dei et hominis," pp. 297–305.

56. *Institutes* (1559) 1.2.1. In debates over Calvin's alleged natural theology (taken up
later in our chapter) much attention has been focused on the words "si integer stetisset
Adam."

57. "Verum, quia se Dominus propinquiore intuitu contemplandum non exhibet, quam
in facie Christi sui, quae ipsa fidei tantum oculis conspicitur: quod de notitia Dei dicendum
restat, in eum locum melius differetur, quo tractabitur fidei intelligentia" (CO 1:304).

58. Dowey argues that this sentence is reworked and appears in its new form in *Institutes* (1559) 1.7.5, where it again alerts the reader that the subject of knowledge is not yet
complete (*Knowledge of God in Calvin's Theology*, p. 254). However, the sentence to which
he refers, now appearing in *Institutes* (1559) 1.7.5 actually derives from 1550 and can in
no way be considered as the sentence that concluded chapter 1 in the editions of 1539–
1554 (see OS 3:71; CO 1:206). This statement indeed alerts the reader to a future discussion
of the Spirit as the agent of certainty of scriptural authority. Battles locates this discussion
in book 3 (*Institutes* [1559], vol. 1, p. 81, note 18; compare p. 74, note 2). However, it
should be recalled that in 1550 the discussion of the Spirit appeared primarily in Calvin's
treatment of the third article of the Creed (CO 1:536–38). The "alibi" could also point to
the later discussions of the authority of scripture in the church in Calvin's exposition of
the fourth article of the Creed and in his discussion of the power of the church (CO 1:
630–33 and 1041–45; compare *Institutes* [1559], 4.8.5–14).

59. Dowey points out that Karl Barth and Emil Brunner, in their famous debate over
Calvin's theology, confused the problem of relating this section to the condemning force
of nature's witness in *Institutes* (1559) 1.1–5, with the problem of relating this section to
the knowledge of God the redeemer contained in books 2–4 (*Knowledge of God in Calvin's
Theology*, p. 265).

60. "Pietatem voco coniunctam cum amore Dei reverentiam quam beneficiorum eius
notita conciliat" (*Institutes* [1559], 1.2.1). Though many of the points made in chapter 2
are from earlier editions of the *Institutes*, Calvin has reworked the discussion to such a
degree that it is with only a few exceptions almost impossible to locate these passages in
the earlier editions. The actual definition of piety quoted here is new in 1559.

61. *Institutes* (1559) 1.2.1. Portions of this statement are considered by the editors of
the OS to derive from the second sentence of the 1536 edition as revised in 1539: "Illa
[cognitio] scilicet, quae non modo unum esse Deum ostendat, quem ab omnibus oporteat
coli et adorari: sed simul etaim doceat, illum unum omnis veritatis, sapientiae, bonitatis,
iustitiae, iudiciae, misericordiae, potentiae, sanctitatis fontem esse" (OS 3:34–35; CO 1:
279).

62. "The natural order was that the fabric of the universe should be the school in
which we were to learn piety, and from it pass over to eternal life and perfect felicity. But

after man's rebellion, our eyes, wherever they turn, encounter God's curse. This curse while it seizes and envelops innocent creatures through our fault, must overwhelm our souls with despair. For even if God wills to manifest his fatherly favor to us in many ways, yet we cannot by contemplating the universe infer that he is father. Rather, conscience presses us within and shows in our sin just cause for his disowning us and not regarding or recognizing us as his sons" (*Institutes* [1559], 2.6.1). It is interesting that this addition in 1559 is one of the few places in the *Institutes* where Calvin indicates that the world of nature was affected negatively by the Fall; this is even more explicit in the French edition of 1560: "malediction: laquelle estant espandue sur toutes creatures, et tenant le ciel et la terre comme enveloppez" (OS 3:320). Calvin expounded the fallenness of the natural order in greater detail in his commentaries on Genesis (1554), the Psalms (1557), Isaiah (1558), and Jeremiah (1563); see Schreiner, *Theater of his Glory*, pp. 28–30. Stauffer says that this idea appears in the sermons only in the forty-third sermon on Job (*Dieu, la création et la Providence*, p. 31).

63. *Institutes* (1559), 2.6.4.

64. Gerrish, *Grace and Gratitude*, p. 68; see also "Theology within the Limits of Piety Alone," p. 204 and p. 380, note 43.

65. Gerrish, *Grace and Gratitude*, p. 69.

66. Referring to Ps. 14:1 (cf. 53:1), Calvin says: "But to render their madness more detestable, David represents them as flatly denying God's existence; not that they deprive him of his being, but because, in despoiling him of his judgment and providence, they shut him up idle in heaven" (*Institutes* [1559], 1.4.2). In addition to referring to several psalms, Calvin also mentions 2 Tim. 2:13. Compare also the new discussion in *Institutes* 1.5.4, where Calvin polemicizes against the Epicureans, and in *Institutes* 1.5.5., where he argues against the Aristotelians.

67. *Institutes* (1559), 1.5.1.

68. "Indeed, he not only declares [in Psalm 8] that a clear mirror of God's works is in humankind, but that infants, while they nurse at their mothers' breasts, have tongues so eloquent to preach his glory that there is no need at all of other orators" (*Institutes* [1559], 1.5.3). In this section Calvin also refers to Acts 17:27–28 to prove God's nearness to human beings.

69. *Institutes* (1559), 1.5.14; this passage is verbatim from 1539 (CO 1:291).

70. *Institutes* (1559), 1.6.1.

71. "There is no doubt that Adam, Noah, Abraham, and the rest of the patriarchs with this assistance penetrated to the intimate knowledge of him that in a way distinguished them from unbelievers. I am not yet speaking of the proper doctrine of faith whereby they had been illumined unto the hope of eternal life. For, that they might pass from death to life, it was necessary to recognize God not only as creator but also as redeemer, for undoubtedly they arrived at both from the word" (*Institutes* [1559], 1.6.1). Most of this passage was new in 1559; an earlier version, which shows the previous mingling of soteriological and nonsoteriological elements, appeared in the editions of 1539–1554 as follows: "Hunc enim ordinem ab initio Dominus in servorum suorum vocatione tenuit, ut praeter omnia illa documenta verbum quoque adhiberet, quae multo rectior et familiarior est ad ipsum dignoscendum nota. Sic Adam, sic Noe, sic Abraham et reliqui patres in cognitionem eius interiorem verbo illuminati penetrarunt; sive illis instillabatur per oracula et visiones, sive prioribus ita revelatum, eorum ministerio, quasi per manum illis tradebatur. Neque tamen intererat, quo tandem modo fierent eius verbi participes, modo a Deo profectum esse intelligerent; cuius rei Deus indubiam semper fidem fecit, quoties eius revelationi voluit esse locum. Ergo peculiariter se paucis, evidenti praesentiae suae dato signo, insinuavit, ac salvifica doctrinae thesaurum apud eos deposuit, cuius ipsi rursum ad posteritatem dispensatores

forent. Qualiter Abraham videmus foedus aeternae vitae, apud se coelesti oraculo depositum, et propagasse in totam familiam, et in longam generationem transmittendum curavisse. Atque hoc quidem interstitio, iam tum a reliquis nationibus distinguebatur Abrahae progenies, quod singulari Dei beneficio in istam verbi communionem admissa erat" (CO 1:292; compare OS 3:61–62).

72. *Institutes* (1559), 1.6.1.

73. *Institutes* (1559), 1.6.2.

74. "Now [David] means by the word 'regnant' not the power with which [God] is endowed and which he exercises in governing the whole of nature but the doctrine by which he declares his lawful sovereignty" (*Institutes* [1559], 1.6.3). The editors of the OS provide references to Psalms 93, 96, 97 and 99. In his comments on these psalms, Calvin does not make such a clear distinction between the declaration of sovereignty or power and the palpable manifestations of providence. As I have shown, he frequently makes such a distinction when he takes up the question of the relationship between God's word and God's works in his commentary. However, this particular question is not the focus of his comments on these particular psalms. Still, it is true that in his comments Calvin views the statements about God as regnant as attestations to God's sovereignty that believers should employ as shields against doubt (compare the comments on Ps. 93:1 [CO 32:16–17]). In this way these scriptural pronouncements declare the providential promise that is the focus of providential faith.

75. "Psalm 29 looks to this same end, where the prophet—speaking forth concerning God's awesome voice, which strikes the earth in thunder, winds, rains, whirlwinds and tempests, causes mountains to tremble, shatters the cedars—finally adds at the end that his praises are sung in the sanctuary because the unbelievers are deaf to all the voices of God that resound in the air. Similarly, he thus ends another psalm where he has described the awesome waves of the sea: 'Thy testimonies have been verified, the beauty and holiness of thy temple shall endure forevermore' [compare Ps. 93:5]" (*Institutes* [1559], 1.6.4).

76. *Institutes* (1559), 2.12.1. Willis points out that the words "sine Mediatore" were not translated into the French (*Calvin's Catholic Christology*, p. 69, note 4).

77. *Institutes* (1559), 2.12.6–7. Calvin's main objection to Osiander is to the speculative nature of his questioning.

78. Willis, *Calvin's Catholic Christology*, p. 69. In the 1559 *Institutes*, Calvin expands his earlier criticisms of Servetus to a section in the discussion of the Trinity. Here he argues against Servetus's view that God was not revealed to Abraham and the other patriarchs but that they worshipped only an angel. In response, Calvin argues that the church's orthodox doctors have held that the "angel" was "God's word, who already at that time, as a sort of foretaste, began to fulfill the office of Mediator" (*Institutes* [1559], 1.13.10; references to Servetus are given in the OS 3:122, notes 2 and 4.

79. "Sed excipimus primum mediatoris nomen Christo quadrare, non solum ex quo carnem induit, vel ex quo munus suscepit reconciliandi cum Deo humani generis, sed ab initio creationis iam vere fuisse mediatorem: quia semper fuit caput ecclesiae, et primatum tenuit etiam super angelos, et primogenitus fuit omnis creaturae (Ephes. 1,2; Col. 1,15 sq. et 2,10). Unde colligimus non modo post Adae lapsum fungi coepisse mediatoris officio, sed quatenus aeterni Dei sermo est, eius gratia coniunctos fuisse Deo tam angelos quam homines, ut intergri perstarent" (*Responsum ad Fratres Polonos, quomodo mediator sit Christus, ad refutandum Stancari errorem*, CO 9:338; translated in Willis, *Calvin's Catholic Christology*, p. 70; compare a further quotation from the same treatise on pp. 70–71). For a discussion and translation of Calvin's first response to the Polish brethren, see Joseph Tylanda, "Christ the Mediator: Calvin versus Stancaro," *Calvin Theological Journal* 8 (1973): 5–16; rpt. in Gamble, *Articles* 5:161–72. Calvin's response was directed toward the assertion

of Francesco Stancaro (b. 1501) that Christ was a mediator not with respect to his divine nature but only because of his human nature. This view was developed, ironically, in a tract that Stancaro wrote against Osiander's view that Christ was the mediator only according to his divinity (*Apologia contra Osiandrum*, 1552). Calvin first learned of this argument in a letter from Francis Dryander, dated 30 October 1552, but did not get involved until he received an appeal from Polish ministers in 1560. Finally, it is worthwhile to note that Calvin bases his notion of Christ's dual mediation on *Pauline* proof texts.

80. *Institutes* (1559), 2.14.3 (emphasis mine).

81. Compare, from Calvin's exegesis of 1 Cor. 15:27–28: "when the veil has been removed, we will see God openly reigning in majesty; and no longer will the means be Christ's humanity, which holds us back from a nearer vision of God [*neque amplius media erit Christi humanitas quae nos ab ulteriore Dei conspectu cohibeat*]" (CO 49:549). See Willis's discussion, *Calvin's Catholic Christology*, pp. 97–99. Willis points out that Calvin does not say that Christ will relinquish his humanity but says only that he will transfer his reign—and, presumably, his mediatorial office—from his humanity to his divinity.

82. The following was inserted into the discussion from 1539: "I do not yet touch upon the special covenant by which [God] distinguished the race of Abraham from the rest of the nations. For, even then in receiving by free adoption as sons those who were enemies, he showed himself to be their redeemer. We, however, are still concerned with that knowledge which stops at the creation of the world and does not mount up to Christ the mediator. But even if it shall be worthwhile a little later to cite certain passages from the New Testament, in which the power of God the creator and of his providence in the preservation of primal nature are proved, yet I wish to warn my readers what I now intend to do, lest they overleap the limits set for them. Finally, at present let it be enough to grasp how God, the maker of heaven and earth, governs the universe founded by him. Indeed, both his fatherly goodness and his beneficently inclined will are repeatedly extolled; and examples of his severity are given, which show him to be the righteous avenger of evil deeds, especially where his forbearance toward the obstinate is of no effect" (*Institutes*, 1.10.1).

83. See Schreiner, *Theater of His Glory*, chap. 3.

84. For a discussion of Calvin's teaching on the angels and the role of this topic in his doctrine of creation, see Schreiner, *Theater of His Glory*, chap. 2. Schreiner notes that Calvin's defense of the existence of angels was an important component in his polemic against the Libertines in 1545. The Libertines held a pantheistic view of the universe that led to a denial of the essence of both human and angelic natures (p. 46).

85. "Then the visible works of God follow, in which we are bid to recognize the artificer himself: heaven, earth, sea, and whatever these contain. For, as I have elsewhere said, although it is not the chief evidence for faith, yet it is the first evidence in the order of nature, to be mindful that wherever we cast our eyes, all things they meet are works of God, and at the same time to ponder with pious meditation to what end God created them" (CO 1:508; compare *Institutes* [1559], 1.14.20).

86. *Institutes* (1559), 1.14.1.

87. "In short, let us remember that that invisible God, whose wisdom, power, and righteousness are incomprehensible, sets before us Moses' history as a mirror in which his living likeness glows. For just as eyes, when dimmed with age or weakness or by some other defect, unless aided by spectacles, discern nothing distinctly; so, such is our feebleness, unless scripture guides us in seeking God, we immediately vanish in a fog" (*Institutes* [1559], 1.14.1).

88. See Schreiner, *Theater of His Glory*, pp. 15–16.

89. *Institutes* (1559), 1.14.2.

90. The details of Calvin's angelology and demonology do not concern me here in-

asmuch as these are invisible realities that, apparently, the faithful perceive only in the rarest of circumstances. Nonetheless, a knowledge of angels and demons as set forth in scripture is important and necessary for faith. In an addition to his prefatory comments to this 1543 discussion, Calvin states one of his reasons: "For if we desire to recognize God from his works, we ought be no means to overlook such an illustrious and noble example" (*Institutes* [1559], 1.14.3).

91. "Nothing is to be gained by further discussing what direction the contemplation of God's works should take and to what goal such contemplation ought to be applied, inasmuch as the greater part of this topic has been disposed of in another place, and it is possible to accomplish in a few words whatever concerns our present purpose" (*Institutes* [1559], 1.14.21). Earlier versions of the sentence were substantively the same and pointed back to the discussion in chapter 1 of the editions of 1539–1554.

92. *Institutes* (1559), 1.14.21. The changes from the earlier editions (1543–1554) are extremely minor; compare CO 1:508.

93. *Institutes* (1559), 1.14.22; compare CO 1:509.

94. See Schreiner, *Theater of His Glory*, pp. 16–21.

95. Parker, *Calvin's Doctrine of the Knowledge of God*, p. 41.

96. See Calvin's discussion in *Institutes* (1559), 1.16.1 and 1.16.5.

97. *Institutes* (1559), 1.16.9; compare CO 1:891.

98. *Institutes* (1559), 1.16.9 (my emphasis).

99. *Institutes* (1559), 1.16.9.

100. *Institutes* (1559), 1.16.9.

101. *Institutes* (1559), 1.17.1.

102. *Institutes* (1559), 1.17.1.

103. "Hic enim obstrepit sensus, dum ipsos natales praevenit calamitas, acsi Deus parum clementer immeritos sic affligeret. Atqui in hoc spectaculo fulgere gloriam Patris sui testatur Christus, modo puri sint nobis oculi" (*Institutes* [1559], 1.17.1).

104. *Institutes* (1559), 1.17.1.

105. *Institutes* (1559), 1.17.2.

106. Calvin returns to this point in *Institutes* (1559), 1.18.3–4. Virtually this entire chapter is new in 1559. It deals in polemical fashion with several of the implications of Calvin's doctrine of God's omnicompetence: ordination versus permission, determination versus freedom of the human will, the question of the unity of God's will, and the relationship of God and evil. Calvin is concerned here to advance clear scriptural proofs for his position on these issues. These are clearly elements of knowledge of God as creator that exceed human mental capacity and therefore are known only by faith. However, I have left these out of consideration for the present since my main concern is to explore the extent to which the scriptural teaching about God's providence allows faith to view God's creative and sustaining activity in nature and history. Book 1, chapter 18, sheds little light on this particular issue.

107. *Institutes* (1559), 1.17.2. On Calvin's understanding of the distinction between God's absolute and ordained power, see Steinmetz, "Calvin and the Absolute Power of God."

108. *Institutes* (1559), 1.17.2.

109. Calvin cites and comments on Job 26:14, 28:21, and 28:28; he also quotes from Augustine, *On Diverse Questions*, question 27 (PL 40:18).

110. "[S]uscipere fidei oculis Dei providentiam, quae animis nostris ad patientiam compositis, constanter nos in pietate retineat" (CO 31:358, verse 2).

111. *Institutes* (1559), 1.17.4–5; compare CO 1:892–94.

112. *Institutes* (1559), 1.17.6–9; compare CO 1:894–98.

113. *Institutes* (1559), 1.17.10–11; compare CO 1:898–99.

114. See Gerrish, *Grace and Gratitude*, p. 70. Stuermann also is interested in faith's restorative power: "Therefore, when Calvin speaks of faith, one should understand that he is speaking of a relationship to God which restores to fallen man all the parts of that original felicity" (*Calvin's Concept of Faith*, p. 17). "Faith thus begins the restoration of felicity to man; for through it he once again comes to know God, to obey his Lord, to have his nature increasingly purified, and to enter into a new harmonious relationship to his fellow creatures *and to nature.* . . . Faith *sees* things under the aspect of eternity; it therefore *sees* the things and events of this terrestrial life in their true dimensions and *perceives* their proper uses" (*Calvin's Concept of Faith*, pp. 25–26; my emphasis).

115. "Nam hic virtutum Dei sensus nobis idoneus est pietatis magister, ex qua religio nascitur" (*Institutes* [1559], 1.2.1).

116. CO 31:729.

117. Emil Brunner, "Nature and Grace," and Karl Barth, "No! Answer to Emil Brunner," trans. Peter Fraenkel, in *Natural Theology* (London: Centenary Press, 1946); Emil Brunner, *Natur und Gnade*, 2d ed. (Tübingen: J. C. B. Mohr, 1935); Peter Barth, *Das Problem der natürlichen Theologie bei Calvin*, Theologische Existenz Heute, Heft 18 (Munich: Kaiser Verlag, 1935); Günter Gloede, *Theologia naturalis bei Calvin*, Tübinger Studien zur Systematischen Theologie 5 (Stuttgart: Kohlhammer, 1935); Pierre Maury, "La Théologie naturelle chez Calvin," *Bulletin de la Société de l'Histoire du Protestantisme Français* 84 (April–June 1935): 267–279; Wilhelm Niesel, review of G. Gloede, *Theologia naturalis bei Calvin*, in *Theologische Literaturbeilage der reformierten Kirchenzeitung* (October 1936): 15–16; *Die Theologie Calvins*; Dowey, *Knowledge of God in Calvin's Theology* (1994), especially pp. 265–67 (pp. 247–49 in earlier editions).

118. Brunner, *Natur und Gnade*, 2nd ed., p. 53.

119. P. Barth, *Das Problem der natürlichen Theologie*, pp. 9–10.

120. "Es ist unzweifelhaft: durch die Schrift wird uns eine zweite, sozusagen verschüttete, Quelle der Gotteserkenntnis aufgetan und nutzbar gemacht" (Brunner, *Natur und Gnade*, 2d ed., p. 54).

121. Dowey, *Knowledge of God in Calvin's Theology*, p. 266 (p. 248 in earlier editions).

122. Serene Jones points to failings of a different sort in *Calvin and the Rhetoric of Piety*, Columbia Series in Reformed Theology (Louisville: Westminster/John Knox Press, 1995), pp. 111–14.

123. Barth, "No!" p. 105.

124. Willis, *Calvin's Catholic Christology*, is an important exception; see especially pp. 124–28 and note his citations from Calvin's commentary on Genesis.

125. *Institutes* (1559), 1.2.1. Note that this, as well as Calvin's argument against Osiander for inferring that if Adam had never fallen the incarnation would still have taken place (2.12.5–7), are both new in 1559. As noted earlier, Calvin's main objection is to Osiander's speculation, since Calvin's own supralapsarianism demands that God also decreed the incarnation by an eternal decree. Nevertheless, Calvin does hold that "if Adam's uprightness had not failed, he along with the angels would have been like God; and it would not have been necessary for the Son of God to become either man or angel [*quia si non collapsa fuisset Adae integritas, similis fuisset Deo cum Angelis: neque tamen propterea necesse fuisset Filium Dei fieri vel hominem vel Angelum*]" (*Institutes* [1559], 2.12.7). Gerrish observes that Calvin's view that life was always in Christ, i.e., mediated by the word, "is in harmony with his conviction that the incarnation of the Word does not make God benevolent but *manifests* God's benevolence" (*Grace and Gratitude*, p. 69, note 81 [emphasis in original]).

126. Willis, *Calvin's Catholic Christology*, p. 127.

127. Thomas Torrance, *Calvin's Doctrine of Man* (London: Lutterworth Press, 1949), pp. 33–34 and 40–41.

128. The first fruits of such an investigation can be found in Susan Schreiner, " 'The Spiritual Man Judges all Things': Calvin and the Exegetical Debates about Certainty in the Reformation."

129. David Foxgrover argues that the idea of temporary faith does not undermine Calvin's insistence on certainty (" 'Temporary Faith' and the Certainty of Salvation"). Zachman also discusses these sections, from the perspective of assurance, with detail on temporary faith (*The Assurance of Faith*, pp. 181–83).

130. "To the Unknown God," pp. 142–43; emphasis in original.

131. *Institutes* (1559), 1.16.9; OS 3:201 (my emphasis).

132. For a thorough investigation into Calvin's Job sermons, see, in addition to her earlier articles, Susan E. Schreiner, *Where Shall Wisdom Be Found?* As in the Psalms commentary, in the Job sermons Calvin does not ascribe to faith or the eyes of faith an ability to grasp the reasons for God's actions. However, it appears that he presents faith more as a blind trust *that* God is provident rather than the ability to recognize the divine hand even without an understanding of the meaning of certain events; see pp. 128–130.

133. An initial step toward this is C. J. Kinlaw's "Determinism and the Hiddenness of God in Calvin's Theology," *Religious Studies* 24 (1988): 497–509; rpt. in Gamble, *Articles*, 9:161–73.

134. That the *Institutes* (1559) as a whole presents Calvin's doctrine of God has been noted especially by Gerrish; see "The Mirror God God's Goodness," p. 150, and "Theology within the Limits of Piety Alone," especially 199–201 and 203.

Bibliography

Primary Sources by Calvin

EDITIONS

Calvin's Commentary on Seneca's de Clementia. Edited and translated with an introduction and notes by Ford Lewis Battles and André Malan Hugo. Leiden: E. J. Brill, 1969.

Les Commentaires à l'Ancien et au Nouveau Testament. Publication sous les auspices de la Société calviniste de France. Geneva: Labor et Fides, 1960–.

Commentarii in Pauli Epistolas ad Galatas, ad Ephesios, ad Philippenses, ad Colossenses. Ed. Helmut Feld. Vol. 16 of *Ioannis Calvini Opera Omnia: Series 2: Opera Exegetica Veteris et Novi Testamenti.* Geneva: Librairie Droz, 1992.

Commentarii in secundam Pauli Epistolam ad Corinthios. Ed. Helmut Feld. Vol. 15 of *Ioannis Calvini Opera Omnia: Series 2: Opera Exegetica Veteris et Novi Testamenti.* Geneva: Librairie Droz, 1994.

Commentarius in Epistolam ad Hebraeos. Ed. T. H. L. Parker. Vol. 19 of *Ioannis Calvini Opera Omnia: Series 2: Opera Exegetica Veteris et Novi Testamenti.* Geneva: Librairie Droz, 1996.

In Evangelium Secundum Johannem Commentarius Pars Prior. Ed. Helmut Feld. Vol. 11/1 of *Ioannis Calvini Opera Omnia: Series 2: Opera Exegetica Veteris et Novi Testamenti.* Geneva: Librairie Droz, 1997.

Institution de la religion chrestienne [1541]. Ed. J. Pannier. 4 vols. Paris: Societé les belles lettres, 1936; reprint, 1961.

Iohannis Calvini: Commentarius in Epistolam Pauli ad Romanos. Ed. T. H. L. Parker. Studies in the History of Christian Thought 22. Leiden: E. J. Brill, 1981.

Ioannis Calvini Opera Omnia. Geneva: Librairie Droz, 1992–.

Ioannis Calvini opera quae supersunt omnia. Ed. Wilhelm Baum, Edward Cunitz, and Edward Reuss. 59 vols. *Corpus Reformatorum,* vols. 29–87. Brunswick: C. A. Schwetschke and Son (M. Bruhn), 1863–1900.

Ioannis Calvini opera selecta. Ed. Peter Barth, Wilhelm Niesel, and Dora Scheuner. 5 vols. Munich: Chr. Kaiser, 1926–1952.

Psychopannychia. Ed. W. Zimmerli. Quellenschriften zur Geschichte des Protestantismus 13. Leipzig: Deichert, 1932.

Supplementa Calviniana: Sermons inedits. Neukirchen: 1936–.

TRANSLATIONS

The Bondage and Liberation of the Will: A Defence of the Orthodox Doctrine of Human Choice against Pighius. Ed. A. N. S. Lane. Trans. G. Davies. Texts and Studies in Reformation and Post-Reformation Thought 2. Grand Rapids: Baker Books, 1996.

Calvin: Commentaries. Ed. and trans. Joseph Haroutunian. Library of Christian Classics, vol. 23. Philadelphia: Westminster Press, 1958.

Calvin's Commentaries. 45 vols. Edinburgh: Calvin Translation Society, 1844–1856; reprint in 22 vols., Grand Rapids: Baker Book House, 1981.

Calvin's New Testament Commentaries. 12 vols. Ed. D. W. Torrance and T. F. Torrance. Grand Rapids: Eerdmans, 1959–1972.

Concerning the Eternal Predestination of God. Trans. J. K. S. Reid. Cambridge: James Clarke, 1961; reprint, Louisville: Westminster/John Knox, 1997.

The Epistles of Paul the Apostle to the Romans and to the Thessalonians. Trans. Ross Mackenzie. Grand Rapids: Eerdmans, 1961.

Institutes of the Christian Religion: 1536 Edition. Translated and annotated by Ford Lewis Battles. 1975; rev. ed., Grand Rapids: Eerdmans, 1986.

Calvin: Institutes of the Christian Religion [1559]. Ed. John T. McNeill. Trans. Ford Lewis Battles. 2 vols. Library of Christian Classics, vols. 20–21. Philadelphia: Westminster Press, 1960.

Instruction in Faith [1537]. Trans. Paul J. Fuhrmann. 1949; reprint, Louisville: Westminster/John Knox, 1992.

John Calvin and Jacopo Sadoleto: A Reformation Debate. Ed. John C. Olin. 1966; reprint, Grand Rapids: Baker Book House, 1976.

Der Psalter auf der Kanzel Calvins. Edited with an introduction by E. Mühlhaupt. Neukirchen: Neukirchener, 1959.

Tracts and Treatises. 3 vols. Trans. Henry Beveridge. Edinburgh, 1844–1851; reprint, Grand Rapids: Eerdmans, 1958.

"A Warning against Judiciary Astrology and other Prevalent Curiosities, by John Calvin." Translated with an introduction by Mary Potter. *Calvin Theological Journal* 18 (1983): 157–89.

Other Primary Sources

Augustine of Hippo. *De diversis Quaestionibus octoginta tribus liber unus.* In vol. 40 of *Patrologiae Cursus Completus, Series Latina.* Ed. J.-P. Migne. Paris: 1887.

———. *Enarrationes in Psalmos.* Ed. Dekkers and Fraipont. Vols. 38–40 of *Corpus Christianorum: Series Latina.* Turnhout: Brepols, 1956.

———. *Epistola CXLIII.* In vol. 33 of *Patrologiae Cursus Completus, Series Latina.* Ed. J.-P. Migne, cols. 585–90. Paris: 1902.

———. *Epistolae ad Romanos inchoata Exposito.* In vol. 35 of *Patrologiae Cursus Completus, Series Latina.* Ed. J.-P. Migne, cols. 2087–104. Paris: 1902.

———. *Expositio quarumdam propositionum ex Epistola ad Romanos.* In vol. 35 of *Patrologiae Cursus Completus, Series Latina.* Ed. J.-P. Migne, cols. 2063–86. Paris: 1902.

———. *Expositio quarumdam propositionum ex Epistola ad Romanos* and *Epistolae ad Romanos inchoata Expositio.* In *Augustine on Romans.* Text and translation by Paula Fredriksen Landes. Chico, Calif.: Scholars Press, 1982.

———. *In Iohannis Evangelium Tractatus CXXIV.* Vol. 36 of *Corpus Christianorum: Series Latina.* Turnhout: Brepols, 1954.

————. *Sermones ad populum.* Vol. 38 of *Patrologiae Cursus Completus, Series Latina.* Ed. J.-P. Migne. Paris: 1841.

————. *De Spiritu et littera.* In vol. 44 of *Patrologiae Cursus Completus, Series Latina.* Ed. J.-P. Migne, cols. 199–246. Paris: 1865.

————. *The Spirit and the Letter.* In *Augustine: Later Works.* Library of Christian Classics, vol. 7, pp. 182–259. Philadephia: Westminster Press, 1955.

————. *De Vivendo Deo Liber, Seu Epistola CXLVII.* In vol. 33 of *Patrologiae Cursus Completus, Series Latina.* Ed. J.-P. Migne, cols. 596–622. Paris: 1902. Also in vol. 44 of *Corpus scriptorum ecclesiasticorum latinorum,* pp. 274–332. Vienna: 1866–.

Biblia cum glosa ordinaria, Nicolai de Lyra postilla, moralitatibus eiusdem, Pauli Burgensis additionibus, Matthiae Thoring [= Doering] replicis. Basel, 1506–1508.

Bucer, Martin. *Common Places of Martin Bucer.* Trans. and ed. D. F. Wright. Courtenay Library of Reformation Classics 4. Appleford, England: Sutton Courtenay Press, 1972.

————. *Enarratio in Evangelion Iohannis (1528, 1530, 1536).* Ed. Irena Backus. Vol. 2 of *Martin Buceri Opera Latina, Martin Bucer Opera omnia,* series 2. Leiden: E. J. Brill, 1987.

————. *Metaphrases et enarrationes perpetuae epistolarum D. Pauli Apostoli . . . Tomus primus. Continens metaphrasim et enarrationem in Epistolam ad Romanos.* Strasbourg, 1536; 2d ed., Basel, 1562.

————. *Sacrorum Psalmorum libri quinque.* Strasbourg, 1529; 1532; Basel, 1547.

————. [*Selections*]. In *Melanchthon and Bucer.* Ed. Wilhelm Pauck. Library of Christian Classics, vol. 19. Philadelphia: Westminster Press, 1969.

Canons and Decrees of the Council of Trent. Text and translation by H. J. Schroeder. St. Louis: B. Herder, 1941.

Cicero. *De natura deorum.* Trans. H. Rackham. Ed. E. H. Warmington. Loeb Classical Library. Cambridge, Mass.: Harvard University Press, 1967.

Concilium Tridentinum: Diariorum, Actorum, Epistularum, Tractatuum Nova Collectio. 13 vols. Freiburg: Herder, 1964–.

Cyril of Jerusalem. *Catecheses.* In vol. 1 of *Cyrilli Hierosolymarum archiepiscopi opera quae supersunt omnia.* 2 vols. Ed. W. C. Reischl and J. Rupp. Munich, 1848; reprint, Hildesheim: Georg Olms, 1967.

————. "Lenten Lectures." In vol. 1 of *The Works of St. Cyril of Jerusalem.* Trans. Leo P. McCauley and Anthony A. Stephenson. Vol. 61 of *The Fathers of the Church.* Washington: Catholic University of America Press, 1969.

Denis the Carthusian. *Enarratio in Evangelium secundum Joannem.* Vol. 12 of *Doctoris estatici D. Dionysii Cartusiani Opera omnia.* 42 vols. in 44. Ed. Monks of the Carthusian Order. Monstrolii S. M. De Pratis, 1901.

————. *Super librum Psalmorum.* In *Doctoris estatici D. Dionysii Cartusiani Opera Omnia.* 42 vols. in 44. Ed. Monks of the Carthusian Order, 5:389–690, 6:1–48. Monstrolii S. M. De Pratis, 1896–1913, 1935.

Erasmus, Desiderius. *In epistolam Pauli Apostoli ad Romanos paraphrasis.* In English in *Paraphrases on Romans and Galatians.* Ed. Robert D. Sider. Translated and annotated by John B. Payne et al. Vol. 42 of *Collected Works of Erasmus.* Toronto: University of Toronto Press, 1984.

Filastrius of Brescia. *Diversarum haereseon liber.* In vol. 9 of *Corpus Christianorum: Series Latina,* pp. 217–324. Turnhout: Brepols, 1957.

————. *Ephiph Haer.* In vol. 31 of *Die griecheschen christlichen Schriftsteller der ersten drei Jahrhunderte.* Leipzig: Hinrichs, 1897–.

Gerhoh of Reichersberg. *Commentarius Aureus in Psalmos.* In vols. 194–95 of *Patrologiae*

Cursus Completus, Series Latina. Ed. J.-P. Migne, cols. 619–1814; 9–998. Paris: 1854–1855.

John Chrysostom. *Homiliae XXXII in Epistolam Ad Romanos*. In vol. 60 of *Patrologiae Cursus Completus, Series Graeca*. Ed. J.-P. Migne, cols. 13–384. Paris, 1858–1860. Reprint, Turnhout: Brepols, 1978.

———. *Homiliae XLIV in Epistolam Primam Ad Corinthios*. In vol. 61 of *Patrologiae Cursus Completus, Series Graeca*. Ed. J.-P. Migne, cols. 9–380. Paris, 1858–1860; reprint, Turnhout: Brepols, 1978.

———. *Homiliae XXX in Epistolam Secundam Ad Corinthios*. In vol. 61 of *Patrologiae Cursus Completus, Series Graeca*. Ed. J.-P. Migne, cols. 381–610. Paris, 1858–1860; reprint, Turnhout: Brepols, 1978.

———. *Homilies on the Acts of the Apostles and the Epistle to the Romans*. A Select Library of the Nicene and Post-Nicene Fathers of the Christian Church, series 1, vol. 11. 1889; reprint, Grand Rapids: Eerdmans, 1979.

———. *Homilies on First and Second Corinthians*. A Select Library of the Nicene and Post-Nicene Fathers of the Christian Church, series 1, vol. 12. 1889; reprint, Grand Rapids: Eerdmans, 1979.

Luther, Martin. *D. Martin Luthers Werke: Kritische Gesamtausgabe*. Weimar: Böhlaus, 1883–1957.

———. "Großer Katechismus/Catechismus major." In *Die Bekenntnisschriften der evangelisch-lutherischen Kirche*, pp. 545–733. Göttingen: Vandenhoeck and Ruprecht, 1986.

———. "Large Catechism." In *The Book of Concord: The Confessions of the Evangelical Lutheran Church*. Trans. and ed. Theodore G. Tappert, pp. 357–461. Philadelphia: Fortress Press, 1959.

———. *Luther's Works*. Ed. Jaroslav Pelikan and Helmut T. Lehmann. 55 vols. St. Louis: Concordia Publishing House and Philadelphia: Fortress Press, 1955–1986.

———. *Operationes in Psalmos* [1519–1521]. Ed. Gerhard Hammer and Manfred Biersack. In *Archiv zur Weimarer Ausgabe der Werke Martin Luthers*. Cologne: Böhlau, 1981–.

Melanchthon, Philip. *Commentarii in Epistolam Pauli ad Romanos* [1540]. In vol. 15 of *Philippi Melanchthonis Opera quae supersunt omnia*. Ed. C. G. Bretschneider and H. E. Bindsell. 28 vols. *Corpus Reformatorum*, vols. 1–28. Brunswick: C. A. Schwetschke and Son (M. Bruhn), 1848; reprint, 1963.

———. *Commentary on Romans* [1540]. Trans. Fred Kramer. St. Louis: Concordia Publishing, 1992.

———. *Loci communes theologici* [1521, 1535]. In vol. 21 of *Philippi Melanchthonis Opera quae supersunt omnia*. Ed. C. G. Bretschneider and H. E. Bindsell. 28 vols. *Corpus Reformatorum*, vols. 1–28. Brunswick: C. A. Schwetschke and Son (M. Bruhn), 1854; reprint, 1963.

———. *Loci communes theologici*. In *Melanchthon and Bucer*. Ed. Wilhem Pauck. Library of Christian Classics, vol. 19. Philadelphia: Westminster Press, 1969.

———. *Römerbrief-Kommentar 1532*. Ed. Rolf Schäfer. Vol. 5 of *Melanchthons Werke in Auswahl*. Gütersloh: Gerd Mohn, 1965.

Musculus, Wolfgang. *In sacrosanctum Davidis Psalterium commentarii*. Basel, 1551.

Origen. *Commentarii in Epistulam ad Romanos*. In vol. 14 of *Patrologiae Cursus Completus, Series Graeca*. Ed. J.-P. Migne, cols. 839–1291. Paris, 1857; reprint, Turnhout: Brepols, 1977.

———. *Commentarii in Epistulam ad Romanos/Römerbriefkommentar*. 2 vols. Translated with an introduction by Theresia Heither. New York: Herder, 1991–1992.

———. *Der Römerbriefkommentar des Origenes. Kritische Ausgabe der Übersetzung Rufins,*

Buch 1–3. Ed. Caroline P. H. Bammel. Vetus Latina. Aus der Geschichte der lateinische Bibel, vol. 16. Freiburg: Herder, 1990.

Pighius, Albert. *Controversiarum praecipuarum in comitiis Ratisponensibus tractarum, et quibus nunc potissimum exagitatur Christi fides et religio, diligens et luculenta explicatio.* Cologne, 1542.

———. *De liberio hominis arbitrio et divina gratia libri decem.* Cologne, 1542.

Thomas Aquinas. *Commentary on the Gospel of St. John.* Vol. 4 of Aquinas Scripture Series. Trans. J. A. Weisheipl with F. R. Larcher. Albany, N.Y.: Magi Books, 1980.

———. *Commentum in Matthaeum et Joannem Evangelistas.* Vol. 10 of *Sancti Thomae Aquinatis Doctoris Angelici Ordinis Praedicatorum opera omnia.* Parma: P. Fiaccadori, 1861; reprint, New York: Musurgia Publishers, 1949.

———. *On Faith: Summa Theologiae, Part 2–2, Questions 1–16 of St. Thomas Aquinas.* Trans. Mark D. Jordan. Notre Dame: University of Notre Dame Press, 1990.

———. *Summa Theologiae.* 61 vols. New York: McGraw-Hill, 1963–.

———. *Summa Theologiae.* In *Basic Writings of Saint Thomas Aquinas.* 2 vols. Ed. Anton C. Pegis. New York: Random House, 1945.

Zwingli, Huldrych. *Commentary on True and False Religion.* Ed. Samuel Macauley Jackson and Clarence Nevin Heller. 1929; reprint, Durham, N.C.: Labyrinth Press, 1981.

———. *Enchiridion Psalmorum* [1532]. In *Huldreich Zwinglis Sämtliche Werke.* Ed. Emil Egli et al. *Corpus Reformatorum* 100:467–836. Berlin,: C. A. Schwetschke and Son, 1905–.

———. *De Providentia Dei.* In *Werke. Erste vollständige Ausgabe.* Ed. M. Schuler and J. Schulthess, 4:79–144. Zurich, 1828–1848.

———. *De vera et falsa religione commentarius.* In *Huldreich Zwinglis Sämtliche Werke.* Ed. Emil Egli et al. *Corpus Reformatorum* 90:590–912. Leipzig: C. A. Schwetschke and Son, 1914.

———. *Zwingli: On Providence and Other Essays.* 1922; reprint, Durham, N.C.: Labyrinth Press, 1983.

Secondary Sources

Affeldt, Werner. *Die weltliche Gewalt in der Paulus-Exegese: Röm. 13,1–7 in den Römerbriefkommentaren der lateinischen Kirche bis zum Ende des 13. Jahrhunderts.* Göttingen: Vandenhoeck und Ruprecht, 1969.

Armstrong, Brian G. "*Duplex Cognitio Dei,* Or ? The Problem and Relation of Structure, Form, and Purpose in Calvin's Theology." In *Probing the Reformed Tradition: Historical Studies in Honor of Edward A. Dowey, Jr.* Ed. E. A. McKee and B. G. Armstrong, pp. 135–53. Louisville: Westminster/John Knox, 1989.

Augustijn, Cornelius. "Calvin in Strasbourg." In *Calvinus Sacrae Scripturae Professor: Calvin as Confessor of Holy Scripture.* Ed. Wilhelm H. Neuser, pp. 166–77. Grand Rapids: Eerdmans, 1994.

Bahmann, Manfred K. "Calvin's Controversy with Certain 'Half-Papists.' " *Hartford Quarterly* 5 (1965); reprint, *Articles on Calvin and Calvinism.* Ed. Richard C. Gamble, 5:337–51.

Barth, G. *Pistis, pisteuo.* In *Exegetisches Wörterbuch zum Neuen Testament.* 3 vols. Ed. H. Balz and G. Schneider, 3:224–31. 2d ed. Stuttgart: W. Kohlhammer, 1993.

Barth, Karl. "No! Answer to Emil Brunner." In *Natural Theology.* Trans. Peter Fraenkel, pp. 65–128. London: Centenary Press, 1946.

Barth, Peter. "Fünfundzwanzig Jahre Calvinforschung, 1909–1934." *Theologische Rundschau,* Neue Folge 6 (1934): 161–75, 246–67.

———. *Das Problem der natürlichen Theologie bei Calvin.* Theologische Existence Heute, Heft 18. Munich: Chr. Kaiser, 1935.

Beeke, Joel R. *Assurance of Faith: Calvin, English Puritanism, and the Dutch Second Reformation.* American University Studies, series 7. Theology and Religion 89. New York: Peter Lang, 1991.

Benoit, Jean-Daniel. "The History and Development of the *Institutio*: How Calvin Worked." In *John Calvin: A Collection of Distinguished Essays.* Ed. G. E. Duffield, pp. 102–117. Grand Rapids: Eerdmans, 1966.

Berger, Heinrich. *Calvins Geschichtsauffassung.* Studien zur Dogmengeschichte und systematischen Theologie 6. Zurich: Zwingli, 1955.

Bluhm, Heinz. *Luther: Translator of Paul: Studies in Romans and Galatians.* New York: Peter Lang, 1984.

Blondiaux, Benjamin. *De la notion de la foi d'après l'Institution chrétienne de Calvin.* Montauban: 1874.

Boegner, Alfred. *Quid Joannes Calvinus in libro tertio Institutionis christianae religionis de fide senserit exponitur et aestimatur.* Argentorati: 1876.

Bohatec, Josef. *Budé und Calvin: Studien zur Gedankenwelt des französischen Frühhumanismus.* Graz: Böhlau, 1950.

———. "Calvins Vorsehungslehre." In *Calvinstudien: Festschrift zum 400. Geburtstag Johann Calvins,* pp. 339–441. Leipzig: Rudolph Haupt, 1909.

———. "Gott und die Geschichte nach Calvin." *Philosophia Reformata* 1 (1936): 129–61.

Bouwsma, William J. *John Calvin: A Sixteenth-Century Portrait.* New York: Oxford University Press, 1988.

Brunner, Emil. *Natur und Gnade.* 2d. ed. Tübingen: J. C. B. Mohr [Paul Siebeck], 1935.

———. "Nature and Grace." In *Natural Theology.* Trans. Peter Fraenkel, pp. 16–54. London: The Centenary Press, 1946.

Brunner, Peter. *Vom Glauben bei Calvin: Dargestellet auf Grund der Institutio, des Catechismus Genevensis und unter Heranziehung exegetischer und homiletischer Schriften.* Tübingen: J. C. B. Mohr (Paul Siebeck), 1925.

Bulman, James M. "The Place of Knowledge in Calvin's View of Faith." *Review and Expositor* 50 (1953): 323–29; reprint, *Articles on Calvin and Calvinism.* Ed. Richard C. Gamble, 7:289–97.

Büsser, Fritz. "Bullinger as Calvin's Model in Biblical Exposition: An Examination of Calvin's Preface to the Epistle to the Romans." In *In Honor of John Calvin, 1509–64.* Ed. E. J. Furcha, pp. 64–95. Montreal: Faculty of Religious Studies, McGill University, 1987; reprint, *Articles on Calvin and Calvinism.* Ed. Richard C. Gamble, 6:434–65.

Butin, Philip Walker. *Revelation, Redemption, and Response: Calvin's Trinitarian Understanding of the Divine-Human Relationship.* New York: Oxford University Press, 1995.

Casteel, Theodore W. "Calvin and Trent: Calvin's Reaction to The Council of Trent in the Context of his Conciliar Thought." *Harvard Theological Review* 63 (1970): 91–117.

Chaix, Henri. *Le Psautier Hugenot: sa Formation et son Histoire dans l'Église Réformée.* Geneva: Imprimerie Romet, 1907.

De Jong, James A. " 'An Anatomy of All Parts of the Soul': Insights into Calvin's Spirituality from His Psalms Commentary." In *Calvinus Sacrae Scripturae Professor: Calvin as Confessor of Holy Scripture.* Ed. Wilhelm H. Neuser, pp. 1–14. Grand Rapids: Eerdmans, 1994.

Dee, Simon Pieter. *Het geloofsbegrip van Calvijn.* Kampen: Kok, 1918.

Diehl, Wilhelm. "Calvins Auslegung des Dekalogs in der ersten Ausgabe seiner *Institutio* und Luthers Katechismen." *Theologische Studien und Kritiken* (1898).

Doumergue, Emile. *Jean Calvin, les hommes et les choses de son temps.* 7 vols. Lausanne: Georges Bridel, 1899–1917; Neuilly: Editions de La cause, 1926–1927.

Dowey, Edward A. *The Knowledge of God in Calvin's Theology.* New York: Columbia University Press, 1952; expanded ed., Grand Rapids: Eerdmans, 1994.

———. "The Structure of Calvin's Theological Thought as Influenced by the Two-Fold Knowledge of God." In *Calvinus Ecclesiae Genevensis Custos.* Ed. W. H. Neuser, pp. 135–48. Frankfurt am Main: Peter Lang, 1984. Reprint, as chap. 6, "Influence of the Twofold Knowledge on Calvin's Theology," in *The Knowledge of God in Calvin's Theology.* Grand Rapids: Eerdmanns, 1994.

Ebeling, Gerhard. "Cognitio dei et hominis." In *Geist und Geschichte der Reformation: Festgabe Hanns Rückert zum 65. Geburtstag.* Ed. H. Liebing and K. Scholder, pp. 271–322. Berlin: de Gruyter, 1966.

Emmen, E. *De Christologie van Calvijn.* Amsterdam: H. J. Paris, 1935.

Engel, Mary Potter. *John Calvin's Perspectival Anthropology.* American Academy of Religion Series, Number 52. Atlanta: Scholars Press, 1988.

Farmer, Craig S. *The Gospel of John in the Sixteenth Century: The Johannine Exegesis of Wolfgang Musculus.* New York: Oxford University Press, 1997.

Feld, Helmut. *Martin Luthers und Wendelin Steinbachs Vorlesungen über den Hebräerbrief: Eine Studie zur Geschichte der Neutestamentlichen Exegese und Theologie.* Veröffentlichungen des Instituts für Europäische Geschichte 62. Wiesbaden: Steiner, 1971.

———. "Die Wiedergeburt des Paulinismus im Europäischen Humanismus." *Catholica: Vierteljahresschrift für Oekumenische Theologie* 36. Münster: Aschendorff, 1982: 294–327.

Forstman, H. Jackson. *Word and Spirit: Calvin's Doctrine of Biblical Authority.* Stanford: Stanford University Press, 1962.

Foxgrover, David. " 'Temporary Faith' and the Certainty of Salvation." *Calvin Theological Journal* 15 (1980): 220–32

Frerichs, [?]. "Der Glaube nach Calvins Unterricht in der christlichen Religion." *Reformierte Kirchenzeitung* 69 (1919): 19–22, 26–27.

Friedrich, Gerhard. "Glaube und Verkündigung bei Paulus." In *Glaube im Neuen Testament: Studien zu Ehren von Hermann Binder.* Ed. Ferdinand Hahn and Hans Klein. Neukirchen: Neukirchener, 1982.

Fritz, Johannes. *Der Glaubensbegriff bei Calvin und den Modernisten.* Freiburger Theologische Studien 11. Freiburg: Herdersche, 1913.

Froehlich, Karl. "Which Paul? Observations on the Image of the Apostle in the History of Biblical Exegesis." In *New Perspectives on Historical Theology: Essays in Memory of John Meyendorff.* Ed. Bradley Nassif, pp. 279–299. Grand Rapids: Eerdmans, 1996.

Gamble, Richard C. "Calvin as Theologian and Exegete: Is There Anything New?" *Calvin Theological Journal* 23 (1988): 178–94.

———, ed. *Articles on Calvin and Calvinism.* 14 vols. Hamden, Conn.: Garland, 1992.

Ganoczy, Alexandre. "Calvin als paulinischer Theologe." In *Calvinus Theologus.* Ed. W. H. Neuser, pp. 39–69. Neukirchen: Neukirchener, 1976.

———. *The Young Calvin.* Trans. David Foxgrover and Wade Provo. Philadelphia: Westminster Press, 1987.

Ganoczy, Alexandre, and Stefan Scheld. *Die Hermeneutik Calvins: Geistesgeschichtliche Voraussetzungen und Grundzüge.* Veröffentlichungen des Instituts für Europäische Geschichte 114. Wiesbaden: Steiner, 1983.

Gerrish, B. A. *Grace and Gratitude: The Eucharistic Theology of John Calvin.* Minneapolis: Fortress Press, 1993.

———. *The Old Protestantism and the New: Essays on the Reformation Heritage.* Edinburgh: T. and T. Clark, 1982.

————. "The Pathfinder: Calvin's Image of Martin Luther." In *The Old Protestantism and the New*, pp. 27–48.

————. "Theology within the Limits of Piety Alone: Schleiermacher and Calvin's Notion of God." In *The Old Protestantism and the New*, pp. 196–207.

————. " 'To the Unknown God': Luther and Calvin on the Hiddenness of God." In *The Old Protestantism and the New*, pp. 131–49.

————. "The Word of God and the Words of Scripture: Luther and Calvin on Biblical Authority." In *The Old Protestantism and the New*, pp. 51–68.

Gestrich, Christof. *Zwingli als Theologe: Glaube und Geist beim Zürcher Reformator*. Studien zur Dogmengeschichte und systematischen Theologie 20. Zurich: Zwingli, 1967.

Girardin, Benoit. *Rhétorique et Théologique: Calvin, Le Commentaire de l'Épître aux Romains*. Paris: Éditions Beauchesne, 1979.

Gloede, Günther. *Theologia naturalis bei Calvin*. Tübinger Studien zur Systematischen Theologie 5. Stuttgart: Kohlhammer, 1935.

Gordh, George. "Calvin's Conception of Faith." *Review and Expositor* 50 (1953): 207–15; reprint, *Articles on Calvin and Calvinism*. Ed. Richard C. Gamble, 7:373–82.

Gosselin, E. A. *The King's Progress to Jerusalem: Some Interpretations of David during the Reformation Period and Their Patristic and Medieval Backgrounds*. Malibu, Calif.: Undena Publications, 1976.

Gössmann, Elisabeth. "Glaube. V. Mittelalter." *Theologische Realenzyclopädie*, 17:308–18. New York: de Gruyter, 1977–.

Goumaz, Louis. *La Doctrine du Salut d'après les commentaires de Jean Calvin sur le Nouveau Testament*. Lausanne: Payot, 1917.

Grässer, Erich. *An die Herbräer: 1 Teilband: Hebr 1–6*. Vol. 17/1 of *Evangelisch-Katholischer Kommentar zum Neuen Testament*. Ed. N. Brox et al. Braunschweig: Benzinger and Neukirchen-Vluyn: Neukirchener, 1990.

————. *Der Glaube im Hebräerbrief*. Marburger Theologische Studien, vol. 2. Marburg: N. G. Elwert, 1965.

Greef, Wulfert de. *The Writings of John Calvin: An Introductory Guide*. Trans. Lyle D. Bierma. Grand Rapids: Baker Books, 1993.

Gründler, Otto. "John Calvin: Ingrafting into Christ." In *The Spirituality of Western Christendom*. Ed. E. Rozanne Elder, pp. 169–87. Kalamazoo: Cisterian Publications, 1976.

Hagen, Kenneth. *Hebrews Commenting from Erasmus to Bèze: 1516–1598*. Beiträge zur Geschichte der Biblischen Exegese 23. Tübingen: J. C. B. Mohr (Paul Siebeck), 1981.

————. *A Theology of Testament in the Young Luther: Lectures on Hebrews*. Studies in Medieval and Reformation Thought 12. Leiden: E. J. Brill, 1974.

Hammer, Gerhard, and Karl-Heinz zur Mühlen, eds. *Lutheriana: Zum 500. Geburtstag Martin Luthers*. Vol. 5 of *Archiv zur Weimarer Ausgabe der Werke Martin Luthers*. Cologne: Böhlau, 1984.

Harbison, E. Harris. "Calvin's Sense of History." In *Christianity and History*, pp. 270–88. Princeton: Princeton University Press, 1964.

Hasler, Richard A. "The Influence of David and the Psalms upon John Calvin's Life and Thought." *Hartford Quarterly* 5 (1965); reprint, *Articles on Calvin and Calvinism*. Ed. Richard C. Gamble, 1:87–99.

Hauck, W. A. *Christusglaube und Gottesoffenbarung nach Calvin*. Gütersloh: C. Bertelsmann, 1939.

Hausammann, Susi. " 'Leben aus Glauben' in Reformation, Reformorthodoxie und Pietismus." *Theologische Zeitschrift* 27 (1971): 263–89.

————. *Römerbriefauslegung zwischen Humanismus und Reformation: Eine Studie zu Heinrich Bullingers Römerbriefvorlesung von 1525*. Studien zur Dogmengeschichte und Systematischen Theologie, vol. 27. Zurich: Zwingli, 1970.

Hazen, Harry Booth. "Calvin's Doctrine of Faith." B. D. thesis, University of Chicago, 1903.

Heim, S. Mark. "The Powers of God: Calvin and Late Medieval Thought." *Andover Newton Quarterly* 19 (1979): 156–66; reprint, *Articles on Calvin and Calvinism*. Ed. Richard C. Gamble, 4:3–12.

Hobbs, R. Gerald. "Martin Bucer on Psalm 22: A Study in the Application of Rabbinic Exegesis by a Christian Hebraist." In *Histoire de l'Exégèse au XVI siècle*. Études de philologie et d'Histoire 34. Ed. O. Fatio and P. Fraenkel, pp. 144–64. Geneva: Librairie Droz, 1978.

———. "Hebraica veritas *and* Traditio Apostolica: Saint Paul and the Interpretation of the Psalms in the Sixteenth Century." In *The Bible in the Sixteenth Century*. Ed. David C. Steinmetz, pp. 83–99.

———. "How Firm a Foundation: Martin Bucer's Historical Exegesis of the Psalms." *Church History* 53 (1984): 477–91.

———. "An Introduction to the *Psalms* Commentary of Martin Bucer." Diss., University of Strasbourg, 1971.

———. "Zwingli and the Study of the Old Testament." In *Huldrych Zwingli, 1484–1531: A Legacy of Radical Reform*. Ed. E. J. Furcha, pp. 144–77. Montreal: McGill University Press, 1985.

Hofius, Otfried. "Wort Gottes und Glaube bei Paulus: Wilfrid Werbeck zum 60. Geburtstag." In *Paulusstudien*. Wissenschaftliche Untersuchungen zum Neuen Testament 51, pp. 148–74. Tübingen: J. C. B. Mohr (Paul Siebeck), 1989.

Holfelder, Hans Hermann. *Tentatio et Consolatio: Studien zu Bugenhagens "Interpretatio in Librum Psalmorum"*. Arbeiten zur Kirchengeschichte 45. Berlin: de Gruyter, 1974.

Holladay, William L. *The Psalms through Three Thousand Years: Prayerbook of a Cloud of Witnesses*. Minneapolis: Fortress Press, 1993.

Honig, A. G. "Het Geloofsbegrip van Calvijn." Review of *Het geloofsbegrip van Calvijn*, by S. P. Dee. In *Gereformeerd Theologisch Tijdschrift* 21 (1920): 132–46, 178–86.

Hörcsik, Richard. "John Calvin in Geneva, 1536–38—Some Questions about Calvin's First Stay in Geneva." In *Calvinus Sacrae Scripturae Professor: Calvin as Confessor of Holy Scripture*. Ed. Wilhelm H. Neuser, pp. 155–65. Grand Rapids: Eerdmans, 1994.

Jacobs, Paul. *Prädestination und Verantwortlichkeit bei Calvin*. Kassel: Oncken, 1937.

Jones, J. M. "The Problem of Faith and Reason in the Thought of John Calvin." Diss., Duke University, 1942.

Jones, Serene. *Calvin and the Rhetoric of Piety*. Columbia Series in Reformed Theology. Louisville: Westminster/John Knox, 1995.

Kertelge, Karl. *"Rechtfertigung" bei Paulus: Studien zur Struktur und zum Bedeutungsgehalt des paulinischen Rechtfertigungsbegriffs*. Münster: Aschendorff, 1967.

Kinlaw, C. J. "Determinism and the Hiddenness of God in Calvin's Theology." *Religious Studies* 24 (1988): 497–509; reprint, *Articles on Calvin and Calvinism*. Ed. Richard C. Gamble, 9:161–73.

Klauck, Hans-Josef. *Der erste Johannesbrief*. Vol. 23/1 of *Evangelisch-Katholischer Kommentar zum Neuen Testament*. Ed. N. Brox et al. Braunschweig: Benzinger and Neukirchen-Vluyn: Neukirchener, 1991.

Kok, Joel Edward. "The Influence of Martin Bucer on John Calvin's Interpretation of Romans: A Comparative Case Study." Ph.D. diss., Duke University, 1993.

Kolfhaus, Wilhelm. *Christusgemeinschaft bei Johannes Calvin*. Beiträge zur Geschichte und Lehre der Reformierten Kirche 3. Neukirchen: Buchhandlung des Erziehungsvereins, 1939.

Köstlin, Julius. "Calvins Institutio nach Form und Inhalt, in ihrer geschichtliche Entwicklung." *Theologische Studien und Kritiken* (1868): 6–62, 410–86.

Kraus, Hans-Joachim. *Psalmen*. 2 vols. Erster Teilband: *Psalmen 1–59*. Zweiter Teilband: *Psal-*

men 60–150. Vols. 25/1 and 25/2 of *Biblischer Kommentar Altes Testament*. 1961; 5th ed., Neukirchen: Neukirchener, 1978.

Krusche, Werner. *Das Wirken des heiligen Geistes nach Calvin*. Göttingen: Vandenhoeck und Ruprecht, 1957.

Lang, August. "Die Quellen der Institutio von 1536." *Evangelische Theologie*, 3. Jahrgang. Munich: Chr. Kaiser, 1936; reprint, Amsterdam: John Benjamin, 1969.

———. "Zwingli und Calvin." *Monographien zur Weltgeschichte*, fasc. 31. Bielefeld, 1913.

Lange van Ravenswaay, Jan Marius J. *Augustinus totus noster: das Augustinusverständnis bei Johannes Calvin*. Forschungen zur Kirchen- und Dogmengeschichte 45. Göttingen: Vandenhoeck und Ruprecht, 1990.

Lienhard, Marc. *Luther: Witness to Jesus Christ: Stages and Themes of the Reformer's Christology*. Trans. Edwin H. Robertson. Minneapolis: Augsburg, 1982.

Loewenich, Walter von. *Wahrheit und Bekenntnis im Glauben Luthers dargestellt im Anschluß an Luthers Großen Katechismus*. Institut für Europäische Geschichte Mainz Vorträge 57. Wiesbaden: Steiner, 1972.

Lubac, Henri de. *Exégèse médiévale: les quatres sens de l'écriture*. 4 vols. Paris: Aubier, 1959–1964.

McKane, W. "Calvin as an Old Testament Commentator." *Nederduitse Gereformeerde Teologiese Tydscrif* 25 (1984): 250–59; reprint *Articles on Calvin and Calvinism*. Ed. Richard C. Gamble, 6:250–56.

McKee, Elsie Anne. "Calvin's Exegesis of Romans 12:8—Social, Accidental, or Theological?" *Calvin Theological Journal* 23 (1988): 6–18.

———. "Exegesis, Theology, and Development in Calvin's *Institutio*: A Methodological Suggestion." In *Probing the Reformed Tradition: Historical Studies in Honor of Edward A. Dowey, Jr.* Ed. E. A. McKee and B. G. Armstrong, pp. 154–74. Louisville: Westminster/John Knox Press, 1989.

Marmelstein, Joh. Wilhelm. *Étude comparatives des textes latins et français de l'Institution de la religion chrétienne*. Groningen: J. B. Wolters, 1923.

Martin-Achard, R. "Calvin et les Psaumes." 1960; reprint in *Approche des Psaumes*. Cahiers Theologique 60. Neuchatel: Éditions Delachaux et Niestlé, 1969.

Massot, P. E. *La notion de la foi d'après l'Institution chrétienne de Calvin*. Montauban: 1871.

Maur, H. J. auf der. *Das Psalmenverständnis des Ambrosius von Mailand*. Leiden: E. J. Brill, 1977.

Maury, Pierre. "La Théologie naturelle chez Calvin." *Bulletin de la Société de l'Histoire du Protestantisme Français* 84 (April–June 1935): 267–79.

Millet, Olivier. *Calvin et la dynamique de la parole: Étude de rhétorique réformé*. Bibliothéque Littéraire de la Renaissance, série 3, vol. 28. Paris: Librairie Honoré Champion, 1992.

———. "*Docere/Movere*: Les catégories rhétoriques et leurs sources humanistes dans la doctrine calvinienne de la foi." In *Calvinus Sincerioris Religionis Vindex: Calvin as Protector of the Purer Religion*. Ed. Wilhelm H. Neuser and Brian G. Armstrong, pp. 35–51. Sixteenth Century Essays and Studies, vol. 36. Kirksville, Mo.: Sixteenth Century Journal, 1997.

Moroney, Stephen K. "The Noetic Effects of Sin: An Exposition of Calvin's View and a Constructive Theological Proposal." Ph.D. diss., Duke University, 1995.

Mühlhaupt, E., ed. Introduction to *Der Psalter auf der Kanzel Calvins*, by John Calvin. Neukirchen: Neukirchener, 1959.

Muller, Richard A. "*Fides* and *Cognitio* in Relation to the Problem of Intellect and Will in the Theology of John Calvin." *Calvin Theological Journal* 25/2 (November 1990): 207–24.

———. "The Hermeneutic of Promise and Fulfillment in Calvin's Exegesis of the Old

Testament Prophecies of the Kingdom." In *The Bible in the Sixteenth Century*. Ed. David C. Steinmetz, pp. 68–82.

———. "Scripture as Revealing Word: The Foundation of Calvin's Theology." Erroneously published as "The Foundation of Calvin's Theology: Scripture as Revealing God's Word." *Duke Divinity School Review* 44 (1979): 14–24; reprint, *Articles on Calvin and Calvinism*. Ed. Richard C. Gamble, 6:398–408.

———. *The Unaccommodated Calvin: Studies in the Foundation of a Theological Tradition*. New York: Oxford University Press, 1999.

Niesel, Wilhelm. *Die Theologie Calvins*. Munich: Chr. Kaiser, 1938.

———. Review of *Theologia naturalis bei Calvin*, by G. Gloede. *Theologische Literaturbeilage der reformierten Kirchenzeitung* (October 1936): 15–16.

Noble, T. A. "Our Knowledge of God according to John Calvin." *Evangelical Quarterly* 54 (1982): 2–13; reprint, *Articles on Calvin and Calvinism*. Ed. Richard C. Gamble, 7:320–32.

Oberman, Heiko A. "The 'Extra' Dimension in the Theology of Calvin." 1966, 1970; reprint in *The Dawn of the Reformation: Essays in Late Medieval and Early Reformation Thought*, pp. 234–58. Edinburgh: T. and T. Clark, 1986.

———. *The Harvest of Medieval Theology: Gabriel Biel and Late Medieval Nominalism*. 1963; reprint, Durham, N.C.: Labyrinth Press, 1983.

———. *Initia Calvini: The Matrix of Calvin's Reformation*. Mededelingen van de Afdeling Letterkunde, Nieuwe Reeks 54, no. 4. Amsterdam: Koninklijke Nederlandse Akademie van Wetenschappen, 1991. Reprint in *Calvinus Sacrae Scripturae Professor: Calvin as Confessor of Holy Scripture*. Ed. Wilhelm H. Neuser, pp. 113–54. Grand Rapids: Eerdmans, 1994.

———. " 'Iustitia Christi' and 'Iustitia Dei': Luther and the Scholastic Doctrines of Justification." 1966; reprint in *The Dawn of the Reformation: Essays in Late Medieval and Early Reformation Thought*, pp. 104–25. Edinburgh: T. and T. Clark, 1986.

———. *Luther: Man between God and the Devil*. Trans. E. Walliser-Schwarzbart. New Haven: Yale University Press, 1989.

Parker, T[homas] H[enry] L[ouis]. *Calvin: An Introduction to his Thought*. Louisville: Westminster/John Knox, 1995.

———. *Calvin's Doctrine of the Knowledge of God*. 1952; rev. ed., Grand Rapids: Eerdmans, 1959.

———. *Calvin's New Testament Commentaries*. Grand Rapids: Eerdmans, 1971.

———. *Calvin's Old Testament Commentaries*. Edinburgh: T. and T. Clark, 1986.

———. "Calvin the Exegete: Change and Development." In *Calvin Ecclesiae Doctor*. Ed. W. H. Neuser, pp. 33–46. Kampen: Kok, 1981.

———. *Commentaries on the Epistle to the Romans 1532–1542*. Edinburgh: T. and T. Clark, 1986.

———. *Oracles of God: An Introduction to the Preaching of John Calvin*. London: Lutterworth Press, 1947.

Partee, Charles. *Calvin and Classical Philosophy*. Studies in the History of Christian Thought 14. Leiden: E. J. Brill, 1977.

———. "Calvin's Central Dogma Again." *The Sixteenth Century Journal* 28/2 (Summer 1987): 191–99; reprint, *Articles on Calvin and Calvinism*. Ed. Richard C. Gamble, 7: 75–84.

———. "Farel's Influence on Calvin: A Prolusion." 1983; reprint, *Articles on Calvin and Calvinism*. Ed. Richard C. Gamble, 1:73–85.

Payne, John B. "Erasmus and Lefèvre d'Étaples as Interpreters of Paul." *Archiv für Reformationsgeschichte* 65 (1974): 54–83.

———. "Erasmus: Interpreter of Romans." In *Sixteenth Century Essays and Studies*. Ed. Carl S. Meyer, 2:1–35. St. Louis: Foundation for Reformation Research, 1971.

———. "Interpretations of Paul in the Reformation." *Encounter* 36 (Summer 1975): 196–211.

Peter, Rodolphe. "Calvin and Louis Budé's Translation of the Psalms." In *John Calvin: A Collection of Distinguished Essays*. Ed. G. E. Duffield, pp. 190–209. Grand Rapids: Eerdmans, 1986.

Peter, Rodolphe, and Jean-François Gilmont. *Bibliotheca Calviniana: Les oeuvres de Jean Calvin publiées au XVIe siècle*. Vol. 1. *Écrits théologiques, littéraires et juridiques 1532–1554*. Vol. 2. *Écrits théologiques, littéraires et juridiques 1555–1564*. Travaux d'Humanisme et Renaissance 255 and 281. Geneva: Librairie Droz, 1991 and 1994.

Peyer, Étienne de. "Calvin's Doctrine of Divine Providence." *Evangelical Quarterly* 10 (1938): 30–44.

Pitkin, Barbara. "Imitation of David: David as a Paradigm for Faith in Calvin's Exegesis of the Psalms." *Sixteenth Century Journal* 24/4 (Winter 1993): 843–63.

Preus, J. Samuel. *From Shadow to Promise: Old Testament Interpretation from Augustine to the Young Luther*. Cambridge, Mass.: Harvard University Press, 1969.

Le Psautier de Genève: Images Commentées et Essai de Bibliographie. Geneva: Bibliothèque publique et universitaire, 1986.

Puckett, David L. *John Calvin's Exegesis of the Old Testament*. Columbia Series in Reformed Theology. Louisville: Westminster/John Knox, 1995.

Reuter, K. *Das Grundverständnis der Theologie Calvins*. Neukirchen: Neukirchen des Erziehungsvereins, 1963.

Richard, Lucien Joseph. *The Spirituality of John Calvin*. Atlanta: John Knox Press, 1974.

Russell, S. H. "Calvin and the Messianic Interpretation of the Psalms." *Scottish Journal of Theology* 21 (1968): 37–47; reprint, *Articles on Calvin and Calvinism*. Ed. Richard C. Gamble, 6:261–72.

Schelkle, Karl Hermann. *Paulus, Lehrer der Väter: Die Altkirchliche Auslegung von Römer 1–11*. Düsseldorf: Patmos, 1956.

Schierse, Franz Josef. *Verheißung und Heilsvollendung: Zur Theologischen Grundfrage des Hebräerbriefes*. Münchner Theologische Studien, vol. 9. Munich: Karl Zink, 1955.

Schnackenburg, Rudolf. *Das Johannesevangelium*. 4 vols. In *Herders Theologischer Kommentar zum Neuen Testament*. Freiburg: Herder, 1965–1984.

Schreiner, Susan E. "Exegesis and Double Justice in Calvin's Sermons on Job." *Church History* 58/3 (September 1989): 322–38.

———. "Faith." *The Oxford Encyclopedia of the Reformation*. 4 vols. Ed. Hans Hillerbrand et al., 2:89–93. New York: Oxford University Press, 1996.

———. " 'The Spiritual Man Judges All Things': Calvin and the Exegetical Debates about Certainty in the Reformation." In *Biblical Interpretation in the Era of the Reformation: Essays Presented to David C. Steinmetz in Honor of his Sixtieth Birthday*. Ed. Richard A. Muller and John L. Thompson, pp. 189–215. Grand Rapids: Eerdmanns, 1996.

———. *The Theater of His Glory: Nature and the Natural Order in the Thought of John Calvin*. Studies in Historical Theology 3. Durham, N.C.: Labyrinth Press, 1991.

———. " 'Through a Mirror Dimly': Calvin's Sermons on Job." *Calvin Theological Journal* 21 (November 1986): 175–93.

———. *Where Shall Wisdom Be Found? Calvin's Exegesis of Job from Medieval and Modern Perspectives*. Chicago: University of Chicago Press, 1994.

Schulze, L. F. *Calvin's Reply to Pighius*. Potchefstroom, Republic of South Africa: Pro Rege—Press, 1971.

Schützeichel, Heribert. *Die Glaubenstheologie Calvins.* Beiträge zur Oekumenischen Theologie 9. Ed. Heinrich Fries. Munich: Max Hueber, 1972.

——. "Ein Grundkurs des Glaubens: Calvins Auslegung des 51. Psalms." *Catholica: Vierteljahresschrift für Oekumenische Theologie* 44. Münster: Aschendorff, 1990: 203–19.

Schwarz, Reinhard. *Fides, Spes und Caritas beim jungen Luther. Unter besonderer Berücksichtigung der mittelalterlichen Tradition.* Arbeiten zur Kirchengeschichte 34. Berlin: de Gruyter, 1962.

Sebestyen, Paul. "The Object of Faith in the Theology of Calvin." Ph.D. diss., University of Chicago, 1963.

Selinger, Suzanne. *Calvin against Himself: An Inquiry into Intellectual History.* Hamden, Conn.: Archon Books, 1984.

Shepherd, Victor A. *The Nature and Function of Faith in the Theology of John Calvin.* NABPR Dissertation Series, No. 2. Macon, Ga.: Mercer University Press, 1983.

Smalley, Beryl. *The Study of the Bible in the Middle Ages.* 2d ed. Oxford: Basil Blackwell, 1952.

Souter, Alexander. *The Earliest Latin Commentaries on the Epistles of St. Paul.* Oxford: Clarendon Press, 1927.

Spicq, C. "L'exégèse de Hébr. 11:1 par S. Thomas d'Aquin." *Révue des Sciences Philosophiques et Théologiques* 31 (1947): 229–36.

Stakemeier, Adolf. *Das Konzil von Trient über die Heilsgewißheit.* Heidelberg: F. H. Kerle, 1947.

Stauffer, Richard. *Dieu, la création et la Providence dans la prédication de Calvin.* Basler und Berner Studien zur historischen und systematische Theologie, vol. 33. Las Vegas: Peter Lang, 1978.

Steinmetz, David C. "Calvin and Abraham: The Interpretation of Romans 4 in the Sixteenth Century." *Church History* 57 (1988): 443–55.

——. "Calvin and the Absolute Power of God." *Journal of Medieval and Renaissance Studies* 18/1 (Spring 1988): 65–79.

——. "Calvin and the Natural Knowledge of God." In *Via Augustini: Augustine in the Later Middle Ages, Renaissance, and Reformation.* Ed. Heiko A. Oberman and Frank A. James, III. Studies in Medieval and Reformation Thought, vol. 49, pp. 142–56. Leiden: E. J. Brill, 1991.

——. "Calvin and the Patristic Exegesis of Paul." In *The Bible in the Sixteenth Century.* Ed. Steinmetz, pp. 100–18.

——. *Calvin in Context.* New York: Oxford University Press, 1995.

——. *Luther and Staupitz: An Essay in the Intellectual Origins of the Protestant Reformation.* Durham, N.C.: Duke University Press, 1980.

——. *Luther in Context.* Bloomington, Ind.: Indiana University Press, 1986.

——, ed. *The Bible in the Sixteenth Century.* Durham, N.C.: Duke University Press, 1990.

Strohl, Henri. "La Pensée de Calvin sur la Providence divine au temps oú il était réfugié à Strasbourg." *Revue d'Histoire et de Philosophie Religieuses* 22 (1942): 154–69.

Stuermann, Walter E. *A Critical Study of Calvin's Concept of Faith.* Ann Arbor: Edwards Brothers, 1952.

Thompson, John L. *John Calvin and the Daughters of Sarah: Women in Regular and Exceptional Roles in the Exegesis of Calvin, His Predecessors, and His Contemporaries.* Geneva: Librairie Droz, 1992.

Torrance, Thomas. *Calvin's Doctrine of Man.* London: Lutterworth Press, 1949.

——. *The Hermeneutics of John Calvin.* Edinburgh: Scottish Academic Press, 1988.

——. "Intuitive and Abstractive Knowledge: From Duns Scotus to John Calvin." In

Studia-Scholastico. Congressus Scotisticis Internationalis, 2d., Oxford and Edinburgh, 1966, 4:291–305. Rome: 1968.

———. "Knowledge of God and Speech about Him according to John Calvin." In *Regards Contemporains sur Jean Calvin.* Actes du Colloque Calvin, Strasbourg 1964, pp. 140–60. Paris: Presses Universitaires de France, 1965.

Trinkaus, Charles. "Renaissance Problems in Calvin's Theology." In *Studies in the Renaissance.* Ed. W. Peery, 1:59–80. New York: Renaissance Society of America, 1954.

Tylanda, Joseph. "Christ the Mediator: Calvin versus Stancaro." *Calvin Theological Journal* 8 (1973): 5–16; reprint, *Articles on Calvin and Calvinism.* Ed. Richard C. Gamble, 5: 161–72.

Wallace, Ronald S. *Calvin's Doctrine of the Christian Life.* Grand Rapids: Eerdmans, 1959.

Warfield, Benjamin. *Calvin and Calvinism.* New York: Oxford University Press, 1931.

Wawrykow, Joseph. "John Calvin and Condign Merit." *Archiv für Reformationsgeschichte* 83 (1992): 73–90.

Weijers, Olga. "Some Notes on 'Fides' and Related Words in Medieval Latin." *Archivum Latinitatis Medii Aevi* 40 (1977): 77–102.

Weiser, Artur. *Die Psalmen.* 2 vols. *Erster Teil: Psalm 1–60. Zweiter Teil: Psalm 61–150.* Vols. 14 and 15 of *Das Alte Testament Deutsch.* Göttingen: Vandenhoeck und Ruprecht, 1950.

Wendel, François. *Calvin: The Origins and Development of His Religious Thought.* Trans. Philip Mairet. New York: Harper and Row, 1963; reprint, Durham, N.C.: Labyrinth Press, 1986.

Wengert, Timothy J. *Philip Melanchthon's Annotationes in Johannem in Relation to Its Predecessors and Contemporaries.* Geneva: Librairie Droz, 1987.

Wiles, Maurice. *The Divine Apostle: The Interpretation of St. Paul's Epistles in the Early Church.* Cambridge: Cambridge University Press, 1967.

———. *The Spiritual Gospel: The Interpretation of the Fourth Gospel in the Early Church.* Cambridge: Cambridge University Press, 1960.

Wilckens, Ulrich. *Der Brief an die Römer.* 3 parts. Vol. 6 of *Evangelisch-Katholischer Kommentar zum Neuen Testament.* Zurich: Benzinger and Neukirchen-Vluyn: Neukirchener, 1978–.

Willis, E. David. *Calvin's Catholic Christology: The Function of the So-Called Extra Calvinisticum in Calvin's Theology.* Studies in Medieval and Reformation Thought, vol. 2. Leiden: E. J. Brill, 1966.

———. "The Influence of Laelius Socinus on Calvin's Doctrines of the Merits of Christ and the Assurance of Faith." In *Italian Reformation Studies in Honor of Laelius Socinus.* Ed. John A. Tedeschi. Florence: Felice le Monnier, 1965; reprint, *Articles on Calvin and Calvinism.* Ed. Richard C. Gamble, 5:59–67.

Willis-Watkins, D. "The Unio Mystica and the Assurance of Faith according to Calvin." In *Calvin: Erbe und Auftrag: Festschrift für Wilhelm Heinrich Neuser zum 65. Geburtstag.* Ed. Willem van't Spijker, pp. 77–84. Kampen: Kok, 1991.

Wilterdink, Garret A. "The Fatherhood of God in Calvin's Thought." *Reformed Review* 30 (1976–1977): 9–22; reprint, *Articles on Calvin and Calvinism.* Ed. Richard C. Gamble, 9:175–88.

Woudstra, Marten H. "Calvin Interprets What 'Moses Reports': Observations on Calvin's Commentary on Exodus 1–19." *Calvin Theological Journal* 21 (1986): 151–74.

Wright, David F. "Calvin's Pentateuchal Criticism: Equity, Hardness of Heart, and Divine Accomodation in the Mosaic Harmony Commentary." *Calvin Theological Journal* 21 (1986): 33–50.

Wyatt, Peter. *Jesus Christ and Creation in the Theology of John Calvin.* Princeton Theological Monograph Series 42. Allison Park, Penn.: Pickwick Publications, 1996.

Zachman, Randall A. *The Assurance of Faith: Conscience in the Theology of Martin Luther and John Calvin.* Minneapolis: Fortress Press, 1993.

Ziesler, John. *Pauline Christianity.* Rev. ed. New York: Oxford University Press, 1990.

Zillenbiller, Anette. *Die Einheit der katholischen Kirche. Calvins Cyprianrezeption in seinen ekklesiologischen Schriften.* Veröffentlichungen des Instituts für Europäische Geschichte, vol. 151. Mainz: Philipp von Zabern, 1993.

Index